JUSTICE AND LEGAL CHANGE ON THE SHORES OF LAKE ERIE

Ohio University Press Series on Law, Society, and Politics in the Midwest

Series Editors: Paul Finkelman and L. Diane Barnes

The History of Ohio Law, edited by Michael Les Benedict and John F. Winkler

Frontiers of Freedom: Cincinnati's Black Community, 1802–1868, by Nikki M. Taylor

A Place of Recourse: A History of the U.S. District Court for the Southern District of Ohio, 1803–2003, by Roberta Sue Alexander

The Black Laws: Race and the Legal Process in Early Ohio, by Stephen Middleton

The History of Indiana Law, edited by David J. Bodenhamer and Hon. Randall T. Shepard

The History of Michigan Law, edited by Paul Finkelman and Martin J. Hershock

The Rescue of Joshua Glover: A Fugitive Slave, the Constitution, and the Coming of the Civil War, by H. Robert Baker

The History of Nebraska Law, edited by Alan G. Gless

American Pogrom: The East St. Louis Race Riot and Black Politics, by Charles L. Lumpkins

No Winners Here Tonight: Race, Politics, and Geography in One of the Country's Busiest Death Penalty States, by Andrew Welsh-Huggins

Democracy in Session: A History of the Ohio General Assembly, by David M. Gold

The Dred Scott Case: Historical and Contemporary Perspectives on Race and Law, edited by David Thomas Konig, Paul Finkelman, and Christopher Alan Bracey

The Jury in Lincoln's America, by Stacy Pratt McDermott

Degrees of Allegiance: Harassment and Loyalty in Missouri's German-American Community during World War I, by Petra DeWitt

Justice and Legal Change on the Shores of Lake Erie: A History of the U.S. District Court for the Northern District of Ohio, edited by Paul Finkelman and Roberta Sue Alexander

JUSTICE AND LEGAL CHANGE ON THE SHORES OF LAKE ERIE

A HISTORY OF THE
U.S. DISTRICT COURT
FOR THE NORTHERN
DISTRICT OF OHIO

Edited by Paul Finkelman and Roberta Sue Alexander

Foreword by Solomon Oliver, Jr.

OHIO UNIVERSITY PRESS
Athens

Ohio University Press, Athens, Ohio 45701
ohioswallow.com
© 2012 by Ohio University Press
All rights reserved

Printed in the United States of America
Ohio University Press books are printed on acid-free paper ∞ ™

20 19 18 17 16 15 14 13 12   5 4 3 2 1

Library of Congress Cataloging-in-Publication Data

Justice and legal change on the shores of Lake Erie : A history of the U.S. District Court for the
Northern District of Ohio / edited by Paul Finkelman and Roberta Sue Alexander ; foreword by
Solomon Oliver, Jr.
    p. cm. — (Ohio University Press series on law, society, and politics in the midwest)
Includes bibliographical references and index.
ISBN 978-0-8214-2000-3 (hc : alk. paper) — ISBN 978-0-8214-4416-0 (electronic)
1. United States. District Court (Ohio : Northern District)—History. 2. District courts—Ohio—
History. I. Finkelman, Paul, 1949– II. Alexander, Roberta Sue, 1943–
KF8755.O36J87 2012
347.73'02097712–dc23

2012027255

*This book is dedicated to the men and women who have
served the nation as judges on the U.S. District Court
for the Northern District of Ohio.*

Contents

Contents

Illustrations follow page 334

Foreword

FEDERAL COURTS PLAY a very special role in the American democratic system. They have the responsibility under the Constitution of deciding those categories of cases that are deemed to touch on issues of national significance, for example, cases involving a federal statute or the Constitution, cases between states, cases where the United States is a party, and cases between citizens of different states. In deciding those cases that come before them, judges are not simply to preside over the proceedings; they also have the duty and responsibility to interpret the law, including the Constitution itself. Indeed, in Federalist No. 78, Alexander Hamilton described federal judges as having a duty to be "faithful guardians of the Constitution." As such, judges are responsible, among other things, for determining the constitutionality of legislative acts as well as actions by the executive branch, including the president of the United States. In order to carry out this responsibility, the Framers perceived a need for an independent judiciary. They provided that neither the executive nor the legislative branch would have sole authority over the appointment of judges, that the pay of judges could not be diminished while in office, and that judges would have lifetime appointments subject to good behavior. The view of the Framers in this regard has proven extremely wise. Since their inception, federal courts have been involved in deciding not just ordinary lawsuits, but some entailing the most volatile and intractable issues in society. Those issues have included the right to vote, racial and gender discrimination in various forms, the right to privacy (including abortion rights), separation of powers and executive privilege, freedom of religion and freedom of speech in various permutations, and public corruption. It is now hard to imagine how a federal judicial system — a system that must address such hot-button issues as well as antitrust, intellectual property, immigration, and myriad federal administrative law and state law issues — could carry out its responsibility with a cadre of judges worrying about whether they will be reelected or recalled.

The federal judiciary has a proud history, in part due to its independence. Some of that history is well documented. However, because there are ninety-four trial courts in the federal judicial system, as well as thirteen circuit courts of appeal, including the federal circuit, and the Supreme Court, some of that history is little known by the general public or even by judges. In an effort to address

ix

the lack of a formal history of the U.S. District Court for the Northern District of Ohio, my predecessor as chief judge, James G. Carr, suggested a few years ago that we undertake a court history project. The first aspect of the project was an oral history, which has been completed. The other aspect is this book, which has now come to fruition under the leadership of Paul Finkelman and Roberta Alexander. We are grateful that these two experienced legal historians were willing to serve as editors, to choose the authors of the various chapters, and to contribute chapters of their own. We are indebted to our colleagues Dan Aaron Polster, who served as our primary contact with the editors and publisher, and David D. Dowd Jr. and Lesley Wells, who provided ideas and gave insightful feedback on some of the chapters. We also owe special thanks to Geri Smith, clerk of court; Irene Milan, Sixth Circuit satellite librarian; Dave Zendlo of our automation department; and Melanie Walsh, secretary to the clerk and deputy clerk, all of whom provided invaluable assistance in gathering relevant information.

We agreed with the editors that the book would not be about individual judges but about the history of the court, as revealed in some of the interesting and important cases that have been decided by this court from its inception in 1855 until the present. In so doing, we recognized that space and other limitations would necessarily cause perhaps equally interesting and important cases to go undiscussed. It was our hope that the cases chosen and the stories told through them would shed light on the work of the court as a whole and the fifty-four men and women who have served as judges on it. I think this volume does that well.

The court is proud of its history and the role it has played in the nation and its judicial system, as well as in the state and region it serves, as reflected by these cases. As judges, we realize that, in some sense, every case we hear is important and that our success is determined by whether we fairly and consistently render impartial justice to the litigants who come before us.

Solomon Oliver, Jr.
Chief Judge
U.S. District Court
Northern District of Ohio

Acknowledgments

THIS BOOK BEGAN when James Carr, who was then chief judge of this court, and Paul Finkelman were at a conference on terrorism and civil liberties at the Rand Corporation. Judge Carr mentioned that he and his colleagues wanted to sponsor a history of the U.S. District Court for the Northern District of Ohio. This book emerged from that conversation. The members of the Northern District Court, especially Chief Judge Solomon Oliver, Jr., Judge Dan Aaron Polster, and Judge David Dowd, Jr., were essential in making this book happen. Their enthusiasm for the project was surpassed only by the help they offered in identifying the key issues that have come before the court in the last few decades. The assistance of the court librarian, Irene Milan, and her staff and of Geri Smith, the clerk of court, and her staff was essential for this book. Working with them has been a great pleasure. Similarly, the librarians at Albany Law School were invaluable in helping with the research and cite checking for this book. Paul owes his longtime friend Bob Emery, who retired from the Albany Law School library shortly before we completed the final work on this book.

We owe a great debt to our colleagues and friends who contributed to this book. Funds for this book came from the U.S. District Court's Attorney Admissions Fund, generated from attorney admissions fees, and used for the benefit of the bench and the bar in the administration of justice. By turning to experts on specific subjects, we hope this book provides lawyers, judges, scholars, students, and the general public a window into the workings of the Northern District Court, into its history, and into the way it has affected northern Ohio and the nation.

We owe special debts to the staff at Ohio University Press, particularly Gillian Berchowitz, the superb editorial director of the press, who is pleasantly relentless in the tough tasks of herding cats in the form of academics. Nancy Basmajian, managing editor of the press, has wonderfully coordinated all of the details of the publishing process. We also thank our copyeditor, Joan Sherman; our production manager, Beth Pratt; and our brilliantly talented designer, Chiquita Babb.

Most importantly, Paul's administrative assistant, Fredd Brewer, at Albany Law School was responsible for managing the various chapters and databases necessary for this book. His skills, patience, and good humor made the completion of this book possible.

Paul finished the last tasks on this book while a visiting professor at Duke Law School, where he held the John Hope Franklin Chair in American Legal History. He thanks Duke Law School for its support while he completed the final proofing and editing.

Paul Finkelman
Roberta Alexander

JUSTICE AND LEGAL CHANGE
ON THE SHORES OF LAKE ERIE

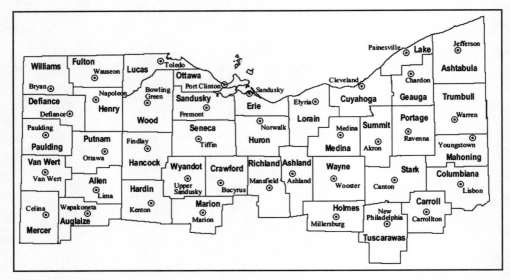

Map of counties served by the Northern District Court of Ohio

Introduction

Paul Finkelman

THIS BOOK EXAMINES the history of a single federal court—the U.S. District Court for the Northern District of Ohio. This is not a comprehensive, day-to-day or year-to-year history of the court. Nor is it a collection of biographies of the many judges who have served on it. Rather, we have chosen to examine a series of cases and topics that illustrate the nature of the court and the wide-ranging work it does. Some chapters focus on famous cases that began in the district court and went on to the Supreme Court—such as the World War I prosecution of the socialist leader Eugene Victor Debs. Other chapters center on equally famous cases and the events surrounding them that never went beyond this court, including the prosecution of scores of abolitionists after the Oberlin-Wellington fugitive slave rescue and the litigation following the shooting of students by the Ohio National Guard on the Kent State University campus in 1970. In addition to essays on great cases and historic events, the authors of these chapters analyze topics and themes such as the role of this district court in fighting political corruption, protecting the environment, or sorting out incredibly complicated social issues, including school desegregation and the relationship of religion to the government under the First Amendment.

1

Congress established Ohio's first federal district court on February 19, 1803.[1] Initially, the court met in Chillicothe, but in 1820, it moved to Columbus when that city became the state capital.[2] In its first fifty years of statehood, Ohio grew at an astounding pace. In 1800, there were only about 42,000 settlers in what would become Ohio. The first census after statehood found some 231, 000 people in the state. By 1830, Ohio's population had grown to about 938,000, and in the next twenty years, the state would more than double to 1,980,000 in 1850. On the eve of the Civil War, Ohio was the nation's third-largest state, with a population of about 2,340,000. The growth in northern Ohio was particularly dramatic in the four decades leading to the Civil War. For example, in 1820, Cleveland was a mere village, with a population of 600. With an astounding growth of 7,100 percent over the next forty years, the city had more than 43,000 people by 1860. Cincinnati remained the largest city in the state, with just over 160,000 people, but its rate of growth had slowed, especially in contrast to northern Ohio. In 1830, Cincinnati was about twenty times the size of Cleveland; by 1860, its population was a little more than three times Cleveland's. Cincinnati was the nation's sixth-largest city in 1850, but that is where it peaked. By 1920, it would drop to sixteenth, well below Cleveland. Congress could not, of course, have known this outcome in 1855, but it was clear northern Ohio was the focus of the state's growth and thus the region needed its own federal court.

The rapid growth of Cleveland, as well as the emergence of other northern Ohio cities such as Akron, Canton, Toledo, and Youngstown, led to increased legal business in the region. The expansion of Great Lakes shipping meant even more legal business for northern Ohio. Shipping led to admiralty disputes, which often required speedy access to courts. The presence of a federal court in northern Ohio seemed essential to the growing business, lake commerce, and population of that part of the state. On February 10, 1855, Congress recognized these changing needs by creating two separate district courts in the state. The existing court moved to Cincinnati and was now called the U.S. District Court for the Southern District of Ohio; the new court—the U.S. District Court for the Northern District of Ohio—would meet in Cleveland.[3] Thus, the history of this court begins in the 1850s. However, before turning to that history, it is important to explore the origin and role of federal districts courts in American society.

FEDERAL district courts have played a complicated role in American history. Before the modern era, they were often the embodiment of the national government at the local level. Until the Civil War, there was very little federal presence in most communities, and the majority of Americans rarely encountered a federal official other than the postmaster. In port cities—such as New York, Boston, or Philadelphia—there were large customhouses, collecting revenue to help run the national government, and on the frontier, there were federal land offices. But these offices were mostly administrative, and the people who ran them—postmasters, customs collectors, and land commissioners—were by and large administrators. There was little sense of the power or prestige of the national government attached to them.

From the beginning, the lower federal courts created a more commanding national presence. The district courts offered a forum for the resolution of disputes and the prosecution of lawbreakers. The courts provided a safe and orderly venue where Americans could sort out their differences. A federal district court was, as historian Roberta Sue Alexander has noted, "a place of recourse" for Americans to settle disputes.[4] But a federal judge was more than a referee for disputes; he was also a human face representing the authority and reputation of the national government. Dressed in magisterial robes, presiding over solemn proceedings in often impressive courthouses, surrounded by bailiffs and clerks and marshals, the district judges symbolized the power and prestige of the national government.

One significant role of the district courts was to oversee the process of naturalizing aliens. In a nation of immigrants, this aspect of the court's business has always been particularly significant. For immigrants seeking naturalization, the federal district court was not a place to be feared or a palace of oppression—like the courts in much of Europe. Rather, the federal district court was a temple of justice where the tired and poor, "the huddled masses" of the world "yearning to be free,"[5] became American citizens, with the right to vote and participate in self-government.[6]

From the beginning of the American nation, the idea of national courts was both important and controversial. Initially, there was no system of national courts. Most leaders in the new nation saw this as one of the defects of the government under the Articles of Confederation. Indeed, the Framers of the Constitution in 1787 insisted that national courts be established to resolve disputes between citizens of different states, to enforce the laws of the nation, and to provide a mechanism for bringing the authority of the national government to the people.

When the Constitutional Convention began in late May 1787, Governor Edmund Randolph of Virginia offered an outline for a new system of government. Called the Randolph Plan or the Virginia Plan, this document, largely written by James Madison, proposed that "a National Judiciary be established to consist of one or more supreme tribunals, and of inferior tribunals to be chosen by the National Legislature."[7] On June 4, the convention unanimously agreed that "a National Judiciary be established." Without any debate, the delegates also agreed that the judiciary should consist of "one supreme tribunal, and of one or more inferior tribunals."[8] The next day, the convention had a full-blown debate over the court system. The convention began by eliminating the clause that required the creation of "inferior tribunals"—that is, what would eventually become the lower federal courts. The vote was close, with five states voting for the change, four against, and two delegations divided. Significantly, the three Deep South states opposed the idea of federal district courts, as did two small northern states, Connecticut and New Jersey. Edward Rutledge, a wealthy South Carolina slave owner, argued that the state courts "[are the most proper] to decide in all cases of first instance."[9] The South Carolinians, always fearful of national power, initially resisted the creation of federal courts. After a long debate over the nature of a national court system, James Madison of Virginia and James Wilson of Pennsylvania proposed "that the National Legislature be empowered to institute inferior tribunals." Under their proposal, the creation of lower federal courts would be discretionary, not mandatory. This debate revealed both the importance of district courts to the Framers and the high quality of their deliberations. In what was essentially a reconsideration of the earlier vote, eight states now voted for federal courts, one state (New York) remained divided, and only South Carolina and Connecticut voted no.[10]

On July 18, 1787, the convention once again considered the creation of courts under the new national government. The provision before the convention was the one Madison and Wilson had proposed a month earlier: "Resol: that Natl. (Legislature) be empowered to appoint inferior tribunals."[11] Like his South Carolina colleague Rutledge, Pierce Butler opposed the motion, noting he "could see no necessity for such tribunals." Butler believed that the state courts "might do the business" of the federal government. He supported a strong national government, but at the same time, as a wealthy slave owner who vociferously argued throughout the convention for the protection of slavery, he may have had at least some fear of national courts.[12] After Butler made his objection to federal courts, Luther Martin, who would ultimately oppose the Constitution and argue against ratification, supported him. Martin believed national courts would "create jealousies" in the states because the national courts would interfere with state jurisdiction.

There is some irony in the opposition to federal courts on the part of the southerners, especially Butler. Near the end of the convention, Butler authored the fugitive slave clause of the Constitution, which ultimately embroiled the federal courts in enormous conflicts with some northern states, as the federal courts were used to *protect* the interests of slave owners.[13] In the 1850s, there would indeed be conflicts and jealousies between federal district courts and the state courts because the federal courts would be the primary forums for the enforcement of the Fugitive Slave Law of 1850. Meanwhile, some state courts in the 1850s would be called on to stymie that law in order to protect the liberty of free blacks or fugitive slaves in the northern states or to protect abolitionists — black and white — who resisted the law. In 1854, the Wisconsin Supreme Court directly challenged the jurisdiction of the federal courts in fugitive slave cases.[14] Because of state jealousies, it would take five years for this case to reach the U.S. Supreme Court: the Wisconsin Supreme Court simply refused to forward the record of the case to the U.S. Supreme Court. Thus, the nation's highest court was unable to decide the matter until the Wisconsin Supreme Court published its opinions. Then, the U.S. Supreme Court unanimously overruled the state court.[15] The prediction that federal courts would stimulate state jealousies also proved true for the Northern District of Ohio. Indeed, the first great case to come before that court was the prosecution of abolitionists after the Oberlin-Wellington fugitive slave rescue. While the rescue cases were pending in the Northern District Court, the Ohio Supreme Court was considering whether to issue a writ of habeas corpus ordering the U.S. marshal to bring the Oberlin rescuers into the state courts. In *Ex parte Bushnell, Ex parte Langston*,[16] the Ohio Supreme Court, by a single vote, failed to challenge the jurisdiction of the federal courts. Had there been a different ruling, there might have been a constitutional crisis of enormous proportions emanating from the Northern District.

These conflicts between northern state courts and federal district courts over slavery were of course not on the horizon as the delegates in Philadelphia debated whether to have national courts sitting in the states. In the debate at the Philadelphia convention, Nathaniel Gorham of Massachusetts noted that there were "already" national courts established under the Articles of Confederation to adjudicate cases of piracy and that "no complaints have been made by the States or the Courts of the States." Lower federal courts, he believed, would get the same respect and function in the same way. Governor Randolph of Virginia was even more emphatic about the need for a system of lower federal courts, declaring that the state courts "can not be trusted with the administration of the

National laws." He envisioned a conflict between state and national laws and understood that national courts were necessary to ensure the enforcement of national laws. He may have also understood from personal experience that the Virginia courts might not be willing to enforce federal law, especially if they were under the control of staunch opponents of a strong national government, such as Patrick Henry. His Virginia colleague, George Mason, was skeptical about a strong national government and ultimately would not sign the Constitution. Yet he too supported the idea of lower federal courts, noting that "many circumstances might arise not now to be foreseen, which might render such a power absolutely necessary."[17] Thus, at that point in the deliberations, all the state delegations at the convention unanimously endorsed the idea of Congress having the discretionary power to create lower federal courts.

A month later, on August 17, the convention agreed without debate or dissent that Congress would have the power to "constitute inferior tribunals."[18] On August 27, the delegates considered what was emerging as the final language of the Constitution: "The Judicial Power of the United States shall be vested in one Supreme Court, and in such inferior Courts as shall, when necessary, from time to time, be constituted by the Legislature of the United States." By then, even the South Carolina delegates supported the clause.[19] It may be that these Deep South delegates were finally persuaded that lower federal courts were necessary. But the vote may also have reflected South Carolina's huge victory in the previous session, when the convention had adopted the slave trade clause, preventing Congress from ending the African slave trade until at least 1808.[20] On August 29, two days after approving a system of federal courts, the convention adopted, without debate, what became the fugitive slave clause of the Constitution. As I noted earlier, this clause would eventually have an enormous impact on the federal courts and lead to the jealousies that delegates such as Pierce Butler feared.

THE members of the First Congress quickly used their constitutionally created discretion to devise a court system that included lower federal courts. The first substantive measure introduced in the Senate led to the Judiciary Act of 1789. The bill quickly moved through the Senate but took longer in the House. On September 24, President George Washington finally signed the bill creating the federal courts. This was the twentieth act passed by Congress. The 1789 act created a three-tiered system. At the top was the Supreme Court, with six justices.

At the bottom were the district courts and their judges. Initially, every state had one district judge, except for Massachusetts and Virginia. At the time, the modern state of Maine was part of Massachusetts and the modern state of Kentucky was part of Virginia. The First Congress recognized that the geography of these two states required an extra district judge for Maine and Kentucky. As new states entered the Union, Congress would create new district judges. Thus, in 1803, Congress created a district court for Ohio.

In addition to the district courts and the Supreme Court, Congress created a hybrid circuit court. Initially this consisted of a district judge sitting with two Supreme Court justices. With confusing nomenclature, the district judge would be called the circuit judge when sitting in the circuit court, and a Supreme Court justice riding circuit would be called the circuit justice. After 1802, only a single Supreme Court justice was assigned to the circuit court. More important, under this law the district judge could preside over the circuit court even if no Supreme Court justice was present. As a consequence, the distinction between the district court and the circuit court was not particularly clear to the average American. Often, the same individual presided over both courts on the same day. In the morning, he might be a district judge, and in the afternoon, he might be the circuit judge.[21] The main difference between the two courts centered on the kinds of cases they heard and the importance of those cases. Most of the district courts' early cases consisted of private suits where the matter in controversy involved $500 or less and minor criminal cases where the fine was not more than $100 or the possible jail time not more than six months. District judges also heard admiralty cases. The circuit courts had jurisdiction over larger private suits as well as more significant criminal cases.

Over the next seventy-five years, Congress tinkered with the court system, expanding the jurisdiction of the district courts. For example, in 1842, the district courts were given concurrent jurisdiction with the circuit courts for all noncapital federal crimes.[22] In addition to changing the jurisdiction of the courts, Congress increased the number of these courts and the number of judges. Starting in 1801, it divided some district courts, recognizing that it was almost impossible for people in certain areas to reach the only district court in their state. Under this process, a district judge would hold court in different sections of a state, and though there might be court clerks, bailiffs, or other functionaries in more than one place, the judge himself had to travel. By 1838, for example, Tennessee had three district courts, all served by the same judge.[23] In 1812, Congress authorized the appointment of a second district judge in New York, recognizing that the nation's largest state had such a huge docket of cases that no single judge could handle it.[24] Eastern and western districts or northern and southern districts soon appeared in a number of states.[25] Meanwhile, starting with Tennessee in 1802, Congress began to create multiple districts in the same state.[26]

By 1850, Ohio, with nearly 2 million people, was ripe for a new federal court. Residents of Columbus not surprisingly objected to the creation of a second district court because this would hurt business in their city. The federal court supplied clients for local attorneys, while litigants, witnesses, and visiting lawyers patronized hotels, restaurants, and other enterprises. Opening a new federal court in Cleveland would take some of this commerce out of Columbus. But in the context of the nineteenth century, the creation of the U.S. District Court for the Northern District of Ohio was an obvious and logical outcome of the phenomenal growth of the state and the rapid expansion of its northern part. The creation of the new court also symbolized the change that had taken place in Ohio in the previous half century. At statehood, Ohio was an outcropping of the South, with a plurality of its settlers coming from Virginia and Kentucky and most of its population focused on Ohio River traffic and the growing city of Cincinnati, which by 1830 was the eighth-biggest city in the nation. But by 1850, the population in the northern part of the state was growing faster, with most of that section's residents coming from New England, New York, or Europe.[27] Lake traffic now competed with river traffic as canals fed commerce north to Lake Erie as well as south to the Ohio River.[28] For many in the state, the focus of commerce and transportation was no longer the Ohio River, the Mississippi River, and the port of New Orleans. Rather, it was the state's huge canal system and the Cuyahoga River, flowing into Lake Erie and taking the produce of the state to New York's Erie Canal and ultimately the port of New York.

The creation of the new court in Cleveland symbolized the shift in population and power in the state. Four American presidents—Rutherford Hayes, James Garfield, William McKinley, and Warren Harding—would come out of the counties that constituted the Northern District of Ohio. In the next century and a half, northern Ohio would become an industrial powerhouse—the home and even the birthplace of new industries, businesses, and technologies. Glass, steel, and rubber would flow from Toledo, Youngstown, Cleveland, and Akron. Before World War I, factories in northern Ohio would run second only to those in Detroit in the production of automobiles. Scales from Toledo would help weigh the produce of the nation, oatmeal boxed in Akron with a smiling Quaker as its logo became an American standard, and more Americans lit their morning stoves with matches manufactured in nearby Barberton than from any other city. Much of the grain, ore, and finished goods from Ohio and the American heartland traveled on giant transports built at Lake Erie shipyards. The industry that provided the major fuel for the new industrial American economy would be born in Cleveland in 1870, when a local entrepreneur, John D. Rockefeller, created the Standard Oil Company, which quickly became the largest refiner of petroleum products in the United States.

As the economy of northern Ohio expanded, the demographics of the region changed. Most of the region was first settled by New Englanders, relocating to northeast Ohio to claim land in the Western Reserve. In 1840, northern Ohio was almost entirely populated by white Protestants from New England and upstate New York whose ancestors had migrated from Great Britain. But starting in the 1840s, Irish, German, and central European immigrants began moving to the region. After 1870, millions of immigrants and migrants from eastern and southern Europe, the Middle East, Appalachia, and the American South poured into northern Ohio. A century later, the region had one of the most ethnically, racially, and religiously heterogeneous populations in the nation. In 1860, Cleveland ranked twenty-first among American cities; by 1920, it was fifth. And as late as 1950, with just under a million people, it would rank seventh in the nation. In that year, Toledo, Youngstown, Akron, and Canton were also among the hundred largest cities in the country.

With all this change came enormously complicated and interesting legal issues. Cases involving the rights of workers, the changing notions of land use, pollution and environmental waste, demands for racial justice, immigration, expanding notions of due process and criminal justice, protests over the draft and national foreign policy during World War I and the Vietnam War, the changing and expanding rights of women, conflicts over religion and public life, and political corruption all were adjudicated in the U.S. District Court for the Northern District of Ohio. The chapters in this book teach us how that court developed and grew, how it affected the region and the nation, and how in turn it changed as the region and the nation changed. In essence, these essays tell some of the story of America at the local level. It is a story that instructs us about our past, enhances our understanding of our present, and helps us prepare for our future.

Notes

1. 2 Stat. 201 (1803). For a history of the U.S. District Court for the Southern District of Ohio, see Roberta Sue Alexander, *A Place of Recourse: A History of the U.S. District Court for the Southern District of Ohio, 1803–2003* (Athens: Ohio University Press, 2005).

2. An act altering the place of holding the circuit and district court of the district of Ohio, 3 Stat. 544 (1820).

3. 10 Stat. 604 (1855). For a history of the Ohio federal court before this division, see Alexander, *Place of Recourse*. See also chapter 1 of this volume.

4. Alexander, *Place of Recourse*.

5. Emma Lazarus, "The New Colossus" (1883).

6. However, as the case on John Demjanjuk shows, the court can also be a place where fraudulent paths to citizenship can be undone and where those who do not merit inclusion in society can face deportation. See chapter 12.

7. Max Farrand, ed., *The Records of the Federal Convention of 1787*, 4 vols. (New Haven, Conn.: Yale University Press, 1966), 1:21.

8. Ibid., 1:104–5.

9. Ibid., 1:119.

10. Ibid., 1:125.

11. Ibid., 2:45. The quotations in the rest of this paragraph come from this source (2:45–47).

12. Ibid., 2:45. Earlier in the convention, John Rutledge of South Carolina had also opposed the creation of lower federal courts; see Farrand, *Records*, 1:119. For a discussion of Butler's proslavery arguments at the convention, see Paul Finkelman, *Slavery and the Founders: Race and Liberty in the Age of Jefferson*, 2nd ed. (Armonk, N.Y.: M. E. Sharpe, 2001), chap. 1.

13. Finkelman, *Slavery and the Founders*, chap. 4.

14. In re Booth and Rycraft, 1 Wis. 3 (1854). For a history of this case, see H. Robert Baker, *The Rescue of Joshua Glover: A Fugitive Slave, the Constitution, and the Coming of the Civil War* (Athens: Ohio University Press, 2006).

15. Ableman v. Booth, 62 U.S. 506 (1859).

16. 9 Ohio St. 77 (1859).

17. Farrand, *Records*, 2:45–47.

18. Ibid., 2:314

19. Ibid., 2:428.

20. Ibid., 2:416.

21. In Pollard v. Dwight, 8 U.S. (4 Cr.) 421 (1808), the Supreme Court affirmed that a district judge could preside over the circuit court without a U.S. Supreme Court justice being present and a Supreme Court justice could preside over a circuit court without a district judge being present. See also chapter 1 of this volume.

22. Act of August 23, 1842, 5 Stat. 517 (1842).

23. See Erwin C. Surrency, *History of the Federal Courts*, 2nd ed. (Dobbs Ferry, N.Y.: Oceana Press, 2002), 69.

24. Act of April 29, 1812, 2 Stat. 719 (1812).

25. See Surrency, *History of the Federal Courts*, 2nd ed., 69.

26. Act of April 29, 1802, 2 Stat. 165. For greater details on the creation of the new court, see chapter 1.

27. The changing demographics of the state and the emerging power of its northern part can be seen in Ohio's regulation of race. Shortly after achieving statehood, Ohio passed

a series of racially discriminatory laws, known as Black Laws, that were designed to limit, as much as possible, the growth of the state's black population. In 1849, almost all these laws were repealed, illustrating the power of antislavery in the state as well as the growing influence and increasing population of northern Ohio. See Paul Finkelman, "Race, Slavery, and the Law in Antebellum Ohio," in *The History of Ohio Law*, 2 vols., ed. Michael Les Benedict and John F. Winkler (Athens: Ohio University Press, 2004), 2:748–81, and Finkelman, "The Strange Career of Race Discrimination in Antebellum Ohio," *Case Western Reserve Law Review* 55 (2004): 373–408.

28. For a classic study that helps explain the growth of Ohio and the eventual need for a northern district court, see Harry N. Scheiber, *Ohio Canal Era: A Case Study of Government and the Economy, 1820–1861* (Athens: Ohio University Press, 1969).

PART 1

Beginnings

1

The Willson Era

The Inception of the Northern District of Ohio, 1855–67

Roberta Sue Alexander

IN THE MID-1850s, lawyers, newspapers, and civil boosters across northern Ohio campaigned for the creation of a new federal court in the region. As Cleveland's *Plain Dealer* noted: "The interest of the people of Northern Ohio imperatively demand a new U.S. Judicial District. Ohio should be divided into a Northern and Southern district, with the court of the Northern half held at [Cleveland]."[1] In 1855, this campaign was successful, as Congress created the U.S. District Court for the Northern District of Ohio (NDOh).

In 1803, when Ohio became the seventeenth state of the Union, Congress created the U.S. District Court for the District of Ohio, located in Chillicothe, then the state capital.[2] When Ohio moved its capital to Columbus in 1820, Congress relocated the federal court there.[3] But as the state continued to grow, with increased commerce, immigration, and industry, the citizens of Cleveland and Cincinnati, the leading cities, became more and more resentful of Columbus's domination of the political and judicial life of their state. They complained that "the people on the Lakes and on the Rivers" were "compelled" to travel "away from where nearly all the business rises . . . , making expenses so onerous as to defeat the end of justice."[4] Moreover, even if lawyers undertook the "tedious journeys to Columbus" to obtain the necessary papers to collect money owed them from a shipping dispute, it was almost impossible to enforce their liens, for they often returned home only to find that the vessels involved in the lawyers' cases had "slipped away."[5]

Despite the active lobbying by the bench and bar of both Cincinnati and Cleveland and support from many in the state legislature, there was enough controversy to cause Congress to take over a year to pass the bill—introduced in the Senate by Salmon Portland Chase, a Cincinnatian, on December 21, 1853 —that would divide the state into two federal districts.[6] Columbus's leading citizens worked feverishly to defeat the bill in hopes of avoiding the loss of the prestige and patronage that they reaped from housing a federal district court.[7] Some argued that political differences played a role in slowing the bill's progress. The *Plain Dealer*, Cleveland's Democratic newspaper, placed the blame for opposition to a federal court in Cleveland on the "fact" that northern Ohio was represented by abolitionists, among them Benjamin Wade and Joshua Giddings, who were sacrificing the welfare of the region "on the altar of 'God and Liberty.'" Who, the *Plain Dealer* asked rhetorically, would support a U.S. district court planted in a city where federal laws such as the Fugitive Slave Act "are repudiated and so openly defied and resisted"?[8] Further, rumors persisted that some Cincinnati and Cleveland leaders either opposed or were lukewarm about the division of the district court.[9]

The Cleveland Bar fought back, appointing one of the city's leading attorneys, Hiram V. Willson, to go to Washington to work for the bill's passage.[10] Members of the bar also unanimously passed resolutions supporting "the division of Ohio into two U. S. Judicial Districts, believing that the convenience and interests of the citizens of the State imperatively demand such division."[11] Finally, on February 10, 1855, President Franklin Pierce signed into law the bill that created the Northern District of Ohio, assigning to it the northern forty-eight counties of the state.[12] The *Plain Dealer* saw this victory as so important to the future of Cleveland that it published the entire statute, along with an editorial explaining what the federal courts did so that citizens would understand the "advantages which Cleveland is destined to derive from this wise arrangement."[13] It predicted that the new court would be "a windfall to our city equal to half a dozen Rail Roads." The district and circuit courts would bring to the city "not only lawyers from all parts of the State . . . , but suitors and witnesses; who, unlike rail road patrons, *stop* instead of going *through* town." Further, the business of the Northern District would be at least as great as it had been for the entire district of Ohio, since many had previously "abandoned" potential suits rather than travel to Columbus.[14]

The day he signed the act, President Pierce also nominated Hiram Willson, a fellow Democrat, to be the new judge for the district. The Senate quickly confirmed Willson "without dissent."[15] Most applauded his appointment. As the *Toledo Blade*, a Whig newspaper, noted, he had lobbied "in season and out of season, to bring about a division of this District." Moreover, Willson, an "active and successful" member of the Cleveland Bar, although "an ardent politician," was far preferable to others who had been considered, "being the least rabid and ultra." "A gentleman of generous impulses" who worked hard to advance "the public good" and sought "to build up rather than tear down," Willson, the *Blade* concluded, would "raise above any party influences, and scorn to pander to any political prejudices."[16]

Willson entered upon his duties on March 16. Described by his friends as "a large fine looking man,"[17] with "a massive head and dark countenance,"[18] and by his enemies as "a large, obese, gray-haired man who looked older than his fifty years,"[19] Willson had moved to Cleveland from New York in the 1830s, forming a law firm that would become one of the area's most successful. He also became politically active. In 1852, he ran for Congress as a Democrat, losing to his law partner at the time, the Free-Soil candidate Edward Wade.[20] In 1854, he, along with a group of commissioners from Cleveland and Ohio City, worked out the details for annexing Ohio City to Cleveland, making Cleveland a major metropolis.[21]

Despite the fact that Willson—like every judge—sought to administer the law impartially and without any political partisanship, federal courts were entwined with politics. The numerous appointments made by the president and the court's personnel were often accompanied by accusations of political intrigue and manipulation, bringing to the public's attention, with some regularity, the realization that federal courts could become embroiled in the heated debates of the day. For example, President James Buchanan's appointment of Matthew Johnson in 1858 to replace Jabez W. Fitch as U.S. marshal was surrounded by controversy and led to "an open rupture" between Buchanan and Senator George Pugh, the Democratic U.S. senator from the Cincinnati area. This move was part of an effort to ensure the admission of Kansas into the Union as a slave state under the Lecompton Constitution, even though a strong majority of voters in

Kansas opposed slavery and the new constitution. Buchanan also wanted to punish Democrats such as Pugh who had sided with Stephen A. Douglas of Illinois in opposing the Lecompton Constitution because it had been fraudulently written and ratified. Thus, Buchanan ignored Pugh's choice for U.S. marshal and threatened to withhold patronage from all who opposed him; simultaneously, he made promises of patronage and appointments as a reward for those who would support his position.[22]

In office, court officials often used patronage to increase support for their party. For instance, in 1859, the *Plain Dealer* accused Marshal Johnson of corruptly and inappropriately using his patronage to support Buchanan and his policies by "secretly commissioning some half dozen persons in each county as Deputy Marshals, each appointed unknown to the other and each expecting . . . that they shall take the census of their respective counties," provided that they enrolled a large number of subscribers for a "pro-Lecompton Anti-Douglas" newspaper that Johnson started.[23] A year earlier, Cleveland's Republican newspaper, the *Leader,* had accused the court's clerk and the U.S. marshal, when selecting grand and petit jurors, of using "every opportunity to pack" the juries "with political partisans."[24]

On March 20, Willson convened the U.S. District Court for the Northern District of Ohio for its first session.[25] He proclaimed the rules of the court for civil, criminal, and admiralty cases as well as procedures for admitting attorneys to practice before the federal court.[26] After completing these initial tasks, Willson, through the end of the term on April 2, convened court daily and then immediately adjourned, there being no business to conduct.[27] Initially, the court operated out of temporary offices in a rented building until the new courthouse was completed.[28] It would not be until January 1859 that the court moved into its permanent new building.[29] When completed, the building was everything the city newspapers had campaigned for.[30] Located on Park, Superior, and Rockwell Streets, the three-story structure was half surrounded by pavement of "East Cleveland stone." Willson's office was big enough to accommodate his "large library." There were also consultation rooms for lawyers, jury rooms, rooms for the grand jury, and offices for all of the court's personnel. The "imposing" courtroom, located on the third floor, was over ninety feet high, "the ceiling having four large iron columns with Corinthian capitals for its support." This was a building that would "endure" for "a long time."[31]

As district judge, Willson presided over the U.S. District Court and, with U.S. Supreme Court justice John McLean, sat on the U.S. Seventh Circuit

Court for the District of Ohio when it met in Cleveland.[32] Because the aged McLean was often unable to travel to Ohio to sit as the circuit justice, Willson usually presided over both courts. When the courts met during the same term, he would hold one in the morning and one in the afternoon or hold both courts together, taking cases as they came up.[33] To the general public, both courts were *the* federal court in Cleveland, and the newspapers made few distinctions when reporting on their activities.[34] What the Cleveland newspapers did do was make the public aware of the federal courts and the role they played in citizens' lives, regularly reporting on the convening of the courts, the impaneling of the petit and grand juries, the dockets of the courts, and the results of many of the cases.[35]

The first full session of the U.S. District Court for the Northern District of Ohio opened on July 2, 1855.[36] Willson's most important task at this session was delivering his charge to the grand jury, for this provided the means by which he could educate the citizens of northern Ohio about the role of the federal court and their obligations to help enforce the law. He explained that the duties of the grand jurors were "as plain and as simple . . . as they are important." The federal court examined all violations of acts of Congress, the most significant of which were laws against counterfeiting coin and tampering with the U.S. mail and laws involving violations of the public trust by public officials.[37] But in his charge to the grand jury at the start of the November 1856 term, just after the hotly contested presidential election, Willson enunciated another role. Despite his pronouncements of political neutrality, he launched into an attack on Free-Soil Republicans. Jurors as well as "others" in the community, he exhorted, had to rise above the political passions that were "shaking the great national fabric in its centre" and, he claimed, "threatening the stability of the government itself." "Sober judgment," "free from prejudice, free from passions and free from the influence of the angry elements around us," was essential to counter the "dangerous political contagion" that had been "rampant in our country."[38]

The docket of the district court during the Willson years was dominated by admiralty cases. Criminal matters comprised the next largest category of cases for the court. Most dealt with counterfeiting or robbing the U.S. mails, but the most dramatic dealt with violations of the 1850 Fugitive Slave Act. There were only a handful of civil, equity, and patent cases. Finally, Willson also spent considerable time naturalizing immigrants.

In May 1855, he established a procedure for naturalization, ordering his clerk to procure a journal in which he would list all those who were naturalized.[39] The court sat in special session on the first Monday of every month to afford aliens the opportunity to become citizens. In addition, Willson performed naturalization tasks anytime the court met in regular session.[40] Aliens typically appeared before Judge Willson, provided "satisfaction" to the court that they had complied with all the requirements of federal law relating to naturalization, and then took the oath prescribed by law to become a citizen of the United States. Hundreds became citizens in this manner, all being adult free white males, as required by federal law.[41] Most came from Germany and Ireland. Although the numbers remained fairly steady up until the Civil War, when they fell sharply, the number of aliens seeking citizenship rose dramatically just before elections, illustrating the role political parties played in this process.[42] For example, in 1856, a presidential election year, Willson naturalized 1,189 aliens, ten times the number naturalized one year earlier. Perhaps even more significant, only five of these naturalizations took place after the election.[43]

The district court heard few civil cases. An examination of the civil docket books for the Northern District of Ohio from 1855 through 1867 revealed only twenty-five debt or bond cases and four forfeitures of recognizance bonds.[44] Perhaps the case that created the most press was an equity matter known as the "bridge case." Charles Avery, a prominent Clevelander, and two other city residents sued the city to prevent the construction of a bridge across the Cuyahoga River at the foot of Lighthouse Street. At issue was whether the city of Cleveland had the legislative authority to build a bridge over a navigable river and whether the bridge, if constructed, would be a nuisance, damaging the plaintiffs' private property. At the preliminary ex parte hearing, Willson did not rule on the merits of the case—that is, whether the bridge actually obstructed commerce on the river or damaged the plaintiffs' property—but in issuing a preliminary injunction, he clearly upheld both federal and state power over commerce at the expense of cities and localities. He first declared that it was well settled that the Cuyahoga was navigable water and that only Congress had the power to authorize obstructions. Second, he declared that a city had no authority to erect a bridge over navigable water unless specifically authorized or licensed by the state board of public works, a "wise" policy designed to preserve the state's control over internal improvements.[45] Thus, he determined, until the city received permission from the state's regulatory board, the preliminary injunction would stand. After the city received permission from the state to erect the bridge, it sought dissolution of Willson's injunction. But after hearing "hundreds of witnesses" on both sides arguing over whether the bridge would be a public and private nuisance and, more important, whether it would obstruct navigation on the river, Willson ordered the injunction to continue until the master he appointed took additional testimony to ascertain whether the proposed bridge would become "a material obstruction to navigation and a nuisance to the harbor."[46]

On the criminal side, counterfeiting cases dominated the court's docket. An examination of the criminal docket books from 1855 through 1867 indicated that the court averaged ten to twelve cases a year pertaining to making or passing counterfeit currency.[47] And at every term, the city's newspapers reported arrests of counterfeiters, alerting citizens to the "epidemic" in this criminal area and warning them to be wary.[48] One writer claimed that "the woods were full" of counterfeiters, some of whom were prominent citizens, "well known and saluted on the streets."[49] Willson generally sentenced convicted counterfeiters to two or three years in the state penitentiary, there being no federal penitentiaries at the time.[50] But during the Civil War, in at least one case, he offered to suspend the five-year sentence he had imposed if the defendant enlisted in the army. The defendant, however, declined, preferring to pay his fine and serve his prison term.[51]

Next to counterfeiting in prevalence, matters involving robbing or obstructing the U.S. mails, forgery, and embezzlement of public moneys filled the criminal docket and were regularly reported in the newspapers.[52] Perhaps the most interesting was a case of first impressions in which two businessmen, armed with a writ of attachment and accompanied by a county sheriff, prevented a train from moving for almost an hour because the railroad owed them money. After the train left Cleveland, the federal government prosecuted the businessmen for interfering with the U.S. mails. At trial, U.S. Attorney George W. Belden argued that no one "for any private purpose" had the right "to obstruct and hinder the transit of the U.S. Mails, whether acting under color of civil process or otherwise; that the faithful administration of the Federal Government demands and requires that its official communications as they are constantly passing through the mails be not hindered or delayed." Further, he maintained, the "interests of the community . . . in this area of the public service require that there be no hindrance in the transmission of its business correspondence." The defense argued that no corporation could be exempt from attachments to satisfy debts just because it was transmitting the mail. The jury sided with the prosecution, finding the defendants guilty and fining each $10 and costs.[53] During the Civil War, Willson came down hard on one defendant who was convicted of taking letters from a post office and embezzling their contents. Because soldiers and seamen had sent the letters "to their families at home," he sentenced the culprit to three years in the penitentiary.[54]

In addition to presiding over these rather routine criminal cases, Willson was called upon to settle a key legal question in the case of *United States v. Joseph S. Wilson*. The defendant had been charged with robbing the U.S. mail. His attorney filed a motion to quash because only fourteen grand jurors voted on the bill of indictment, one juror being absent when the bill was found. Willson "delivered an elaborate opinion" to support his ruling denying the defense's motion. Citing numerous precedents, he held that as long as the grand jury was "legally empanelled and composed of good and lawful men," he would uphold the principle established in earlier cases that "if twelve grand jurors agree in finding an indictment it cannot be invalidated on account of the misconduct of one of the grand jurors."[55]

But the most "celebrated"[56] criminal case heard during Willson's tenure and the one that produced "the most intense excitement in the community"[57] had nothing to do with routine crime. In the Oberlin-Wellington rescue case, a grand jury indicted thirty-seven men, including a faculty member and several students at Oberlin College, along with other prominent citizens, white and black, for rescuing an escaped slave in violation of the 1850 Fugitive Slave Act.[58] The grand jury acted after Willson delivered his charge attacking those who advocated a "higher law" theory. He granted that the Fugitive Slave Act "unquestionably" contained provisions "repugnant to the moral sense of many good . . . people." Still, it was the law of the land and "ours is a government of laws"; a higher law philosophy "should find no place or favor in the Grand Jury room" because "its tendency leads to the subversion of all law and a consequent insecurity of all the constitutional rights of the citizen."[59]

Depending on one's politics, Willson's charge was praised or damned. The Democratic *Plain Dealer* called it a "clear" and "able" explanation of the relevant sections of the Fugitive Slave Act as well as a welcome critique of those who advocated obedience to a higher law.[60] The Republican *Leader,* by contrast, called it an "assault . . . upon respectable white citizens, and upon the whole community." It was an example of how "corrupt politicians and partisan judges pander to an institution and a law based upon the worst existing form of injustice and oppression."[61]

Although the rescue took place in early September 1858, the indictments came down several months later, in early December. The trials did not begin until April 1859. By May 11, two men—a white printer and bookseller, Simeon Bushnell, and a black schoolteacher, Charles Langston—had been separately tried and convicted. The court then went into recess, and when it reopened in July, an elaborate plea bargain ended the trials.[62] The Oberlin case is discussed at length in chapter 2 of this book.

When the trials began, "business almost ceased as citizens crowded into the Federal Building."[63] "Eminent" citizens sympathetic to the defendants' cause visited the jail, and "prominent ladies" brought the defendants food, "delicacies," and "fragrant flowers."[64] People all over the Western Reserve region held protest meetings, and many arrived by "'trainload and wagonload' to parade before the jail" in support of the "martyrs." Leading opponents of the Fugitive Slave Act, including Ohio governor Salmon P. Chase, Judge Daniel R. Tilden, and Joshua R. Giddings, addressed mass meetings, held daily in the public square.[65] Some feared violence.

Judge Willson received threats and criticism, being seen as an "instrument" of "the slave power."[66] The *Leader* attacked him as well as the jurors, claiming the jurors were "a counterpart of the Judge—old, broken down, party hacks, with the scabs and marks of the party harness still on them; selected solely and for no purpose but to do the thing they did."[67] The Republican press also attacked U.S. Attorney Belden as "a man of small intellect" who "glories in his infamy." But the Democrats praised Willson and the jurors.[68]

The case brought national attention to northern Ohio and almost brought the federal courts into a direct conflict with the state government. By a single vote, the Ohio Supreme Court declined to issue a writ of habeas corpus to free the Oberlin rescuers from federal custody. Had the state court issued the writ, Governor Chase was prepared to use the Ohio militia to enforce it.[69]

The most vital work Willson performed was in the area of admiralty law, which dominated the district court docket.[70] Because most of the cases he heard involved vessels traveling on the Great Lakes rather than on the high seas, he had the opportunity to establish many precedents.[71] As the *Plain Dealer* noted, in that area Willson's "judgements have added large and valuable contributions."[72] Indeed, one authority claimed that his decisions were some of "the clearest expositions of the law to be found in the books."[73]

The admiralty docket began slowly, with only 10 cases filed in 1855. But two years later, 99 cases were filed, and in 1858, a total of 134 admiralty suits filled the docket. One of Willson's most significant tasks was to define the scope of federal maritime authority over vessels sailing on the Great Lakes. The first case in which he clearly articulated the broad sweep of federal power, *Wolverton v. Lacey,* was an action in debt, not an admiralty case. In 1855, the schooner *Yorktown* hired a crew of ten to make a trip from Cleveland to Chicago and back. Four of those crew members sued the vessel's master for failure to comply with a federal statute requiring all seamen to sign shipping articles before they sailed. At issue was whether this statute applied to merchant trade on the Great Lakes. The defendant insisted that the 1790 statute was intended only to cover admiralty cases—that is, cases on the high seas—and that the act of 1845, extending the jurisdiction of the district courts to certain cases upon the lakes and providing that U.S. maritime law applied equally to such cases—did not extend to this action. The defendant argued that to apply the 1790 statute to traffic on the lakes would be "detrimental alike to seamen and owners of vessel property" as well as against "public policy." Willson held for the plaintiffs, citing the Supreme Court's decision in *The Genesee Chief v. Fitzhugh,* which rejected English precedents and established the principle that admiralty jurisdiction was not confined to tidewater but extended to all "public navigable waters." Willson maintained that because commerce on lakes and rivers was increasing so rapidly, the courts recognized that there was no reason to distinguish "great lake commerce from the other maritime commerce." Further, as a matter of public policy, it was important that rules like those requiring seamen to sign shipping articles be enforced everywhere. He pointed out that the loss of life and property on the lakes was mounting annually and that a recent grand jury concluded that these disasters were caused in large measure by the failure of vessels to comply with federal statutes regulating vessels and seamen, including the signing of shipping articles. If such provisions were not enforced, men abandoned vessels, leaving the ships undermanned; insubordination resulted, and safety was jeopardized. Thus, Willson ordered the ship's master to pay the penalties prescribed by law.[74]

Throughout his years on the bench, Willson was repeatedly called upon to rule on the extent of federal jurisdiction in admiralty cases. In almost all of these instances, he upheld and broadened, when possible, the district courts' scope of powers.[75] In 1860, he again asserted the broad power federal courts exercised under admiralty jurisdiction, in what the *Plain Dealer* claimed was an "important" case addressing new questions.[76] The "revenue cutter case" dragged on in his court for two years before he rendered his decision. The many libelants, men who had furnished materials used in building six revenue cutters for the government, filed over thirty separate libels to collect moneys the government owed them.[77] First, the government claimed that the court had no jurisdiction because government property could not be seized. Willson dismissed that claim, asserting that because the government purchased the revenue cutters with liens on them, the government "acquires no better title than that possessed by its vendor. If the property is legally incumbered by mortgage or other liens, the transfer of title does not divest it of those incumbrances."[78] The most significant matter, however, was the question of jurisdiction of the federal court over vessels not licensed or engaged in the coasting trade or in the business of commerce or navigation between different states. The government argued that the federal act of February 26, 1845, extending the jurisdiction of district courts to certain cases upon the lakes and navigable waters connecting the same, limited district court jurisdiction. After carefully examining provisions of the Constitution and federal law, Willson ruled against the federal government. He determined that district courts were granted complete admiralty and maritime power by virtue of Section 2 of Article 3 of the Constitution and the Judiciary Act of 1789 and that those powers were independent of and unrestricted by the statute of 1845. Therefore, district courts could exercise equally complete power over ships on the Great Lakes and ships on tidewaters, including ships of war; the determination was not limited to cases involving vessels engaged in the coasting trade or commerce between the states.[79]

Further, in *Lyon v. The Brig Isabella*, he held that because the U.S. district courts had, by virtue of the powers granted them by the Constitution and acts of Congress, "exclusive original cognizance of all civil causes of admiralty and maritime jurisdiction," state courts were "precluded from proceeding *in rem* [that is, against a thing rather than a person] to enforce . . . maritime claims."[80] Thus, even though certain seamen had obtained, under the authority of certain Ohio statutes, a lien in state court against the *Isabella* for wages earned but not paid, they could not be precluded from acquiring another lien against the boat in federal district court. Willson concluded that a "lien of seamen for their wages is prior and paramount to all other claims on the vessel" and that "the only court that has jurisdiction over this lien, or authorized to enforce it, is the court of admiralty, and it is the duty of that court to do so." No state court could "enforce or displace this lien."[81] Thus, the purchaser of the boat, at a judicial sale such as the one that occurred in this case in state court, "takes the property *cum onere*," that is, subject to a charge or burden.[82]

Such jurisdictional cases gave Willson the opportunity to establish key precedents and make the weight of federal authority felt throughout the economic world of northern Ohio. But most of the admiralty docket consisted of collision cases and contract disputes. The contract disputes were fairly routine. They generally involved suppliers and contractors suing to collect for materials provided in the construction, repairing, or manning of vessels or seamen suing for unpaid wages. Typically in such cases, either the owners of the vessels paid the amount due, once that amount was established, or the vessels were seized and sold to pay the debts. The most difficult part was assessing a vessel's worth.[83] Disputes of this type were so common that the *Plain Dealer,* in every issue, printed notices of seizures and sales of various vessels involved in admiralty litigation.[84]

Most important, the federal court served as an arbiter, and Willson, perhaps because of his Democratic principles, tended to support seamen in their disputes with their masters. For example, in early 1865 when the owner of the schooner *White Squall* refused to pay his crew, claiming they had mutinied and deserted (although they "were returned to the vessel" and then completed the voyage back to Cleveland), Willson held for the seamen. After hearing elaborate arguments by attorneys on both sides, citing "authorities on the subject of revolts, desertion, disobedience of orders," and the like, he ruled that what occurred "did not amount to a mutiny or revolt in the maritime sense, but only to a temporary disobedience of orders, which was perhaps induced by indiscreet conduct and manner on the part of the master." Showing compassion for the seamen, he held that "while the law holds seamen to implicit obedience to all proper orders, it may sometimes make allowance where the disobedience is only temporary . . . and followed by a prompt return to duty."[85]

Collision cases were much more difficult because either Willson or a jury had to determine not only the value of the lost vessels but also who was at fault. In *Waldorf et al. v. The New York,* Willson clearly delineated the procedures the judge or the jury needed to undertake and the standards that should be applied. Here, the steam propeller *New York* struck the schooner *Dawn,* sinking it, "the crew barely able to escape with their lives."[86] After hearing the testimony and the arguments by counsel on both sides, which the *Leader* claimed were "among the most learned and able ever delivered in our courts,"[87] Willson first determined that the *Dawn,* in changing course at the last minute, was not at fault; even though the propeller had "a right to assume that the sailing vessel will keep her course," the *Dawn* was "justified by the impending danger of collision." The next inquiry, Willson explained, was "whether this collision was a casualty for which no blame should be imputed to either party" or whether it

resulted "from the carelessness . . . of those in charge of the propeller." In deciding this issue, he noted, one had to apply the standards established in numerous
precedents, that is, "when a steamer approaches a sailing vessel, the steamer
is required to exercise the necessary precautions to avoid a collision." If a collision occurred, it was "prima facie" the steamboat's fault.[88] Here, Willson came
down hard on the officer in charge of the propeller, chastising him for his "ig-
norance and unskillfulness" in not avoiding the collision. After finding the
propeller at fault, he assessed damages, calculating the worth of the *Dawn* based
on cost of construction, maintenance expenses, and current market value, "giving due weight to the testimony of those witnesses who have the best means
of knowledge."[89]

During the Civil War, the federal court faced new challenges and new issues.
As Willson explained to one wartime grand jury, the court's criminal docket
before the conflict consisted almost solely of "cases of counterfeiting coin . . .
and for violation of the post office laws." But during the war, Congress passed "a
large number of laws, some of them novel in their character," that the federal
courts had to enforce.[90] Indeed, in November 1859, even before the war began—
with tensions high after John Brown's October raid of the U.S. arsenal at Harpers
Ferry, Virginia, in an attempt to spread a slave rebellion across the South, as
well as after the several fugitive slave cases—Willson defined the law of treason
in a charge to the grand jury that was so significant it was reported nationally.[91]
It was vital, he said, for the jurors to understand "the character and essential elements" of the "heinous offence" of treason "lest [they] might be induced to
improper action by extraneous influences." In particular, Willson thought the
government might charge some who met in Cleveland the previous May during the Oberlin-Wellington trial with treason, the U.S. attorney believing that
their purpose was to plan "open and violent resistance to the execution of a
public law of the United States." As he did during the Wellington-Oberlin trial,
Willson condemned those who, he claimed, felt they could judge for themselves which laws to obey "*according to their own individual tastes and opinions.*" The role of the grand jury, he emphasized, was to uphold congressional
law, especially laws "which are . . . violated under the influence of popular
excitement, and without . . . reflection [as to] their serious consequences to individuals and to the public." He cautioned that the heresy of the higher law
theory, if "unchecked . . . tends directly to the subversion of all law . . . and the
destruction of those sacred guarantees, under which the people of the United
States have reposed with peace and confidence . . . for three quarters of a

century." But Willson drew a sharp distinction between a meeting held to express opinions hostile to the government and a gathering to plot the violent overthrow of the government. If people engaged in such a conspiracy, courts should show them no mercy, no matter what their motives. But if people assembled merely to denounce "the national government, its laws, and its public functionaries" and to pass "resolutions of disfavor," that was not treason.[92]

In 1861, Willson issued another charge to another grand jury in which he again defined the law regarding conspiracy and treason.[93] This time, however, he directed his attention not to abolitionists, who tended to support the Republican Party, but to the many Southern sympathizers in Ohio, some of whom were suspected of providing aid to the rebellion and who tended to support the Democratic Party. Willson had been a devout Democrat before his appointment to the bench, and his jurisprudence at times clearly reflected that, including his unswerving support for the fugitive slave laws. But when the war began, opposition to the national government and federal law came from Democrats. Indeed, the leading Democrat in Ohio, Clement Vallandigham, was tried by a military tribunal and imprisoned during the war for his attempts to interfere with the draft. Willson, however, broke with the Peace Democrats and urged all citizens to support *the law*, as he saw it, even when it went against those who had once been his political allies. As a federal judge, he saw his role as educating the public on the dangers of treason and the need for strict obedience to the law and support of the Union cause.

In his charge to the grand jury, Willson emphasized the importance of supporting the war effort. "The loyal people of this great nation have enjoyed the blessings of our excellent Constitution too long and too well to be insensible of its value or to permit its destruction." This "bold and mad rebellion . . . is a rebellion without cause and without justification. . . . Let the motives of the conspirators be what they may, this open, organized, and armed resistance to the Government of the United States is *treason*, and those engaged in it justly merit the penalty denounced against traitors." The notion "of the reserved right of the States to secede from the Union . . . is false in theory . . . and without the semblance of authority in the Constitution." "If this Union is to be perpetuated," he declared, "and the Government itself is to exist as a power among the nations, its laws must be enforced at all hazards and at any cost. And especially should courts and juries do their whole duty, without respect to persons, when crimes are committed, tending to the subversion of the Government and the destruction of our cherished institutions."[94]

As the war progressed, the court continued to stress that citizens had a patriotic obligation to support the war and the new congressional laws enacted to further the war effort. Early on, Willson heard several habeas corpus cases in which he released recruits who had enlisted or who had been illegally detained by enrollment officers, the recruits being under the age of eighteen.[95] But when Congress enacted a draft on March 3, 1863, a new type of case landed in federal court. Many Northerners opposed the draft, and many judges denounced it as unconstitutional, arguing that it violated both individual liberties and states' rights.[96] Willson faced several cases of draft dodging, desertion, and obstructing marshals who were trying to arrest deserters and force those subject to the draft into the army.[97] In January 1864, he delivered a charge to the grand jury unequivocally supporting the draft. After outlining the provisions of the draft statute in detail, he proclaimed that an examination of the Constitution—its history, purposes, and text—led to the conclusion that the conscription act "as a whole and in all of its provisions, is fully sanctioned by the Constitution of the United States." He then emphasized not only that the draft was constitutional but also that the crimes of resisting the draft, counseling others to resist, obstructing the draft's execution in any way (including resisting, obstructing, or assaulting an enrollment officer), and enticing soldiers to desert were all violations of the statute that had to be stopped. He especially criticized those who had engaged in the lucrative business of enticing soldiers to leave one regiment in order to enlist in another, thus collecting additional bounty money.[98]

Of the many draft cases Willson and the juries of the Northern District of Ohio had to deal with, perhaps the most serious was the Holmes County draft riot, referred to as the "battle of Fort Fizzle." In June 1863, "a mob" attacked an enrollment officer. After the provost marshal arrested four leaders, another group of citizens freed them. Then, approximately nine hundred to a thousand men helped build Fort Fizzle to protect local citizens from the draft. It took over four hundred federal soldiers to disarm the men and enforce the draft in the area.[99] Twelve of the rioters, who had been indicted in July 1863, faced trial during the court's May 1864 term. Only Laurant Blanchard was found guilty. Willson sentenced him to six months at hard labor in the Ohio penitentiary, but President Abraham Lincoln pardoned him prior to the completion of the sentence. The government eventually dropped the prosecution of the other cases.[100]

Another new category of cases that Willson faced during the Civil War involved smuggling. The smuggling cases appeared after Congress proclaimed the Southern states to be in rebellion, prohibiting trade with them and enacting new revenue laws, including the taxation of distilled spirits. The procedure to deal with smuggling was simple. After the U.S. marshal seized the smuggled goods, he publicized the seizure, and if no complaint was made, the court condemned them as forfeited and sold them, with the proceeds going to the U.S. Treasury.[101] The court also heard a few cases involving the confiscation of property, under the congressional act of 1862 that decreed the forfeiture of property located in the North but owned by disloyal men residing in the South.[102]

After the war, the court's docket returned to its normal cases, except for the so-called Fenian Invasion. The Fenians were members of an organization seeking to end British rule in Ireland and to establish an independent republic there. With such a large number of Irish immigrants in northern Ohio, the court took seriously the U.S. State Department's warning to U.S. attorneys and marshals to watch out for Fenians. On June 7, 1866, Marshal Earl Bill arrested the officers of the Fenian Brotherhood in Cleveland, charging them with aiding and abetting violators of the neutrality laws of the United States. Further, Bill was ordered to watch for any attempted expedition from Cleveland by the Fenians. If any boats went a mile or two from the city, they were to be "blown up." One U.S. ship lay in the Cuyahoga River, ready to execute this executive order. However, nothing more came of this situation.[103]

With Judge Willson's death from tuberculosis on November 11, 1866,[104] an era ended. For eleven years, Willson had carried out his duties with "industry and fidelity,"[105] having "abandoned the field of partisan politics" to preside impartially.[106] The Cleveland Bar lauded him as an "upright and fearless Judge" who treated all with "courtesy" and respect, especially new members of the bar, whom he encouraged, aided, and treated with kindness.[107] The *Leader* summed up the unanimous feeling of those in the Northern District when it simply noted that "his loss will be seriously felt" and he will be "sincerely mourned."[108] Willson established the court in the Northern District of Ohio,[109] and he ruled on many pivotal issues, especially those related to admiralty and commerce. He also brought home to the citizens of northern Ohio the role of the court not only in trade and commerce but also in maintaining law and order, especially during the perilous Civil War years. Further, by naturalizing so many immigrants at a time when foreigners flooded into the area, the federal court helped integrate recent migrants into the body politic. Thus, the court played a vital part in arbitrating commercial, political, and social issues that helped foster the economic and demographic growth of Cleveland and the rest of the Northern District.

Notes

1. Cleveland *Plain Dealer*, October 7, 1854, 2. See also resolution of the Bar of Cuyahoga County "unanimously in favor of the division," quoted in *Plain Dealer*, March 10, 1854, 3. And see *Toledo Blade*, February 14, 1855, 2.

2. Roberta Sue Alexander, *A Place of Recourse: A History of the U.S. District Court for the Southern District of Ohio, 1803–2003* (Athens: Ohio University Press, 2005), 7. See chap. 1 of that book for a history of this court's early years.

3. An Act altering the place of holding the circuit and district court in the district of Ohio, 3 Stat. 544 (1820).

4. *Plain Dealer*, February 9, 1855, 2. See also *Plain Dealer*, October 7, 1854, 2, and February 9, 1855, 2. The *Toledo Blade*, February 14, 1855, 2, agreed that not having a court in Cleveland had caused the northern area's "commercial interests" to suffer "for want of convenient courts."

5. *Plain Dealer*, February 8, 1854, 2.

6. *Senate Journal*, 33d Cong., 1st sess., 59 (December 21, 1853), 85 (January 9, 1854), and 110 (January 18, 1854); *House Journal*, 33d Cong., 1st sess., 248 (January 19, 1854), 253 (January 23, 1854), 682 (April 24, 1854), and 422 (April 27, 1854); *Mahoning Free Democrat* (Youngstown, Ohio), January 4, 1854, 3; *Plain Dealer*, March 10, 1854, 3.

7. See, e.g., *Ohio State Journal*, January 11, 1854, 2, February 17, 1854, 2, February 10, 1855, 2, and February 12, 1855, 2.

8. *Plain Dealer*, July 13, 1854, 2. See also *Plain Dealer*, August 12, 1854, 2, and October 7, 1854, 2.

9. See, e.g., *Plain Dealer*, March 10, 1854, 3, and March 13, 1854, 2.

10. George Irving Reed, ed., *Bench and Bar of Ohio: A Compendium of History and Biography* (Chicago: Century Publishing and Engraving, 1897), 2:37. Indeed, O. J. Hodge argued that Willson "commenced" the movement to divide the state into two districts. See O. J. Hodge, *Reminiscences* (Cleveland: Brooks, 1910), 2:94. See also *Plain Dealer*, March 10, 1854, 3.

11. *Plain Dealer*, March 10, 1854, 3, and March 13, 1854, 2.

12. 10 Stat. 605 (1855). The Northern District was to be composed of all counties north of the counties of Belmont, Guernsey, Muskingum, Licking, Franklin, Madison, Champaign, Shelby, and Mercer.

13. *Plain Dealer*, February 15, 1855, 2.

14. *Plain Dealer*, February 13, 1855, 2.

15. *Akron Beacon Journal*, February 28, 1855, 2. See also www.ohnd.uscourts.gov. It was rumored that the influential Ohio senator from Cincinnati, George E. Pugh, and a number of other Democrats opposed Willson, with some, at least, preferring Rufus P. Ranney, a justice on the Ohio Supreme Court. *New York Times*, February 13, 1855; *Plain Dealer*, February 19, 1855, 2, and February 21, 1855, 2; "Editorial Notes," *Magazine of Western History* 12, no. 2 (June 1890): 218.

16. *Toledo Blade*, February 14, 1855, 2. See also *Plain Dealer*, February 20, 1855, 2; *Ohio State Journal*, February 12, 1855, 2.

17. Hodge, *Reminiscences*, 2:94.

18. "Editorial Notes," quoting F. T. Wallace, a member of the Cleveland Bar.

19. Nat Brandt, *The Town That Started the Civil War* (Syracuse, N.Y.: Syracuse University Press, 1990), 115.

20. Maurice Joblin, *Cleveland: Past and Present—Its Representative Men* (Cleveland: Fairbanks, Benedict, 1869), 191; "Hiram V. Willson," available at www.ca6.uscourts.gov/lib_hist/history.html.

21. "Willson, Hiram V.," *The Encyclopedia of Cleveland History*, available at ech.cwru .edu/ech-cgi/article.pl?id+WHV. Willson was also active in his community, serving as director of the Cleveland Female Seminary, an officer of the University Heights Congregational Church, and a contributor to the Cleveland Law Library Association. To honor his achievements, the city named the street upon which he lived Willson Avenue (now E. 55th Street). Ibid. See also *Plain Dealer*, February 12, 1855, 2, for a list of civic projects to which he devoted himself. For a complete biography of Willson, see James Harrison Kennedy and Wilson M. Day, *The Bench and Bar of Cleveland* (Cleveland: Cleveland Printing and Publishing, 1889), 273; Reed, *Bench and Bar of Ohio*, 2:37; William R. Coats, *A History of Cuyahoga County and the City of Cleveland* (Chicago: American Historical Society, 1924), 1:436–37; and Crisfield Johnson, *History of Cuyahoga County, Ohio, with Portraits and Biographical Sketches of Its Prominent Men and Pioneers* (Philadelphia: D. W. Ensign, 1879), 320.

22. *New York Times*, February 13, 1858, 1, February 16, 1858, 2, May 5, 1858, 4, and May 10, 1858, 1. See also *Plain Dealer*, May 5, 1858, 3, and May 10, 1858, 2.

23. *Plain Dealer*, October 12, 1859, 2, October 17, 1859, 2, and October 26, 1859, 1.

24. *Leader*, December 29, 1858, 2.

25. District Court Journal, vol. 1 (1855–59), March 20, 1855, General Records, Eastern Division, Records of the U.S. District Court, Northern District of Ohio, Record Group (RG) 21, National Archives Branch Depository, Great Lakes Region, Chicago (hereafter cited as Journal). In the notes that follow, all the records of the U.S. District Court, Northern District of Ohio, will be identified simply as RG 21.

26. Ibid., March 21, 1855. The *Plain Dealer*. May 9, 1855, 3, printed a notice that those interested could purchase the court's Rules and Regulations for $.50.

27. Journal, March 21–April 2, 1855.

28. *Plain Dealer*, February 13, 1855, 2.

29. *Leader*, August 23, 1858, 3.

30. Both the *Plain Dealer* and the *Leader* had pushed for a grand courthouse, "a super structure" that would be "as fine . . . as any city in the West." But they had fought over its location. The *Plain Dealer* wanted the courthouse built on Superior Street, "as the most *central*" location and "one which nine-tenths of the people interested would approve as best accommodating all interests . . . on both sides of the river," or any location near the docks and central business area. The *Leader* preferred the east side of the Public Square as the most central location. The *Plain Dealer* even accused "land speculators" of pushing for a location that would benefit only their interests and chastised the *Leader* for supporting these men. See, e.g., *Plain Dealer*, February 13, 1855, 2, February 19, 1855, 2, February 21, 1855, 2, February 24, 1855, 2, May 15, 1855, 2, September 1, 1855, 3, February 11, 1857, 2, and July 7, 1857, 2; *Leader*, February 9, 1856, 2, and July 13, 1857, 2.

31. *Plain Dealer*, November 28, 1858, 3; *Leader*, January 24, 1859, 3.

32. The Judiciary Act of 1789, under which the federal courts were organized, created a three-tier court system. Below the Supreme Court, both the district and circuit courts served as trial courts. The circuit courts had appellate jurisdiction over some cases begun at the district level as well as trial responsibilities for major federal civil and criminal cases. In addition, defendants in diversity cases could remove their cases from state to federal court if the jurisdictional amount exceeded $500. The Judiciary Act restricted the district courts' criminal and civil jurisdiction to minor cases. But they had exclusive jurisdiction over all admiralty and maritime cases and over suits brought by the United States to collect penalties or to enforce forfeitures imposed on defendants who had been found to have violated federal law.

33. See *Plain Dealer*, January 25, 1859, 3, for an example of the courts meeting together, and November 8, 1859, 3, for an example of one court meeting in the morning and the other in the afternoon.

34. See, e.g., *Plain Dealer*, July 10, 1855, 3, July 25, 1855, 3, July 30, 1855, 3, July 12, 1858, 3, November 8, 1858, 3, and January 25, 1859, 3. On one occasion, the *Plain Dealer*, November 23, 1855, 3, reported that the circuit court was engaged in an admiralty trial. But since the district court had exclusive jurisdiction in admiralty cases, it is clear that, at least occasionally, newspapers got the proceedings of the two courts mixed up.

35. *Plain Dealer*, 1855–66, passim; *Leader*, 1856–66, passim.

36. Journal, July 2, 1855. The court had met briefly in May and June to hear a few admiralty cases and to begin naturalization proceedings, but these were special sessions. See Journal, May and June 1855, passim.

37. *Plain Dealer*, July 12, 1855, 2.

38. Quoted in *Plain Dealer*, November 13, 1856, 3.

39. Journal, May 7, 1855. See also May 1855, passim.

40. *Plain Dealer*, May 9, 1855, 3; Journal, 1855–66, passim.

41. Naturalization Journals, 1855–66, Naturalization Records, RG 21. See also Journal, 1855–66, passim. Cleveland newspapers also regularly reported on naturalization proceedings. See, e.g., *Plain Dealer*, 1855–66, passim, and *Leader*, 1855–66, passim.

42. Naturalization Journals, passim. The Cleveland newspapers seemed to encourage aliens to seek naturalization, regularly announcing that the court was open, "affording an opportunity for persons desiring [it] to obtain their naturalization papers"; *Leader*, March 10, 1859, 3. Just before the 1856 election, the *Plain Dealer*, October 31, 1856, 2, announced that the court would be open all day and evening "for the purpose of giving facilities to naturalization. All persons who have not obtained their citizen's papers, and are entitled to them, should lose no time." See also *Plain Dealer*, September 1, 1855, 3, and 1855–66, passim.

43. Naturalization Journals, 1855 and 1856 (computations mine).

44. See, e.g., Civil and Criminal Docket Books, 1855–67, passim, RG 21 (computations mine); *Plain Dealer*, March 3, 1857, 3; *Leader*, November 13, 1861, 3, November 22, 1862, 3, and November 26, 1862, 3; Ely et al. v. Hanks, 8 F. Cas. 600 (1858), Holmes et al. v. Cleveland, Columbus & Cincinnati Railroad Company et al., 93 F. 100 (1861).

45. *Plain Dealer*, May 24, 1856, 3. See also *Plain Dealer*, May 19, 1856, 3; Kennedy and Day, *Bench and Bar of Cleveland*, 38; Joblin, *Cleveland: Past and Present*, 193.

46. *Plain Dealer*, July 29, 1856, 3, January 21, 1857, 3, and February 14, 1857, 3.

47. Civil and Criminal Docket Books, 1855–67, passim (computations mine). See also Journal, 1855–66, passim.

48. See, e.g., *Plain Dealer*, August 20, 1859, 2, November 3, 1859, 3, and 1855–66, passim; *Leader*, May 10, 1865, 4, May 19, 1865, 4, July 21, 1866, 4, and 1855–66, passim. See also *Toledo Blade*, July 20, 1865, 2.

49. Kennedy and Day, *Bench and Bar of Cleveland*, 37.

50. See, e.g., *Plain Dealer*, February 26, 1857, 3, February 28, 1857, 3, and July 25, 1859, 3; *Leader*, July 26, 1859, 3, and October 12, 1863, 3. The first federal penitentiaries were created by the Three Prisons Act of 1891, which established penitentiaries in Leavenworth, Kansas; Atlanta, Georgia; and McNeil Island, Washington. See http://www.archives.gov/southeast/exhibit/3.php.

51. *Leader*, July 3, 1864, 4.

52. Civil and Criminal Docket Books, 1855–67, passim; Criminal Record Books, November Term 1855, July Term 1858, and July Term 1860, RG 21; Journal, 1855–66, passim; *Plain Dealer*, 1855–66, passim; *Leader*, 1855–66, passim.

53. *Plain Dealer*, November 22, 1858, 3, and November 24, 1858, 2; Journal, December 2, 1858, December 21, 1858, December 23, 1858, and December 24, 1858. The result of the original case to collect moneys owed from the railroad is not known.

54. *Plain Dealer*, December 9, 1861, 3, December 11, 1861, 3, and December 13, 1861, 3.

55. *Plain Dealer*, November 23, 1855, 3. See also Coats, *History of Cuyahoga County*, 1:393.

56. Coats, *History of Cuyahoga County*, 1:451.

57. Kennedy and Day, *Bench and Bar of Cleveland*, 37.

58. Journal, December 6 and December 8, 1858, and 1858–59 passim.

59. Quoted in *Plain Dealer*, November 11, 1858, 3.

60. *Plain Dealer*, November 10, 1858, 3.

61. *Leader*, December 8, 1858, 2. The *Leader*, December 29, 1858, 2, also accused the clerk and marshal of the court of packing the grand and petit juries with "political partisans." For other criticisms of Willson, see *Leader*, January–May 1859, passim.

62. Almost immediately after the government discontinued prosecution in the Oberlin cases, the trial of over twenty men for preventing the arrest of Lucy, an escaped slave from Virginia, took place. The case was continued throughout 1861 and finally dropped. Journal, December 7, 1860, January 3, 1861, March 18, 1861, July Term 1861, and 1861–62, passim. See also *Plain Dealer*, March 13, 1861, 3.

63. William Ganson Rose, *Cleveland: The Making of a City* (Cleveland: World Publishing, 1950), 290.

64. Kennedy and Day, *Bench and Bar of Cleveland*, 37.

65. Rose, *Cleveland*, 290.

66. Kennedy and Day, *Bench and Bar of Cleveland*, 98; *Plain Dealer*, February 28, 1859, 3; *Leader*, May 14, 1859, 1.

67. *Leader*, May 12, 1859, 2. At the time, many severely criticized Willson for his complicity in enforcing the 1850 law in an extremely biased way, but after his death, members of the bar praised the judge for the calm and dispassionate way he presided over the case and credited him with preserving law and order and a peaceful community during those tense times. See, e.g., Reed, *Bench and Bar of Ohio*, 2:37; Kennedy and Day, *Bench and Bar of Cleveland*, 98–99.

68. See, e.g., *Plain Dealer*, April 14, 1859, 2, April 15, 1859, 2, April 16, 1859, 2, April 20, 1859, 3, April 21, 1859, 2, April 22, 1859, 2, May 2, 1859, 2, May 11, 1859, 1, 2, May 12, 1859, 2, May 13, 1859, 2, and May 19, 1859, 2.

69. Paul Finkelman, "Race, Slavery and the Law in Antebellum Ohio," in *A History of Ohio Law*, ed. Michael Les Benedict and John F. Winkler (Athens: Ohio University Press, 2004), 2:769–73.

70. *Encyclopedia of Cleveland Law*, available at ech.case.edu/ech-cgi/article.pl?id=L6.

71. Bicentennial Committee of the Judicial Conference of the United States, *History of the Sixth Circuit: A Bicentennial Project* (Washington, D.C.: Bicentennial Committee of the Judicial Conference of the United States, 1977), 209.

72. *Plain Dealer*, November 12, 1866, 2. See also Reed, *Bench and Bar of Ohio*, 2:37, praising Willson for his vast knowledge in this area of law.

73. Reed, *Bench and Bar of Ohio*, 2:37.

74. Wolverton v. Lacey, 30 F. Cas. 417–420 (N.D. Ohio February 1856). See also Journal, November 23, 1855, and February 2, 1856; Criminal Record Books, November Term 1855. And see *Plain Dealer*, November 23, 1855, 3.

75. See, e.g., The Clarion, 5 F. Cas. 832 (N.D. Ohio 1859), Admiralty Records 1855–1902, vol. 2, November Term 1859, Admiralty Records, RG 21 (hereafter cited as Admiralty Records), and *Plain Dealer*, March 17, 1859, 3; James T. Brown v. The Steam Boat Troy,

James Cable v. The Steam Boat Troy, Leonard Reis v. The Steam Boat Troy, Esau Thorp v. The Steam Boat Troy, and T. I. Wardell v. Steam Boat Troy, Admiralty Records 1855–1902, vol. 2, January Special Term 1860, June Term 1860. But in Kynoch v. The S. C. Ives, Willson ruled that the court had no jurisdiction in this contract dispute because the contract was an executory rather than an executed one and that courts of admiralty "have no general jurisdiction to administer relief as courts of equity." Kynoch v. The S. C. Ives, 14 F. Cas. 888, 891 (N.D. Ohio 1856). See also Journal, August 4 and 5, 1856.

76. *Plain Dealer*, July 20, 1858, 3.

77. The Revenue Cutter No. 1, 20 F. Cas. 560 (N.D. Ohio 1860). See also Admiralty Records, vol. 2 January Special Term 1859.

78. The Revenue Cutter No. 1, 20 F. Cas. at 560, 563.

79. Ibid., 565–68. The case was so significant that the *Plain Dealer* printed Willson's decision in total on its front page on March 15, 1860.

80. Lyon v. The Isabella, 13 F. Cas. 158 (N.D. Ohio 1860). See also Admiralty Records, March Special Term 1860. The case was an important one, reported in detail in the *Plain Dealer*, March 16, 1860, 3. The *Plain Dealer*, March 23, 1860, 3, noted that the judgment was carried out a week later, the *Isabella* being sold to pay off its liens.

81. Lyon v. The Isabella, 13 F. Cas. at 159.

82. Ibid., 161. Willson did, on occasion, uphold state authority. See, e.g., Wick v. The Samuel Strong, 29 F. Cas. 1130.

83. See Admiralty Records, vols. 1–2, passim; Journal, August 4, 1856, September 22, 1856, September 23, 1856, and March-April Term 1857, passim, and especially April 28, 1857, and June 9, 1857. See also *Leader*, March 9, 1859, 3; *Plain Dealer*, March 17, 1859, 3, May 9, 1860, 3, and June 4, 1860, 3.

84. See, e.g., *Plain Dealer*, June 7, 1855, 4, June 8, 1855, 4, June 22, 1855, 4, June 23, 1855, 4, and 1855–66, passim.

85. *Plain Dealer*, January 13, 1865, 3. Willson also decided cases of physical assaults between seamen and between seamen and their captains. See, e.g., Criminal Records Books, November Term 1858 and July Term 1861; Journal, November 24, 1858, November 27, 1858, November 30, 1858, December 1, 1858, December 2, 1858, June 4, 1861, and July 10, 1861; *Plain Dealer*, July 11, 1861, 3; *Leader*, August 16, 1861, 3.

86. Admiralty Records, vol. 2, April Term 1860. See also Waldorf et al. v. The New York, 28 F. Cas. 1360, 1361 (N.D. Ohio 1862).

87. *Leader*, February 21, 1860, 3.

88. Waldorf et al. v. The New York, 28 F. Cas. at 1362, 1363. In *Cleveland: Past and Present*, 193, Joblin claimed that in *Hoag v. the Propeller Cataract*, Willson also set forth the law of collision, citing numerous precedents. That collision, where the propellor *Cataract* sank the brig *Oxford*, received much attention because of its tragic nature. Not only did the *Cataract* sink the *Oxford*, with the loss of the ship and cargo, but the master of the ship, his wife, his child, and three seaman were lost at sea. After the case dragged on for almost a year, Willson finally held that the damages "ought to be equally apportioned" between the libelants and the claimant. See also Admiralty Records, vol. 1, May Special Term 1857; Journal, September 20, 1856, October 6, 1856, March 11, 1857, April 29, 1857, March 20, 1857, and June 9, 1857; *Plain Dealer*, March 13, 1857, 3.

89. Waldorf et al. v. The New York, 28 F. Cas. at 1363–64. In another case, Willson used similar analysis and precedents to hold the sailing ship at fault. See Lake Erie & Buffalo Steamboat Co. v. The Son & Heir, 14 F. Cas. 948 (N.D. Ohio 1863); Admiralty Records, vol. 3, June Term 1862.

90. Willson's charge to the Grand Jury in the Circuit Court of the United States, Northern District of Ohio, January Term, 1864, published in *Plain Dealer*, January 6, 1864, 2.

91. *New York Times*, November 15, 1859, 2.

92. Ibid.; *Plain Dealer*, November 10, 1859, 1.

93. *Leader*, November 14, 1861, 3.

94. Cited in Joblin, *Cleveland: Past and Present*, 195–96. Throughout the war years, Willson used his judicial position to support the war, and beyond that, in many private activities he indicated his support for the Northern cause. See *Leader*, September 3, 1863, 3, and May 20, 1864, 4.

95. See, e.g., Journal, September 19, 1861, November 22, 1861, and passim; August 4, August 18, and August 19, 1863; *Plain Dealer*, November 6, 1861, 3; *Leader*, October 25, 1861, 4, and August 20, 1863, 1.

96. *Plain Dealer*, January 6, 1864, 2.

97. See, e.g., Journal, November 1861 and February 6, 1862; *Plain Dealer*, May 8, 1863, 3, January 6, 1864, 3, January 7, 1864, 3, May 18, 1864, 3, May 21, 1864, 3, May 28, 1864, 3, January 18, 1865, 3, January 23, 1865, 3, and January 26, 1865, 3; *Leader*, April 7, 1863, 1, July 3, 1863, 3, July 11, 1863, 1, July 16, 1863, 3, July 25, 1863, 3, October 16, 1863, 3, January 19, 1865, 4, and July 12, 1866, 4.

98. *Plain Dealer*, January 6, 1864, 2.

99. Ohio History Central, available at www.ohiohistorycentral.org/entry.php?rec=474, and Ohio Historical Markers, available at www.ohiochannel.org/your_state/remarkable_ohio/marker_details.cfm?marker_id= 993.

100. *Leader*, July 3, 1863, 3; *Plain Dealer*, May 21, 1864, 3; and also see en.wikipedia.org/wiki/Battle_ of_Fort_Fizzle. In May 1864, nine men from Knox County were indicted for conspiracy to resist the draft. However, after the jury was sworn, the district attorney entered a nolo contendere and the defendants were discharged. *Plain Dealer*, May 28, 1864, 3.

101. See, e.g., Journal, May 1862. The civil and criminal dockets listed seven cases in 1865 and three more in 1866; Civil and Criminal Docket Books, 1865–67. See also *Plain Dealer*, August 8, 1865, 3, September 6, 1865, 3, and July 12, 1866, 3; *Leader*, July 18, 1866, 4, August 6, 1866, 4, October 5, 1866, 4, and October 31, 1866, 4.

102. *Plain Dealer*, July 12, 1866, 3.

103. *Leader*, June 7, 1866, 4, and September 6, 1866, 1. See also *Plain Dealer*, September 26, 1866, 3. And see Journal, vol. 3, January 11, 1867. During Willson's illness, Solomon L. Withy, district judge for the Western District of Michigan, presided over the District Court for the Northern District of Ohio. Journal, vol. 3, January 10, 1866.

104. *Plain Dealer*, November 12, 1866, 2; *Leader*, November 13, 1866, 2; *Toledo Blade*, November 15, 1866, 2; *New York Times*, November 13, 1866.

105. *Plain Dealer*, November 12, 1866, 2.

106. Reed, *Bench and Bar of Ohio*, 2:37. See also *Leader*, November 13, 1866, 1.

107. *Plain Dealer*, November 13, 1866, 2, and November 12, 1866, 2.

108. *Leader*, November 13, 1866, 1.

109. One resolution passed by the Cleveland Bar acknowledged its "obligations" to Willson, "by whose influence and labors the Courts of the United States were established in our midst." *Plain Dealer*, November 13, 1866, 2.

2

A Political Show Trial in the Northern District

The Oberlin-Wellington Fugitive Slave Rescue Case

Paul Finkelman

O N MONDAY, SEPTEMBER 13, 1858, William Shakespeare Boynton, the thirteen-year-old son of an Oberlin farmer, asked John Price, a fugitive slave living in Oberlin, if he wanted to earn some money harvesting potatoes. Price declined but agreed to accompany Boynton to the house of another black he thought would be interested in the work. Although Price was a fugitive slave, he saw no threat from young Boynton and readily hopped into his buggy. But Boynton was in fact working for Anderson Jennings, a Kentucky slave catcher who was operating under a power of attorney from John Bacon, Price's owner. Jennings also had a warrant for Price under the Fugitive Slave Law of 1850, issued by a commissioner from the U.S. District Court for the Southern District of Ohio. For $20—a significant sum at the time—Boynton had agreed to lure Price out of Oberlin so he could be quietly seized. About a mile outside Oberlin, Jacob K. Lowe, a U.S. deputy marshal from Columbus—together with Samuel Davis, a deputy sheriff from Franklin County, and Richard P. Mitchell, Bacon's Kentucky neighbor who was moonlighting as a slave catcher—overtook Boynton, seized Price, and then headed to Wellington, Ohio, about ten miles away. In

Wellington, they took Price to the Wadsworth Hotel to wait for the next train to Columbus, where Price would be formally remanded to Jennings under the Fugitive Slave Law. Meanwhile, Jennings remained in Oberlin until Boynton returned. He then paid the young teenager and set out for Wellington at a leisurely pace.[1]

These carefully calculated plans might have worked, except that shortly after Price's capture, the buggy carrying Price and his captors passed two Oberlin residents who were heading home. Price yelled to them for help. Neither offered any assistance, but when they reached Oberlin, one of them, Ansel W. Lyman, an Oberlin College student who had served with John Brown in Kansas, immediately spread word about the "kidnapping"—as abolitionists referred to the seizure of fugitive slaves. Within minutes, Oberlin residents—students, college professors, shopkeepers, laborers—were gathering vehicles and horses, as well as rifles and pistols, and heading to Wellington.

By the end of the day, Price would be rescued and quickly sent to Canada, where he would remain free. Shortly after the rescue, the federal prosecutor secured grand jury indictments of thirty-seven men for violating the Fugitive Slave Law of 1850. Presiding over the grand jury was Judge Hiram Willson, a loyal Democrat who had been appointed to the newly created U.S. District Court for the Northern District of Ohio in 1855. Like his sponsor, President Franklin Pierce, Willson was a classic doughface Democrat—a northern man with southern principles. He was a strong booster of Cleveland and northern Ohio and earned his seat on the court by lobbying heavily for the creation of the new district.[2] But he was also deeply loyal to the proslavery agenda of northern Democrats, such as Pierce and James Buchanan, who seethed at the hostility to the Fugitive Slave Law coming out of their own constituencies. Willson's charge to the grand jury condemned opponents of the law, asserting that theirs was "a sentiment semi-religious in its development, and almost invariably characterized by intolerance and bigotry."[3] Willson apparently saw no irony in accusing those who opposed the Fugitive Slave Law of "intolerance and bigotry," even though the law was directed at only one group of people—African Americans —and was utterly intolerant of their legal rights.

The indictments that came from Judge Willson's charge would lead to the first significant trials in Ohio's newly created Northern District Court. More than a century and a half later, these prosecutions remain among the court's most famous cases. To understand the Oberlin cases, we must begin in the town and state where Price was seized.

The Fugitive Slave Law of 1850 and the Rescue of John Price

Fugitives from Virginia and Kentucky regularly escaped across the Ohio River into the Buckeye State. The Ohio River was a great highway to freedom for countless blacks, many of whom went no farther than Cincinnati. Despite obvious discrimination, the occasional antiblack race riot, and the threat from Kentucky slave catchers, the Queen City had more blacks than any other place in the state and a higher percentage of blacks than the rest of the state.[4]

Although Cincinnati offered blacks a large community, a vibrant economy, and the cultural advantages of a major urban center, tiny Oberlin, in northern Ohio, offered them real and substantial opportunity. Located in Ohio's Western Reserve, which had been settled by New Englanders who were overwhelmingly hostile to slavery, Oberlin quickly became a haven for fugitive slaves and free blacks. Here, African Americans could raise their children without the stigma of segregated public schools. In 1833, evangelical opponents of slavery established Oberlin College as an integrated institution, with blacks and women admitted on equal terms with white men. While blacks could not vote in Ohio, the state constitution did not prevent them from holding office, and in Oberlin and Lorain County, the antislavery voters chose John Mercer Langston, the son of a slave and her Virginia master, for a number of offices. Langston was not the first African American elected to public office in the United States,[5] but he was the first black to hold elective office in the Midwest. In 1858, he was serving as a township clerk.[6]

At that time, Oberlin had about four hundred free black residents and a hundred or so fugitive slaves. For most blacks and the whites in Oberlin, it was a matter of great pride that no fugitive slave had ever been successfully removed from the town or from Lorain County. Many of the town's fugitive slaves, like John Price, were on the margins of society, possessing few skills and little property. The free black community had many poor and unskilled people as well, but it also contained business owners, tradesmen, skilled workers, and some professionals, including the lawyer John Mercer Langston and his brother Charles, who was a teacher.

Blacks throughout the North were particularly concerned about their liberty after the passage of the Fugitive Slave Law of 1850. Technically an amendment to the Fugitive Slave Law of 1793, this measure created the first federal law enforcement bureaucracy in the nation's history. The law provided for the appointment of federal commissioners in every county to issue warrants for the seizure of alleged fugitives, to hear cases under the law, and to call out the army and the state militia or raise a local posse to enforce it. An alleged fugitive was given a juryless hearing before a federal judge or U.S. commissioner. The individual was not allowed to testify at this summary proceeding, although out-of-court statements by the alleged fugitive were often introduced, to his or her detriment. Thus, even before Chief Justice Roger Taney held in *Dred Scott v. Sandford* that blacks had no rights under the Constitution,[7] Congress concluded that they could have no voice when courts considered if they were free people or slaves. The law further prohibited any judge, at the state or federal level, from issuing a writ of habeas corpus to remove the alleged slave from the custody of a federal marshal or a slave catcher. Most outrageously, federal commissioners received $5 if they determined the person brought to them was not a slave but $10 if they remanded the captured black to slavery. Anyone convicted of interfering with the return of a fugitive could be sentenced to six months in jail and be subject to a $1,000 fine plus court costs.

The law was designed to speedily send people back to slavery without any meaningful due process. Once seized under the law, a northern black had little chance of regaining his or her freedom except by escaping the clutches of the slave catchers. John Price's fate rested in the hands of others who were willing to risk heavy fines and jail terms to rescue him.

Thus, when news reached Oberlin that Price had been seized by slave catchers, hundreds of the town's residents rode off to Wellington, where a standoff quickly developed. Price was held in the attic of the Wadsworth Hotel, guarded by a handful of armed men. By 3:00 PM, the public square outside the hotel was filled with people, probably three or four hundred, although the slave catcher, Jennings, thought there were a thousand. Most were from Oberlin and Wellington, with some from nearby farms. The crowd was overwhelmingly white, although about two dozen blacks were also mingling in front of the hotel. A significant number of men, black and white, were armed.[8] For the Kentuckians guarding Price, the sight of armed blacks must have been shocking and frightening.

The slave catchers were outnumbered and outgunned. Some of the abolitionists were pacifists,[9] and others were unwilling to use violence against a federal deputy. But it is unlikely the men inside the hotel knew this. They only saw a huge crowd with many armed men. They also knew that without some settlement or outside help, it would be impossible for them to get to the train station for the 5:13 PM train to Columbus.[10] At the same time, people in the crowd feared the train would bring reinforcements, including the militia, the regular army, or more federal deputies, to aid the slave catchers; the men in the hotel hoped this would be the case.

A few members of the crowd eventually made their way into the hotel to negotiate an end to the standoff. A local constable, Barnabas Meacham, tried to serve a warrant on the slave catchers for kidnapping. Meacham wanted those holding Price to go before a local judge to prove they had proper legal process to seize him as well as some evidence that he was a fugitive slave and, moreover, that he was *the* fugitive slave named in the papers. Meacham failed to serve the warrant when warned that interfering with the enforcement of the Fugitive Slave Law could lead to a $1,000 fine and six months in jail. He briefly examined the papers Jennings had and thought they appeared to be in order, though he noted they lacked an official seal. But Meacham was just a constable, not a judge or a lawyer. The slave catchers refused to appear before any judge in Wellington and also refused to show their papers to any judge. It would later turn out that the papers and warrants had some irregularities in them.

Had this been a simple arrest in a criminal case, the law enforcement personnel would probably have consented to go before a local judge to prove their prima facie claim to their prisoner. Or they would have responded to a writ of habeas corpus issued by a local judge. But the 1850 law was designed to circumvent any state or local interference with the return of fugitive slaves. Thus, the confrontation in Wellington was real and not easily defused. Most in the crowd thought Price was about to be carted off to bondage without any meaningful opportunity to defend his rights. Many believed that under the law of God, if not the law of man, no one had a right to reduce another human being to slavery. Price's captors, however, believed strongly that they had the law and fundamental justice on their side. Bacon, the Kentucky slave owner, had a substantial economic investment in his slave and was entitled to his property under the laws and Constitution of the United States. Although the antislavery men in the crowd believed that returning a fugitive slave was unjust and unchristian, the slave catchers might have responded that just as Saint Paul had returned the fugitive slave Onesimus to Philemon,[11] so too should the religious Christians in Oberlin have cooperated in the return of Price to his owner.

The chaos of the moment — and the mutual fears of all concerned — made any serious evaluation of the legal issues impossible. In fact, though there were problems with the paperwork of the slave catchers, they did have a warrant from the U.S. commissioner in Columbus, which should have been sufficient for them to take Price out of town. But there was no possibility of ascertaining any of this because the slave catchers were unwilling to leave the safety of the hotel.

After Meacham departed, U.S. Deputy Marshal Lowe asked Charles Langston, the black schoolteacher from Oberlin, and the brother of the black office-holder John Mercer Langston, to come to the hotel. Lowe knew Langston from previous trips to Oberlin and considered him to be "a reasonable man."[12] Lowe also understood that Langston was a leader of the community: if he could be persuaded to allow the legal process to move forward, the marshal might be able to still the crowd.

Inside the hotel, the conversation did not go well. Lowe tried to convince Langston that he had complete legal authority to remove Price to Columbus. At some point, he told Langston there was "no use of talking, we are going to hold him as long as we can." Lowe later testified that Langston responded, "We will have him any how."[13]

The meaning of this conversation—and its content—is subject to multiple interpretations. The federal prosecutors saw Langston's words as a blatant threat to rescue Price. Yet Langston did not actually participate in the rescue, and there is no evidence he worked directly with the rescuers themselves. Langston claimed he did not say "*we* will have him" but rather simply warned Lowe that many in "the crowd were much excited, many of them averse to longer delay and bent upon rescue at all hazards." Langston told Lowe this because the marshal was "an old acquaintance and friend": thus, the schoolteacher said, he was "anxious to extricate him from the dangerous position he occupied, and therefore advised that he urge Jennings to give the boy up." Langston openly advocated a legal response to the crisis, using a writ of habeas corpus to bring Price before a judge. And he said that if he used language similar to what Lowe alleged, it was to tell Lowe that "they will have him," not that "*we* will have him." This, of course, changes the entire meaning of what Lowe claimed took place.[14] Langston argued that he was simply being predictive. With hundreds of angry and armed abolitionists in the front of the hotel, he was just stating the obvious—that the abolitionists would rescue Price.

And so they did. Shortly after the 5:13 train arrived, with no reinforcements, two groups of men forced their way into the hotel. William E. Lincoln, an Oberlin College student deeply dedicated to antislavery, asked for volunteers, but despite the huge number of men in front of the hotel and their overwhelming opposition to slavery, only five other armed men—three whites (including Ansel Lyman, the veteran of Bleeding Kansas) and two blacks—joined him.

Meanwhile, John Scott, a free black harness maker from Oberlin, organized a group of blacks, including John Copland, Henry Evans, and the fugitive slave Jerry Fox, to rescue Price. Langston followed them to the hotel, but he did not go upstairs where Price was being held and did not participate in his actual rescue.

Both groups of men quickly forced their way into the hotel. There was a brief skirmish, with no one seriously injured and no guns fired. The slave catchers may have had the law on their side and Price was clearly a valuable catch, but none of the Kentuckians or their Ohio confederates were ready to die (or even be seriously injured) just to return a slave to the South. The rescue took only a few minutes. Price was carried out of the hotel, and Simeon Bushnell, a white typesetter, drove him back to Oberlin. Bushnell first stopped at the home of his brother-in-law (and employer) James Fitch, a bookseller and printer. Bushnell then took Price to the home of Professor James Fairchild, who was deeply antislavery but publicly opposed to breaking the Fugitive Slave Law. This made him "the logical person to hide [Price]" until he could be taken out of town and across Lake Erie,[15] where he disappeared into the large fugitive slave community in Upper Canada. As his freedom was being secured by the laws and power of Queen Victoria's government, the liberty of his rescuers was more problematic, since they had so blatantly broken the laws of the United States and challenged the power of President James Buchanan.

The Indictments

Oberlin rejoiced at the rescue. The rescuers were local heroes who had vindicated the town's honor. But the honor of the Buchanan administration had been stained, and in Washington and Cleveland, federal officials planned to vindicate their own honor and their proslavery politics.

Since its passage in 1850, the Fugitive Slave Law had bedeviled every presidential administration. In 1851, President Millard Fillmore and Secretary of State Daniel Webster arranged for the arrest of a fugitive named Jerry McHenry while a Liberty Party convention was taking place in Syracuse, New York. The Fillmore administration made no provisions for extra deputies or military force to secure the fugitive. This absurd attempt to embarrass the antislavery movement in heavily abolitionist central New York backfired when a huge mob rescued Jerry, who soon ended up in Canada. A series of prosecutions went nowhere, and the abolitionist Frederick Douglass declared that the Fugitive Slave Act was virtually a "dead letter" in central New York.[16] After fugitives at Christiana, Pennsylvania, successfully resisted being seized, Fillmore personally ordered the U.S. district attorney in Philadelphia to bring treason indictments against forty-seven men who simply refused to aid the U.S. marshal. These prosecutions also embarrassed the administration when Supreme Court Justice Robert Grier, while riding circuit, ruled that whatever the bystanders had done, they were clearly not making war against the United States and thus they could not be charged with treason. Fillmore and Secretary of State Webster also oversaw seemingly endless prosecutions of black and white abolitionists in Boston after a group of free blacks helped the slave Shadrach escape from federal custody and later in the year almost liberated Thomas Sims from custody. None of the trials resulted in convictions.[17]

Franklin Pierce was only marginally more successful than Fillmore in enforcing the Fugitive Slave Law. In 1854, the Pierce administration arranged for the arrest of the fugitive slave Anthony Burns in Boston. The administration used federal troops, the local militia, and more than one hundred special deputies to prevent a rescue of Burns and then used a coast guard cutter to send him back to Virginia. Abolitionists unsuccessfully stormed the jail where Burns was being held, but they were unable to rescue him. Prosecutions of the would-be rescuers produced no convictions, but the federal government spent nearly $100,000 to return Burns to Virginia, where he was subsequently auctioned off for just over $900.

The Oberlin case provided Buchanan with the opportunity to prove his support for slavery, the South, and the Fugitive Slave Law. The administration had not planned the arrest of Price, and the commissioner and marshal from the Southern District of Ohio had not worked with their counterparts in the new Northern District to ensure sufficient force to effectuate the seizure. Indeed, the ease of his rescue illustrated the failure of federal officials in this case. But once the rescue took place, the administration had to aggressively respond to this challenge to the 1850 law. In addition, the rescue provided supporters of the administration in northern Ohio with an opportunity to use their political power and the court system to punish not only the rescuers but also well-known abolitionists and members of the recently formed Republican Party, who publicly challenged the law and opposed Buchanan.

Within days of the event, U.S. District Judge Hiram V. Willson called a grand jury into session to investigate the rescue. Gathering the grand jurors was in the hands of U.S. Marshal Matthew Johnson, while U.S. Attorney George W. Belden worked closely with him in preparing evidence for the grand jury.

The grand jury did not represent the Northern District of Ohio, and its makeup suggests the highly political nature of these trials. Northern Ohio was overwhelmingly Republican and antislavery. In 1856, the brand-new Republican Party carried ten of eleven congressional districts in northern Ohio. Northeastern Ohio sent three committed abolitionists—Joshua R. Giddings, Edward Wade, and John A. Bingham—to Congress, and the state, on the basis of Republican power in the north, sent the radical abolitionist Benjamin F. Wade to the Senate.[18] The Republican presidential candidate, John C. Frémont, carried the sixteen northeastern counties in a landslide, winning more than 60 percent of the vote.[19] Frémont won 81 percent of the vote in Ashtabula and Geauga counties, 78 percent in Lake, 71 percent in Lorain, 68 percent in Trumbull, 66 percent in Huron, 64 percent in Summit, 62 percent in Medina, 61 percent in Erie, and 57 percent in Cuyahoga.[20] The only significant Democratic officeholders in the area were federal appointees tied to the proslavery Buchanan administration. All of the important elected officials in the region were Republicans, hostile to slavery. Yet every member of the grand jury was a Democrat who supported the Buchanan administration, and in a stunning departure from due process and traditional legal ethics, one of the grand jurors, Lewis Boynton, was personally involved in the case. Jennings had visited Boynton's farm and had hired his teenage son, Shakespeare, to lure Price out of town. The impropriety of putting Boynton on the grand jury underscores the lax ethical standards of Johnson, Belden, and Judge Willson. It is perhaps not surprising that the prosecutor would want to stack the grand jury. But Judge Willson should have known better. That he did not indicates his own partisan hostility to antislavery and his willingness to ignore basic standards of due process.

Much of northern Ohio had been settled by New Englanders, who were culturally antislavery, but Willson came from Buffalo, New York, where there was substantially less antislavery sentiment. In 1841 while in Buffalo, he helped trick a black into leaving the state so he could be sent to Louisiana. Willson was subsequently charged with kidnapping. While these charges were pending, he fled to Ohio.[21] Judge Willson's grand jury charge reflected his roots and his hostility to antislavery and New Englanders. He properly and appropriately set out the nature of what constituted a violation under the Fugitive Slave Act of 1850. But then he abandoned his guise as a nonpartisan jurist and launched into a political harangue and mini-sermon, condemning the "sentiment . . . which arrogates to human conduct a standard of right above, and independent of, human laws; and it makes the CONSCIENCE of each individual in society the TEST of his own ACCOUNTABILITY to the laws of the land." Willson then compared opponents of the Fugitive Slave Law to "prelates of the dark ages," saying they were "versed in all they consider useful and sanctified learning—trained in certain schools in New England to manage words" and "skilled in practicing upon the superstition and credulity of others—FALSE, as it is natural a man should be whose dogmas impose upon all who are not saints according to HIS CREED the necessity of being hypocrites." Willson told the grand jury that opposition to the Fugitive Slave Act "leads to the subversion of all, and a consequent insecurity of all the constitutional rights of the citizens."[22]

This charge appealed to religious and political prejudices and was directed at anyone who opposed the law, without regard to any specific actions. Almost all the witnesses at the grand jury were vetted by the handful of Democrats from Oberlin, led by U.S. Deputy Marshal Anson Dayton (whom Charles Langston's brother, John Mercer Langston, had defeated in the recent election for town supervisor). These Democrats also provided Belden with a list of potential suspects to be indicted.[23] On December 7, the grand jury brought indictments against thirty-seven men. Twenty-five were from Oberlin, and twelve of these were black. Another twelve were from Wellington. Oddly, Professor Fairchild, who had harbored Price, was not indicted. None of the indicted men were Democrats, although at least one Oberlin Democrat, Norris Wood, had openly bragged about playing a role in the rescue, including climbing a ladder to gain entry to the attic where Price was being held. The *Cleveland Morning Leader* believed that politics, not apparent guilt, was the key to determining who was indicted. Three of the indicted Oberlin men—Henry E. Peck, Ralph Plumb, and James M. Fitch—were not in Wellington at the time of the rescue, and the government had no evidence tying them to helping Price after the rescue.[24] But they were leading and vocal opponents of the Fugitive Slave Law. Similarly, eight of the twelve indicted from Wellington were known opponents of the law and allegedly active in the Underground Railroad. For some of these defendants, the connection to the rescue was minimal. A seventy-four-year-old Wellington farmer had merely urged the owner of the Wadsworth Hotel to open the doors so the rescuers could gain entrance and thus avoid violence or property destruction. Another individual, Matthew De Wolfe, had tried to raise money to indemnify Constable Meacham if he served the writ of habeas corpus on the slave catchers. Neither took part in the rescue, but both were well known for their opposition to the Fugitive Slave Law and allegedly had helped fugitive slaves in the past.

The events at Wellington were unplanned and chaotic. Before the rescue, numerous men, including a number who would later be indicted, tried to negotiate a settlement. Their relationship to the rescue was unclear, tangential, or nonexistent. Judge Willson and the grand jury might have reasonably concluded that those who were trying to negotiate a settlement were not interfering with the law. In theory, the offer to bring Deputy Marshal Lowe to a judge to have his paperwork examined might have led to a peaceful removal of Price. When negotiations failed, two separate groups of men rushed the hotel with no coordination or planning. The rescuers had not been in contact with the negotiators, so there was no conspiracy and no rescue plan if the negotiations failed. Nor did the negotiators directly incite the rescuers or join them. Obviously, those in Oberlin could not possibly have had any impact on what happened in Wellington.

Nevertheless, Judge Willson and District Attorney Belden cast a wide net, charging rescuers, free blacks, fugitive slaves, suspected Underground Railroad conductors, leaders of the Oberlin community, and bystanders. When Belden could not produce any evidence or testimony tying Peck, Plumb, and Fitch to the rescue, Judge Willson recessed the grand jury until the district attorney could find someone to testify to a statement or act by the men that might plausibly indicate they had aided or abetted the rescue that took place miles from where they were.[25]

Buchanan, like Fillmore and Pierce, was anxious to conduct political show trials in Ohio in order to persecute abolitionists, pressure those who helped fugitive slaves, and if possible convict some people who had actually helped Price escape. Yet Judge Willson was no pawn in the machinations of the Buchanan administration. Only recently appointed to the court, he was as committed as anyone in the administration to punishing those who violated the law, but like most Buchanan Democrats, he was also openly hostile to anyone who publicly opposed the Fugitive Slave Act.

The First Trial

The indictments were issued on December 6, 1858, when Marshal Johnson went to Oberlin with "a large packet" of twenty-five warrants."[26] He started at the home of Professor Henry E. Peck, who cordially met with him in his study.

47

Peck then guided Johnson through Oberlin so he could serve his papers. Most of the defendants were easily found, although a few were out of town because the college was on winter break. The three indicted fugitive slaves had wisely left town and would never be located. Johnson asked Peck and the other Oberlin defendants to go to Cleveland the next day to be arraigned. They all left together, with a large crowd cheering them at the train station. In Cleveland, they met with their three-man legal team, which was led by Rufus P. Spalding, a former speaker of the Ohio House of Representatives and a former justice on the Ohio Supreme Court. Spalding had started his career as a Democrat and was a close friend of Governor Salmon P. Chase, another former Democrat who had become one of the most prominent opponents of slavery in the new Republican Party. (In his closing argument in Bushnell's case, Spalding would cite his own Democratic roots to appeal to the twelve Democrats on the jury.) Joining Spalding were Albert Gallatin Riddle, a former county prosecutor who had also served in the Ohio legislature, and Seneca O. Griswold, a relatively young lawyer who was also an Oberlin graduate.

So far, everything about the proceedings seemed surreal. The lead defendant had helped the U.S. marshal locate his quarry; in fact, Marshal Johnson told a newspaper that in Oberlin he had been met "with the utmost courtesy and good feeling."[27] Most of the defendants had enthusiastically proceeded, at their own expense, to Cleveland. But at the arraignment, this cordiality began to disappear. Spalding asked that the trial begin that day. He was ready to defend his clients and assumed that U.S. Attorney Belden was prepared to prosecute them, since Belden had been preparing his case for weeks. In the nineteenth century, such quick trials were common, so there was nothing extraordinary about starting a trial almost immediately after arraignment. However, Belden was not ready for trial. To prove his case, he had to show that Price was indeed a fugitive slave, owned by Bacon, and that he had been taken from the custody of Bacon's lawful agent, Jennings. Only the testimony of Bacon and Jennings could prove this. But they were in Kentucky.

Thus, Belden "begged" the court for a two-week continuance. Spalding sarcastically countered that "citizens of Ohio might think two weeks some time to lie in jail for the convenience of citizens of Kentucky." Willson responded that would not be necessary because he would set bail, but Spalding argued that many of his clients were poor and could not post bail. Belden, while asking to postpone the trial, nevertheless insisted on bail, and Willson set it at $500, which he said was a modest amount. In fact, $500 was a significant amount and

48

a sum that many of the defendants did not have. After conferring with his clients, Spalding told Willson that they had no intention of posting bail, boldly declaring, "The accused were ready for, and demanded immediate trial. The United States had summoned them to appear for trial, and it was the business of the United States to be ready to proceed with the trial without delay." Spalding proposed that they be set free on their own recognizance. After a private conversation with Belden, Willson returned with a face-saving compromise. Each defendant would be freed on an "individual recognizance" with a penalty of $1,000 if he did not show up for trial. The court then adjourned, but not for the two weeks Belden wanted. Instead, the court would reconvene on March 8, after its winter recess.[28]

In the next three months, Belden continued to prepare his case. He sought funds from Attorney General Jeremiah Black to hire outside counsel to help him with the case.[29] This suggests that his request for a continuance may have been a ruse to gain more time for preparing his case, to add another lawyer to his team, and perhaps to leave the defendants in a state of limbo. The Buchanan administration already understood this was a high-profile case, with multiple defendants and trials, and so Black authorized special counsel. Belden then hired George Bliss, a former congressman and former state judge. On March 8, Belden appeared in court but once again asked for a postponement, pleading "private and professional engagements."[30] Willson, who almost always indulged the prosecution, postponed the case until April 5.

When the court reconvened on the morning of April 5, the defense team had added a fourth lawyer, Franklin T. Backus, who had served in both houses of the Ohio legislature and as the district attorney for Cuyahoga County. Oddly, one of the prosecution witnesses, Robert A. Cochran, was allowed to sit with the court officers because he was the clerk of Mason County, Kentucky, and would be called to help prove the facts of Bacon's ownership of Price. As a matter of courtesy, Judge Willson allowed Cochran to sit with his own court clerk. It is unlikely that the clerk of the Northern District influenced Cochran's testimony, but the seating arrangement might have prejudiced how the testimony would be understood by the jury. Cochran would be called to the stand as some sort of special witness with a seat of honor and privilege in the courtroom. The defense did not object to this, although it should have. More important, Willson should have prohibited this unusual seating arrangement, which certainly prejudiced the defense. But Willson, whose grand jury charge indicated his own hostility to the defendants, appeared oblivious to the impropriety of this arrangement.

Both sides agreed to a struck jury, which allowed each side to eliminate twelve potential jurors. The next twelve men on the list would then make up the jury. Had the jury been randomly chosen within the Northern District, this process would have helped the defendants, since the district was overwhelmingly antislavery. But of the forty men the clerk of the court, Frederick William Green, summoned, only ten were Republicans or antislavery. The other thirty were reliable Democrats. Green, a Democrat originally from Maryland, had served one term in Congress and voted to open Kansas and Nebraska to slavery. A classic doughface like the president he served, Green played his part to guarantee a conviction. His list of thirty Democrats and only ten opponents of slavery allowed Belden to use his strikes to eliminate everyone who opposed slavery. The result was an entirely Democratic, proslavery jury in a district that was overwhelmingly Republican and antislavery. Thus, the outcome of the trial was almost preordained by the jury pool the clerk called. The tainted nature of the jury pool became even more apparent six days into the trial, when the defense discovered that one of the jurors was also a U.S. deputy marshal. This information had been hidden from the defense attorneys, but it was undoubtedly known to the clerk, the prosecution, and probably Judge Willson, since the marshals were officers of the court itself. When the defense team alerted the court, Judge Willson "did not see fit to take any action in regard to the matter,"[31] even though it was surely improper for an officer of the court to serve on the jury.

With the jury chosen, the trial should have commenced, but once again, Belden requested a postponement because twenty-nine of his witnesses were absent. The defense asked that the jurors be sworn in immediately and that they be "put upon their oaths" not to discuss the case outside the courtroom. Belden objected, and Willson, accommodating the prosecution as always, did not require an oath at this time but simply admonished the jurors "to avoid all conversation among themselves."[32] That afternoon, the court reconvened and Willson swore in the jurors. Although Belden still lacked thirteen witnesses, Simeon Bushnell's trial began.

The government prosecuted Bushnell first because he was the easiest person to convict. Bushnell had driven John Price from Wellington to Oberlin after the rescue, and a number of witnesses could testify to this fact. Similarly, other witnesses placed Bushnell in Oberlin gathering a crowd to go to Wellington. *If* John Price was the slave of John Bacon of Kentucky and *if* Jennings had the proper power of attorney to seize Bacon's fugitive slave, then Bushnell was certainly guilty of interfering with a rendition under the 1850 law.

Less easy to prove was that the man Bushnell drove was the same man Bacon owned. Since Bacon never saw Price in Ohio, the prosecution had to rely on the testimony of the Kentuckians who *had* seen him. There were complications with this proof. In his affidavit giving Jennings the power of attorney, Bacon had described his slave John—without a last name—as "dark copper color."[33] However, Anderson Jennings, his Kentucky neighbor, described John Price as "a full blooded negro, not a drop of white blood in him." On cross-examination, Jennings explained that in Kentucky, there were "different names for different colored niggers" and that a "copper color is between black and light mulatto." Jennings asserted that "some would call John copper color, but should call him black." Jennings also made clear that the person seized in Oberlin was black and not copper colored.[34] Richard Mitchell, another Kentuckian who testified on the identity of Bacon's slave, whom he knew in Kentucky, called him "dark copper colored, not a jet black."[35] Equally confusing was the description of John's size. Bacon's affidavit described him as "five feet eight or ten inches high; weighs about 150 or 160 pounds," and Richard Mitchell described Bacon's slave the same way.[36] But Ohioans who knew John Price in Oberlin described him as dark black, no more than five feet five, and at the time only about 135 pounds because he had been sick. One witness specifically said he was "up to my ear, five feet four or five inches."[37] In his closing argument, Jacob Riddle noted the conflicting testimony: "When he left Kentucky at the age of eighteen, he was five feet eight or ten inches high, and would weigh 165 or 170 pounds, and was copper colored. At Oberlin they arrest a John, who is positively sworn by a number of unimpeachable witnesses, who had the best means of knowing, to have been not over five feet five or six inches tall, weighing from 135 to 140 pounds, and so black that he *shone!*"[38]

There was one other potential method of proving that John Price was Bacon's slave John—to report the admissions Price himself made to his captors. Such testimony might have been objected to as hearsay. But the defense raised a different kind of objection. When Belden asked Jennings if Price "recognized you," the defense argued that "the acts of this piece of property, this chattel, this *thing*, were nothing to charge the defendant by, unless he, the defendant were a party to them. The recognition of his master's agent by this chattel was no more than the recognition a dog might make by the wagging of the tail." The defense asserted it was "absurd" for the "Government to attempt to charge the defendant by so frivolous and incompetent testimony as was sought to be introduced here."[39] This declaration was not a racist outburst from an attorney representing a number of black defendants. Rather, it was a sarcastic and pointed argument about the lack of rights possessed by blacks in general and alleged fugitives in particular. The 1850 law flatly prohibited the alleged slave from taking the stand to defend his freedom. Surely, the Oberlin defendants argued, the court could not take the secondhand, hearsay evidence of what the prisoner allegedly said in order to convict the defendants. This was especially true because had there been a hearing on Price's status, he would not have been allowed to speak at it. In addition, slaves were property under southern law and in the federal courts during a fugitive slave case. Property—"this chattel, this *thing*"—could not provide evidence to convict a free person of a crime. Finally, this argument was a veiled reference to the recent decision in *Dred Scott v. Sandford*,[40] where the Supreme Court held that blacks had "no rights" under the Constitution. If blacks were property, chattel, then surely their secondhand testimony was meaningless.

Judge Willson upheld the defense objection to Jennings testifying about what Price said.[41] However, the next day, Willson reversed himself, allowing Jacob Wheeler, a local postmaster who held a Democratic patronage office under the Buchanan administration, to testify that Price told him he was "from Kentucky" and "belonged to a man by the name of Bacon." The defense once again "objected to the testimony of what this property said," but Willson overruled the objection. Then, Wheeler testified that Price said he had tried to return to Kentucky and got as far as Columbus, where "the folks from Oberlin overtook him and brought him back!" The absurdity of this assertion led to laughter across the courtroom. Throughout his testimony, Wheeler referred to Price as "the nigger."[42]

Wheeler's testimony underscored the danger of allowing the hearsay evidence of the alleged slave. These conversations, if they took place at all, happened when Price was surrounded by armed men who were intent on taking him to Kentucky. His safety, his personal security, and even his life depended on pleasing them. Under such circumstances, if Price talked at all he would have said whatever he thought would please his captors. The fact that the prosecution could find no other evidence to show that he once tried to return to Kentucky but only got as far as Columbus suggests either that Wheeler was lying about what Price said or that Price was spinning stories just to please his captors. Either way, the testimony undermined the rights of the defendants.

The prosecution also had to prove that if John Price was Bacon's slave, Jennings had the authority to seize him. However, Robert Cochran, the clerk for Mason County, Kentucky, testified that the signature on the power of attorney from Bacon was not his but had been forged by his deputy. Cochran said he did not know the alleged fugitive slave and knew nothing about the case. Oddly, the defense did not cross-examine Cochran. But the point was clear. If the power of attorney was fraudulent, then Jennings had no legal authority to seize Price and Bushnell could not have committed a crime by rescuing him. This issue went directly to the defense claim that no one in Wellington *knew* if this was a legal seizure under the 1850 law, and the refusal of Jennings and Lowe to appear before a judge underscored the reasonable belief that this was actually a lawless kidnapping. In his closing argument, Rufus Spalding came back to this point, noting that the power of attorney was not "certified as required by the Act of Congress." After reading from the 1850 statute, he insisted that "the requirements of the law, therefore, must be lived up to."[43] If the prosecution insisted on upholding the 1850 law against the defendants, then the court should insist upon a strict application for those who would bring a black man from Ohio to Kentucky as a slave.

Other than these issues, the prosecution easily proved Bushnell's role in the rescue. The defense chipped away at the prosecution but with little effect. The defendants were handicapped by their own politics. The Oberlin rescuers were proud of what they had done. They could not and would not deny the rescue. Indeed, most considered their indictment a badge of honor. The defense focused on the fact that one of the key prosecution witnesses, Seth Bartholomew, was a notorious liar with a criminal record.[44] The defense also tried to show, with limited success, that Bushnell was not a key organizer of the rescue and had been late getting to Wellington. This of course may have been true, but it did not refute the fact that he had driven Price back to Oberlin.

The closing arguments of both sides differed considerably. Belden's was straightforward: Price had been rescued and the 1850 law had been violated. Bushnell was guilty. The prosecution's summation took less than three hours.[45] By contrast, the defense spent nearly two days on its closing. Bushnell's lawyers pointed out inadequacies in the indictments and the power of attorney, as well as the failure of the prosecution to prove that John was claimed as a slave under Kentucky law, that Kentucky law allowed slavery, or that Bacon had good title to John. In his charge to the jury, Judge Willson asserted that none of these issues were relevant except the legitimacy of the power of attorney because the court took "judicial notice" that slavery existed in Kentucky. Beyond this were defense counsels' long discussions about the immorality of slavery, the injustice of the Fugitive Slave Law, and the unconstitutionality of the act, interwoven with a history of the Constitutional Convention of 1787 and the Northwest Ordinance. The lawyers openly declared their support for a "higher law" theory of constitutionalism. Essentially, they asked the jury to put the institution of slavery on trial and to nullify the law of 1850. This strategy might have worked with a jury randomly chosen from the people of northern Ohio, but it had no chance with what was essentially a handpicked panel of Buchanan Democrats.

The strongest defense argument focused on the identity of the alleged fugitive: "A copper-colored fled, an ebony was captured; a youth of eighteen weighing 165 or 175 pounds fled, a man weighing 135 or 140 was taken; a boy of the grenadier height of five feet eight or ten inches escaped; and one dwarfed to five feet five arrested! Can he be the same?"[46] The case might have been won on this argument if the jurors had been open-minded or if the defense had narrowly focused on this and a few other issues. But two days of abolitionist rhetoric and higher law constitutional theory from two different lawyers, dripping with sarcasm and anger, doubtless ensured that none of the jurors would support the defense. What began as a political trial initiated by the federal prosecutor and supported by the district judge ended as a political harangue by the abolitionist defense lawyers. The defense's closing may have thrilled the defendants and most of the spectators, but it was at best useless for their case and perhaps counterproductive. Like Willson and Belden, the defense attorneys turned the proceedings into a political trial for their own benefit.

On Friday, April 15, the case went to the jury. Judge Willson's charge was partially about the law and partially a refutation of the defense arguments. He summarized the Supreme Court's doctrine on the Fugitive Slave Law, noting that the Constitution "imposes a specific duty upon the national government" to facilitate the return of fugitive slaves. He rejected the idea that a district court had the power to consider the constitutionality of the law and emphatically rejected claims that the grand jury was improperly called. The only issue for the jury to consider, he said, was whether Bushnell "knowingly and willingly rescued the slave from the agent of the owner."[47] The charge was restrained and nonpolitical. But it worked. The jury quickly found Bushnell guilty. This outcome did not surprise the defendants or those in the courtroom. What followed, however, shocked the defendants and much of the general public.

The Second Trial

Immediately after the verdict, Belden called Charles Langston to the bar, to begin his trial. The defense understood from previous discussions with Belden that the second person tried would be Professor Henry Peck. Accordingly, Rufus Spalding said the defense was only prepared to move forward on Peck's case. Belden, however, insisted on immediately trying Langston, a move that Willson supported. These events stood in stark contrast to the two delays Judge Willson had given the prosecution in Bushnell's case. Spalding responded that if necessary, his team "might be ready with that case by the time the new Jury was ready to proceed."[48]

But to Spalding's shock, Willson declared that "the present Jury was one struck and selected for the term, and it was proper that they should try all the cases." Franklin Backus, who had been a county prosecutor, told Willson he was "astonished" by this because the jury had already heard all the evidence in the case and "rendered a verdict" unfavorable to the defense and "their minds are made up and fixed upon all the important points." Backus thought this was a "mockery of that justice which should prevail in every Court." Somewhat extravagantly, he declared this was a "villainous outrage on the sense of justice of the civilized world" and would be a "monstrous proceeding, the like of which had never been known since courts were first in existence."[49]

Unmoved, Willson told Backus that "the Jury would decide each case upon the evidence offered in that particular case, and there was no occasion for excitement or intemperate zeal to be exhibited, as the rule would be enforced." Spalding, the former state supreme court justice, declared that if this was the case, the district attorney "could call the accused up as fast as he pleased and try them, for neither would they call any witnesses for the defense nor appear by attorney before such a jury."[50]

Belden responded by asking the court to revoke the recognizances of the defendants and send them all to jail until they could be tried. Judge Willson immediately ordered all the defendants arrested and sent to jail for the weekend, until the court would resume on Monday. Spalding then declared he would be in court that day to challenge the jury.[51]

At that point, Belden may have realized the absurdity of his position or the political fallout it might cause, and he "moved that the defendants be released from the custody of the marshal on their own recognizances with sureties to the satisfaction of the clerk."[52] Judge Willson, perhaps regretting his hasty revocation of the original recognizances, modified Belden's demand and said he would release them on their own "personal recognizances" to appear the following Monday for the new trial.[53] Willson then left the court with the prisoners still in the custody of Marshal Johnson, who asked them to enter into recognizances to return on Monday. But the defendants refused to do this, arguing that they had been remanded to the marshal by the court and could only be released by the

55

court. Petulantly, Henry Peck, as spokesman for the defendants, asserted that "inasmuch as the District-Attorney had placed them in [the marshal's] custody they would remain there until relieved by due court of law" and "would give no bail, enter no recognizances, and make no promises to return to Court."[54]

When the court convened on Monday, April 18, the issue of the jury was sidetracked by a debate over what had happened the previous Friday. Judge Willson had entered into the record that the defendants "had surrendered themselves" and discharged their recognizances. The defendants insisted that the recognizances had been withdrawn against their will on Belden's motion and Willson's order. The judge offered to give them back their recognizances, but he insisted they ask for them and enter into new bonds. The defendants refused, arguing that "self-respect forbade their entering into new bonds." The rescuers publicly announced that to ask for new bonds "would have encouraged the Prosecution in the belief that they were effectually humbled, and that they had forsaken their cause as being lost."[55]

Both sides were clearly politicizing the trial, with mixed costs and benefits. Judge Willson appeared reasonable in offering a new bond, even as he refused to make the written record of the case reflect his own complicity in Belden's high-handed demand that the bonds be revoked. Though having a patina of reasonableness, Willson and the prosecutor sent a clear signal that Democrats in northern Ohio would be tough on abolitionists and staunch supporters of the rights of slave owners. Doughfaces throughout the North could gloat to their southern friends that the "fanatics" from Oberlin were in jail even before they were convicted. This narrative may have played well in Washington and the South, but it undermined the credibility of Buchanan and his party throughout Ohio, even among moderates who had little love for the higher law doctrines taught at Oberlin.

The bail issue also played directly into the political campaign of the defendants. The Oberlin rescuers would remain in jail for eighty-three days, until July 6, when the trials ended—a heavy price to pay and not one any of them imagined when they refused to seek a new recognizance. But for devout Protestants, steeped in a culture of Christian martyrdom, these eighty-three days may have been the most important of their lives. Professor Henry Cowles, writing in the *Oberlin Evangelist*, compared the defendants to the New Testament martyrs Paul and Silas, jailed by the Romans,[56] which was surely a comparison they loved. Out of jail, they were defendants, commuting to Cleveland each week for the trial. In jail, they were martyrs to the cause of freedom and adored by most of their neighbors, who visited them, sent them food, and cheered them on. The federal government rented jail space from Cuyahoga County, and the county sheriff, Matthew Wrightman, reflected the politics of northern Ohio—he was an antislavery Republican who told his prisoners, "I open my doors to you, not as criminals, but as guests. I cannot regard you as criminals for doing only what I should do myself under similar circumstances."[57] Thus, in jail, the prisoners were treated more like hotel guests. On his first Sunday behind bars, Henry Peck conducted a Sabbath service in the prison yard, with some six or seven hundred "visitors" present and others on the streets outside the jail walls or watching from nearby buildings. Famously, the defendants were allowed to publish their own newspaper, and shortly before their release, a single four-page issue of *The Rescuer* appeared, with a print run of five thousand copies.[58] Thus, despite the hardship of being kept from their families and the huge financial cost of not working or running their businesses, the rescuers' martyrdom was hardly oppressive and, in fact, played directly into their own political goals.

One of the rescuers initially claimed they were "very happy" in jail and were there "for declining to intrust our liberty to the keeping of twelve men who had just announced under oath, their fixed opinion of the merits of our case."[59] If this were really the only reason they were in jail, a compromise might easily have been reached after their first weekend in jail. But that would not happen. On Monday morning, Willson refused to budge on the official record. As the court finished its business that afternoon, Albert Riddle once again asked the judge to revise the record of the previous Friday to indicate that the defendants had not voluntarily surrendered their recognizance bonds but had been forced to do so. Willson stubbornly replied, "They could go out again upon signing new recognizances, as before."[60] Riddle declared they would not do this, and so they remained in jail.

The rescuers would claim that they were held in jail by the arbitrary acts of the judge and district attorney. Scholars have accepted this claim. Thus, the only full-length modern study of the case declares: "The die was cast. The only recourse the Rescuers now had was to appeal to the Ohio Supreme Court for writs of habeas corpus for their release," which would nearly lead to a head-on conflict between the state of Ohio and the federal government.[61] But this analysis is not correct. If the rescuers had signed new recognizance bonds, they would have been released. They chose not to do so for political reasons, just as Belden had insisted on revoking their bonds for political reasons.

While Willson refused to budge on the official record of why the rescuers were jailed, he completely reversed himself on the issue of the jury. When Langston's case was called on Monday morning, Spalding and Riddle made arguments against keeping the same jury. Riddle, the former prosecutor, told Willson of one case where a judge used three different juries to try three men, all charged with the same crime. Perhaps this argument swayed Willson. Just as likely, it provided him with forensic cover to reverse his earlier ruling. After having a weekend to reflect on Friday's events, he probably realized that it was legally inappropriate and politically suicidal to use the same jury over and over again. Willson thus asked Belden if the charge against Langston was the same as that against Bushnell, "with the mere substitution of one name for another." If so, he said he would dismiss Bushnell's jurors. Without waiting for Belden to reply, Willson let the old jurors go.[62] Oddly, the charges against Langston were different, as was the evidence the government would offer. Bushnell had been convicted of driving Price to Oberlin, a charge the government was able to easily prove. Langston, however, was charged with the rescue itself, which was far more problematic, since in fact he had not gone upstairs to rescue Price and may have had nothing to do with getting him out of the building.

That afternoon, Marshal Johnson presented twelve men as jurors. Clearly, the court officials knew in advance that a new jury was to be called and had gathered names and individuals who fit the profile the clerk and prosecution wanted. Oddly, the defense did not demand a pool of at least thirty-six so there could be a struck jury. Instead, each juror was questioned. Belden challenged one juror, who was dismissed, but Willson would not dismiss one challenged by Backus for the defense, even though he had attended the first trial. Nor would Willson allow Backus to question this juror about the case. When another juror said he believed that Price was a fugitive slave, Willson would not dismiss him, even though a key defense argument was that John Price was *not* Bacon's slave John. The court finally dismissed this juror when "he supposed the slave did escape and was illegally rescued." By the end of the process, six of the proposed jurors were excused and six were kept.[63]

When Judge Willson agreed to seat a new jury, Franklin Backus expressed his hope that their "political proclivities" would be less objectionable, but this did not happen. As Jacob Shipherd noted, "The politics of this Jury were too marked to escape notice." There were "nine Administration Democrats, two Fillmore Whigs, and one Republican, who had no objections to the Fugitive Slave Law."[64] Clearly, the court clerk and the marshal had done their homework, coming up with yet another jury pool of Democrats and others who supported the Fugitive Slave Act. This jury did not bode well for Langston, and in fact he would be easily convicted. But the makeup of the jury also did not bode well for the prosecution in future cases. With thirty-seven men under indict-ment, the composition of this jury suggested that the court would soon run out of Buchanan Democrats and others who supported the 1850 law. Future juries would undoubtedly include Republicans and abolitionists, who might vote to acquit the Oberlin defendants.

With a new jury seated, Langston's trial finally began. John Bacon's testimony was "substantially the same" as in the last trial, proving his ownership of a slave named John. But as in the first trial, Bacon had never seen the man seized in Ohio, so he could not positively assert that John Price was his slave John. In the first trial and presumably the second, Bacon described his slave as "copper color" and about "five feet eight inches high."[65]

Bacon's earlier testimony, which he repeated at Langston's trial, also played directly into the defense strategy of exposing to people in Ohio the nature of slavery. Bacon firmly asserted "John is my property" and "he is still mine, *bone and flesh.*"[66] Such language must surely have shocked many who were watching the trial, even if it did not affect the jury. Similarly, the constant use of the word "nigger" by Bacon, Jennings, and Mitchell as well as other prosecution witnesses stood in sharp contrast to the use of "Negro" by the defense witnesses.

Next, the Mason County clerk and Anderson Jennings testified. This time, the court allowed Jennings to recount the actions of Price but not his words. Jennings explained that Langston came into the room where Price was held and that Jennings thought he was a lawyer. At a number of points, he said he could not positively identify Langston as being in the crowd before or after he entered the hotel.

A key aspect of the case was whether Langston threatened to rescue Price. Significantly, Jennings's spin on the conversation was markedly different than the prosecution's. He recalled Langston as saying, "You might as well give the negro up, as *they* are going to have him anyway."[67]

The other Kentucky slave catcher, Bacon's neighbor Richard Mitchell, then testified, as he had in the first case, that Bacon's slave was a "full blooded negro" and that he was satisfied that the man they seized in Ohio was Bacon's slave.[68] Everyone agreed that John Price was a full-blooded Negro, with very dark skin. But Bacon had just testified that his slave was copper colored. This discrepancy in the identification of Bacon's slave might well have raised questions among the jurors.

Other witnesses placed Langston in the crowd in Wellington, but this of course did not prove his direct complicity in the rescue. One prosecution witness said he did not hear Langston say anything to anyone, so he could not prove the defendant was involving in planning the rescue. He did, though, implicate other defendants (who were not yet on trial), testifying that they had said they would "have" Price "any how," whether by a writ of habeas corpus or by force.[69] Similarly, another prosecution witness said, "I won't be certain whether Langston went in or not" during the rescue, although he too identified other defendants who did enter the hotel to effectuate the rescue.[70]

In the midst of this testimony, a series of truly bizarre events took place in the courtroom. As Mitchell was leaving the witness stand, Richard Whitney, the deputy sheriff of Lorain County, L. C. Thayer, an attorney from nearby Elyria, and a number of sheriff's deputies walked to the front of the courtroom. There, Whitney arrested Mitchell and Anderson for kidnapping, with a warrant issued by the Lorain County Court of Common Pleas. U.S. Marshal Johnson immediately countered with a warrant from Belden to hold both men in federal custody until the end of the trials. Thayer then clarified that the Lorain County officials had no intention of interfering with the federal trial; they only wanted to make sure that when Jennings and Mitchell "should be discharged" by the federal court "they would be delivered into the custody of the Lorain Sheriff."[71] Belden obviously anticipated something like this, and probably he had advance warning that his two star witnesses had been indicted in Lorain County, which explains why he had a bench warrant to hold them in federal custody. However, Judge Willson, who also may have known of the Lorain indictment, was startled and angered by the attempt to arrest the witnesses in his federal court on state charges. He curtly told the Lorain deputies he would "take the matter under advisement."[72]

The Lorain lawmen took chairs next to Jennings and Mitchell, who were sitting inside the bar at the front of the courtroom. The next witness was called, but in the middle of his testimony, Marshall Johnson removed Jennings and Mitchell to the left side of the judge, outside the bar of the court, and ordered the Lorain contingent to sit behind the bar with all other spectators to the right of the judge. Deputy Marshal Lowe, who was also a prosecution witness, remained inside the bar, near the prosecuting attorneys. Albert Riddle then interrupted the proceeding to ask if Lowe was an attorney, implying that otherwise he could not sit inside the bar, unless the Lorain deputies could sit there as well. Marshal Johnson replied the Lowe was "his deputy, appointed that afternoon, and had a right to remain within the bar circle."[73] This was a new development. Lowe was a key prosecution witness. Now he was being given special treatment, sitting with the prosecutors, which might lend greater moral authority to his testimony. It was surely odd that Lowe, who had a job as deputy U.S. marshal in the Southern District, was suddenly a deputy in the Northern District.

Testimony continued for the rest of the afternoon without any other interruptions, but before the court adjourned for the day, Willson ordered Jennings and Mitchell remanded to Marshal Johnson under his bench warrant. They were to be held in his custody unless they could post bail, which they lacked the funds to do.[74] Ironically, even though Willson had been willing to give the defendants a recognizance bond, he would not do so, at Belden's insistence, for the main prosecution witnesses. Thayer then "renewed his request that the Court order those men to be held subject to the arrest as made by the Lorain County Sheriff," expressing his fear that otherwise they might be "spirited away, and thus escape the officers of Lorain County." Willson responded that this "unheard-of proceeding" was a "contempt," making Thayer "liable to arrest." Thayer calmly assured the judge that he had "no intention of disturbing the Court," but he pointed out that "it was well known that Jennings and Mitchell had not been out of the building for two weeks, and no other opportunity was offered for their arrest on the indictment found against them in Lorain." He reaffirmed that the Lorain arrest was only meant to take place after the "prior claim" to them by the federal court. This explanation apparently mollified Willson enough so that he did not cite Thayer for contempt but merely remanded the men to Marshal Johnson and said that when all the witnesses had been called, "it would be time to argue the matter."[75]

The next day, the trial resumed without any dramatic interruptions. Norris Wood testified that Langston urged Lowe to give up John because "we will have him any way."[76] Another witness said that Langston gave a speech in Oberlin that night, but he could not say if Langston claimed to have rescued Price or if he just told the crowd what happened. Another witness remembered Langston saying that Deputy Lowe had asked him to "assist him in pacifying the crowd" but that Langston declared he would "not assist—would have nothing to do with it; that it was no use for them to try to keep John, for they would have him anyway."[77] Surprisingly, the Democratic postmaster, Jacob Wheeler, testified that Langston had urged people to "keep cool" and had said that the "only proper way to get him [Price] would be to take out a writ of habeas corpus."[78]

On Friday, the following day, the proceedings once again began to unravel, as Belden asked for an immediate recess to attend to unexpected business in

Columbus. He had just received a writ from the Ohio Supreme Court ordering him to appear the next day in Columbus to explain why the state court should not issue a writ of habeas corpus on behalf of the Oberlin defendants. At the same time, Marshal Johnson removed Bushnell from the immediate custody of David Wrightman, the Cuyahoga County sheriff, to hold him in closer custody. But because there was no federal jail in Cleveland, Bushnell ended up in a room in Judge Willson's own home, where ironically Jennings and Mitchell were also being held. As the *Cleveland Plain Dealer* observed, "Misfortune indeed, makes strange bed-fellows."[79]

Arguments in Columbus continued on Monday. Meanwhile, Belden and Attorney General Black communicated back and forth on this issue, with Black telling Belden to "be as careful as possible not to give any just cause of offence to the state authorities" but also to refuse to surrender the prisoners to the state.[80] On Thursday, the Ohio Supreme Court declined to intervene in the matter because all the cases were pending, including Bushnell's, since he had not yet been sentenced.

While the Ohio Supreme Court considered the application for a writ of habeas corpus, Langston's trial was suspended. However, that week, George Bliss, the special counsel Belden had hired, asked the court to drop the charges against two Oberlin defendants, Jacob R. Shipherd and Ordindatus Wall, because their names had been misspelled in the indictments. The prosecution had known about these errors for months, but Belden had ignored the problem. The release of the two men was legally proper, although they could presumably be indicted again.

Their release may have been an indication that the court and the prosecutor had to find some face-saving device to end the trials. The first arrests had taken place in early December. It was now the end of April, and only one trial had been completed. The first trial had used up at least thirty-six potential jurors. The second had used up another eighteen. At that rate, the prosecution would soon run out of reliable Democrats and Fillmore Whigs (truly a rare breed by then) to put on the jury. If the juries began to reflect the actual population of the Northern District, there would be acquittals. The identity of Price, what the defendants actually said and did in Wellington, and other facts were all in dispute, and different juries might see the evidence in a new light. In addition, the prosecution witnesses were restless. The Kentuckians could not be expected to spend weeks at a time in Cleveland over the next two years. Furthermore, while under indictment in Lorain County, they had to be carefully guarded and protected. After releasing Wall and Shipherd, the prosecutor cut deals with almost all the defendants from Wellington, releasing them on bail and then accepting pleas with fines of $20 plus court costs — significantly less than the $1,000 and six months incarceration they faced if convicted. Although this strategy cleared some of the prisoners out of jail, it also put greater pressure on the Oberlin defendants, whose solidarity was now under attack. But the Oberlin inmates, despite being separated from families and work, were being treated very leniently by Sheriff Wrightman, an elected local official in sympathy with their politics. Their families were allowed to visit them almost at will, and they had the full run of the jail. They could claim to be martyrs to the cause while actually not suffering very much.

While the Wellington rescuers were released, Bushnell languished without being sentenced. Rejecting Spalding's request, Willson refused to sentence him but promised — a promise he later broke — that any time spent in jail before sentencing would be applied as time served against any sentence.[81] By not sentencing Bushnell, Willson prevented the Ohio Supreme Court from issuing a writ of habeas corpus while subtly pressuring those under indictment. If he was going to count Bushnell's jail time against his sentence, then by not sentencing him, Willson was indicating that he might be giving out long sentences.

Meanwhile, Langston's trial continued, with various interruptions. One prosecution witness after another reported that the defendant had essentially threatened a rescue, repeating that he had said, "We will have him."

The defense offered eighteen witnesses, almost all of them testifying that Langston was opposed to violence and was looking for a legal solution to the problem. At the beginning of the proceedings on Friday, May 6, Willson delayed testimony to take pleas of nolo contendere from four of the Wellington defendants. Each was fined $20 plus costs and sentenced to one day in jail. In fact, they did not go to jail but were allowed to spend the night in a local hotel before heading home.[82] The last of the testimony was then taken, and closing arguments began. They would continue until May 10, when Willson charged the jury.

Willson's charge was simultaneously straightforward and bizarre. He began by noting the difficulty of asking jurors to "act in a case where political partialities or prejudices are invoked to sway" their vote. But of course, Willson ignored that the entire proceedings had been politicized, including the way the jury was chosen and his own revocation of bail for the defendants. Attempting to justify the Fugitive Slave Law, he noted that other legislation had been passed that was "distasteful" to the South, giving as an example "the laws enacted to suppress the slave-trade." However, this statement was historically inaccurate, since most southerners supported the ban on the African slave trade, a ban signed into law by the slaveholding Thomas Jefferson.[83] Clumsily, Willson compared banning the importation of slaves (which had strong national support and significant support in much of the South) with a law that denied due process to blacks—whether fugitive or free—and was roundly condemned throughout much of the North. He then summarized the evidence to favor the prosecution. He noted that if Price was Bacon's slave, then Jennings had a right to take him back to Kentucky. Yet he did not mention any of the evidence—even the conflicting testimony of the prosecution—on the actual identity of Price that suggested he did not fit the description provided by Bacon and the power of attorney that Jennings held. Nor did he remind the jurors of the conflicting evidence over what Langston said, or did not say, when talking to Deputy Lowe. With this charge, it took only half an hour for the jury to reach a verdict of guilty.[84]

By the standards of the mid-nineteenth century, this had been an extraordinarily long trial, with fifteen days of testimony, as well as legal arguments and summations spread over twenty-five days. Even though most of the Wellington defendants had pled nolo contendere and two Oberlin defendants had been dismissed from the indictment, there were still more than twenty men to be tried. At that pace, it would take the court more than a year and a half to complete the prosecutions.

With this in the background, the court reconvened on Wednesday, May 11. Willson began by sentencing Bushnell to sixty days in jail and a huge, $600 fine plus the costs of the prosecution, which were more than the fine.[85] Bushnell was relatively poor, owned no land, and had few assets. He would never be able to raise this money on his own. In sentencing him, Willson reneged on his promise to count Bushnell's twenty-six days in jail since his conviction against the sentence.

Having sentenced Bushnell, Willson asked for "any farther motion." Albert Riddle requested that the next defendant, John Watson, be placed on trial. All along, the defense had been asking for swift trials. But once again, the prosecution asked for a postponement. Belden reported that Jennings, Mitchell, and Deputy Lowe had been arrested by the sheriff of Lorain County on kidnapping charges. Belden has been appointed to defend the three men and could not continue the cases against the rescuers. He further reported that Bushnell would be applying for a new writ of habeas corpus now that he had been sentenced, and Belden anticipated having to spend time in Columbus defending the federal government against this state action.

Spalding answered that Belden's arguments were a "sham" because Jennings, Lowe, and Mitchell could be brought back to the federal court at moment's notice on a writ of habeas corpus, could give their testimony, and could then be returned to the Lorain County sheriff. The defense believed that Belden's endless delays, together with Willson's complicity in them, were part of a strategy of both the prosecution and the court to wear down the defendants while keeping them in jail. Spalding insisted that the case against Watson start immediately or that Belden submit a motion in writing, swearing to why he needed a postponement. Belden replied that "his official character would give power enough to the bare motion to postpone." Spalding retorted, "Your official character can add nothing to that statement" and added "Nor to your blackguardism" and to "your private character still less."[86] Belden then asserted that one of the defendants, Ralph Plumb, had berated the Lorain County sheriff for not arresting Jennings and his cohorts sooner. Plumb denied this, and stunningly, Marshal Johnson supported Plumb. This nasty exchange illustrated that the defense was in effect striking back at the prosecution on a number of fronts. Johnson's support of Plumb indicated that even the U.S. marshal had lost patience with the U.S. attorney.

That afternoon, Belden presented an affidavit explaining why he needed a continuance. Immediately, a new attorney for the defendants, Judge Daniel Rose Tilden, appeared with a motion demanding that John Watson be put on trial at once. But Judge Willson would not even hear arguments on this motion and simply ruled that the U.S. attorney would have his continuance. This ruling led Albert Riddle to once more ask that the defendants be released on their own recognizances, as they previously had been. In response, Belden offered to release them on $500 bonds, which he considered to be generous. Willson endorsed Belden's proposal. In other words, the U.S. attorney demanded endless continuances, and Judge Willson broke his promise about granting "time served" to those convicted when sentencing them while at the same time accepting Belden's new demands for a bail amount that most of the defendants did not have.

Belden declared that the defendants had voluntarily surrendered to him. Riddle interrupted by claiming, "That's false, utterly false," and Spalding followed, asserting, "That's a lie." Belden denied that he had demanded that the court revoke their recognizances, when in fact he had. When Riddle asked permission to correct Belden's statements, Judge Willson ruled him out of order. After more very tense arguments, Spalding asked how long the continuance would last, and Wilson declared it would go on until the July term began, which was nearly two months away.[87]

The next day, Willson began to sentence Langston, but he was apparently so rattled by the situation that he asked, "[Is] Mr. Bushnell . . . in the house?" The U.S. marshal responded that Bushnell had been sentenced the day before and said, "Perhaps your Honor refers to Mr. Langston?" Willson acknowledged that he meant Langston and ask him to rise. After declaring he had been found guilty, Willson asked Langston if he had anything to say.[88]

Langston responded with a long and powerful speech, noting he had never been in court before and declaring that he doubted anything he would say would alter Willson's "predetermined line of action." He spoke of the "cruel masters" and of their "blood thirsty patrols" and "bloodhounds and horses" used to hunt fugitive slaves. He called Price "a *man*, a *brother* who had a right to his liberty under the laws of God, under the laws of Nature, and under the Declaration of Independence." He said he "identified" with Price "by color, by race, by manhood, by sympathies, such as God had implanted in us all." He claimed his actions were also motivated by what he had learned from his "Revolutionary father"—the white slave owner who had freed him. He argued that his acts derived from "the fundamental doctrine of this government" that "*all* men have a right to life and liberty." He noted that the U.S. Constitution promised "a trial by an *impartial* jury" to "*all persons*" and then declared, "I have had no such trial." He reminded Willson that "the colored man is oppressed by certain universal and deeply fixed *prejudices*" and that the jury "shared largely in those prejudices." Langston waxed eloquent about American history and the rights guaranteed under the Constitution. But he also constantly referred to America's support for slavery, noting that even though he was a free man, he could be seized as a fugitive slave and have no right to even speak in his own defense. He quoted Chief Justice Taney's opinion in *Dred Scott* that "BLACK MEN HAVE NO RIGHTS WHICH WHITE MEN ARE BOUND TO RESPECT." He asked Willson "to place yourself in my situation, and you will say with me, that if your brother, if your friend, if your wife, if your child, had been seized by men who claimed them as fugitives and the law of the land forbade you to ask any investigation, and precluded the possibility of any legal protection or redress,—then you will say with me, that you could not only demand the protection of the law, but you would call in your neighbors and friends, and would ask them to say with you, that these your friends *could not* be taken into slavery." He told the prosecutors and Willson that "we have common humanity." He declared that if he were seized as a slave, "I would call upon you, your Honor, to help me," and Langston asserted, "you would do so; your manhood would require it; and no matter what the laws might be, you would honor yourself for doing it; your friends would honor you for doing it; and every good and honest man would say, you have done *right*."[89]

Langston's speech clearly affected the court. The spectators applauded so long and hard that Willson and the marshal had a hard time restoring order. Then, Willson told Langston that he had "done injustice to the Court" by "thinking that nothing you might say could effect a mitigation of your sentence. You have presented considerations to which I shall attach much weight." Obviously shaken by Langston's penetrating condemnation of the court, the Fugitive Slave Law, the entire American judicial system, and slavery itself, Willson acknowledged the defendant's "condition" and sentenced him to only twenty days in jail, a $100 fine, and court costs.[90] The court costs undercut the leniency, since they were set at more than $800, in part because of the many delays Belden had demanded. Immediately after sentencing Langston, three Wellington defendants pled nolo contendere and were sentenced to a $20 fine and twenty-four hours in jail.

The Ending

Although no one knew it at the time, Langston's sentencing was the beginning of the end of these trials. Everything else was postponed until July, as Willson went on vacation and Belden went off to defend his key witnesses in Lorain County and fight the habeas corpus action in the Ohio Supreme Court. Arguments and deliberation in Columbus took the rest of the month. The printed report of the case, *Ex parte Bushnell, Ex parte Langston*, would run more than three hundred pages. The Ohio Supreme Court justices agonized over the issue before them. In the end, the Republican chief justice, Joseph R. Swan, sided with two Democrats, holding that the state had no jurisdiction to order the U.S. marshal to release Bushnell and Langston. The ruling came down on May 30. It was certainly a correct decision under the federal constitution, but it cost Swan his career.[91] Had the court ruled the other way, Governor Salmon P. Chase was prepared to send the state militia to Cleveland to force the marshal to release the prisoners.

Meanwhile, Jennings, Mitchell, and Lowe spent eight days in the Lorain County jail before being released on $800 bail. Their trial was set for July 6. Belden also obtained a writ of habeas corpus to better secure his witnesses. But

U.S. Marshal Johnson found it impossible to serve the writ because the Lorain County sheriff was nowhere to be found. Demonstrations in front of the jail in Cleveland where the rescuers were held drew thousands of citizens and many leading politicians. In the Cuyahoga County jail, the rescuers began to work on their own newspaper. The first and, as it turned out, the only issue of *The Rescuer* appeared on July 4. The trials were set to begin again on July 12. But by that time, the administration had had its fill of the fiasco in Cleveland. Marshal Johnson and Belden had been to Washington, where they were told to settle the case. The trials of Anderson, Mitchell, and Lowe were set to begin, and the two Kentuckians had had enough. Their counsel complained to Belden that unless the Lorain prosecutions ended, the Kentuckians would never return to Ohio. A deal was struck. Belden, much against his will, entered *nolle prosequi* against the remaining defendants, and the Lorain County prosecutor did the same against the two Kentucky kidnappers and Deputy Marshal Lowe. The Oberlin cases were finally over.

The Aftermath

But of course, they were not completely over. The Buchanan administration had not fared well in the Oberlin cases. Huge amounts of money had been spent, and the cases accomplished little more than making martyrs of the rescuers and probably increasing support for the Republicans in Ohio and elsewhere. The cases brought national attention to Oberlin and embarrassed the administration. The fugitive slave had escaped, Bacon had received no compensation, and a few men had spent a relatively short time in jail. Most of the rescuers went free and returned to Oberlin as heroes. Moreover, Willson had undermined the credibility of the federal court in northern Ohio, although his lenient sentencing of Langston probably gained him some support.

Although the trials were over, Bushnell had a few more days to serve on his sentence, and he remained in jail until July 11. There would be no more jailings, but there were fines and court costs to collect. In addition, the national government had to pay for the costs of defending its case before the Ohio Supreme Court. In that proceeding, the Buchanan administration, knowing that it needed a better lawyer than Belden, had hired Noah H. Swayne, who would later serve on the U.S. Supreme Court. Hiring Swayne was something of a humiliation for the administration, since he was an antislavery Republican who had actively supported Buchanan's opponent, John C. Frémont, in the 1856 presidential election. In July, Swayne requested payment for his work, but as late as December 1859, he was still trying to get Attorney General Black to send him the $1,000 he was owed.[92] Meanwhile, Belden sought $2,000 for his work on the habeas corpus cases. In February 1861, just before Buchanan left office, Judge Willson wrote a letter supporting Belden's claim.[93]

While the lawyers who worked for the national government were having trouble getting paid, the rescuers actively avoided paying their fines and court costs. In August, Marshal Johnson tried to collect Bushnell's fine of $600 plus court costs of $786.28 and another $1.50 in interest. On November 14, 1860, with Abraham Lincoln just elected president, the marshal obtained a new writ to get the fine and costs plus $5.28 in interest. At the same time, he sought to collect fees and fines from various other defendants. But Bushnell had no money, and the marshal reported he had no goods or anything else of value.[94] Johnson sought the execution on various goods and chattels owned by the defendants but with mixed luck. Daniel Williams gave bond to Johnson after the marshal started to seize Williams's ten cows. But on January 2, 1861, Johnson reported that he was unable to get any money from Henry Niles because he had "no goods, or chattels, lands or tenements."[95] By that time, Johnson was desperate to collect this money. Most of it was fees that he was due, and he needed to collect the money soon. With Lincoln about to take office, Marshal Johnson understood he would soon be removed from his patronage job and be replaced by a Republican who would have little interest in collecting money from the Oberlin rescuers.

The final failure of these cases came just as the Buchanan administration was leaving office. Charles Langston refused to pay his $100 fine or his court costs of $872.70. Langston was not rich, but he owned a town lot in Columbus. The Northern District Court forwarded the paperwork to its counterpart in the Southern District, and U.S. Marshal Lewis Sifford advertised the sale of the town lot, appraised at $1,200. The sale was set for February 19, 1861. By then, seven states had declared themselves out of the Union; Lincoln was about to become president; Governor Chase of Ohio was on his way to Lincoln's cabinet as secretary of the Treasury; and Belden, Johnson, and the other Buchanan patronage officeholders were about to be unemployed. The nation was careening toward a crisis, which northerners fully understood had been caused by slavery and the incessant demands of the slavocracy. The oppressive Fugitive Slave Law was one of the causes of this crisis.

Under these circumstances, Marshal Sifford conducted an auction on the property owned by Charles Langston. He then reported back to the District Court for the Northern District of Ohio: "I caused the described real estate to be appraised" and advertised the sale, but "it was not sold for want of bidders. No other goods nor chattels, lands nor tenements are found whereon to levy." Langston would keep his land and not pay his fine or court costs, and Sifford sent a bill to Judge Willson for $27.15 to cover his expenses and fees, which the Northern District Court was obligated to pay him.[96] It was a fitting and ironic end to the Oberlin cases.

Notes

1. This paragraph is based on the secondary account set out in Nat Brandt, *The Town That Started the Civil War* (Syracuse, N.Y.: Syracuse University Press, 1990), 54–64.

2. See chapter 1 in this volume.

3. Charge to Grand Jury, quoted in Jacob R. Shipherd, *History of the Oberlin-Wellington Rescue* (Boston: John P. Jewett, 1859), 3.

4. Paul Finkelman, "Race, Slavery, and the Law in Antebellum Ohio," in *The History of Ohio Law*, ed. Michael Les Benedict and John F. Winkler (Athens: Ohio University Press, 2004), 2:748–81; Nikki M. Taylor, *Frontiers of Freedom: Cincinnati's Black Community, 1802–1868* (Athens: Ohio University Press, 2005).

5. Brandt, *Town That Started the Civil War*, 45, erroneously asserts this.

6. Langston defeated the incumbent Anson P. Dayton in 1857. After losing the election, Dayton ingratiated himself with the notoriously proslavery administration of President James Buchanan and gained a patronage appointment as a U.S. deputy marshal. In that capacity, he could be called upon to seize and remand fugitive slaves. In Oberlin, he was generally seen as a pariah, feared but also treated with contempt by the town's black population and most whites as well.

7. 60 U.S. (19 How.) 393 (1857).

8. Brandt, *Town That Started the Civil War*, 89–90.

9. Robert M. Baumann, *The 1858 Oberlin-Wellington Rescue: A Reappraisal* (Lorain, Ohio: Bodnar Printing, 2003), stresses the nonviolent response in Oberlin to fugitive slave cases. However, it is clear that some in Oberlin, such as Ansel W. Lyman, who had ridden with John Brown, were prepared to use violence to protect black freedom. Some of the blacks in the mob had previously used force or threatened force, to prevent the capture of fugitives. A significant number of those who came from Oberlin were armed.

10. Baumann, *1858 Oberlin-Wellington Rescue*, and Brandt, *Town That Started the Civil War*, provide the microdetails of the day, such as the time of the expected train.

11. Epistle to Philemon. On proslavery thought in general, see Paul Finkelman, *Defending Slavery: Proslavery Thought in the Old South* (Boston: Bedford Books, 2006).

12. Shipherd, *History of the Oberlin-Wellington Rescue*, 119.

13. Ibid.

14. Charles H. Langston, *Should Colored Men Be Subject to the Pains and Penalties of the Fugitive Slave Law? Speech of Charles H. Langston before the U.S. District Court for the Northern District of Ohio, May 12, 1859* (Cleveland: Ohio State Anti-Slavery Society, 1859), 11.

15. Brandt, *Town That Started the Civil War*, 108.

16. Frederick Douglass, *The Life and Times of Frederick Douglass* (New York: Macmillan, 1962), 282.

17. On the Fillmore era trials, see Paul Finkelman, *Millard Fillmore* (New York: Times Books, 2011).

18. Kenneth C. Maris, *The Historical Atlas of Political Parties in the United States Congress, 1789–1989* (New York: Macmillan, 1989), 110–11.

19. See http://www.dispatchpolitics.com/content/downloads/1856_Ohio_President_Map.pdf.

20. See http://www.dispatchpolitics.com/content/downloads/1856_Ohio_President_County_Results.pdf.

21. Shipherd, *History of the Oberlin-Wellington Rescue*, 235–39.

22. Willson's grand jury charge is reprinted in ibid., 3–4.

23. William Cheek and Aimee Lee Cheek, *John Mercer Langston and the Fight for Black Freedom, 1829–1865* (Urbana: University of Illinois Press, 1996), 329.

24. Fitch had in fact briefly harbored Price, but the prosecution did not know this.

25. Brandt, *Town That Started the Civil War*, 125.

26. Shipherd, *History of the Oberlin-Wellington Rescue*, 4.

27. *Cleveland Leader*, quoted in Brandt, *Town That Started the Civil War*, 126.

28. Shipherd, *History of the Oberlin-Wellington Rescue*, 4–5.

29. G. W. Belden to Jeremiah S. Black, February 26, 1859, National Archives, Record Group (RG) 60, Container 126, Folder 9, Northern District of Ohio.

30. Shipherd, *History of the Oberlin-Wellington Rescue*, 13.

31. Ibid., 38.

32. Ibid., 14.

33. Ibid., 1

34. Ibid., 21.

35. Ibid., 28.

36. Ibid., 16, 30.

37. Ibid., 34–35, 41.

38. Ibid., 52.

39. Ibid., 18.

40. 60 U.S. (19 How.) 393 (1857).

41. Shipherd, *History of the Oberlin-Wellington Rescue*, 18.

42. Ibid., 26.

43. Ibid., 76.

44. Ibid., 41, 22.

45. Ibid., 45.

46. Ibid., 54.

47. Ibid., 83, 84. Oddly, Bushnell had not actually "rescued" Price but only driven him back to Oberlin after others rescued him. But this detail was ignored by Judge Willson in his charge and by the jury.

48. Shipherd, *History of the Oberlin-Wellington Rescue*, 88.

49. Ibid., 88–89.

50. Ibid.

51. Ibid.

52. Ibid., 89.

53. Ibid.

54. Ibid.

55. Ibid., 182–84.

56. Cowles, writing in the *Oberlin Evangelist*, quoted in Brandt, *Town That Started the Civil War*, 168.

57. Wrightman, quoted in ibid., 161.

58. Ibid., 231.

59. Ibid., 162.

60. Shipherd, *History of the Oberlin-Wellington Rescue*, 99.

61. Brandt, *Town That Started the Civil War*, 168.

62. Shipherd, *History of the Oberlin-Wellington Rescue*, 95–96.

63. Ibid., 96–97.

64. Ibid.

65. Ibid., 17.

66. Ibid., 16.

67. Ibid., 102.

68. Ibid.

69. Ibid., 104.

70. Ibid.

71. Ibid., 103.

72. Ibid.

73. Ibid., 103–4.

74. Ibid., 105.

75. Ibid.

76. Ibid., 106.

77. Ibid.

78. Ibid., 107.

79. Ibid., 107–9; Brandt, *Town That Started the Civil War*, 173–75, and *Plain Dealer*, quoted on p. 174.

80. Black to Johnson, April 26, 1859, National Archives, RG 60, Northern District of Ohio.

81. Shipherd, *History of the Oberlin-Wellington Rescue*, 114.

82. Ibid., 126.

83. For a discussion of the closing of the African slave trade, see Paul Finkelman, "The American Suppression of the African Slave Trade: Lessons on Legal Change, Social Policy, and Legislation," *Akron Law Review* 42 (2008–9): 431–67; Paul Finkelman, "Regulating the African Slave Trade," *Civil War History* 54 (2008): 379–405. On Jefferson's relationship to slavery see Paul Finkelman, *Slavery and the Founders: Race and Liberty in the Age of Jefferson*, 2nd ed. (Armonk, N.Y.: M. E. Sharpe, 2001).

84. Shipherd, *History of the Oberlin-Wellington Rescue*, 166–69.

85. Ibid., 170; To the Marshal of the North District of Ohio, In re Simeon Bushnell, August 17, 1859, Records of the U.S. District Court for the Northern District of Ohio, RG 60, National Archives and Records Administration, Chicago Branch (hereinafter cited as NARA Chicago). The costs were $786.28.

86. Shipherd, *History of the Oberlin-Wellington Rescue*, 170.

87. Ibid., 174.

88. Ibid., 175.

89. Langston, *Should Colored Men Be Subject*, 1–16. Also printed in Shipherd, *History of the Oberlin-Wellington Rescue*, 175–78.

90. Shipherd, *History of the Oberlin-Wellington Rescue*, 178.

91. Robert M. Cover, *Justice Accused: Antislavery and the Judicial Process* (New Haven, Conn.: Yale University Press, 1974).

92. N. H. Swayne to Attorney General Black, July 28, 1859, and December 2, 1859, container 126, folder 9, Department of Justice Letters Received, Ohio, National Archives, RG 60.

93. Hiram Willson to Belden, February 12, 1861, and Belden to Black, February 18, 1861, Attorney General Letters Received, National Archives, RG 60.

94. To the Marshal of the North District of Ohio, In re Simeon Bushnell, August 17, 1859, and November 14, 1859, and same for John Mandeville, Matthew De Wolfe, Daniel Williams, Henry D. Niles, and Robert Cummings, Records of the U.S. District Court for the Northern District of Ohio, RG 2, NARA Chicago.

95. Ibid.

96. To the Marshal of the Southern District of Ohio, dated January 5, 1861, on the first page, Records of the U.S. District Court for the Northern District of Ohio, RG 21, NARA Chicago.

3

The Impact of the Northern District of Ohio
on Industrialization and Labor

*Liability Law and Labor Injunctions in the U.S. District Court
for the Northern District of Ohio, 1870–1932*

Melvyn Dubofsky

S INCE THE MID-1980S, scholars in legal history and related fields have insisted that rulings by the American judiciary shaped the character, beliefs,
and goals of the American labor movement and its affiliated trade unions. Judge-
made law caused unions to conclude that political reform had become a dead
end for workers and that instead of relying on political action to improve working conditions, unions should build their own power. Moreover, the judiciary
defined the meaning of free labor, implemented the doctrine of employment at
will, and sanctified the concept of individual liberty of contract as the corner-
stone of the employment relationship. Workers and unions existed in a world
created and defined by judges.[1]

The federal district court for northern Ohio reflected the reality that judges
played a decisive role in determining the fate of workers and their unions. Two
dominant labor issues occupied the judges who sat on that bench from the
1870s into the 1930s. The most common variety of labor case that came before
the district court concerned claims made by injured employees or surviving
dependents for compensation from employers deemed responsible for the injury or death; such cases fell under the rubric of master-servant law. But per-

haps more significant in revealing judicial attitudes toward workers and their organizations were the cases that occupied the district judges far more irregularly —cases that arose from industrial conflicts during which employers sought judicial protection against collective action by their employees. These latter cases tended to fall within common-law categories of criminal conspiracy, illegal restraint of trade, and equity proceedings that might provide injunctive relief. In instances of personal injury and industrial conflict, the district court took jurisdiction on one of two grounds: either diversity of citizenship, meaning plaintiff and defendant were citizens of different states, or under the federal government's power to regulate interstate commerce.

One obstacle complicates our ability to discern clearly and fully the pattern of labor law jurisprudence as applied in the district court. Not all of the cases and rulings heard under the rubric of master-servant law were reported. Indeed, many such cases only entered the reported record when the Sixth Circuit Court ruled on appeals of the district court's original decisions. In those instances, the appeals court rulings offer evidence of decisions originally made at the district level. Because the cases that arose from collective action during strikes were far less common and usually more contentious legally and politically (and also not presented to juries), they resulted in more complete recorded reports.

Ten different judges sat on the northern Ohio district court between the 1870s and the passage of the Norris-LaGuardia Act in 1932. In 1878, Congress divided the district in two, creating separate judgeships for an eastern half and a western half. Eight of the ten judges were appointed by Republican presidents and had been active in Republican Party politics at the state and local levels. The other two were appointed by Woodrow Wilson and had figured prominently in Ohio Democratic Party affairs. Two judges from other districts in the Sixth Circuit heard significant labor cases that came before Ohio's Northern District. Both were appointed by a Republican president, although one who sat on the bench for the Western District of Tennessee had been a Southern Democrat and Confederate military officer. All twelve judges were white males of Protestant faith. Their family origins and circumstances were largely similar. They enjoyed comfortable family circumstances that ranged from solidly middle-class or respectably bourgeois to upper-class elite. All were well educated, and most had attended prestigious private colleges, though not all graduated. The majority prepared for the law by matriculating in law schools, although several trained in what was then the traditional manner of reading the law in the office of an older practicing attorney, sometimes a family member. Given their similarities in family background, education, legal training, religion, political activity, and memberships in an array of fraternal organizations, it should come as no surprise that the men who sat on Ohio's Northern District court—with one exception, a judge who resigned after a brief term of service—shared a common approach and philosophy in their rulings on labor law.[2]

A close examination of the cases that these judges heard over a sixty-year period shows their clear, consistent tendency, whenever possible, to offer employers the benefit of doubt in tort actions and liability claims while distrusting the juries' ability to render proper judgments. A similar pattern prevailed in the smaller number of cases that they considered in which employers sought injunctions against union action. Here, the judges without exception frowned upon collective action; perceived unions as institutions that sought to elevate private law above public or legitimate legal authority; and treated liberty of contract as an individual, not a collective, right.

Ohio's federal district judges, whether self-educated through apprenticeships in law offices or formally instructed in schools of law, imbibed what Daniel Ernst characterized as a Victorian legal culture that deified individualism, demanded personal rectitude, policed private practices in the interest of community well-being, and lauded natural law. The code allowed neither employers nor employees to diminish the rights of others; group or collective interests had no standing at the law. Private property rights did not cede to businesspeople the power to restrain competition, impair free markets, or exact monopoly prices from consumers. The free labor doctrine and its concomitant, employment at will, denied workers an unlimited right to withhold their labor (that is, to strike or boycott) if such action infringed on the equal rights of other workers, harmed the community, or "illegally" diluted the value and use of employers' private property. Courts issued rulings and injunctions that restrained both employers and workers from acting to injure others through combinations (collective or group action) that violated the rules of the marketplace.[3] In practice, however, workers bore a heavier burden under the Victorian legal code, a code that prevailed in the northern Ohio federal district court from the 1870s into the first half of the 1930s.

Few tort or liability cases entered the docket of the district court prior to the end of the nineteenth century. Such suits brought by injured workers ordinarily were pursued in local and state courts that had primary jurisdiction in such matters. The cases considered by federal courts most often arose from work-related injuries or deaths on interstate railroads and in interstate and foreign

maritime shipping. Since the vast majority of maritime claims for worker compensation arose from transoceanic and intercoastal shipping, Ohio's Northern
District Court was not a common venue in which to pursue such suits. Nonetheless, Cleveland and Toledo both served as Great Lakes port cities, and one of
the earliest recorded employee injury suits heard by the district court was brought
by a worker employed on a lakes ship. Otherwise, the vast majority of these
cases arose from worker injuries incurred on the several interstate railroads that
crossed northern Ohio. Occasionally, moreover, an employee injured in a manufacturing enterprise whose corporate headquarters existed in another state brought
suit on the basis of diversity of citizenship.

For much of the late nineteenth century, the traditional rules of common
law governed compensation claims pursued by injured workers. Under the prevailing code of master-servant law, a master remained responsible for the proper
care and treatment of his or her servants. A servant seeking compensation for a
work-related injury had to establish the master's full responsibility in order to
obtain damages. The common law provided masters with three grounds for defense: (1) contributory negligence by the claimant, (2) a fellow servant's responsibility for the injury, or (3) assumption of risk on the part of the servant.[4]

By the end of the nineteenth century and the opening decades of the twentieth, however, both state and federal governments had enacted employers' liability and workers' compensation laws that weakened masters' defenses under
the three common-law principles just cited. Employer liability laws placed the
burden of proof on masters to establish that their governance of servants was in
no way responsible for work- or service-related employee injuries. The aim of
such laws was to ensure that juries, which tended to favor the claims of employees, were less likely to be instructed by judges to reject worker claims for compensation on the basis of contributory negligence, assumption of risk, or fellow
servant responsibility. Workers' compensation legislation sought to eliminate
entirely the necessity for injured employees or the surviving spouses and dependents of deceased workers to go to court in order to obtain compensation. Such
laws treated work-related injuries and deaths as normal and ordinary occurrences
in the course of modern work regimes, and they set standard rates of financial
compensation for claimants based on the severity of injury or the death of an
employee. Neither employer liability statutes nor workers' compensation laws,
however, eliminated the pursuit of claims in court by aggrieved employees or
their survivors. Under the new employer liability statutes that weakened the
traditional common-law defenses for masters and employers, claimants hoped

to obtain more substantial financial awards from sympathetic juries. In the case of workers' compensation awards, claimants sought damages in excess of the payment schedules established by law. Thus, such cases continued to appear on the docket of the district court.[5]

An examination of all the reported cases for work-related compensation brought before the district court under the category of master-servant law as well as those originally tried at the district court level but reported only at the appeals court level shows a pattern in which three threads interweave. First, juries clearly sympathized with injured plaintiffs. Second, the introduction of employer liability laws and federal railroad safety statutes caused district court judges to tread more gingerly in considering common-law defenses raised by employer defendants. And third, judges tended to evince their distrust of jury judgment; to render narrow readings of federal employer liability and safety legislation; and to continue to instruct juries that contributory negligence by employees, fellow servant negligence, and assumption of risk offered reasonable bases of defense for employers.

The first notable reported case was heard by Judge Martin Welker, who sympathized with the aggrieved plaintiff (servant) rather than the defendant (master). He instructed the jury that the common-law defenses of contributory negligence and fellow servant action in the case of a seaman who fell into an open hatch at night did not apply in this instance. It was, he stated, the clear obligation of the master to assume responsibility for negligence by a fellow servant who caused injury to a fellow worker. So instructed, the jury awarded damages to the plaintiff.[6] That case, however, proved to be the exception rather than the rule as judges instructed juries in comparable proceedings.

Just six years later in a case in which an employee of the Wabash Railroad died on the job as a result of the company's failure to implement a state safety law, Eli Hammond—a former Confederate officer and sitting judge for the Western District of Tennessee who was temporarily serving in northern Ohio— instructed the jury that if the deceased worker contributed in any way to his own death, the railroad was innocent. He further advised jury members to consider the need to balance the safety law's requirements with the railroad's demand for efficiency.[7] Suggesting to jurors that they weigh the economic necessities of an enterprise against the claims of an employee plaintiff was a common refrain for many of the district court's judges. A year later, in 1890, Judge Augustus Ricks presided over a case in which a twelve-year-old boy employed in violation of Ohio's child labor law had lost an arm, suffered serious disfigurement of his face, and incurred grave chest injuries. His mother brought suit for damages against the employer, the American Iron and Tube Company. In his charge to the jury, Ricks stressed that the company had violated the child labor law only from a charitable instinct to offer employment and hence income to the boy's mother, a penurious widow. He even suggested the possibility of exonerating the company as a consequence of the boy's contributory negligence. "I . . . feel it proper and prudent to warn you," Ricks charged, "that the rights of parties in courts of justice are to be determined on well-defined legal principles of law, and not upon impulses of generous hearts, however well prompted." Nevertheless, the jury awarded the plaintiff $6,000 and legal costs.[8]

In his remaining years on the bench, Ricks followed the pattern that he had set in 1890. Dealing with an 1895 case in which the defendant, a railroad company, was guilty of gross negligence in causing the deaths of an engineer and fireman, he reduced the awards to the survivors of the engineer and the fireman by more than 10 percent from the amount awarded by the court-appointed master because other states had set lower maximum awards for negligent death.[9]

Other district judges emulated Ricks in seeking grounds to exonerate employers of responsibility for injury to their employees or, if that was impossible, to reduce the amount of damages awarded. In 1904, Judge Francis J. Wing heard a case in which a plaintiff brought suit for a wrongful death caused when a railroad engineer negligently crashed his train into another and killed the second train's fireman, legally an inferior employee. Ohio's employer liability law held employers responsible for actions by superior employees over lesser employees. Wing directed an acquittal for the defendant on the grounds that the Ohio law was unconstitutional. According to the judge, the Ohio constitution made no distinctions among employees or citizens on the basis of rank. All employees, whether in superior or inferior positions, were fellow servants unless they were too young to offer proper legal consent to such a relationship. Hence, the common law's stricture about fellow servant negligence absolved the employer from responsibility for the fireman's death.[10] Wing's directed dismissals in this case and in a second case in which he also ruled for the defendant employer on the basis of fellow servant negligence were overruled by the circuit court of appeals. The appeals court judges determined that where employers failed to provide, as required by state law, safe appliances or apparatuses for employees, they were legally negligent. Both of Wing's directed dismissals were remanded back to the district court for retrial.[11] The appeals court responded similarly in other cases in which district court judges directed verdicts for the defense based on common-law defenses despite state laws that eliminated such employer defense options.[12]

Just when most state legislatures and Congress had come to conclude that the traditional common law of master-servant liability was not a good fit with a modern industrial economy and that employers had a positive duty to ensure a safe workplace, thus eliminating their traditional grounds for defense, judges on Ohio's Northern District Court cited contributory negligence and assumption of risk as valid defenses for employers. The same jurists also loosened employers' obligation to provide a safe workplace. And they discovered other ways to strip federal railway safety and employer liability laws of their protections for employees. In fact, nearly all the work injury compensation cases heard by the court involved workers employed by interstate railroads. Repeatedly, judges instructed juries to rule for defendants because plaintiffs had negligently contributed to their work-related injuries even when federal and state employer liability laws eliminated that as a basis for legal defense.[13] Several judges disregarded the actual terms of the federal railroad safety appliance law that conferred absolute liability on a company for either using defective required appliances or failing to provide the required appliances. For example, in the case of a Pennsylvania Railroad Company employee who died on the job as a result of a defective safety appliance, Judge David C. Westenhaver ruled that the federal employer liability law, rather than the safety appliance law, was applicable. And because the employee had negligently contributed to his own death, Westenhaver absolved the company of responsibility.[14]

Judges proved ingenious in discovering grounds to relieve employers of responsibility for workplace accidents. In a case in which a railroad worker was injured while repairing damaged cars, Judge John Killits ordered a directed verdict for the defense because an employer could not be negligent when a dangerous work assignment occurred for unforeseen reasons.[15] In a second case, Killits used a widely applied judicial tactic for exonerating railroad companies of responsibility for workplace havoc. Federal law applied to interstate commerce, and only a minority of the employees who worked for interstate railroads crossed state lines in the performance of their duties. Hence, Killits often ruled that railroad employees who labored in a fixed workplace did not fall under the protection of federal law. In such cases, he and other jurists directed verdicts for the defense.[16]

Federal judges in Ohio also persisted in ruling that under the common-law doctrine of assumption of risk, employees could not be compensated for injuries sustained at work. In one particularly egregious instance, a circuit court upheld the district court's directed verdict for the defense, a unanimous panel declaring that an employee injured while engaging in dangerous work under direct threat of discharge had done so voluntarily.[17] Similarly, Ohio's Northern District Court judges rendered the federal railroad safety appliance act toothless in several rulings that suggested—absent absolute proof that the appliance in question was defective or that the worker had not contributed to the appliance's failure to operate properly—a directed verdict had to absolve the company of responsibility.[18]

The only judge to differ from his colleagues in these matters was William L. Day, a respectable establishment Republican who was the son of U.S. Supreme Court Justice William R. Day and a graduate of the University of Michigan and its law school. Appointed to the bench by William Howard Taft, Day seemed exceptionally solicitous of the claims pursued by plaintiffs in personal injury suits. In a case in which an employer appealed a generous jury award, claiming that the state workers' compensation award was sufficient in the absence of excessive company negligence, Day responded that plaintiff's counsel had read the Ohio statute too narrowly. "I cannot believe," he asserted, "that the Legislature intended that the term 'willful act' should be narrowed down to mean a deliberate attempt to do bodily injury and nothing else. This compensation act was passed for a purpose; its primary purpose was to protect the men engaged in the various occupations in Ohio." Hence, he sustained the jury's original award, a decision subsequently affirmed by the circuit court.[19] In case after case, Judge Day sympathized with plaintiffs and sustained juries' generous financial awards.[20] He served on the court for only three years, apparently resigning because his salary proved insufficient.

A similar pattern prevailed when the district judges dealt with cases that arose as a result of industrial conflict. There too, they typically adhered to common-law traditions that rejected collective efforts to restrain trade, and they likewise read new legislation parsimoniously. Over the entire period from the 1880s into the 1930s, the judges sitting on the federal district court for northern Ohio hewed to a consistent line in their rulings in cases involving employer plaintiffs or public prosecutors who sought to enjoin unionized workers from practicing forms of collective action. Far fewer cases of this type reached the district court than those involving work-related injuries, but the rulings in the former instances were of more significance. In none of the opinions or rulings rendered in cases arising from industrial conflict did the northern Ohio federal jurists note the opinions of their judicial colleagues elsewhere who had begun to shift their jurisprudence in the matter of collective action by workers.[21] Nor did the judges of the Northern District Court give credence to the testimony of municipal officials and police or to the policies they implemented. These jurists persistently ruled in favor of employers and against unionized workers.

As was true with matters of liability law, most judicial decisions affecting workers, unions, and industrial conflict were handed down at the state and local levels. Federal courts could only act when interstate commerce or diversity of citizenship provided causes for action. Industrial conflicts tended to occur in waves; the vast majority passed with little notice especially by courts, and only a rare few were of sufficient scope and turbulence to involve federal courts. Thus, over the span of several years, the district court for northern Ohio might never consider a single case that arose as a result of industrial conflict, Yet it was not unusual for many such cases to appear on the docket in a single year or two.

The first case of this type to appear before the district court occurred in 1893 during a peak moment of industrial conflict—including such turbulent disputes as the Homestead lockout and strike; the Cripple Creek, Colorado, labor war; the Pullman strike and boycott; and the many strikes that hampered traffic on interstate railroads prior to the Pullman dispute. Judge Augustus Ricks, who had proved especially solicitous to employers in his workplace injury rulings, acted similarly in enjoining workers from interfering with the business of railroads. Traditionally, injunctions could be issued only to restrain criminal acts or to avert the possibility of irreparable harm to persons or property. By the late nineteenth century, however, jurists had come to define property rights as adhering to more than material possessions or facilities. An enterprise's reputation as well as its ability to maintain production, to trade its products, to offer services, and to turn a profit from its activities had all been incorporated within the law's definition of property rights.[22] Ricks had little difficulty declaring a member of the Brotherhood of Locomotive Engineers in contempt of court because, following the rules established by his union, he had refused to transfer cars that he was transporting to another railroad that the engineers' union had struck. The Sixth Circuit Court had previously ordered unionized railroad engineers to transfer freight to railroad companies that continued to operate even when their union employees had walked off the job.[23] Under both the common-law strictures against conspiracies in restraint of trade and the Interstate Commerce Act, actions that impeded the free flow of interstate commerce were enjoinable. In the immediate case before Ricks, the engineer, prior to transferring cars from his line to another, quit service to his employer. Ricks ruled that such behavior was a subterfuge to escape the provisions of an existing injunction, and he found the engineer guilty of contempt and fined him $50. Ricks also ruled that the injunction would remain in force and that future violators might face even more severe penalties.[24]

As the nineteenth century drew to its end and a new century opened, two other judges hearing cases involving strike injunctions that came before the U.S. District Court for the Northern District of Ohio expanded substantially on Ricks's and Taft's ruling in the railroad cases. Both injunctions involved strikes declared by a craft union against Cleveland metal industry firms. In 1897, a local union declared a strike against the Consolidated Steel and Wire Company because it refused to recognize the local, bargain with it, or pay Cleveland area union wage rates. The union picketed the work site, and the strikers sought to convince laborers not to work for a nonunion enterprise. Clearly, the picketing and the persuasion interfered with the company's ability to hire and to keep a nonunion labor force. So, Consolidated Steel went to court seeking an injunction that outlawed picketing and what it contended was coercive intimidation of its employees rather than peaceful persuasion. The company claimed that its employees were satisfied with their wages, that they voluntarily refused to join the union, and that the union had engaged in mass picketing that intimidated its workers. Unable to keep a stable labor force in such circumstances, Consolidated Steel shut down operations for several months and then reopened the plant, offering employment to all workers willing to accept company terms. The union once again declared a strike, organized pickets who behaved violently according to the company, and threatened worse violence. On that basis, the district court granted the company a preliminary injunction to halt what it cited as a violent conspiracy.[25] Precisely on what basis the federal court assumed jurisdiction remains unclear. Under established legal principles, manufacturing was not part of the stream of interstate commerce; most likely, then, jurisdiction derived from diversity of citizenship based on the firm's incorporation in a state other than Ohio. The court issued an original preliminary injunction in an ex parte proceeding and then called for a full hearing at which the issuance of a permanent injunction would be considered.

At the second hearing at which plaintiffs (the company) and defendants (the union and its members) were represented, both parties presented briefs and evidence to prove their claims. The company provided depositions from its employees claiming that they had been threatened by pickets and had been the victims of union-sponsored violence. The union's attorneys presented their own depositions from pickets, who insisted that they had behaved in an orderly fashion, and from three Cleveland city policemen assigned to patrol the plant's premises, who attested to the absence of mass picketing or any form of disorderly behavior. Judge George Sage, who normally sat on Ohio's Southern District Court, declared at the outset of his ruling that the defendants' affidavits and depositions, including those from the police, were "to be utterly discredited . . . and to be altogether unworthy of belief."[26] Citing innumerable state judicial rulings declaring that strikes to enforce union demands were illegal boycotts that breached the law and subverted an individual's right to contract as he or she pleased, Sage ruled that business ownership was a property right that brooked no interference or restraint by other private parties, especially if the latter behaved illegally, and he made his injunction permanent. One of the state cases that he particularly cited as precedent, *Vegelahn v. Gunter*—a case that other judges on the Northern District would cite in a similar manner—has also been cited by a number of legal scholars and historians. However, they have focused on a dissent by Oliver Wendell Holmes Jr. in which the justice enunciated a competing version of equity law as it affected industrial relations, a perspective that Ohio's district court jurists dismissed out of hand.[27] Sage insisted that employees and their union "must not interfere with the rights of employers to manage their own businesses in their own way."[28] Then, addressing specifically what he claimed to be the union's mode of behavior, he declared, "The courts will be ready for the emergency whenever and wherever the spirit of anarchy may manifest itself, whether within or without the lodges [union locals], and the American people, if need be, will rise in their majesty and their might, and crush it as a triphammer would crush an eggshell."[29]

A year later, in 1898, in the second case in which a union declared a strike against a firm manufacturing steel wire and engaged in picketing to dissuade nonunion employees from continuing to work, Judge Eli Hammond, who ordinarily heard cases coming before the federal district court for western Tennessee, reiterated Sage's legal principles. Hammond insisted that courts did not act as strikebreakers by issuing ex parte preliminary injunctions because such injunctions merely enforced the law. If strikers abandoned their cause because they chose to obey the law, the courts would not have broken the strike. In Hammond's words, "For that abandonment the courts are in no wise responsible, nor should that fact influence its judgment."[30] The only choice strikers had, he insisted, was to obey the law or to suffer the consequences. "Even 'scabs,'" he declared, "and those who employ 'scabs' have rights which the strikers are bound by law to respect."[31] The primary legal right that strikers had to respect was liberty of contract, every citizen's essential birthright—a right that even legislators were forbidden to limit. "The truth is," he expostulated, "that the most potential and unlawful force or violence may exist without lifting a finger against any man, or uttering a word of threat against him." Such was the mere presence of pickets, which alone interfered with a worker's right to enter his or her place of work. Hammond directed pointed criticism at Cleveland's mayor and the city's police force for refusing to bar strikers from congregating in streets near the mill and for failing to guarantee free passage for strikebreakers through city streets. Like Sage, Hammond cited *Vegelahn v. Gunter*, and he even cited Holmes's dissent as precedent for his injunction.[32]

The alacrity of Sage and Hammond in citing *Vegelahn* and in the latter's instance alluding to Holmes's dissent as establishing precedent for their injunction rulings rings odd. It is true that, as with the Ohio cases heard by Sage and Hammond, the Massachusetts case concerned a strike in which union members seeking to enforce a closed shop against a recalcitrant employer engaged in picketing to dissuade workers from taking their places at work. Moreover, clearly, the majority opinion in the Massachusetts case supported the injunctions issued by Sage and Hammond. But unlike most other comparable cases, *Vegelahn* prompted two vigorous dissents, most notably the one by Holmes.[33] Holmes agreed that courts of equity could issue injunctions to restrain criminal or violent behavior, but he maintained that picketing and vigorous persuasion by strikers to influence strikebreakers were not in themselves criminal or illegal acts. Holmes's language captured an emerging and alternative jurisprudence of labor law. "One of the eternal conflicts out of which life is made up is that between the effort of every man to get the most he can for his services, and that of society, disguised under the name of capital, to get his services for the least possible return. Combination on the one side," Holmes proceeded, "is patent and powerful. Combination on the other is the necessary and desirable counterpart, if the battle is to be carried on in a fair and equal way." Workers could combine to get as much as possible for their labor, Holmes maintained, "just as capital may combine with a view to getting the greatest possible return." Labor, then, had to have

> the same liberty that combined capital had to support its interests by argument, persuasion, and the bestowal or refusal of those advantages it otherwise lawfully controlled. I can remember when many people thought that . . . strikes

were wicked, as organized refusals to work. I suppose that intelligent economists and legislators have given up that notion to-day. I feel pretty confident that they equally will abandon the idea that an organized refusal by workmen of social intercourse with a man who shall enter their antagonist's employ is wrong, if it is dissociated from any threat of violence, and is made for the sole object of prevailing if possible in a contest with their employer about the rate of wages. The fact, that the immediate object of the act by which the benefit to themselves is to be gained is to injure their antagonist, does not necessarily make it unlawful, any more than when a great house lowers the price of certain goods for the purpose, and with the effect, of driving a smaller competitor from the business.[34]

None of Ohio's Northern District Court judges paid heed to Holmes's alternative labor jurisprudence—not in the 1890s and not afterward.

Indeed, in several cases judges in the Northern District went beyond the majority opinion in *Vegelahn*, which condemned and enjoined only violent or coercive strike actions. In a ruling he delivered in July 1901, Judge Francis Wing declared it illegal for a union to demand that an employer hire only union members for a particular type of work and then to picket in an attempt to persuade nonunion workers from laboring for the Otis Steel Company.[35] Even if such an action was peaceful, Wing ruled, it amounted to an attempt by the union to enforce a higher law than that which was administered by courts. He added "that a self-constituted body of men, deriving no authority from recognized law, should not be permitted to originate edicts for the government of others, and attempt to enforce them by any means whatsoever."[36] Wing then defined picketing, however conducted, as an illegitimate form of coercion. By definition, his opinion proceeded, picketing was a method of warfare, even in this instance in which the union pickets allowed 90 percent of all employees free ingress and egress from the plant. The union instead sought to bar access only to the roughly 10 percent of employees (between fifty and sixty-eight workers) who served as skilled molders. To Wing, most of those nonunion molders who resided and boarded in the plant during the strike or were escorted to and from the premises by private armed guards were simply common workers exercising their constitutional right to do with their labor as they pleased. Intimidation, he pronounced, could not be disguised as persuasion, for "persuasion, too emphatic or too long and persistently continued, may itself become a nuisance, and its use a form of unlawful coercion."[37] Hence, Wing enjoined all picketing near the company's premises.

Only five years later, a second district judge enjoined picketing by a machinists' union local involved in a dispute with an automobile manufacturing company. Although the judge in this instance, Robert Tayler, declared peaceful picketing lawful in theory, he found that the union's use of the tactic amounted to unlawful coercion. To the company's appeal for an injunction against the pickets, Tayler issued a temporary restraining order intended to protect the right of the nonunion machinists to labor as they chose under individual freedom as guaranteed by U.S. laws and the Constitution.[38] It was for a judge and a judge alone to decide the facts in the case and determine whether union activity transgressed the law.

The next and last wave of industrial dispute cases that came before judges in the Northern District of Ohio arose from the labor militancy precipitated by U.S. entry into World War I and the ensuing postwar upheaval. These cases occurred regularly between the years 1917 and 1923 and coincided with a number of federal circuit court and U.S. Supreme Court rulings on the same issues at law. By then, however, the federal judiciary's ability to enjoin strikes and to ban picketing had been limited by the clauses in the 1914 Clayton Anti-trust Act that said labor was not a commodity of commerce and that legitimated collective union action. Or so thought union officers and members, as evidenced in the words of Samuel Gompers, president of the American Federation of Labor, who declared the Clayton Act "labor's Magna Carta."[39]

In short order, Ohio's unions and their members discovered that the Clayton Act had not emancipated workers from federal judicial supervision. They first learned that lesson in Judge John Killits's opinion in *Stephens et al. v. Ohio State Telephone Co.*, which arose from a dispute between a local of the International Brotherhood of Electrical Workers and the Ohio State Telephone Company. The union declared a strike against the company in 1916 when its managers refused to bargain with union representatives, to recognize the right of its employees to choose to be represented by union officials, or to meet the union's conditions for wages and hours. As was usually the case, the union and its members resorted to picketing in order to dissuade nonunion employees from reporting for work. The telephone company turned to the district court for an injunction to ban picketing, and Killits provided it. In response to union attorneys who cited the Clayton Act as grounds to deny the company's request, Killits asserted that the clause of the act in question guaranteed rights to employers and the public as well as to labor unions. In fact, he stressed, clause 20 of the Clayton Act forbade labor to infringe on the rights of employers and the public. If it provided special rights to labor, Killits added, it was class legislation and hence unconstitutional.[40] But, he concluded, the law provided no such special rights to labor, as it legitimated only lawful, peaceful, nonviolent labor actions. In other words, it simply confirmed common-law legal traditions and precedents that enabled courts to enjoin illegal picketing. No court, Killits proclaimed, had ever restrained peaceful union action. When pickets called nonunion employees "rats," "scabs," "thieves," and "outcasts" and spoke to them without invitation, shadowed them, and intimidated them, they broke the law.[41]

Killits revealed his nonobjective, or nonjudicial, temperament in explaining the basis on which he found the union's actions to be illegal. In his ruling, he conceded that hard evidence had not been provided to establish that pickets had engaged in criminal activity, but he observed that everybody knew violent actions such as cutting phone lines and assaulting innocent employees happened during strikes. Therefore, he could infer that such actions occurred in the course of the current dispute, and newspaper stories supported such suspicions.[42] That being the case, Killits ruled that union members could not exercise their right to free speech unless they respected the replacement workers' right to privacy and freedom from molestation at home, at work, and on the streets. The Clayton Act, he declared, allowed no such free speech unless the audience to which it was directed proved receptive. "These propositions are so elemental that it would seem a waste of time to state them," he said; after all, "the existence of a strike does not make that lawful which would otherwise be unlawful."[43] Moreover, anything that the union or its members did to limit telephone services would be illegal because the company served the public. The only right held by union members, Killits concluded, was the right to withdraw their labor but not to infringe the company's business. The public always came first! And to prove that he was merely implementing the law as commonly understood, Killits cited as precedent a recent circuit court opinion in a comparable case based on the Clayton Act.[44]

Killits's ruling in the case left the union in a classic catch-22 dilemma. If union action actually impeded the phone company's operations, it was prima facie unlawful. If union behavior allowed the company to operate without hindrance, the strike was lost. That remained the pattern of rulings in the remaining comparable cases.

These rulings were made by judges who had been appointed by Republican presidents and who themselves had been active in Republican Party politics prior to ascending to the bench. Yet the longest-serving Democratic judge on the court, David C. Westenhaver, hewed to the pattern set by his Republican colleagues—despite being appointed by Woodrow Wilson and being a former associate of Newton D. Baker, Wilson's secretary of war, and Tom Johnson, a former reform mayor of Cleveland, both of whom were progressive Democrats sympathetic to the labor movement. In a case that arose from the turbulent 1919 national steel strike, Westenhaver, like Killits, Tayler, Sage, and Hammond before him, enjoined the mayor and the police chief of the city of Cleveland from interfering with a company's right to employ strikebreakers.[45] The mayor and the police chief, ostensibly in order to preserve public peace, limited the steel company's ability to replace strikers with workers recruited from out of town. According to Westenhaver, the police apprehended strikebreakers without warrants or reasonable grounds for suspicion, held them captive at police stations for several hours while checking their records, informed them of the ongoing dispute between the company and its workers, and sought to dissuade them from taking employment. "The officer's statement that, upon being informed that a strike was in progress, they voluntarily expressed a desire to return [home] is," declared the judge, "to put it mildly, not worthy of credit."[46]

Having ruled that the testimony by police was without foundation, Westenhaver accepted, without question, all the testimony and depositions provided by the company. Public officials, he stated, had no right to warn prospective employees about a strike in progress, for the plaintiff conducted a lawful business and should have been free to conduct it without unlawful interference by strikers or others.[47] In a remarkable obiter dictum, Westenhaver added that municipal action to forestall public disorder that interfered with the right of a lawful business to function could be enjoined but that comparable public actions to limit free speech or cultural performances that threatened public disruption could not be enjoined.[48] And this was from the same jurist who tried Eugene V. Debs for a speech delivered at a public park in Canton, Ohio; who instructed the jury that Debs's words had violated the 1917 Espionage Act; and who sentenced Debs to an extended term in federal prison.[49]

A particularly interesting case arose that same year because the parties to the dispute, the Willys-Overland Automobile Company and the unions representing striking workers, could not establish diversity of citizenship or a direct link to interstate commerce that would enable either party to bring suit in federal court. Instead, a North Carolina automobile dealership that sold Willys-Overland vehicles brought suit against the company and the unions, claiming that the strike interfered with its business and threatened its survival.[50] In its brief to the court, the plaintiff alleged that the Toledo unions, by striking in violation of the Constitution, engaged in a violent criminal conspiracy in restraint of interstate commerce that threatened to halt the manufacture of vehicles and their parts unless the Willys-Overland company met union demands. The North Carolina dealer asked the court to restrain the union from continuing its criminal behavior and to require the city of Toledo and its police to protect the rights of nonunion workers. Instead, city officials had asked company executives to shut the plant in order to preserve public peace, a request that the company honored.

After an initial temporary restraining order (TRO) failed to restore production at the plant, Killits issued a permanent injunction against the unions and ordered Willys-Overland to resume production under its aegis and the protection provided by U.S. marshals. Killits cited as precedent for his permanent injunction previous antiunion, antistrike, antiboycott rulings issued by circuit courts and the Supreme Court. Indeed, he suggested, the actions undertaken by the unions in Toledo were even more heinous and immoral than those in the cases he cited. Therefore, the Clayton Act offered no relief to unions that engaged in violent, illegal, conspiratorial actions — actions that defendants admitted were intended to stop production and hence to restrain interstate commerce, making them illegal under the Sherman Act as well as the Clayton Act. He consequently ruled that a permanent injunction would restrain the union more firmly. Whereas the TRO allowed a limited number of pickets near the plant premises, the permanent injunction banned all picketing and other union activities associated with the strike. In Killits's opinion, a strike no longer existed, as production had been resumed with a replacement labor force. To be sure, union attorneys claimed that a company lockout had precipitated the renewed picketing by the union, but Killits, in response, claimed that the terms *strike* and *lockout* were synonymous because in both instances, employees made a choice. In one case, they left work voluntarily, and in the other, they refused to return to work voluntarily on the employers' terms.[51] That being the present case, union members, he ruled, no longer had a right to picket, even peacefully, as they were no longer employees covered by the Clayton Act. Killits made his meaning abundantly clear, warning union members that "every court recognizes that 'picketing' suggests aggression — that it is always a hint of unlawful interference with rights entitled to protection."[52]

That same year, Killits proved equally decisive in enjoining a union from picketing an employer that it deemed unfair.[53] In this case, even the judge conceded that the pickets did no more than use their right to speak. Nevertheless, he found that such speech was threatening, insulting, embarrassing, and obscene and hence illegal, even though city police testified otherwise. As usual, Killits declared such testimony unsound and even accused the police of perjury. We can't expect rude, uneducated workmen to stop at strong language, he observed, because such language inevitably leads to direct action and "peaceful persuasion takes its flight." In reality, there was no such thing as peaceful picketing. Both in the text of his opinion and in its subtext, Killits suggested that unions should not be allowed to interfere, ever or in any way, with a company's lawful business.[54] If such behavior as undertaken by Toledo's unions was tolerated, he ruled, society was on the road to socialism and the union had become a "soviet." "Congress surely never intended to so cripple the industries of the country—to so broadly and unfairly discriminate in favor of a class—to so violate the clearest public policy," declaimed the judge.[55] Killits made it plain that he personally considered the Clayton Act an unconstitutional piece of class legislation, although, as a lowly district court judge, he lacked the authority to reject it as unconstitutional. Still, he reminded those in his courtroom that judges alone had to determine how far class legislation might free a special class from the ordinary strictures of the law.[56]

Two final cases illustrated how inchoate the law had become when judges dealt with industrial conflict or labor-management relations. Judge Westenhaver heard both cases. In the first, a company that had contracted with the city of Cleveland to install metal windows, door frames, and sashes at the city municipal hospital brought suit against a local of the sheet metal workers' union and city officials for pursuing actions that interfered with the right of the company to fulfill its contract.[57] The company had employed members of the carpenters' union to install the materials, but under the terms of the union's charter from the American Federation of Labor, the sheet metal workers had primary jurisdiction of such work. Union officials demanded that the city require the company to employ sheet metal workers for the job, and when municipal officials and company managers denied the union's request, the union declared a strike and ordered all its members then working on other city building projects to walk off the job. In response, city officials acceded to the sheet metal union's wishes, and when the company refused to discharge the carpenters, the city sent police to terminate work at the hospital. The company then went to court and asked Westenhaver to issue an injunction limiting the ability of the union and the city to stop work at the hospital.

In his ruling on the request, Westenhaver declared that a municipal contract was an essential protected property right, just like a person's home. Defendants thus had engaged in a conspiracy to deprive plaintiffs of their property and to injure their business. The union had induced the city to breach its contract, clearly an unlawful action that violated the company's rights under the Fifth and Fourteenth Amendments. Westenhaver declared that no dispute existed between employers and employees and that "in no legal sense is this a labor dispute." Hence, the Clayton Act's clauses concerning labor injunctions failed to apply, and higher courts, almost without exception, had found sympathy strikes and secondary boycotts, the practices committed by the sheet metal workers' union in this case, to be unlawful forms of coercion. Even legal acts, the judge declared, became illegal when such methods were used, so if the company had employed nonunion labor rather than members of the carpenters' union, as it had done, the sheet metal workers' action would have remained unlawful.[58]

The second case decided by Westenhaver was perhaps even more interesting in its implications because the suit had been brought by the U.S. Department of Justice. The case arose from an agreement voluntarily negotiated between the Window Glass Manufacturers' Association and the Window Glass Workers' Union to regulate production and employment in their industry. The members of the manufacturers' association and the union produced handblown glass manufactured in the traditional way—a process that was rapidly losing market share to machine-manufactured glass, which cost less to produce and sold for a much lower price. To bring a measure of stability to a declining industry, companies and the union agreed to limit production (half the firms would operate the first half of the year and the remaining firms the second half) with the opportunity to earn wages year-round. The government brought suit under the terms of the Sherman Act, claiming that the agreement between the association and the union represented an unconstitutional and illegal restraint of interstate commerce.[59] Accepting all the government's stipulations in the case, Westenhaver ruled in its favor, declaring that the Clayton Act did not apply because the labor agreement at issue did not involve working conditions but instead endeavored to restrain trade beyond the "rule of reason" that exempted enterprises from liability under the Sherman Act. Moreover, turning to classical economic theory as then taught in most college introductory economics courses and textbooks rather than to factual evidence, Westenhaver ruled that association-union agreement could only result in reduced production, lower employment, and higher prices for the product. To be sure, none of that had been contested by defendants. After all, the purpose of the agreement was to limit production and employment in an effort to manage market share and maintain some price stability. In Westenhaver's estimation, however, the agreement violated the public interest by restraining competition, raising prices for consumers, and harming union members. In the judge's theoretical world, machine-manufactured glass had not intensified market competition, nor offered consumers lower prices, nor cost handblown glass workers thousands of jobs. It was as if the parties to the agreement were not desperately seeking to rescue a declining industry and a vanishing craft from utter collapse but instead were conspiring to extort consumers. From such misunderstandings of the real world of economic activity and such misapplications of economic theory did Ohio's Northern District Court judges apply the law in cases arising from labor disputes.

Remarkably, for the latter half of the 1920s and the first half of the 1930s there are no reported cases for the Northern District of Ohio that involved labor conflicts, union actions, and worker employment rights. For the pre–New Deal years and for the years that followed passage of the Norris-LaGuardia anti-injunction law, the absence of such cases on the court's docket might be easily explained. From 1924 through 1932, strikes declined substantially. The coal industry continued to be battered by conflict even as other sectors of the economy operated practically strike free. So, Ohio's Southern District Court continued to hear labor cases, since the state's coal mines were concentrated in its southern region.

For a half century, then, the U.S. District Court for the Northern District of Ohio and its judges remained consistent in their interpretation and implementation of labor law. The rulings issued by the district's judges, whether Republican or Democratic, reflected none of the shifting perspectives about labor law that had emerged in other state and federal courts as early as the opening decade of the twentieth century and that spread more widely among jurists over the two succeeding decades. Down to 1932, the Ohio judges remained committed to nineteenth-century understandings of economic theory, constitutional law, liberty of contract as a citizen's fundamental right, and a belief that the law could offer no special privileges to a class as a collective category. Ohio's federal district court persisted in acting on a principle enunciated by contemporary legal scholar Richard Epstein: "The risk of judicial abuse is an acceptable price to pay to control the legislative abuses that all too often do occur."[60]

Notes

1. Among the large number of books that detail and analyze the impact of judge-interpreted and judge-made law on workers and their unions, the following are some of the best: William E. Forbath, *Law and the Shaping of the Labor Movement* (Cambridge, Mass.: Harvard University Press, 1991); Victoria C. Hattam, *Labor Visions and State Power: The Origins of Business Unionism in the United States* (Princeton, N.J.: Princeton University Press, 1993); Karen Orren, *Belated Feudalism: Labor, the Law, and Liberal Development in the United States* (New York: Cambridge, University Press, 1991); Christopher L. Tomlins, *The State and the Unions: Labor Relations, Law, and the Labor Movement in America, 1880–1960* (New York: Cambridge University Press, 1986); Tomlins, *Law, Labor, and Ideology in the Early American Republic* (Chapel Hill: University of North Carolina Press, 1993); Robert J. Steinfeld, *The Invention of Free Labor: The Employment Relation in English and American Law and Culture* (Chapel Hill: University of North Carolina Press, 1991); James Atleson, *Values and Assumptions in American Labor Law* (Amherst: University of Massachusetts Press, 1983); and Herbert Hovenkamp, *Enterprise and American Law, 1836–1937* (Cambridge, Mass.: Harvard University Press, 1991). For two interesting older books, see Felix Frankfurter and Nathan Greene, *The Labor Injunction* (Gloucester, Mass.: Peter Smith, 1963), and Edward E. Witte, *The Government in Labor Disputes* (New York: Arno Reprint, 1969). There is also an enormous literature on the subject in law reviews and historical journals too numerous to cite.

2. The material on the biographies of the district court judges has been drawn from "History of the Sixth Circuit," available at www.cab.uscours.gov/lib_hist/courts/district%20court/OH/NDOH/judges/html (accessed August 25, 2010). Similar information can be found at www.judgepedia/org/index/php (accessed August 25, 2010).

3. Daniel R. Ernst, *Lawyers and the Labor Trust: A History of the American Antiboycott Association* (Urbana: University of Illinois Press, 1995); Hovenkamp, *Enterprise and American Law*; cf. Haggai Hurvitz, "American Labor Law and the Doctrine of Entrepreneurial Property Rights: Boycott, Courts, and the Juridical Reorientation of 1886–1895," *Industrial Relations Law Journal* 8, no. 3 (1986): 307–61.

4. Tomlins, *Law, Labor, and Ideology*, provides an excellent guide to the common law of employer, or master, liability.

5. The best recent book on the subject is John Fabian Witt, *The Accidental Republic: Crippled Workingmen, Destitute Widows, and the Remaking of American Law* (Cambridge, Mass.: Harvard University Press, 2004). See also two books on the subject by the econometrician Price V. Fishback: *A Prelude to the Welfare State: The Origins of Workers' Compensation* (Chicago: University of Chicago Press, 2000), and *The Adoption of Workers' Compensation in the United States, 1900–1930* (Cambridge, Mass.: Harvard University Press, 1996), as well as two articles by Robert Asher: "Business and Workers' Welfare in the Progressive Era: Workmen's Compensation Reform in Massachusetts, 1880–1911," *Business History Review* 43 (Winter 1969): 452–75, and "Failure and Fulfillment: Agitation for Employers' Liability Legislation and the Origins of Workmen's Compensation in New York State, 1876–1910," *Labor History* 24 (Spring 1983): 198–222.

6. Sweeney v. Holt, Ex'r, etc., 15 F. 880–84 (1883).

7. Atkyn v. Wabash Ry. Co., 41 F. 193–201 (1889). With these instructions, it was not surprising that the jury found for the defendant.

8. Evans v. American Iron & Tube Co., 42 F. 519–25 (1890), quotation at 525.

9. Farmers' Loan & Trust Company et al. v. Toledo, A. A. & N. M. Ry. Co. et al., 67 F. 73–82 (1895).

10. Kane v. Erie R. Co., 128 F. 474–77 (1904).

11. Chambers v. American Tin Plate Co., 129 F. 561–64 (1904); Kane v. Erie R. Co., 142 F. 682–90 (1906).

12. Mitchell v. Toledo, St. Louis & W. R. Co., 197 F. 528 (1912).

13. Heskett v. Pennsylvania Co., 245 F. 326–30 (1917); McCalmont v. Pennsylvania Co., 273 F. 231–40 (1921); Blunt v. Pennsylvania R. Co., 9 F.2d 395–96 (1925); Michigan Central R. Co. v. Zimmerman, 24 F.2d 23–26 (1928); Lowery v. Hocking Valley Ry. Co., 60 F.2d 78–80 (1932); Line v. Erie R. Co., 62 F.2d 657–58 (1933).

14. McCalmont v. Pennsylvania Co.

15. Noftz v. B. & O. Ry. Co., 13 F.2d 389–90 (1926).

16. Sullivan v. Wabash Ry. Co., 23 F.2d 323–24 (1928); Michigan Central R. Co. v. Zimmerman; Hallstein v. Pennsylvania R. Co., 30 F.2d 594–97 (1929).

17. Hallstein v. Pennsylvania R. Co.; McDougal v. New York, Chicago, and St. Louis Railroad Company, 15 F.2d 283–85 (1926); Pennsylvania R. Co. v. Brubaker, 31 F.2d 939–40 (1929); Emch v. Pennsylvania R. Co., 37 F.2d 828–30 (1930).

18. Burnett v. Pennsylvania R. Co., 33 F.2d 579–80 (1929); Didinger v. Pennsylvania R. Co., 39 1930 F.2d 798–800; Erie R. Co. v. Vajo, 41 F.2d 738 (1930); Reitz v. Chicago & E. R. Co., 46 F.2d 50–53.

19. McWeeny v. Standard Boiler & Plate Co., 210 F. 507–12 (1914), quotation at 512; Standard Boiler & Plate Co. v. McWeeny, 218 F. 361–64. For another ruling by Judge Day sustaining a generous jury award to a plaintiff, see Bolton-Pratt Co. v. Chester, 210 F. 253–57 (1914).

20. Pennsylvania Co. v. Cole, 214 F.2d 948 (1914); Kurtz v. Lake Shore Electric Ry., 218 F. 188–89 (1914).

21. On this point, see Melvyn Dubofsky, "The Federal Judiciary, Free Labor, and Equal Rights," in *The Pullman Strike and the Crisis of the 1890s: Essays on Labor and Politics,* ed. Richard Schneirov, Shelton Stromquist, and Nick Salvatore (Urbana: University of Illinois Press, 1999), 159–78.

22. See Hurvitz, "American Labor Law."

23. Toledo, A. A. & N. M. Ry. Co. v. Pennsylvania Co. et al., 54 F. 730–45 (1893). In his opinion, Taft declared that the union's rule requiring engineers to support their brother union members on strike to be on its face a command to commit a crime.

24. Ibid., 746–58.

25. Consolidated Steel & Wire Co. v. Murray et al., 80 F. 811–29 (1897).

26. Ibid., 815. For a more complete discussion of Sage, who became "the first Federal judge [to blaze] the way for that class of decisions which have since become so well known as 'Government by injunction,'" see Roberta Sue Alexander, *A Place of Recourse: A History of the U.S. District Court for the Southern District of Ohio, 1803–2003* (Athens: Ohio University Press, 2005), 71–73.

27. See a brief discussion of Holmes's dissent and its implications later in this chapter.

28. Consolidated Steel v. Murray, 828.

29. Ibid., 829.

30. American Steel & Wire Co. v. Wire Drawers' & Die Makers' Unions, Nos. 1 & 3, et al., 90 F. 598–622 (1898), quotation at 604.

31. Ibid., 612.

32. Ibid., 614.

33. 167 Mass. 92 (1896), available at http://www.lexisnexis.com.proxy.binghamton.edu/lnacui2api/frame.do (accessed September 16, 2010).

34. Ibid., 11. See also G. Edward White, *Justice Oliver Wendell Holmes: Law and the Inner Self* (New York: Oxford University Press, 1993), 288.

35. Otis Steel Company, Ltd. v. Local Union No. 218, of Cleveland, Ohio, of Iron Molders' Union of North America et al., 110 F. 698–702 (1901).

36. Ibid., 700.

37. Ibid., 702.

38. Pope Motor Car Co. v. Keegan et al., 150 F. 148–52 (1906); see also Donald G. Bahna, "The Pope-Toledo Strike of 1907," *Northwest Ohio Quarterly* 35 (Summer 1963): 138ff, for background on the dispute.

39. Daniel R. Ernst, "The Labor Exemption, 1908–1914," *Iowa Law Review* 74 (July 1989): 1151–73; Stanley I. Kutler, "Labor, the Clayton Act, and the Supreme Court," *Labor History* 3 (Winter 1962): 19–38.

40. Stephens et al. v. Ohio State Telephone Co., 240 F. 759–79 (1917).

41. Ibid., 771.

42. Ibid., 772–73. For how judges consistently used tropes of violence to characterize union behavior, see Dianne Avery, "Images of Violence in Labor Jurisprudence: The Regulation of Picketing and Boycotts, 1894–1921," *Buffalo Law Review* 37 (Winter 1988–89): 3–117.

43. Stephens v. Ohio Phone Co., 774.

44. Tri-city Central Trades Council v. American Steel Foundries, 238 F. 738 (1916–17).

45. American Steel & Wire Co. of New Jersey v. Davis, Mayor, et al., 261 F. 800–806 (1919).

46. Ibid., 803.

47. Ibid., 804.

48. Ibid., 805–6.

49. See chapter 4.

50. Dail-Overland Co. v. Willys-Overland, Inc., et al., 263 F. 171–92 (1919–20).

51. Ibid., 187.

52. Ibid., 191; Killits again cited the Tri-cities case as precedent, this time alluding to a Second Circuit Court opinion, Tri-cities Trades Council v. American Steel Foundries, 274 F. 56–66. For background on the strike, see David A. McMurray, "The Willys-Overland Strike, 1919," *Northwest Ohio Quarterly* 36 (Autumn 1964): 171–80.

53. Vonnegut Machinery Co. v. Toledo Machine & Tool Co. et al., 263 F. 192–204 (1920).

54. Ibid., 199.

55. Ibid., 202. Such was Killits's reading of the Clayton Act's nefarious aim.

56. Killits's tendency toward judicial overkill and to take jurisdiction in questionable circumstances in this case led the full Sixth Circuit Court to overrule his decision because the parties to the suit lacked diversity of citizenship and a direct link to interstate commerce. 274 F. 56–76 (1921).

57. Central Metal Products Corporation v. O'Brien et al., 278 F. 827–32 (1922).

58. Ibid., 830. The cases that Westenhaver cited as precedent included: American Steel Foundries v. Tri-cities Central Trades Council, 257 U.S. 184 (1921); Duplex v. Deering, 254 U.S. 443 (1921); Truax v. Corrigan, 257 U.S. 312 (1921); and Hitchman Coal & Coke Co. v. Mitchell et al., 245 U.S. 229 (1917).

59. United States v. National Ass'n. of Window Glass Mfgers. et al., 287 F. 228–39 (1923).

60. Richard A. Epstein, *Bargaining with the State* (Princeton, N.J.: Princeton University Press, 1993), 19.

4

The Trial of Eugene V. Debs, 1918

Melvin I. Urofsky

O N THE AFTERNOON of June 16, 1918, Eugene Victor Debs, the four-time presidential candidate of the American Socialist Party, arrived at Nimisilla Park in Canton, Ohio, to address more than a thousand of the party faithful gathered for their annual picnic. In addition to local socialists, the crowd also included federal agents, newspaper reporters, and a stenographer who would record the speech for prosecutors considering criminal charges. Local vigilantes also worked the crowd looking for slackers, and whenever they spotted a young man, they insisted on seeing his draft card.

Eugene Victor Debs (1855–1926) dominated the American socialist movement for much of his adult life.[1] In 1896, he helped found the Social Democratic Party, which then elected him chairman of the executive board. In 1900, he ran for president for the first time on the Socialist ticket, receiving 88,000 votes. Debs would run again in 1904, 1908, and 1912, and in the last election, he received 913,693 votes, the largest number ever garnered by a Socialist Party candidate.[2]

During that period, Debs supported himself and his wife by giving speeches and writing articles for newspapers and magazines. He was a charismatic speaker who often employed both the vocabulary and the style of evangelical Christianity, even though he personally disdained organized religion. The columnist Heywood Broun, in his eulogy of Debs, quoted a fellow socialist who said: "That old man with the burning eyes actually believes that there can be such a thing as the brotherhood of man. And that's not the funniest part. As long as he's around I believe it myself."[3]

At the beginning of World War I in 1914, Debs and the Socialist Party swam in the mainstream of American public opinion in wanting the United States to stay out of the conflict. Socialism by definition is pacifist, and American socialists hoped that their brethren in Europe would stand up for their principles and oppose the war. Instead, socialist groups in Germany, France, and England all chose to support what the German socialists called national "self-defense" over the international solidarity of the working class. Within the American party, the debate raged over what should be done, and as Debs traveled the country, he grappled with what the war meant—for the nation, for its people, and for the socialist movement. Sometimes, he seemed to argue that nothing could be done to stop the fighting; at other times, he indicated that perhaps there might be a chance to mediate a peace. At all times, however, he blamed the war on the capitalist system. "Capitalist nations not only exploit the workers," he told his audiences, "but ruthlessly invade, plunder and ravage one another. The profit system is responsible for it all." As the radical journalist John Reed put it, "This is not Our War."[4]

Debs, Reed, and other socialists and pacifists could say this safely while the United States remained neutral. Between August 1914 and April 1917, Debs constantly attacked the war as well as the idea that the United States should get involved. War would kill young men and enrich the capitalists. "Never Be a Soldier," he wrote. The army would turn a man into a "vile and abject thing, the hired assassin of his capitalist master." Occasionally, his prose took on a somewhat purplish hue. He would let himself be shot before he would defend American capitalism, he declared, and he told members of the master class to "rip out their own loins and livers, riot in their own blood and entrails and offer up their own mangled and putrescent carcasses on the blood-drenched altar of Mars and Mammon."[5] By the spring of 1917, however, public opinion had moved sharply in favor of the Allies, and when President Woodrow Wilson asked for a declaration of war against Germany, most of the country cheered.

Ironically, the war to make the world safe for democracy triggered one of the worst invasions of civil liberties in American history. The government obviously had to protect itself from subversion, but many of the laws passed by Congress at the urging of the Wilson administration seemed aimed as much at suppressing criticism of government policy as at ferreting out spies. The 1918 Sedition Act, for example, passed at the behest of senators opposed to the Industrial Workers of the World (IWW), struck out at a variety of "undesirable" activities and forbade "uttering, printing, writing, or publishing any disloyal, profane, scurrilous, or abusive language."[6]

A government must protect itself from active subversion, especially in wartime. But the evidence indicates that Wilson, preoccupied first with mobilization and then with peace making, gave little thought to the problem and deferred to his conservative advisers, especially Postmaster General Albert Sidney Burleson, a reactionary who considered any criticism of the government unpatriotic. The federal laws and analogous state statutes caught radicals, pacifists, and other dissenters in an extensive web, and the total number of indictments ran into the thousands.[7] Debs certainly knew of this when he accepted the invitation to speak in Canton.

The talk in Canton would be the first that Debs had given in nearly a year. He had collapsed from physical and nervous exhaustion the previous summer and spent most of the next year resting, recuperating, and watching as the Wilson administration clamped down on radicals, pacifists, and others opposed to the war.[8] In the spring of 1918, the Socialist Party announced that he would give a few talks in Indiana near his home, and if his strength held up and the police did not interfere, he would go to Canton, Ohio, in mid-June to attend the state party's annual picnic and give the featured address. Debs showed great caution in his Indiana appearances. Claude Bowers, an Indiana Democrat and historian, heard Debs at one outing and said, "It seemed to me that he had prepared his speech with the realization that every word would be microscopically examined by secret agents." There is also evidence that Debs expected, perhaps even hoped, to be arrested: "I'll take about two jumps and they'll nail me, but that's all right."[9]

Because of his illness and his absence from public life for almost a year, when Debs arrived in Canton he had not yet publicly endorsed or rejected the antiwar platform adopted by the Socialist Party at the St. Louis convention the week after Wilson's war message to Congress. The delegates adopted a proclamation declaring their "unalterable opposition" to the war and condemning it as "a crime against the people of the United States." Instead of making the world safer for democracy, it would just send thousands of young men to die in a "mad orgy of death and destruction." The St. Louis Proclamation, as it came to be called, urged socialists to join in "continuous, active, and public opposition to the war," including the draft and the sale of war bonds. Debs also knew of the minority report, prepared by John Spargo, that had urged socialists to accept the war as an unavoidable "fact" and to work with the government to mitigate the suffering the war would cause.[10] Though Debs had privately endorsed the majority report, there had been no opportunity for him to do so publicly.

A complicating factor, however, was the Russian Revolution, which all socialists welcomed. Some members of the party were now urging support for the war against Germany, since doing so would protect the revolution in Russia.[11] Debs, aware of this argument, had not commented on it publicly, and the audience in Canton that afternoon did not know what he would say. He and they understood, however, that if he espoused the antiwar St. Louis Proclamation in his speech, he would surely be arrested.

Debs began by noting that "in speaking to you this afternoon, there are certain limitations placed upon the right of free speech. I must be exceedingly careful, prudent, as to what I say, and even more careful and prudent as to how I say it." The audience understood exactly what he meant and cheered when he then said, "I may not be able to say all I think, but I am not going to say anything I do not think. I would rather a thousand times be a free soul in jail than to be a sycophant and coward in the streets."[12]

In later years, the Canton speech would take on mythic proportions in Socialist Party lore as the greatest antiwar speech ever delivered, but in fact Debs spent relatively little time on the war. For the most part, he urged his listeners "to keep foursquare with the principles of the international Socialist movement."[13] As even the Supreme Court later acknowledged when it reviewed the case, much of the talk was standard socialist fare.[14] But eventually, he got to the war, first declaring that he and all other socialists were patriots and always had been and then lambasting Theodore Roosevelt for his admiration of Kaiser Wilhelm and for telling him, after reviewing German troops, "If I had that kind of an army, I could conquer the world."[15]

He then moved on to the major casualties of the conflict—truth and civil liberties. Kate Richards O'Hare, whom he considered a sister, had just been sentenced to five years in prison. "Think of sentencing a woman to the penitentiary for simply talking," he exclaimed; then he accused her persecutors of deliberately distorting what she had said.[16] Scott Nearing had been dismissed from the University of Pennsylvania for daring to teach his students the truth about world economics. Max Eastman had been indicted and his paper, *The Masses*, suppressed. "The Man of Galilee, the Carpenter," Debs reminded his audience, "the workingman who became the revolutionary agitator of his day soon found himself to be an undesirable citizen in the eyes of the ruling knaves and they had him crucified."[17]

As Debs ran down the reasons why socialists should be against war, he made no reference to the draft law, nor, for that matter, did he ever really talk about the war in Europe. He spoke in terms of broad historical reference and actually spent more time on the plight of serfs in medieval times than on proletarians in modern-day Ohio. But he certainly edged into dangerous territory when he roused the crowd with the following statement:

> The master class has always declared the wars; the subject class has always fought the battles. The master class has all to gain and nothing to lose, while the subject class has nothing to gain and all to lose—especially their lives. They have always taught and trained you to believe it to be your patriotic duty to go to war and to have yourselves slaughtered at their command. But in all the history of the world you, the people, have never had a voice in declaring war, and strange as it certainly appears, no war by any nation in any age has been declared by the people. And here let me emphasize the fact—and it cannot be repeated too often—that the working class who fight all the battles, the working class who make the supreme sacrifices, the working class who freely shed their blood and furnish the corpses, have never yet had a voice in either declaring war or making peace. . . . Yours not to reason why. Yours but to do or die. . . . If war is right let it be declared by the people. You who have your lives to lose, you certainly above all others have the right to declare the momentous issue of war or peace.[18]

He completed his talk by exhorting his listeners to go out and work even harder for socialism. "Do not worry over the charge of treason to your masters, but be concerned about the treason that involves yourselves. Be true to yourself and you cannot be a traitor to any good cause on earth." The sun was setting on the old system and rising on a socialist world. All had to join in and ensure its triumph.[19]

In the audience, Clyde Miller, a reporter for the *Cleveland Plain Dealer*, scratched his head. After listening to the speech, he said he could not tell if Debs was "extremely vicious or extremely misguided." But Miller had been on an antiradical crusade, and so, after filing his story, he called his friend Edwin Wertz, the U.S. attorney for the Northern District of Ohio, and urged him to prosecute Debs. Wertz needed little convincing, since he had been the one to arrange for a stenographer to attend the Canton meeting. He assured Miller that he would seek an indictment.[20]

But after getting a transcript of the talk, Wertz wondered if he had any grounds on which to indict Debs. He went through the transcript, marked passages he thought violated the law, and sent it to John Lord O'Brien, a special assistant in the Justice Department in charge of prosecutions under the Espionage Act. O'Brien replied that many of the offending passages were, in his opinion, protected speech. "Criticism of the courts for their administration of the war laws," he explained, "can hardly be called an attack on the 'form of government of the United States.'" Moreover, Debs had never referred directly to the St. Louis antiwar platform, and his comments were "not sufficiently clear and definite." As far as the Espionage Act went, O'Brien understood it to mean that Debs was entirely free to "abuse the actions of the plutocrats of this country, real or imaginary."[21] (It is also possible that O'Brien considered the case so weak that a jury might acquit Debs, rendering a verdict that would greatly embarrass the government.)

Debs may have been personally ambivalent regarding what socialists should do about the war and technically correct on what he had actually said. But even though Justice Department lawyers told Wertz they did not think it advisable to indict Debs, as a U.S. attorney Wertz had a fair amount of leeway. Under pressure from Ohio newspapers, he decided to go ahead. On July 1, 1918, Debs went to Cleveland to give a speech; there, he was approached by a group of U.S. marshals. "I am glad to meet you, Mr. Debs," Deputy Marshal Charles Boehme said, adding, "I have a warrant for your arrest." "All right," Debs responded with a smile, "I'll come along." Before anyone in his party could react, Debs had been placed under arrest and taken to the federal building and then to the county jail, where he spent the night. Wertz crowed when he told the press, "No man is too big to be held responsible for his actions under the Espionage Act or any other law of the United States."[22] The next day, Debs was released on $10,000 bail, put up by Marguerite Prevey (who had chaired the Canton meeting) and Adolph W. Moskowitz, a well-to-do socialist sympathizer from Cleveland.[23]

The government charged Debs with ten counts of sedition.[24] Debs met with his lawyers in Cleveland on September 9, the day before the trial began, and told them that he did not want to defend himself by claiming his words had been distorted by the press. Instead, he would present no defense of any sort and claim that the Espionage Act violated the First Amendment and was therefore unconstitutional. Moreover, Debs had no doubt he would be convicted, and he did not want to waste time on legal strategy. "I am expecting nothing but a conviction," he wrote to a colleague, "under a law flagrantly unconstitutional and which was framed especially for the suppression of free speech."[25] He then left for Detroit, where he addressed a cheering crowd of three thousand supporters. "I may be sent to prison by the powers of militarism," he declared. "My message from behind bars will be all the more powerful. I would much rather be a man in jail than a coward outside of it."[26]

The trial opened in an air of tension. Only a week earlier, four people had been killed and dozens injured when a suitcase bomb had exploded in the Chicago federal building, the scene of the mass trial of IWW members. Socialists from all over the country flocked to Cleveland, hoping to witness the trial of their beloved leader, and as they tried to get into the courtroom, they were frisked for weapons by volunteers from the local chapter of the American Protective League.[27]

The courtroom struck some observers as overly ornate; others thought it was just what a court of law should look like. Oak and marble abounded, and light flooded in from two-story-high windows, reflecting off a ceiling painted in gold. The large judge's desk stood elevated above the well, where the prosecution and defense teams each had a large table. Behind the judge, a mural by Edwin Blashfield took up the entire wall, a painting of angels with beautiful bodies and stern faces, holding swords of flame and guarding the foundational documents of Anglo-American law—including the Ten Commandments and the Magna Carta—while images of great lawgivers—Moses, Mahomet, Justinian, and Lord Mansfield—looked down on the proceedings.[28] Max Eastman described the courtroom as a sort of "flamboyant solemnity" and noted that at the other end of the room, "a solid crowd of poor people" filled the spectators' seats and the balcony.[29]

Presiding over the trial was Judge David Courtney Westenhaver. Eastman wrote, "I always want to like the judge when I go into a court room. It is such an opportunity for human nature to be beautiful." But the bald, jowly, bespectacled Westenhaver struck him as having the "soul of a small-town lawyer."[30] Eastman and the other radicals packing the courtroom considered Westenhaver a lackey of the ruling class; after all, Debs had often said that federal judges were not chosen by the working class but by "the corporations and the trusts [that] dictate their appointment."[31]

In fact, the fifty-three-year-old Westenhaver had been born in modest circumstances in 1865 in Berkeley County, West Virginia. After graduating from Georgetown Law School in 1886, he had practiced in Berkeley County and had been elected as a prosecuting attorney and a member of the Martinsburg City

Council. In 1903, he had moved his practice to Cleveland and had been counsel to Tom Johnson, the progressive reformer and controversial Cleveland mayor. He had also been a law partner of another progressive, Newton D. Baker, a former pacifist who was then serving as secretary of war, and like Baker, he took a rather lenient approach to conscientious objectors. A scholar of sorts, Westenhaver wrote a number of articles on economic and legal subjects and served as president of the Cleveland Board of Education. His handling of difficult patent litigation brought him praise from judges and lawyers alike. A Democrat, he had only recently been appointed to the federal bench by Woodrow Wilson, replacing John Hessian Clarke, whom Wilson had named to the Supreme Court. Westenhaver served as a judge on the U.S. District Court for the Northern District of Ohio until his death from heart disease in 1928.[32]

The grand jury had handed down ten charges against Debs, but the government decided it would be impossible to prove five of them and thus dropped them from the indictment. The judge dropped a sixth, which alleged that Debs in his Canton speech had used "false reports and false statements" to undermine the war effort. Whether Debs had spoken truth or falsehood or even just opinion made no difference, and neither the judge nor the prosecution wanted to give him a chance to prove any of his allegations about the war. The remaining four charges all relied on inference, that is, whether a reasonable man could believe that Debs had made remarks "calculated to promote insubordination" or "propagate obstruction of the draft." These were questions of "fact" that a jury would determine, and it seemed clear that the jurors were more than willing to find that Debs, as the assistant prosecutor F. B. Kavanaugh claimed in his opening statement, was indeed a dangerous man who "opposed the ideals for which the American flag stands."[33]

Debs had originally not wanted his lawyers to make an opening statement, but Seymour Stedman had insisted, and Debs relented. In the half hour he spoke, Stedman tried to set up the questions that he hoped would determine Debs's fate. It did not matter, he declared, "what this jury thinks about the war, or about socialism, or about anything other than this one thing: 'What does this jury think about the right of Free Speech?' What is this jury going to do about the right of Gene Debs to express to all men the promptings of his soul?" The prosecutor had said that Debs should be judged not by his words but by his works: "The defense accepts the challenge. You shall know him by his works, by the works of his whole life."

At that point, Debs's supporters in the galleries burst into applause and cheering, and a stunned Westenhaver allowed the clamor to go on for a minute before gaveling the crowd into silence. He then chastised those who would turn his courtroom into a socialist rally, and he ordered the bailiff to bring the clappers before the bar. Some of the seven seized protested their innocence; others openly confessed their contempt of the court. One of Debs's lawyers, William Cunnea, directly chided the judge, stating, "I don't like to see you sit up there and play God to your fellow men." Amazingly, Westenhaver, who had every right to hold the noisemakers in contempt, relented, admitting that he had been "unduly vexed." He ordered the clappers to be charged but released without bail; then he adjourned the court for the day. The next day, instead of jailing the offenders, he imposed a modest fine.[34]

On the first day of testimony, the prosecutors planned to introduce the contents of Debs's Canton speech to prove the validity of the charges, and they immediately ran into a problem. The stenographer that Wertz had sent to the picnic, Virgil Steiner, was a car salesman who had limited experience in stenography. Not long after Debs began his speech, Steiner had lost his way and then had missed long stretches of the talk, jumping in when he thought he heard something traitorous. "My practice has been taking letters," he explained. "I have not had experience in taking speeches." The judge nonetheless allowed Steiner's admittedly partial notes into evidence.[35]

Given the unreliability of Steiner's notes, the case might have been thrown out of court had it not been for the fact that the socialists had arranged for a more competent stenographer to record the speech, perhaps hoping that by having an accurate transcription, Debs would be able to refute charges of sedition. Edward Sterling had a dozen years of stenographic experience, but although he was hired by the socialists, he had little sympathy for them. He had dressed very carefully for the trial, wanting to appear "respectable," and he was happy to work with the prosecutor. He read out his transcription in court, even adding dramatic flourishes and emphasizing what he considered treasonous passages.[36] Thus, despite the fact that Debs's partisans believed Sterling's reading had helped their hero, it actually confirmed those parts of Steiner's material that supported the charges against Debs.

After the jury heard what Debs had said, the prosecution set about proving what he had *intended*. Wertz, who now took over from Kavanaugh, needed to convince the jury that no matter how seemingly innocent Debs's words might have appeared, he in truth wanted to obstruct military recruitment. Acting on advice from the Justice Department, Wertz planned to place the Canton speech in the larger context of Debs's previous antiwar statements and especially his support of the St. Louis Proclamation. To do this, he called to the stand the newsman Clyde Miller, who had done so much to instigate the proceedings against Debs. Miller related an encounter with Debs in the lobby of his Canton hotel earlier on the day of the speech, recalling how, in response to a question, Debs had reaffirmed his support for the St. Louis declaration. Then he told the jury how he had been in the federal marshal's office on the day Debs had been arrested and again had asked him about the St. Louis Proclamation. Once more, Debs had reaffirmed his support and in fact had declared that he was willing "to die for those principles." Miller's testimony was critical in the prosecution strategy to link the Canton speech to a wider antiwar position.[37]

The jury then heard from Charles Ruthenberg, one of three socialists Debs had visited in the Canton jail before he delivered his speech and who was now in prison. (Ruthenberg was well known in Cleveland, having run for mayor in the preceding election.) Wertz really did not need Ruthenberg's testimony—confirmation that Debs was a socialist who endorsed the party's St. Louis platform—but he used him as a prop, to associate Debs in the jury's mind with a notorious antiwar agitator now in prison.[38] After that, Joseph Turner, a special agent working for Naval Intelligence, reported that he had attended a meeting in Chicago two months after the Canton speech and heard a militant Debs assert his support for the St. Louis Proclamation and his intention to keep on with the class struggle against the master-class warmongers.[39]

Throughout the first two days of the trial, Stedman raised objections time and again, hoping to lay the basis for an appeal to the Supreme Court.[40] The St. Louis Proclamation was inadmissible in evidence, he claimed. The words *military and naval forces* in the Espionage Act meant the same as in the April 1917 declaration of war, that is, those forces organized and in service, not those merely registered and subject to future enrollment in service. Simply talking to men not already in uniform could not be a violation of the Espionage Act. Moreover, Stedman asserted, none of this really mattered, since the First Amendment protected all of his client's comments.[41]

Debs, however, did not believe that an appeal could succeed, anymore than he believed that the jury would find him not guilty. In fact, making objections to testimony and trial procedures seemed to him to acknowledge the government's right to try him for his ideas. He determined to concede nothing and to offer no apologies or explanations, stating, "All I have said I believe to be true." He wanted to put the Sedition Act itself on trial.[42]

The prosecution concluded its case just before noon on September 11. Stedman rose and informed the court that the defense would call no witnesses, but he asked instead that Debs be allowed to address the court in his own behalf. Judge Westenhaver granted the unusual request and then called a brief recess. No one in the crowded courtroom moved, afraid of losing a precious seat and the opportunity to hear Debs speak. After court resumed, Westenhaver sternly warned the audience against any partisan outbursts.

Debs spoke for nearly two hours. He began by declaring, "I am not a lawyer. I know little about court procedures, about rules of evidence or legal practice."[43] He knew little and cared less because he intended to appeal to a higher moral authority, a standard of justice that went far beyond the power of Judge Westenhaver and his jury.

That jury, he told its members, could certainly send him to jail, where he might spend the rest of his life. "I do not fear to face you in this hour of accusation, nor do I shrink from the consequences of my utterances or my acts," he affirmed. To the contrary, he said, "I can look the Court in the face, I can look you in the face, I can look the world in the face, for in my conscience, in my soul, there is festering no accusation of guilt." He admitted freely "the truth of all that has been testified to in this proceeding. . . . I would not retract a word that I have uttered that I believe to be true to save myself from going to the penitentiary for the rest of my days." The prosecutors, he joked, could have saved themselves a lot of trouble in proving things he would not have denied.[44]

Debs asserted that the real issue of the trial—and the entire meaning of his life's work—was the conflict between the reactionary forces of wealth and progressive demands for industrial democracy. He had been put on trial because he believed in socialism, and he would defend that belief no matter the consequences. "There is not a single falsehood in that speech," he told the jurors. "If there is a single statement in it that will not bear the light of truth, I will retract it. I will make all of the reparation in my power. But if what I said is true, and I believe it is, then whatever fate or fortune may have in store for me I shall preserve inviolate the integrity of my soul and stand by it to the end."[45]

Debs then turned to the crux of the government's case against him: "I have been accused of having obstructed the war. I admit it. Gentlemen, I abhor war. I would oppose the war if I stood alone." He did not, however, consider himself alone, and he saw the episode of his arrest for the Canton speech as just another chapter in the long history of men and women who stood against "the tragic history of the race." Jesus had also been convicted for the dangerous doctrine of human love and the threat it posed to "the profiteers, high priests, the lawyers, the judges, the merchants, the bankers." Socrates had likewise been martyred for his advocacy of new ideas. Debs then praised the Bolsheviks, comparing them to the revolutionaries who had given the American colonies their independence.

Prosecutor Wertz jumped to his feet and called on the judge to force Debs to "confine his remarks to the evidence." Westenhaver had made it clear that he did not intend to let Debs turn his courtroom into a socialist soapbox, but he allowed Debs to continue, especially since it sounded as if the defendant had just offered a full and open confession. The court would "let him talk in his own way."[46]

As Debs spoke, Westenhaver occasionally shook his head from side to side, and Max Eastman reported that the judge had an "amused, attentive, patronizing smile." In one of the few comments that we have from Westenhaver in regard to the proceedings, he told Attorney General A. Mitchell Palmer after the trial that he had found Debs's "humane and patriotic remarks" a smokescreen to obscure his real agenda, that of a "revolutionary internationalist." The longer Debs spoke, the clearer it became to Westenhaver that the defendant had nothing but contempt for a citizen's "patriotic obligations" to obey the law. Debs may have claimed that he believed in peaceful democratic change, but the judge concluded that he had devoted his life to a workers' revolution that could only be achieved through violence.[47]

Still, Westenhaver, along with others in attendance, listened quietly as Debs then moved beyond the particulars of the case and lauded socialism as the logical extension of the moral views of the founders of the country. The Revolutionary generation had been despised radicals in their time, he said, and prior to the Civil War, many Americans regarded the abolitionists as "monsters of depravity." Now children were taught to revere both groups. As the abolitionists had fought to do away with chattel slavery, so socialists now fought to eliminate wage slavery.

As for his love of country, he stated, "I believe in patriotism. I have never uttered a word against the flag. I love the flag as a symbol of freedom." During the war, however, patriotism had been used for "base purposes" and love of country had been twisted into hatred of others. The prosecution had tried to make the St. Louis platform into an attack on America, when it so clearly was but one more expression of the socialist faith in universal brotherhood. The

Socialist Party had never intended to subvert the American war effort but wanted instead to rally workers everywhere to end all wars.

Partway through, Debs offered what he considered the critical part of his defense. "I believe in free speech, in war as well as in peace. I would not, under any circumstances, gag the lips of my bitterest enemy. I would under no circumstances suppress free speech. It is far more dangerous to attempt to gag the people than to allow them to speak freely of what is in their hearts." The real danger to America was not his Canton speech but the Espionage Act itself and the government's efforts to "gag a free people. . . . If the Espionage Law stands, then the Constitution of the United States is dead."[48]

"I am the smallest part of this trial," he concluded. "What you may choose to do to me will be of small consequence after all. I am not on trial here. There is an infinitely greater issue that is being tried today in this court, though you may not be conscious of it. American institutions are on trial before a court of American citizens. My fate is in your hands. I am prepared for your verdict." He thanked the jury members for their patience, bowed to them, and went back to his seat. Stedman recognized that he could not improve on what Debs had said and indicated to the judge that his client's statement would serve as the defense summation for the jury.[49]

Edwin Wertz realized that he had just heard a master work the crowd, and he knew there was no way he could match Eugene Debs in oratory. In fact, he told the jury in his summation that having a great power to move crowds was what made Debs so dangerous. Wertz tried a folksier approach. While driving in the country one day, he related, he had seen a barn on fire. The farmer was trying to save his sheep by herding them out the door. But as soon as he did, "an old ewe at the head of the flock started around the barn as fast as she could go, and every sheep took after her into the barn on the other side where the flames were the worst."

Debs was the old ewe. Congress had passed laws to protect the American people, and if Debs wanted to violate the law, he should go to the penitentiary. But he had no right, Wertz insisted, to take the rest of the flock to prison and make them traitors as well. As for Debs's First Amendment claim, Wertz pointed out that despite the wording of the speech clause, the law had always recognized limits on speech, such as cases of libel, slander, obscenity, and threats to the public's safety. Interestingly, he used an expression that six months later would catch national attention when used by Justice Oliver Wendell Holmes Jr. in the Supreme Court. According to Debs, Wertz claimed, "a man could go into a crowded theatre . . . and yell 'fire' when there was no fire, and people trampled to death, and he would not be punished for it because the Constitution says he has the right of free speech."[50]

Wertz also denigrated Debs's claim that he and the other socialists were just following a long line of great patriots and radicals going back to biblical times. "Is there any doubt what he was trying to do when he took this 'holier than thou' attitude, assuming to be the Jesus Christ of these other fellows that did something in this country?" If this was any other country, Wertz concluded, "he would be facing a firing squad, after a trial on the head of a drum, and not after days and days of pain and effort to give him a fair, just and equitable trial."[51]

This diatribe apparently embarrassed even the judge. Max Eastman, watching from the gallery, wrote that "as clearly as Debs symbolized in his presence the hope of evolution, this man was the mud from which it moves."[52] Debs left the courtroom thronged by admirers. One young girl pushed through the crowd to present him with a bouquet of roses and promptly fainted into his arms.[53]

The next morning, Judge Westenhaver charged the jury, reminding the twelve men that Eugene Debs was not on trial for his political views, although both sides had focused on those in their final comments. The jury should also not be blinded by patriotic fervor or the "righteous indignation" inevitable in wartime. There was a specific charge—violation of a federal law—and the defendant was entitled to the same careful review of evidence, the same due process, in a time of war as in a time of peace.

Under the First Amendment, the judge explained, Debs could freely criticize the government's prosecution of the war, and "disapproval of war is, of course, not a crime, nor is advocacy of peace." The question for the jury was what Debs had *intended* to do in his Canton speech. Was he simply explaining his political views, or did he want young men to evade the draft? Did he provide information on an important public matter, or was he trying to incite his audience to break the law?

Under the legal standards of the time, the government did not have to prove that Debs had succeeded in fomenting overt resistance to the war. They did not have to produce a single witness to say he had acted unlawfully after hearing Debs talk. The prosecution only had to convince the jury that the defendant had tried. The "scraps" of evidence that the government had introduced, such as the St. Louis Proclamation, were not on trial, nor was Debs's belief in them. The prosecution's sole purpose was to establish "the state of mind of the defendant" when he gave the speech.

Finally, Westenhaver instructed the jury to disregard the defense argument that the Espionage Act violated the basic constitutional right of free speech. "The law was on the statute book," he stated, "and it was the part of no man to question its authenticity." The law did not contravene the First Amendment, since Congress had always retained the right to curtail speech in wartime so that the government could protect the public safety. The judge went on, however, to note that if he was wrong on this question, then the nine members of the U.S. Supreme Court would correct him.[54]

In many other Espionage Act cases, federal judges had used the jury charge to vent their personal indignation against the defendants, practically ordering the jurors to find them guilty. But both Stedman and Debs believed that Westenhaver had been quite fair—remarkably so. Moreover, he had been correct in his charge to the jury that they had no business determining the constitutionality of the law. The jury's responsibility was to agree on the facts of a case; the judge determined the law. Westenhaver had decided the Espionage Act did not violate the First Amendment, and he indicated that if he were wrong, then that decision could be remedied on appeal.

The jury left the courtroom at eleven and did not return until five in the afternoon, a fairly long time for juries in such cases. As the judge called for the verdict, Rose Pastor Stokes went up to sit at the defendant's table and held Debs's hand. The jury foreman, Cyrus H. Stoner, announced that the jury had found Debs guilty on three counts. In his speech at Canton, he had "attempted to incite insubordination, disloyalty, mutiny, and refusal of duty in the military and naval forces." He had also obstructed or attempted to obstruct the recruiting and enlistment of men into the armed services. And finally, he had used "language intended to incite, provoke, and encourage resistance to the United States and to promote the cause of their enemy." The jury found Debs innocent of the last charge, "opposition to the cause of the United States." Debs listened calmly as the foreman spoke, even though the three guilty verdicts carried a maximum penalty of twenty years—in effect, a life sentence for the sixty-three-year-old man.[55]

At the sentencing hearing the next day, Westenhaver asked Debs if he had any last words before his sentence was pronounced. Debs, never one to miss a chance to extol socialism, replied that he had a few things to say. Heywood Broun, a liberal journalist and not a Debs partisan, would observe that what Debs then delivered was "one of the most beautiful and moving passages in the English language. He was for that one afternoon touched with inspiration. If anyone told me that tongues of fire danced upon his shoulders as he spoke, I would believe it."[56] Debs stated:

> Your honor, years ago I recognized my kinship with all living beings, and I made up my mind that I was not one bit better than the meanest of the earth. I said then, I say now, that while there is a lower class, I am in it; while there is a criminal element, I am of it; while there is a soul in prison, I am not free. . . .
>
> Your honor, I ask no mercy, I plead for no immunity. I realize that finally the right must prevail. I never more fully comprehended than now the great struggle between the powers of greed on the one hand and upon the other the rising hosts of freedom. I can see the dawn of a better day of humanity. The people are awakening. In due course of time they will come into their own.
>
> When the mariner, sailing over tropic seas, looks for relief from his weary watch, he turns his eyes toward the Southern Cross, burning luridly above the tempest-vexed ocean. As the midnight approaches the Southern Cross begins to bend, and the whirling worlds change their places, and with starry finger-points the Almighty marks the passage of Time upon the dial of the universe; and though no bell may beat the glad tidings, the look-out knows that the midnight is passing—that relief and rest are close at hand.
>
> Let the people take heart and hope everywhere, for the cross is bending, midnight is passing, and joy cometh with the morning.[57]

Westenhaver listened patiently, as he had during the trial. In fact, although it became clear that the judge had no use either for Debs or for his ideas, he understood the political nature of this trial. He would not give the defense any grounds to appeal on the basis of judicial prejudice, and thus, he let Debs speak unhindered. But Debs was now finished speaking, and Westenhaver concluded that however sincere the man might be, he was preaching anarchy. As for his idealism, the judge told him, it was no "higher, purer, nobler than the idealisms of thousands of young men I have seen marching down the streets of Cleveland to defend our country." The judge did not see the socialist leader as a champion of the downtrodden but as a man trying to tear down all that had made the nation great. He sentenced Debs to three concurrent ten-year terms. Because all of the federal prisons were overcrowded thanks to the raids on aliens and dissenters, Westenhaver ordered him sent to the West Virginia state penitentiary in Moundsville.[58] Stedman and his associates immediately began preparing their appeal to the U.S. Supreme Court.

Debs v. United States was the third of the Espionage Act cases heard by the Supreme Court in January 1919.[59] At the time, there was practically no First

Amendment jurisprudence that explicated the phrase "Congress shall make no law . . . abridging the freedom of speech." The Court still adhered to the view expounded by Sir William Blackstone in his *Commentaries* that the right of free speech precluded prior restraint (that is, the government could not stop a person from speaking or publishing ideas) but that the law could punish speakers and writers if their expression tended to harm public welfare. The leading Supreme Court case was *Patterson v. Colorado* (1907), in which Justice Holmes had closely followed Blackstone's analysis and even dismissed the question of whether the statement uttered had been true: "The preliminary freedom extends to the false as to the true; the subsequent punishment may extend to the true as to the false."[60]

In the first of the Espionage Act cases, *Schenck v. United States* (1919), the Court heard the appeal of the secretary of the Philadelphia Socialist Party, who had been indicted and convicted for urging resistance to the draft.[61] Holmes attempted to develop a standard that, as far as he believed, was more speech protective than the Blackstonian criterion, one based on the common-law rule of proximate causation. In a famous passage, he wrote: "The question in every case is whether the words used are used in such circumstances and are of such a nature as to create a clear and present danger that they will bring about the substantive evils that Congress has a right to prevent. . . . When a nation is at war, many things that might be said in time of peace are such a hindrance to its effort that their utterance will not be endured so long as men fight and no Court could regard them as protected by any constitutional right."[62] Far from being speech protective, however, the standard proved to be very restrictive. "Clear and present danger" was a subjective test, and to conservative jurists, radical statements could always be interpreted as clearly and presently dangerous.

Debs's lawyers argued that the indictment had failed to charge the defendant with a real crime; that the use of criminal records from other cases was inadmissible, as was the content of the St. Louis platform; and that the definition of military forces used by the trial court was erroneous.[63] Holmes dismissed these arguments as inconsequential. When Debs's lawyers tried to argue that his speech had been protected by the First Amendment, a unanimous Court rejected the argument, and Holmes's opinion revealed quite clearly the restrictive nature of the clear and present danger test. In his opinion, Holmes fairly summarized what Debs had said and characterized the main theme as "socialism, its growth, and a prophecy of its ultimate success."[64] He then cited two additional pieces of evidence. The first was Debs's statement to the jury: "I have been accused of obstructing the war. I admit it. Gentlemen, I abhor war. I would oppose the war if I stood alone." The second was the St. Louis platform, in which the Socialist Party called for "continuous, active, and public opposition to the war, through demonstrations, mass petitions, and all other means within our power."[65]

That Debs endorsed the platform and saw it as his duty to obstruct the war when he made his speech in Canton, Holmes wrote, "is evidence that if in that speech he used words tending to obstruct the recruiting service he meant that they should have that effect." Moreover, the jury had been instructed not to find Debs guilty "unless the words used had as their natural tendency and reasonably probable effect to obstruct the recruiting services, &c., and unless the defendant had the specific intent to do so in mind."[66]

The constitutional issue, Holmes declared, had been settled in *Schenck,* and he did not even ask if Debs's speech created a clear and present danger. The "natural tendency" and "reasonably probable effect" of his words were all that mattered. The jury had found that Debs's militant antiwar speech had been intended to interfere with the war effort, and the Court saw no reason to overturn that verdict.[67]

Although the decision came down on March 10, 1919, federal officials did not order Debs to report for imprisonment until a month later. The socialist leader began his ten-year sentence at the facility in Moundsville, West Virginia, but two months later, when space opened up, the Justice Department had him transferred to the federal penitentiary in Atlanta. While in prison, Debs wrote a series of columns deeply critical of the prison system, which ran in sanitized form in the Bell Syndicate and in his only book, *Walls and Bars,* published posthumously.[68] He also ran for president again in 1920. Prisoner #9653 received 913,664 write-in votes, slightly fewer than he had garnered in the 1912 election.[69]

There has been speculation about Woodrow Wilson and whether he in fact intended to grant clemency to those who had been convicted and imprisoned for speaking out against the war. On his way home from the Paris Peace Conference, the president cabled his secretary that he intended to grant "complete amnesty and pardon to all American citizens in prison or under arrest on account of anything they have said in speech or print concerning their personal opinions with regard to the activities of the Government of the United States during the period of the war."[70]

After his stroke and the defeat of the Versailles Treaty, however, Wilson grew more vindictive, and at one point, he wrote: "While the flower of American youth was pouring out its blood to vindicate the cause of civilization, this man,

Debs, stood behind the lines sniping, attacking, and denouncing them. . . . This man was a traitor to his country and he will never be pardoned during my administration."[71] In January 1921, Palmer, citing Debs's deteriorating health, proposed to Wilson that Debs receive a presidential pardon that would free him on February 12, Lincoln's birthday. Wilson returned the paperwork after writing "Denied" across it.[72]

On December 23, 1921, President Warren G. Harding commuted Debs's sentence to time served, effective Christmas Day, but he did not issue a pardon. A White House statement summarized the administration's view of Debs's case: "There is no question of his guilt. . . . He is an old man, not strong physically. He is a man of much personal charm and impressive personality, which qualifications make him a dangerous man calculated to mislead the unthinking and affording excuse for those with criminal intent."[73]

When Debs was released from the Atlanta penitentiary, the other prisoners sent him off with "a roar of cheers," and a crowd of fifty thousand greeted his return to Terre Haute to the accompaniment of band music. En route home, Debs was warmly received at the White House by Harding, who welcomed him by saying, "Well, I've heard so damned much about you, Mr. Debs, that I am now glad to meet you personally."[74]

Although he took to the lecture circuit again, things had changed greatly since before the war. Many of his old socialist colleagues had deserted the party, and national membership had dwindled to less than ten thousand. In many cities, the rancor against his antiwar views made it difficult for him to secure a place to speak, and even when the socialists could find a venue, Debs often faced harassment by local vigilantes. Despite the fact that many people had turned out to welcome him home to Terre Haute, the governor of Indiana, Warren McCray, declared that he was "extremely sorry that the one arch traitor to our country should live in the state of Indiana." He suggested to members of the American Legion that they ought to march on Debs's home and teach him "a lesson."[75]

Eugene Debs's already frail health gave out, and he died in a sanitarium in Elmhurst, Illinois, on October 20, 1926, at age seventy.

The Debs trial has remained an iconic event for socialists and radicals ever since, even as it has become a footnote in American constitutional history—one of those cases decided under the old Blackstonian theory of speech before Oliver Wendell Holmes and Louis Brandeis embarked on explicating a modern speech-protective jurisprudence in *Abrams v. United States*[76] and *Whitney v. California*.[77] The Supreme Court finally buried the whole notion of seditious libel in

1969.[78] Debs would no doubt have approved not only modern antiwar protesters but also the fact that they are free to criticize the country's policies under the First Amendment.

Notes

1. There are a number of books on Debs; one could start with the older but still valuable biography by Ray Ginger, *The Bending Cross* (New Brunswick, N.J.: Rutgers University Press, 1949), but see also Nick Salvatore, *Eugene V. Debs: Citizen and Socialist* (Urbana: University of Illinois Press, 1982).

2. For Debs as a presidential candidate that year, see Lewis L. Gould, *Four Hats in the Ring: The 1912 Election and the Birth of Modern American Politics* (Lawrence: University Press of Kansas, 2008), chap. 5.

3. "Spending Time with Jim McGuiggan," available at http://www.jimmcguiggan .com/reflections3.asp?status=Jesus&id=933 (accessed July 7, 2010).

4. Ernest Freeberg, *Democracy's Prisoner: Eugene V. Debs, the Great War, and the Right to Dissent* (Cambridge, Mass.: Harvard University Press, 2008), 25–26.

5. Eugene V. Debs, "Preparedness I Favor," *Appeal to Reason*, December 11, 1914, quoted in ibid., 31.

6. 40 Stat. 553 (1918).

7. Discussions regarding the extent of the wartime attack on civil liberties can be found in numerous books. See William H. Thomas Jr., *Unsafe for Democracy: World War I and the U.S. Justice Department's Covert Campaign to Suppress Dissent* (Madison: University of Wisconsin Press, 2008); Stephen M. Feldman, *Free Expression and Democracy in America: A History* (Chicago: University of Chicago Press, 2008); Paul L. Murphy, *World War I and the Origins of Civil Liberties in the United States* (New York: W. W. Norton, 1979); and the older but still useful William Preston Jr., *Aliens and Dissenters: Federal Suppression of Radicals, 1903–1933* (Cambridge, Mass.: Harvard University Press, 1963), which fits the wartime repression into a broader context.

8. Freeberg, *Democracy's Prisoner*, 61–62.

9. Ibid., 68–69.

10. Both the majority and minority reports were included in a ballot sent to all members of the party on May 5, 1917, and can be found at http://www.marxists.org/history/usa/ parties/spusa/1917/0505-spa-referendumb1917.pdf (accessed July 8, 2010).

11. For the complicated crosscurrents in American socialism regarding the war, see Ginger, *Bending Cross*, 324ff.

12. Jean Y. Tussey, *Eugene V. Debs Speaks* (New York: Pathfinder Press, 1970), 244. The speech is available in a number of places and is a transcription of the verbatim copy made by a stenographer at the talk and then introduced as evidence in the trial. See the trial record in Debs v. United States, 249 U.S. 211 (1919), in the Thomson-Gale database, *United States Supreme Court Records and Briefs, 1832–1978*, and is part of the testimony of Edward Sterling, the stenographer, at 250–95.

13. Tussey, *Eugene V. Debs Speaks*, 245.

14. "The main theme of the speech was socialism, its growth, and a prophesy of its ultimate success." Debs v. United States, 249 U.S. 211, 212 (1919).

15. Tussey, *Eugene V. Debs Speaks*, 248.

16. Ibid., 253.

17. Ibid., 255–56.

18. Ibid., 260–61.

19. Ibid., 279.

20. Miller later recalled his role in an article entitled "The Man I Sent to Jail," *Progressive* (October 1963); Freeberg, *Democracy's Prisoner*, 77–78.

21. Freeberg, *Democracy's Prisoner*, 78.

22. Ibid., 79.

23. Vacha, "Treason in Canton," 11.

24. The indictment can be found in *Record*, 3ff.

25. Debs to Bolton Hall, July 6, 1918, in *Letters of Debs*, 2:424–25.

26. *New York Times*, September 9, 1918; Scott Nearing, *The Debs Decision* (New York: Rand School, 1919), 14–15.

27. For the atmosphere surrounding the trial, see Freeberg, *Democracy's Prisoner*, 83ff.

28. Mark Cole, *Painting and Sculpture: Howard M. Metzenbaum United States Courthouse* (General Service Administration, n.d.), 12–13, also available at http://www.gsa.gov/graphics/pbs/metz.pdf (accessed December 7, 2010).

29. Max Eastman, *The Trial of Eugene Debs, with Debs's Address to the Court on Receiving Sentence* (New York: Liberator Publishing, 1918), 9.

30. Ibid.

31. He repeated this charge in the Canton speech; see Tussey, *Eugene V. Debs Speaks*, 254.

32. "History of the Federal Judiciary," "Biographical Directory of Federal Judges," Federal Courts Center, available at http://www.fjc.gov/servlet/nGetInfo?jid=2555&cid=999&ctype=na&instate=na; "History of the Sixth Circuit," available at http://www.ca6.uscourts.gov/lib_hist/Courts/district%20court/OH/NDOH/judges/westenhaver.html (accessed December 7, 2010).

33. The best description of the trial can be found in Freeberg, *Democracy's Prisoner*, chap. 5.

34. Ginger, *Bending Cross*, 365; Eastman, *Trial of Eugene Debs*, 10–11.

35. *Record*, 213–50.

36. Eastman, *Trial of Eugene Debs*, 6; *Record*, 250–95.

37. *Record*, 194–213. Something about the old radical had nonetheless touched Miller, perhaps his humility and self-admitted fallibility. His liking for Debs the man and his opposition to his political views led Miller to be somewhat uncomfortable on the witness stand. After Miller had finished testifying, Debs left his chair and put his arms around the man's shoulders. "Mr. Miller, all that you say about me is true," he whispered. "You quoted me straight and accurate. I don't want you ever to feel that you have done me an injury by testifying against me. You had to do it, and you did it like a gentleman." Freeberg, *Democracy's Prisoner*, 94.

38. *Record*, 295–300.

39. Ibid., 304–11.

40. In 1918, one could appeal a conviction in federal court directly to the Supreme Court, without first going through a court of appeals.

41. Debs v. United States, 63 L. Ed. at 566–67.

42. Nearing, *Debs Decision*, 15.

43. Tussey, *Eugene V. Debs Speaks*, 281; the speech takes up pp. 339–69 in the *Record*.

44. Tussey, *Eugene V. Debs Speaks*, 282.

45. Ibid.

46. Freeberg, *Democracy's Prisoner*, 99.

47. Westenhaver to A. Mitchell Palmer, March 21, 1919, quoted in ibid., 100.

48. *Record*, 243–44.

49. Ibid.

50. Debs had made no such absolute claim for First Amendment rights. Holmes wrote: "The most stringent protection of free speech would not protect a man in falsely shouting fire in a theater, and causing a panic." Schenck v. United States, 249 U.S. 47, 52 (1919). There is no evidence that Holmes had read Wertz's speech at the time.

51. *Record*, 369–405.

52. Eastman, *Trial of Eugene Debs*, 20.

53. Ginger, *Bending Cross*, 372.

54. *Record*, 405–44.

55. Freeberg, *Democracy's Prisoner*, 105.

56. David Pietrusza, *1920: The Year of Six Presidents* (New York: Carroll and Graf, 2007), 269.

57. Debs, "Statement to the Court," available at http://www.marxists.org/archive,debs/works/1918/court.htm (accessed July 9, 2010).

58. *New York Times*, September 15, 1918.

59. 249 U.S. 211 (1919).

60. Patterson v. Colorado, 205 U.S. 454, 462 (1907).

61. Schenck v. United States, 249 U.S. 47 (1919).

62. Ibid., at 52.

63. Brief for the Appellant, in Philip B. Kurland and Gerhard Casper, eds., *Landmark Briefs and Arguments in the Supreme Court of the United States: Constitutional Law* (Washington, D.C.: University Publications of America, 1975–), 19:32–34.

64. 249 U.S., at 212.

65. Ibid., at 214, 216.

66. Ibid., at 216.

67. Ibid., at 216–17. Although Louis Brandeis joined the opinion in *Debs*, he would have preferred that it be decided on a war powers basis rather than on the clear-and-present-danger test, since that would have confined espionage legislation, as well as restrictions on speech, to wartime. Melvin I. Urofsky, "The Brandeis-Frankfurter Conversations," *Supreme Court Review*, 1985, 299, 324.

68. Eugene V. Debs, *Walls & Bars: Prisons & Prison Life in the "Land of the Free"* (Chicago: Socialist Party, 1927).

69. For Debs's role in the election, see Pietrusza, *1920*, chap. 16, "Convict No. 9653."

70. Woodrow Wilson to Joseph P. Tumulty, June 28, 1919, in *The Papers of Woodrow Wilson*, 69 vols., ed. Arthur S. Link et al. (Princeton, N.J.: Princeton University Press, 1966–94), 61:351–52.

71. Joseph P. Tumulty, *Woodrow Wilson as I Know Him* (Garden City, N.Y.: Garden City Publishing, 1921), 504–5.

72. Ginger, *Bending Cross*, 405.

73. "Harding Frees Debs and 23 Others Held for War Violations," *New York Times*, December 24, 1921.

74. John Wesley Dean, *Warren G. Harding* (New York: Henry Holt, 2004), 128.

75. Freeberg, *Democracy's Prisoner*, 311–12. Ironically, McCray was soon on his way to the Atlanta penitentiary himself to serve a ten-year sentence for mail fraud.

76. 250 U.S. 616, 624 (1919) (Holmes, J., dissenting).

77. 274 U.S. 357, 372 (1927) (Brandeis, J., concurring).

78. Brandenburg v. Ohio, 395 U.S. 444 (1969).

PART 2

The Modern Court

Introduction to Part 2

Dan Aaron Polster

FEDERAL COURTS ARE often referred to as courts of "limited jurisdiction." Pursuant to statute, a litigant gets to federal court in one of two ways: (1) via federal question jurisdiction, if the case arises under the Constitution or a federal statute, or (2) via diversity jurisdiction, if the plaintiff and defendant are from different states and there is at least $75,000 in controversy. Two hundred years ago, few cases met either of these criteria. Since then and particularly since the 1960s, Congress has expanded the scope of the federal judiciary's work, and today, it impacts virtually every phase of America's social, political, religious, and intellectual life.

It would have been hard in 1960 to anticipate the transformation of the federal district court that has taken place in the ensuing decades. Putting aside the substantial growth in the size of the court—it has expanded from six authorized judgeships to twelve (currently eleven[1]), along with seven magistrate judges who occupy a position that did not exist in 1960[2]—the types of cases making up most of the present dockets were not even known in 1960.

On the criminal side, there were no drug or gun cases, which easily comprise 50 percent of the present dockets. In 1960, "street crime" was the purview of the state criminal justice system, so these cases were handled exclusively by state courts. There were few complex fraud cases, as the role of the Department of Justice in investigating and prosecuting bank fraud, securities fraud, and interstate mail and wire fraud cases had yet to emerge. There were no criminal environmental crime statutes. The Racketeer Influenced and Corrupt Organizations (RICO) Act did not yet exist, and the money-laundering statutes had not yet been drafted. The main crimes prosecuted in federal court were bank robberies and interstate transportation of stolen motor vehicles. Most of the significant federal program and procurement fraud cases prosecuted today result from the expansion of the federal government. There was no Medicare or Medicaid in 1960. And in the late 1970s, the entire U.S. Attorney's Office in Cleveland fit into an area of the courthouse that subsequently was used to create the courtroom and chambers of a single federal judge.

The criminal sentencing process has been transformed since 1987 as well. In 1960, criminal sentencing was a simple matter with an indeterminate system. The sentencing judge had complete and unreviewable discretion to impose any sentence ranging from probation to the statutory maximum. The world changed with the advent of the Federal Sentencing Guidelines in 1987 and the promulgation by Congress of mandatory minimum sentences for drug crimes. Congress also eliminated parole and replaced it with supervised release, which essentially transformed each federal judge into a one-person parole board for every individual the judge sentenced. For more than fifteen years, the sentencing guidelines were mandatory; they are currently advisory. A sentencing hearing is now a very complex process, often requiring factual findings and a written opinion, which frequently leads to an appeal.

In 1960, the state of Ohio did not have the death penalty, so federal judges in the Northern District did not have the task of performing habeas corpus review of inmates on death row. Pursuant to the Constitution and federal statutes, federal courts have jurisdiction to review each state court criminal conviction to ensure there have been no constitutional violations that cast doubt on the validity of the conviction or, in capital cases, the sentence of death. Ohio promulgated the death penalty in 1982; considerable litigation and a number of statutory amendments would follow until the legislature ultimately created the current two-stage process (a guilt stage and a penalty/mitigation stage), which passed Supreme Court muster. Accordingly, federal judges now face the daunting task of reviewing what is typically at least ten to fifteen years of state court litigation in a given case to determine whether there have been any constitutional errors.[3]

The transformation of the civil docket has been just as profound. Approximately 25 percent of the civil docket today is composed of cases alleging violations of the federal age, race, sex, and disability discrimination statutes, which were yet to be passed in 1960. Additionally, there were far fewer patent cases back then. And the Employee Retirement Income Security Act (ERISA) had not yet been passed. This statute regulates pension and benefit funds that employers establish for their workers.

All of these new laws have spawned litigation. The exponential growth of federal regulation on all aspects of commercial activity has led to a corresponding increase in litigation challenging this federal rule making. Americans now see the courts, particularly the federal courts, as the place to turn to vindicate all manner of rights. And it is not just the volume of litigation that has increased but also the complexity of that litigation. The new legislation and the agency rule making are not models of clarity. Many of the cases have multiple parties, and it is now commonplace to have a foreign corporation as one of the parties in civil litigation. Meanwhile, the $75,000 threshold for diversity litigation seems quaint; it is quite difficult to have any sort of dispute in this country today that does not involve at least $75,000, and it is not at all unusual to have millions of dollars riding on the outcome of a federal lawsuit.

Changes in administrative policy have also had a significant impact on the judicial workload. Federal judges have jurisdiction to review denials of disability benefits by the Social Security Administration (SSA). In 1960, such cases comprised a modest part of a judge's docket. The Reagan administration decided to review awards of disability benefits granted by the SSA during the prior four years of the Carter administration and to require each individual recipient to again prove his or her disability. By 1983, Social Security disability appeals had ballooned to make up one-third of a typical judge's civil docket. The federal judiciary voiced its concern, and the administration ultimately reverted to a policy of requiring the SSA to demonstrate that a recipient was no longer disabled in order to terminate benefits.

The U.S. District Court for the Northern District of Ohio has grown into a medium-sized business. There are federal courthouses in Cleveland, Akron, Youngstown, and Toledo. In 1960, there was no court governance structure whatsoever, other than the chief judge. Today, the judges administer the court through regular meetings every two months, augmented by standing committee meetings in alternate months. In 1960, the chief judge and the clerk of court assigned cases as they came up for trial or required attention. Today, there is a sophisticated system to assign cases randomly, which equalizes both the number of cases and the composition of the individual judicial dockets. The annual budget of the court (exclusive of judges' salaries) is more than $23 million, and there are approximately three hundred employees spread throughout chambers, the clerk's office, and the Probation/Pretrial Services Office.

Just as the workload of the federal court has changed dramatically since the 1960s, so too has the face of the court. In 1960, the court was made up exclusively of white males. The first African American district judge, George White, and the first female district judge, Ann Aldrich, were both appointed by President Jimmy Carter in 1980. As of 2011, there were two African American judges and three female judges, along with a senior female judge. The roster of magistrate judges reflects a similar racial and gender diversity.

Finally, the traditional role of the judge as the presider over trials has evolved over time. This court was a pioneer in establishing differentiated case management in the early 1990s, and judges are now responsible for managing their civil dockets actively. Starting with the case management conference, each judge plays a major role in guiding the litigation process. The judge assigns the case to one of three tracks (expedited, standard, or complex) and sets an appropriate discovery schedule. A rapidly declining percentage of civil cases end in trials. The court was also a national pioneer in the early 1990s in developing an alternative dispute resolution (ADR) program, in which attorneys volunteer their time to mediate civil cases.[4] In addition, many of the judges and all the magistrate judges spend a significant amount of time in mediating resolutions in civil cases. This district has been in the national vanguard of a trend to treat the litigation process as a dispute resolution mechanism.

Starting around 2005, the court has become a center for multi-district litigation (MDL) cases, and more than half of the judges currently have at least one MDL case. These are complex cases filed in federal courts across the country that are consolidated for pretrial management in front of a single judge. The MDLs in this district can range from a handful of cases to several thousand, and they require the judge to devote a significant amount of time and skill to ensure that the cases are handled fairly and expeditiously. Frequently, the parties consent to the MDL judge trying a number of the bellwether cases, and the judge often plays an active role in mediating a settlement.

The following chapters illustrate how the court has handled noteworthy and challenging cases in a number of subject areas.

It is in the federal courthouse where the struggle to end segregation in housing and schools has most frequently played out, and the Northern District of Ohio is no exception in this regard. Chapter 5 discusses prominent litigation in this area, including *Reed v. Rhodes*, the bitterly contested Cleveland school desegregation case that led to more than twenty years of court-ordered busing.

Chapter 6 focuses on the pivotal role the district court has played in the struggle for gender equality. When I was in elementary school, my teachers were required to take leaves of absence when they showed visible signs of pregnancy. It was not until the landmark case of *LaFleur v. Cleveland Board of Education* that this discriminatory practice was abolished.

The tension between the free exercise and establishment clauses of the First Amendment has produced much high-profile litigation. Chapter 7 focuses on some of these well-known cases, including the Cleveland voucher case and *ACLU v. Stow*, the challenge to incorporating the cross on the Stow city seal.

Chapter 8 addresses the role of the court in the regulation of physical space. Federal courts have come to play a key part in resolving conflicts between private and public interests in the areas of zoning, regulation, and eminent domain.

Most of the major state and local corruption cases across the country are brought in federal court by federal prosecutors. Chapter 9 touches on some of the more famous public corruption cases of this type in northeast Ohio, including the two prosecutions of Youngstown congressman James Traficant and the massive probe of corruption in Cuyahoga County that has been producing at least one conviction every few weeks for the past year.

The Vietnam War and its aftermath had a profound impact upon the country, and chapters 10 and 11 focus on this turbulent period. The May 1970 killing of four students at Kent State University by National Guard troops galvanized the antiwar movement, and the civil rights trial of several guardsmen that took place in federal court drew national attention as well. *United States v. Schmucker* highlighted the tensions created by the military draft.

The more than thirty-year saga of John Demjanjuk, the Nazi prison guard, was the subject of multiple federal court proceedings in the Northern District of Ohio, and chapter 12 discusses this story of local, national, and international significance.

Federal judges in states such as Ohio that have the death penalty are called on to conduct postconviction habeas corpus review to determine whether there were any constitutional violations that raise serious questions about the validity of the conviction or sentence. Chapter 13 addresses this complex area of litigation.

The Sixth Amendment to the U.S. Constitution provides for a right to counsel in felony trials. The most frequently raised challenge in death penalty cases is that counsel was constitutionally ineffective at either the trial or the appellate level. To prevail, the petitioner must show not only that counsel's performance was seriously deficient but also that what the attorney did or did not do casts serious doubt as to the validity of the conviction or the death sentence that resulted.

Since the 1960s, the court has grown, changed, and evolved to serve the needs of the Northern District. It would have been impossible for the seven judges of this court in 1960 to envision what their successors would be doing in the early years of the twenty-first century. And though it is equally difficult for those of us on the court today to conceive of the challenges our own successors will face decades in the future, we are confident that those men and women will have the intelligence, heart, and fortitude to meet them all.

Notes

1. In November 2010, a temporary judgeship first created in 1991 lapsed, so when Judge Kathleen O'Malley was confirmed in December 2010 to a seat on the Court of Appeals for the Federal Circuit, the vacancy was not filled.

2. Magistrate judges are appointed by the district court to serve for a renewable term of eight years. They conduct preliminary criminal matters, handle civil pretrial matters, and hold civil settlement conferences. Magistrate judges are authorized to conduct criminal misdemeanor (but not felony) trials, and they may try civil cases with the consent of all parties.

3. Chapter 13 contains a discussion of death penalty litigation in the Northern District of Ohio.

4. In 2011, the court modified the ADR program to provide compensation to panel members in most cases.

5

Bringing *Brown* to Cleveland

Richard B. Saphire

Brown and Its Progeny

*B*ROWN V. BOARD *of Education*[1] is widely regarded as one of the most important and transformative decisions of the U.S. Supreme Court in the twentieth century.[2] From a legal point of view, *Brown* rejected the "separate but equal"
doctrine the Court had first articulated in 1896,[3] and it established that schools
that had been segregated by race were "inherently unequal" in violation of the
equal protection clause of the Fourteenth Amendment. But from a political and
moral perspective, *Brown* had perhaps even greater significance. In the words of
current Supreme Court Justice Stephen Breyer, "*Brown* helped us to understand
that the Constitution is 'ours,' whoever we may be."[4] By apparently forbidding
the sort of official racism that had characterized much of American life since the
nation's beginnings, *Brown* seemed to take seriously the idea that the Constitution's promise of the full and equal privileges of citizenship applied to all.[5]

More than half a century has passed since *Brown* was decided, and though
its aspirational significance still seems secure in the American consciousness, its
practical significance remains less certain. Legal scholars are engaged in a robust

debate about whether—and the extent to which—the decision has actually changed much in terms of the day-to-day experience of those who were its primary, intended beneficiaries.[6] But whatever changes *Brown* effected did not come quickly or easily. When the Court, in *Brown II*,[7] turned to the question of how and when schools had to be desegregated, it articulated the now famous—or, by some accounts, infamous—"all deliberate speed" standard. As it turned out, all deliberate speed amounted to no speed at all, or at least very little of it.

The story of how the requirements of *Brown* led to confusion and then mass resistance in parts of the country, especially the Deep South, has been told elsewhere.[8] Suffice it to say that after experiencing several years of evasion and noncompliance, the Court, in a series of decisions, made it clear that all school districts throughout the country were bound by *Brown I*;[9] that segregated school districts had the burden of producing plans that promised "realistically to work *now*";[10] that these districts were required not just to discontinue their unconstitutional practices but also to dismantle segregated schools and establish "unitary" school systems;[11] and that federal courts had broad equitable powers to achieve these goals, with the authority to employ a wide range of remedies, including ordering the use of transportation (busing).[12]

Almost all of these decisions involved schools in the South, where segregation was either formally required or approved by law. The question of what to do with northern school districts, where pervasive segregation came about not as the result of an explicit legal mandate but by more subtle and informal means, proved no less difficult or controversial. In the North, urban areas were frequently characterized by residential segregation and by school officials who adopted "neighborhood school" policies, whereby students were assigned to schools located either in or close to the neighborhoods in which they lived. Combined with a variety of other practices and policies, this often led to schools that *in fact* were segregated, as evidenced by the presence of schools that were racially identifiable (that is, where the student body was either completely or almost completely white or black). The question the courts had to decide was whether the creation and maintenance of such schools violated the principle of *Brown*.

In a series of decisions beginning in the 1970s, the Supreme Court attempted to resolve this question.[13] In an important case out of Denver, Colorado, the Court held that where plaintiffs could establish the existence of unconstitutional segregation affecting a "substantial portion" of a school district, a (rebuttable) presumption would attach that segregation in other parts of the district was also unconstitutional, thus supporting a finding of a dual system.[14] And in one of the most consequential decisions after *Brown,* involving the Detroit school system, the Court rejected the inclusion of suburban school districts in a desegregation remedy unless the plaintiffs could prove that any district so included was *itself* guilty of unconstitutional segregation.[15]

With this as background, the chapter now turns to the efforts to desegregate the Cleveland public school system. These efforts occupied the attention of the U.S. District Court for the Northern District of Ohio—and the Cleveland community—for over thirty years. As will be shown, bringing the principles of *Brown* and its progeny to Cleveland was an enormously difficult and challenging undertaking for both the district court and the community.

Desegregation of the Cleveland Public Schools: Early Efforts

At the time *Brown* was decided in 1954, the city of Cleveland was experiencing significant demographic and social change. The movement of black migrants from the South, begun in earnest during World War I, accelerated during World War II, when the demands of defense production attracted large numbers of mainly unskilled workers in search of manufacturing jobs. As noted by a historian of Cleveland, in the 1940s and 1950s the city's black population more than quadrupled to around 252,000, whereas the city's white population shrank, "leaving a black presence in the city that was becoming more and more sharply defined."[16]

Entering the second half of the twentieth century, the plight of blacks in Cleveland, as well as race relations in general, began to worsen. Although the city was not known as having an especially harsh urban environment relative to other northern cities, with blacks achieving a reasonable measure of political power, housing conditions and the conditions of the public schools were not good.[17]

With respect to education, Cleveland experienced serious strains in its public school system. Many schools were overcrowded, and the system as a whole had become increasingly segregated by race.[18] By the 1962–63 academic year, black students constituted a majority of the pupil population in the Cleveland school system. And the racial concentration or isolation of blacks had become extreme. From 1931 through 1965, the percentage of blacks attending racially identifiable schools—that is, where 91 to 100 percent of the children attending the school were black—skyrocketed from 4.4 percent in 1931 to 78.6 percent in 1965. During the same period, the number of schools where black children constituted a majority rose from 71.7 percent to 94.5 percent. This pattern was especially severe in the elementary schools, where by 1965 over 95 percent of blacks attended racially identifiable schools.[19]

In the years just before and after the *Brown* decision, much of the black community in Cleveland came to view the school system "as a hostile and forbidding structure."[20] In the early 1960s, several local citizen groups, including the National Association for the Advancement of Colored People (NAACP), the Urban League, the Congress of Racial Equality, and the United Freedom Movement, mobilized to challenge discrimination and segregation in the schools. Meetings were held, and protests and marches were organized and staged, several of which turned violent. These groups advocated a set of policies that would, among other things, lead to greater "diffusion," or racial integration, of the school system. When the school board began construction of three new schools to serve only minority areas, demonstrators picketed the construction sites. On April 7, 1964, the Reverend Bruce Klunder, a leader of one of the protest groups, was accidentally run over by a bulldozer and killed during a demonstration.[21] Klunder's death helped to polarize the community further, leading to a school boycott and ultimately to litigation.[22]

In May 1964, the NAACP filed a suit in the U.S. District Court for the Northern District of Ohio on behalf of Charles Craggett and a group of schoolchildren.[23] The case, *Craggett v. Cleveland Board of Education*,[24] was assigned to Judge Girard Kalbfleisch.[25] The suit did not involve a frontal assault on racial segregation in the Cleveland school system. Instead, the plaintiffs asked the court to enjoin the construction of the three "replacement" schools referred to earlier, on the grounds that constructing these schools would result in the resegregation of the schools they would replace.

Although over 160 school districts were ordered desegregated in 1963 and 1964, Cleveland's was not one of them.[26] And although the court in *Craggett* acknowledged that once constructed, the three new schools would be segregated in fact,[27] the court rejected the plaintiffs' request for a preliminary injunction on the grounds that they had not carried their burden of establishing that any segregation associated with the opening of the new schools was brought about by "a deliberate design to segregate."[28] The court credited testimony offered by the defendants to the effect that their actions were not racially motivated. The case was appealed to the U.S. Court of Appeals for the Sixth Circuit, which affirmed Judge Kalbfleisch's decision without dissent.[29]

Although the plaintiffs lost in *Craggett*, the case helped focus public attention on the extremely poor state of public education in Cleveland, in terms of both the quality of education being received by children and the serious problems associated with the leadership and administration of the system. The litigation may also have influenced the Cleveland Board of Education president, Ralph McCallister, to resign, although it did not affect the board's commitment to its neighborhood school policy. Paul Briggs replaced McCallister.[30]

Briggs, who had previously been the superintendent of the suburban Parma school district, quickly established himself as a politically savvy leader, and he cultivated good relations with the local media and political leadership both locally and in Washington.[31] But instead of taking ownership of the racial problems affecting the schools and moving toward any serious efforts to address the problems of segregation, Briggs focused on the general quality of education for all students. And the loss of *Craggett* helped to drain much of the momentum from the civil rights and community groups' efforts to push for the integration of the Cleveland schools. As the city entered the 1970s, school segregation only increased, as did the general racial malaise in the broader community.

Reed v. Rhodes: The Long and Tortured Process of Desegregating the Cleveland Schools

In early 1973, the NAACP formally demanded that the Cleveland Board of Education desegregate its school system.[32] Superintendent Briggs had resisted all demands for voluntary efforts, and he had initiated a plan that he claimed would accomplish significant integration and reduce racial isolation without the disruption more radical measures, such as busing, would entail.[33] However, his plan called for new construction of neighborhood schools, which would only exacerbate existing segregation.[34]

When Briggs and the school board refused the NAACP's demands for more aggressive action, on December 12, 1973, the NAACP filed suit in federal court on behalf of Robert Anthony Reed, a student in the Cleveland Public Schools; the local chapter of the NAACP; and others. Named as defendants were the Cleveland Board of Education, the Ohio State Board of Education, the governor of Ohio, and other state and local officials. The complaint alleged that the defendants had promulgated and implemented policies and practices that had "the purpose and effect of perpetuating racial and economic segregation."[35] The case, styled *Reed v. Rhodes*, was assigned to Frank J. Battisti, who at the time was the chief judge of the U.S. District Court for the Northern District of Ohio.[36]

The *Reed* litigation turned out to be one of the most significant events in the modern history of Cleveland,[37] and it became one of the most contested, protracted, and messy school desegregation cases in the country. Although it was only one of nine such cases that were filed in the federal courts in Ohio during this period,[38] it was probably the most controversial and polarizing.[39] Indeed, in 1994, some twenty-one years after the suit was filed, Judge Battisti was moved to recall "the long (and often bitter) struggle that has accompanied this litigation."[40] Two years earlier, he had observed that "for more than a decade [the defendants] displayed a recalcitrance and hostility toward the laws of the land and the remedial orders of this Court," and he noted the "senseless anger" that the case had generated.[41]

A comprehensive account of *Reed* lies well beyond the scope of this chapter.[42] The main litigation generated some thirteen reported opinions from the district court and six opinions from the Sixth Circuit Court of Appeals.[43] And although Judge Battisti presided over most of the litigation,[44] it also came under the supervision of Judge Robert Krupansky[45] and Chief Judge George White.[46] The balance of this section will address several of the key developments in the case.

The Early Litigation and the Liability Decision

The defendants in *Reed* did not contest the fact that the Cleveland schools were segregated; indeed, given the actual racial characteristics of the schools, any such effort would have been futile. In 1975, for example, 91.5 percent of the black students enrolled in the system were attending one-race schools, defined as schools in which "student population is 90% or more one race."[47] Instead of addressing *whether* the system was segregated, Judge Battisti noted that the question for the court to decide was "to what extent, if any, are the defendants . . . responsible for creating or for maintaining or both the segregated situation in the Cleveland public schools?"[48] It was that issue that occupied the parties' attention during the pretrial, discovery stage, which lasted almost two years. The trial, which began on November 24, 1975, ran into the following March, when closing arguments were presented.[49]

On August 31, 1976, the court issued an opinion that was to fill over ninety pages in the federal reporter. Judge Battisti's factual findings covered a period that extended from 1935 to 1970. The defendants' main argument was that any segregation that existed in the school system came about as a result of "private action over which they had no control and in which they had no involvement."[50]

Essentially, the defendants claimed that the neighborhood school policy upon which the system was structured was racially neutral and that any segregation in the system "just happened" and was attributable to "natural" migration patterns and private residential discrimination, which they could not control. But in sometimes meticulous detail, Battisti traced numerous decisions and practices of the Cleveland school officials that belied this argument. These practices included the use of optional attendance zones, the location of new school construction, the busing of black children,[51] the change of schools' grade structure, the assignment of faculty and school administrators, the use of relay classes and special transfers, and the use of "intact busing"[52] as a method for alleviating overcrowding in black schools. In incident after incident, Battisti found that the defendants used these practices to exacerbate or preserve existing segregation. Where polices or practices could be employed with integrative effects, either they were not considered or they were rejected. When viewed as a whole, the court concluded, the record established that the defendants had "violated the plaintiffs' 14th Amendment right to equal protection under the laws by intentionally creating and maintaining a segregated school system."[53]

In *Brown*, the Supreme Court had emphasized not only that segregation had created unequal educational opportunities for black students but also that the separation of students by race "generates a feeling of inferiority as to their status in the community that may affect their hearts and minds in a way unlikely ever to be undone."[54] Though the opinion in *Reed* did not dwell on the extent to which black students in Cleveland had sustained this sort of psychological or stigmatic harm as a result of the defendants' practices, an example from the record reveals why Judge Battisti described the experience of students subject to intact busing as a "racially segregative nightmare for the children involved."

As noted earlier, one of the practices upon which the plaintiffs focused to show that segregation in the school system came about as a result of purposeful decision making by school officials was the use of intact busing, pursuant to which entire classes of black students and their teachers were transported to white schools that had extra capacity. But instead of being integrated or "diffused" into the receiving school, the black students were kept together and given little if any opportunity to mix with or even meet the white students who regularly attended that school. At trial, Yvonne Flonnoy, one of the black students subject to this practice, tellingly spoke of the effect that the experience had on her and her classmates. She described her third-grade classmates being placed in one row at the back of a classroom. They were not allowed to participate in any activities at the receiving school; they were not permitted to take gym, nor were they allowed to eat lunch. At Christmas, when the white students were "caroling in the hallway," she and the other black children were required to stay in the room with their heads down.[55] From this testimony, the Sixth Circuit drew the conclusion that "one of the lessons which Cleveland's black students learned was that the Cleveland school system assigned to them status inferior to that given white students regardless of the American constitutional promise of 'equal protection of the laws.'"[56]

This testimony represented only a small part of the record established at trial. Judge Battisti's meticulous review of that record painted a picture that made his legal conclusions appear almost inescapable. And the language used to describe much of the school board's conduct was often quite forceful and direct. For instance, perhaps in an implied reference to the practice of racial apartheid elsewhere in the world, the court described the policies and practices of the Cleveland school officials as amounting to the "containment of black students in overwhelmingly black schools."[57] This policy of containment was not employed reluctantly but with "zeal."[58] Elsewhere in the opinion, after reviewing the school officials' manipulation of attendance zones and practices to maintain racial isolation, Judge Battisti characterized the defendants' actions as constituting *"outright theft* of those [black] students' rights to even an equal educational experience" that could "be explained only as the manifestation of an intention to contain blacks at all costs."[59]

The extent to which Judge Battisti was affected by his review of the evidence was further revealed in still other passages from the opinion. For example, after reviewing the school board's use of relay classes and intact busing, he observed that "like other integrative opportunities presented to the Board," options that might have had potential to further integration were not ignored but were *"prostituted* into a segregative device." Still elsewhere, he characterized the defendants' efforts to proffer racially neutral explanations for many of their decisions over time as "desperate," and he referred to their overall conduct as representing "the manifestation of an intention to contain blacks at all costs."[60]

Taken cumulatively, the "damning" evidence presented by the plaintiffs left the court with little doubt that the pervasive segregation in the Cleveland schools resulted from the board's racially motivated conduct, and that conduct violated the constitutional rights of the plaintiffs. Whether individual board members acted malevolently, out of a subjective desire to subordinate or harm black children, or whether they simply caved in to political pressure exerted by their white constituents was legally irrelevant. The school system they had created and operated was "dual" in the constitutional sense, and it had to be dismantled.[61]

The language used by the court in condemning the defendants' conduct may have further assured the prospect of an appeal in *Reed*. But in any event, the defendants appealed to the U.S. Court of Appeals for the Sixth Circuit.[62] In July 1977, that court remanded the case to Judge Battisti for further consideration in light of the decisions of the U.S. Supreme Court in the Dayton and Columbus cases.[63] On February 6, 1978, Judge Battisti issued two decisions. The first of these applied the principles recently laid down by the Supreme Court in the Dayton case and others,[64] and it reaffirmed his prior decision that the Cleveland school officials had engaged in pervasive, systemwide, and intentional discrimination against black children.[65] The second decision set out a remedial order that would end up shocking much of the city's political and educational establishment and affecting the course of the Cleveland school system for the next twenty-five years.

A Remedial Road Map for Dismantling Cleveland's Segregated School System

As was customary in desegregation cases, once Judge Battisti found in favor of the plaintiffs in *Reed*, he ordered the defendants to prepare a desegregation plan. He appointed a special master and two experts to assist in that process, and he issued "instructions and guidelines" to guide the preparation of a plan.[66] The United States declined the court's invitation to intervene in the case to help formulate and implement an appropriate remedy, but it agreed to participate as a friend of the court. Over five and a half months, the Cleveland defendants submitted three proposed plans, none of which the court accepted.[67] The court adopted the special master's report recommending that the faculty and staff of the school system be desegregated by September 1977. After two months of hearings, the special master submitted recommendations for a systemwide remedy that the court, with some modifications, accepted.

In what Judge White later described as a remedial plan that imposed "approximately two to three times the number of remedial obligations as compared to those imposed on any other school district subject to a desegregation order,"[68] some sixteen topics and subtopics were addressed, including student assignments; education programs; cooperation with universities, businesses, and cultural institutions; staff development and student training in human relations;

student rights; school-community relations; transportation; safety and security; financial considerations; and the state's role in implementation.[69] The plan's detail was considerable, with tables organizing various elementary, junior high, and high schools into clusters that occupied over twenty pages of the reported decision.[70]

Space does not permit a detailed account of the remedy imposed by Judge Battisti, but the following are some of its most important—and what proved to be most controversial—features: (1) the schools were to be desegregated at one time, not in phases, as the Cleveland board had proposed; (2) not only would students have to be reassigned to different schools, but the defendants would have to develop programs that would correct the effects of prior discrimination as well; (3) the Cleveland defendants were ordered to institute a "department of desegregation implementation," whose head was required to report not to the Cleveland school superintendent or the school board, but to the newly created deputy superintendent for desegregation implementation, who in turn was to report directly to the court; and (4) extensive transportation of students would be required, with all parties agreeing that over fifty thousand students would have to be bused, and up to six hundred buses would need to purchased by the school district. The transportation requirement was connected to one of the plan's most controversial "objectives": that the "racial composition of the student body of any school within the system shall not substantially deviate from the racial composition of the system as a whole."[71]

Judge Battisti's remedial order did more than lay out a detailed and costly set of requirements. It also revealed, once again, the deep sense of frustration he had displayed in his liability decision, a frustration that was to continue for the many years during which he would preside over the case. He lamented the defendants' "disinclination" to provide responsible financial management of the district. He wrote of the "approximately 16 months of patiently attempting to persuade the defendants of the non-adversary nature of fashioning a remedy." And presciently, he lamented the "continuous necessity for this Court to issue orders before the defendants will perform their constitutional duty."[72] As it turned out, the "ground war" in the battle to bring *Brown v. Board of Education* to Cleveland had only begun.[73]

The Cleveland school board reacted quite harshly to Judge Battisti's remedial order,[74] and it once again appealed to the Sixth Circuit. In August 1979, that court for the most part affirmed Judge Battisti's liability and remedial decisions.[75] For the next fifteen years, in what the judge called "the long (and often bitter) struggle that has accompanied this litigation," the remedial portion of the case slogged on, with the parties returning to the court many times to resolve their disputes. Finally, in 1994 the parties submitted a joint motion seeking the court's approval of a settlement agreement that would "modify the parties' remaining obligations under the remedial orders and define a course to the orderly and just resolution of this litigation."[76]

The Consent Decree

The consent decree came about after the court ordered the parties to meet and discuss a range of issues raised in a series of reports issued by the OSMCR, the office that had been created to monitor compliance with the various remedial decrees and orders.[77] The agreement was negotiated under the auspices of Daniel J. McMullen, the OSMCR director.[78] It incorporated many of the elements of Vision 21, a comprehensive education plan proposed in 1993 by then Superintendent Sammie Campbell Parrish.[79] The central features of the consent decree included the following stipulations: (1) it was to be in effect for six years; (2) it generally preserved the racial balance requirement of the initial remedial order, although it exempted some schools in this regard; (3) it obligated the state to contribute $295 million to support desegregation efforts and committed the school district to provide at least $275 million in matching funds; and (4) the parties were to meet on a regular basis to assess progress, to continue cooperation with the OSMCR, and to submit joint annual reports to the court concerning the ongoing status of implementation and compliance with the decree and all outstanding remedial orders. Importantly, the court agreed to either rescind or modify over five hundred remedial orders issued since the litigation began, including much of the original 1978 remedial order.

The community was heartened by the consent decree. It was variously described as a "road map for ending the case"[80] and as "the first step toward the district getting out entirely from under the federal court order."[81] Judge Battisti described the decree as signaling that the parties had "taken a great stride towards changing this aspirational view [of the end of judicial involvement] into a concrete plan."[82] But one suspects that even though he may have been heartened by what appeared to be a newly cooperative attitude among the parties, he was pragmatic and, in light of the sorry history of the parties' fighting and bickering, realistic enough to realize that much work remained before meaningful desegregation could be achieved.

Judge Battisti's Death, Judge Krupansky's Arrival, and the Declaration of Unitary Status

Five months after he approved the consent decree, Judge Battisti died unexpectedly.[83] Judge Robert Krupansky, who at the time was a senior judge on the U.S. Court of Appeals for the Sixth Circuit, was assigned responsibility for approximately 194 outstanding cases on Battisti's docket, including *Reed v. Rhodes*.[84] Given the consent decree, Judge Krupansky apparently believed that the case would require "minimal monitoring,"[85] but events soon proved otherwise. In November, the voters rejected a school levy by a 3-to-2 margin, and a political storm erupted as a result of serious disagreements between then Superintendent Dr. Parrish and a "mayor–school board alliance."[86] When Parrish suddenly announced that she was resigning, on March 3, 1995,[87] Judge Krupansky called a hearing in *Reed*.[88] The evidence at that hearing persuaded him that the school district was "in total fiscal and administrative collapse."[89] After another hearing held on March 3, he issued an order directing the Ohio Board of Education (still a defendant in the case) to exercise authority conferred by Ohio law and prior court orders to essentially take over the Cleveland schools, a task that Dr. John Sanders assumed.[90]

As Judge Krupansky later described it, within a relatively short time the state leadership he appointed stabilized and restored the integrity of the school system.[91] In January 1996, the defendants filed a motion, opposed by the plaintiffs, to modify the 1994 consent decree and to terminate judicial supervision of student school assignments. In a fifty-page opinion, Krupansky granted the defendants' motion.[92] He concluded that the core principles set out in Vision 21 and incorporated into the consent decree could not be reconciled with the racial balance requirements Judge Battisti had imposed in his 1978 remedial order (which had also been largely retained in the consent decree). Accordingly, he held that the defendants would be relieved from any further obligation to have each school in the system approximate (within 15 percent of the systemwide average) the racial balance of the system as a whole. The remainder of the consent decree would, however, remain in effect. Judge Krupansky went on to declare that, at least with regard to matters related to student assignments, the Cleveland schools had achieved "unitary status" and that the court would relinquish any ongoing jurisdiction over such matters.

Given the extraordinarily contentious history of *Reed*, certain aspects of Judge Krupansky's reasoning seem quite problematic. For example, in order to declare unitary status, Supreme Court precedent required a finding that the defendants had exercised "good faith" in complying with court-ordered student assignment criteria. In finding this requirement satisfied, Judge Krupansky concluded that the Cleveland school district had demonstrated good faith not only in complying with the consent decree, but also in "complying with the seminal desegregation decree since it was entered."[93] How odd this must have sounded to the plaintiffs and others who had followed a case in which Judge Battisti had repeatedly, and for years, chastised the defendants' obstreperous bad faith.[94]

Perhaps to no one's surprise, Judge Krupansky's decision was appealed. But unlike in previous appellate decisions, the Sixth Circuit did not speak with one voice this time.[95] In an opinion for himself and Judge Nancy Edmunds, Judge Gilbert Merritt Jr. affirmed the district court's ruling modifying the consent decree and declaring, in part, that the Cleveland school system had achieved unitary status.[96] In reviewing the "long and complicated" history of the case, Judge Merritt claimed that during the 1980s, the school system became predominantly nonwhite as a result of white flight.[97] He found that by the early 1990s, compliance with outstanding remedial orders had reached a level of "astonishing success."[98] In addition, Merritt cited evidence in the record that after the implementation of the consent decree, an overwhelming majority of parents in the school district, including blacks, valued the right to choose a school more than busing for racial balance. Ultimately, applying the deferential standard of appellate review applicable to such cases, the court found that "it cannot be said that the lower court abused its discretion in modifying" the consent decree.[99]

With respect to the declaration of unitary status, Judge Krupansky's ruling was also affirmed. The court compared the racial balance achieved in Cleveland to that achieved in DeKalb County, Georgia, whose system the Supreme Court had declared unitary in *Freeman* v. *Pitts*.[100] It found that the continued racial imbalance in the Cleveland schools was far less than the imbalance in DeKalb County and that the Cleveland schools compared favorably in terms of a variety of other relevant factors. Finally, the court credited Judge Krupansky's finding that the Cleveland defendants had exhibited "unequivocal good faith" in their desegregation efforts.

Judge R. Guy Cole dissented and launched a ringing and forceful critique of Judge Krupansky and the Sixth Circuit majority. He asked whether, after more than thirty years of state-sanctioned racial isolation of black children in the Cleveland schools and more than twenty years of active resistance to the district court's orders requiring desegregation of those schools, the Cleveland Board of

Education should be allowed to implement an assignment plan that would return the city's schools to a state of racial segregation.[101]

Rejecting any effort to paint a picture of harmony permeating the Cleveland school system, Cole asserted that the record "reveals a much more menacing history, one of resistance, defiance and utter disregard for the district court's orders or, more importantly, the rights of black children." He noted that "from the beginning," the defendants had "actively resisted implementation of the Remedial Order." Moreover, he noted that Judge Krupansky himself, shortly after his assignment to the case, had criticized the school board's "indifference" and "active resistance" that led Judge Battisti to initiate a Department of Justice (DOJ) investigation and civil contempt proceedings. And he recalled Battisti's 1992 observations that the defendants had "inflicted grievous wounds on the community as a whole."[102]

And there was more. Judge Cole accused the court's majority, and, by implication, Judge Krupansky, of "caving in" to public pressure and "rewarding the defendants for their dilatory and improper tactics." He went on to claim that the defendants had consistently "flouted" the mandates of Judge Battisti and the Supreme Court, and he accused his colleagues of "harping" on the age of the case and allowing their "impatience" with the desegregation process to guide their judgment. According to Judge Cole, Krupansky was mistaken in attributing good faith to the defendants. Indeed, for him the only material change in circumstances since the execution of the consent decree and all that had come before it was Judge Krupansky's replacement of Judge Battisti![103]

The Final Phase

In early 1998, *Reed v. Rhodes* entered its final phase. After his decision declaring that the Cleveland school system had achieved partial unitary status, Judge Krupansky returned to his duties as senior circuit judge.[104] Chief Judge George White assumed supervision of *Reed*. The 1994 consent decree included a provision allowing the parties to apply to the court for a determination of unitary status with respect to all requirements of that decree except for those that were specifically designated to continue until July 1, 2000.[105] In July 1997, the defendants moved the court to hold hearings on the question of whether the Cleveland school system had achieved unitary status. After five weeks of hearings, Judge White granted the defendants' motion and declared that the Cleveland schools had indeed achieved that status.[106] His decision was affirmed by the Sixth Circuit in a very brief, unanimous, and unpublished opinion.[107] Judge White subsequently lifted all judicial control of the Cleveland schools in 2000.[108]

Before leaving the area of school desegregation, it may be instructive to contrast the tumultuous experience in Cleveland with the quite different experience in Lorain, Ohio. In the late 1970s, Lorain, located some 30 miles west of Cleveland, was a largely blue-collar industrial town. Its school district operated 19 schools, with an enrollment of just over 14,000 students. In the 1978–79 school year, the racial composition of the schools was 2,574 black, 8,637 white, and 2,762 Hispanic. In September 1979, the NAACP brought a class action suit in the U.S. District Court for the Northern District of Ohio alleging that the Lorain Board of Education and the Ohio Board of Education engaged in a pattern or practice of discrimination against blacks and Hispanics by closing certain school facilities, by engaging in race-based student assignments, and by discriminating in the hiring and assignment of teachers and administrators. The case, originally assigned to Judge Ann Aldrich, was transferred to Judge David Dowd in December 1982.

In contrast to the Cleveland case, where it took over twenty years for the parties to finally agree to a consent decree, the litigants in the Lorain case agreed to settle their dispute in only two years.[109] The consent decree consisted of a "Goal Statement," which outlined a series of goals related to "education," "discipline," "affirmative action and employment opportunity," "school closing considerations," and a "procedure to ensure effective implementation of district goals." In his order of May 15, 1984, preliminarily approving the consent decree, Judge Dowd required the Lorain Board of Education, within three weeks, to develop a plan to achieve these goals, with the expectation that such a plan would be implemented in the following school year. He also ordered the state of Ohio to pay 50 percent of the expenses incurred by Lorain in the design, implementation, administration, and maintenance of the plan, with the state's obligation limited to a period of seven school years and to a maximum contribution of $1 million.

The parties were unable to reach agreement on an implementation plan. A central feature of the consent decree was a requirement that each school in the district establish a composite minority student ratio of +20 or –15 percent from the district's average percentage of each identifiable minority's student racial composition. Lorain's proposed plan would achieve this goal through the establishment of a magnet school program, while the plaintiffs insisted on the involuntary reassignment of students. Ultimately, after holding evidentiary hearings,

Judge Dowd rejected plaintiffs' request for involuntary reassignment and approved those portions of the proposed plan pertaining to the use of magnet schools, although he rejected Lorain's proposal to judge the plan's success on targeted ratios other than those set out in the consent decree. The court also approved Lorain's proposals for the enhancement and implementation of a bilingual educational program (primarily for Hispanic students) and for the hiring of new teachers and other employees on the basis of the consent decree's affirmative action goals, subject to periodic court monitoring.

Over the next six or seven years, the court continued to actively monitor compliance with the desegregation plans. In January 1990, the Lorain Board of Education applied to the court for an order requiring the state of Ohio to increase its share of the costs of implementing and completing the desegregation plan. In August 1990, Judge Dowd ordered the consent decree modified and the parties to enter into negotiations to determine the additional amount the state would contribute. Ultimately, Judge Dowd found that the "highly successful desegregation program has cost a great deal more than it was originally thought the program would cost," and he issued a decision ordering the state to contribute millions of dollars more toward desegregation costs over a five-year period.[110]

Finally, in September 1993, both the Lorain and state defendants filed motions with the court seeking to have the Lorain school system declared unitary and for the court to terminate its jurisdiction over the matter. The plaintiffs contested these motions. While the parties agreed that many of the goals set out in the consent decree, including those related to pupil assignment and bilingual education, largely had been achieved, the plaintiffs argued that the defendants had failed to achieve the minority teacher and staff hiring goals. In an order issued on December 21, 1993, Judge Dowd declared the Lorain City School District unitary and the consent decree of August 1984 terminated.[111]

The Parma Housing Discrimination Case

Brown's impact has far transcended the educational context. The years immediately following the decision saw the Supreme Court disengage from any serious effort to vindicate *Brown's* promise of educational equality. *Brown* was met by massive resistance in many parts of the country (especially in the Deep South) and by a tepid response from the political branches of the national government, as well as by ambivalence and even strong resistance from the lower federal courts. But in Professor Michael J. Klarman's account, the blossoming of civil rights activism that took place in *Brown*'s wake together with the backlash created by the violent efforts of desegregation's opponents to suppress civil rights demonstrations—*Brown*'s "indirect effects"—were largely responsible for the civil rights legislation of the 1960s and 1970s. This legislation included the Civil Rights Act of 1964,[112] which prohibited discrimination in the use of federal funds and in public accommodations and authorized the Justice Department to enforce its antidiscrimination provisions.[113]

Thus, *Brown*, even if indirectly, helped lay a foundation of political support for national legislation intended to help realize the Fourteenth Amendment's newly understood conception of racial equality. Spurred on by race riots across the country in the 1960s and the Kerner Commission's forecast of an America "moving toward two societies—one Black and one white, separate and unequal,"[114] Congress enacted Title VIII of the Civil Rights Act of 1968. Widely known as the Fair Housing Act, its purpose was to help ameliorate the housing and residential discrimination that had come to characterize much of the urban North, including Cleveland, Ohio.

Housing Segregation in Cleveland: The Early 1970s

As Judge Battisti noted in a 1980 opinion, recounting the history of events leading to the creation of a "black ghetto" on the east side of Cleveland "does not make pleasant reading."[115] In a 1989 study analyzing 1980 census data, Professors Douglas Massey and Nancy Denton found that Cleveland was one of the most segregated cities in the country, so much so that they classified the city as "hyper-segregated."[116] This segregation was attributable to a number of factors. As in other major urban areas, at the same time blacks were moving into Cleveland in large numbers, whites were moving out, in even larger numbers, to the suburbs.[117] In addition, there was pervasive racial steering practiced by realtors, widespread use of restrictive racial covenants prohibiting the sale of property to blacks, and Federal Housing Administration (FHA)–sponsored racial discrimination in the placement and rental of public housing.[118] All of these factors, combined with blacks' relatively poor economic circumstances, contributed to the heavy concentration of black families in central cities and in primarily black neighborhoods. Beginning in the early 1970s, these conditions led to a number of suits, brought in federal court in Cleveland, challenging this condition of housing segregation on both constitutional and statutory grounds.

The first of these suits was *Banks v. Perk*,[119] in which a group of plaintiffs sued on behalf of all black and other nonwhite tenants in, and applicants for, federally assisted public housing. Among those named as defendants were the City of Cleveland, Mayor Ralph Perk, and the Cuyahoga (County) Metropolitan Housing Authority (CMHA). The suit charged that the defendants had engaged in illegal racial discrimination when they rejected applications for the construction of certain public housing projects. It also sought to enjoin the defendants from perpetuating unconstitutional discrimination by continuing to operate a racially discriminatory housing system. The case was assigned to Chief Judge Frank Battisti.

In issuing an injunction against both the Cleveland defendants and the CMHA,[120] Judge Battisti noted that it was "almost twenty years since the landmark case of [*Brown*]" and that "unless realistic action is taken within the immediate future . . . we can expect the east side of Cleveland to become almost totally Black, while the West side will remain largely White." To avoid the continuing division of the city and county along racial lines, it was necessary to "place a clear majority of all [of CMHA's] new public housing units in White neighborhoods and largely on the west side of the City."[121] Thus, CMHA was enjoined from considering the placement of any new public housing sites on the east side of the city.

Soon after *Banks* was decided, a number of individuals and a nonprofit housing organization, on behalf of all tenants of and applicants for CMHA housing, filed another housing discrimination suit in federal court. This case, *Mahaley v. Cuyahoga Metropolitan*,[122] was initially assigned to a three-judge court and subsequently assigned to Judge Battisti.[123] The three-judge court, which included Battisti, was required under federal law when plaintiffs sought an injunction against the enforcement of state law on federal constitutional grounds. The plaintiffs challenged a federal law that required local governments to enter into a consent agreement with local housing authorities such as CMHA before low-income housing could be constructed or operated, as well as the refusal of municipalities to enter into such agreements.[124] The effect of such refusals was alleged to have been an embargo on low-income housing, which was disproportionately inhabited by blacks. These practices were alleged to violate the Fifth, Thirteenth, and Fourteenth Amendments to the U.S. Constitution. The court, in an opinion written by Judge Battisti, rejected the plaintiffs' claims, in part reasoning that any racial effects associated with the local consent requirement were not caused by the law itself, but "rather by municipal action or inaction which may have used this provision as a shield to protect its inhabitants from integration by low income Negroes."[125] Judge Lambros dissented, noting that "the effects of racial segregation are destroying the community."[126]

In a quite unorthodox move, the three-judge panel remanded the case to a single judge, Frank Battisti.[127] On the same day that the decision of the three-judge panel was issued, Battisti handed down a *second* opinion, in which he found that the plaintiffs had established a prima facie case that the defendant suburbs' refusal to enter into consent or cooperation agreements with CMHA amounted to unconstitutional discrimination and that the "flimsy and transparent rationalizations" offered by the defendants to justify their conduct as nondiscriminatory failed to rebut this presumption.[128] In terms of a remedy, Judge Battisti ordered the defendants, within ninety days, to prepare a plan for the placement of new public housing that would "reflect the needs of each suburban city for low income and elderly housing."[129] The defendants appealed, and the Sixth Circuit reversed.[130] Judge Edwards dissented.[131]

Both *Banks* and *Mahaley* joined *Reed v. Rhodes* as the first significant efforts to involve the district courts of the Northern District of Ohio in the vindication of *Brown*'s constitutional promise of racial equality. In each of these cases, Judge Battisti struggled to translate this promise to the racial realities confronting the people of Cleveland, Cuyahoga County, and beyond.[132] More than once, he and some of his judicial colleagues noted the pervasiveness of residential segregation in Cleveland and its environs. In *Banks*, Judge Battisti wrote that "the City of Cleveland is a racially divided city."[133] He repeated this observation in his opinion for the court in *Mahaley*, and he went on to note that to live in the inner city was all too often a badge both of poverty and of slavery. He also remarked that "Cuyahoga County has the racial shape of a donut, with the Negroes in the hole and with mostly Whites occupying the ring."[134]

A similar tone was struck in Judge Edwards's dissent from the Sixth Circuit's decision in *Mahaley*, where he characterized the case as one in which the plaintiffs were "attacking the growing evil of apartheid in urban America."[135] And Judge Lambros's dissent from the three-judge panel's decision in that case also reflected this theme. There, he all but accused the suburban defendants of disingenuousness in denying that their refusal even to consider allowing low-income housing into their cities was motivated by race. As Lambros put it, "The situation is significantly one of white versus black," and the resulting "racial segregation is destroying this community."[136]

Nowhere was this picture of racial apartheid more clear than in Parma, Ohio, Cleveland's largest suburb. Parma was known as an ethnic enclave, heavily Catholic and blue collar and populated primarily with people of Eastern European descent. Parma prided itself on its independence, and its political leadership had long maintained a cautious and arm's-length relationship with Cleveland, which many Parma residents viewed warily as a foreboding example of the problems of urban decline.

In the 1960s and 1970s, Parma had "a reputation as a white, ethnic, suburban enclave,"[137] a reputation that it was proud of and enthusiastically cultivated. In 1970, Parma had just over one hundred thousand residents, of whom only fifty (.05 percent) were black. This contrasted sharply with Cleveland, where black migration since the 1930s had caused the black population to swell.[138] To the extent that Parma had almost no black residents, it was safe to say that the city was segregated, a proposition that its leaders did not deny. What they did deny, however, was that any segregation was caused by something other than economics and "the free residential choice of blacks and whites to live with people of common background" and ethnicity.[139]

In April 1973, the U.S. Department of Justice filed suit against the city of Parma, alleging that it had engaged in a pattern and practice of racial discrimination in housing in violation of the Fair Housing Act of 1968.[140] As with *Banks* and *Mahaley*, the case was assigned to Judge Battisti. The government's case focused on a series of actions taken by Parma officials between 1968 and 1975 that were alleged to have inhibited or prevented blacks from moving into the city and that effectively implemented a policy of racial exclusion.

The course and the details of the litigation have been discussed elsewhere.[141] Suffice it to say that the suit had a dramatic effect on Parma and the broader Cleveland area. As had been true with *Reed v. Rhodes*, the *Parma* litigation was long and contentious. At least in its initial phases, it may well have deserved the characterization of a "bigotry-laden battle" accorded to it by one observer.[142] As in *Reed*, the record in *United States v. Parma* reflected a series of actions taken by the defendants over time with the clear and dramatic effect of achieving racial exclusion and containment. But the record also demonstrated more than racially discriminatory effects: the plaintiff introduced evidence of racist statements made by Parma's elected officials that contributed to the perpetuation and intensification of the city's racist reputation as a place that "did not want blacks to live there."[143] These statements, combined with such factors as Parma's adamant opposition to any public housing, its denial of building permits for a low-income senior citizen housing project, and its enactment of ordinances limiting the height of future construction and requiring voter approval of the creation of any public housing, all led the court to conclude "beyond cavil that

Parma has held and practiced a deliberate policy of racial exclusion" in violation of federal law.[144]

As had often been true with the Cleveland Board of Education in *Reed*,
Judge Battisti frequently displayed a lack of sympathy or patience for Parma's
litigation position. In denying a Parma motion for summary judgment, he referred to "the muck and mire of defendants' rhetoric" and to their "painstakingly
loquacious" legal brief.[145] And in his liability decision, in what one observer called
"damning language,"[146] he pointedly characterized Parma's actions as "motivated by racial bigotry."[147] That Parma's litigation position was one of intransigence was also quite clear. As one commentator has noted, "Parma's strategy
was to reject all aspects of the government's case and go on the offensive." The
city treated the United States, in the form of Judge Battisti and the DOJ, as in-
vaders and argued that the government, in bringing the case, was discriminating
against *Parma's citizens* on the basis of their Eastern European national origins.[148]
In a classic "pot and kettle" move, Parma's lawyers accused the government of
seeking to pin the badge of slavery on its citizens. They even analogized the
DOJ to Adolf Hitler and Joe McCarthy!

Six months later, Judge Battisti issued an opinion announcing the remedy
he would impose on Parma.[149] The opinion began by noting that the city had
refused the court's invitation to submit written recommendations for a proposed
remedy, instead submitting a brief quoting "inapposite cases" and employing
"racially incendiary language." Further alluding to the defendant's hostility and
intransigence, he noted that he had "admonished the defendant's present lawyers, both in chambers and from the bench, not to traumatize and incite those
who may be affected by the delicate and necessary steps that the court must take
to remediate the statutory violations which were found in Parma."[150]

The remedy, described by a Parma official as an "H-bomb,"[151] was, as in
Reed, wide-ranging. The defendant was enjoined from further discriminatory
conduct that would promote or perpetuate residential segregation and in connection with matters having to do with the planning and construction of public
housing in the city. The court also required Parma to take a number of concrete
actions, including: developing a fair housing program, adopting a fair housing
resolution, conducting an advertising campaign promoting the city as an open
community, and pursuing actions aimed at increasing the supply of low-income
housing.[152] In addition, the court required Parma to submit a proposal to Housing
and Urban Development (HUD) for federal funds to pursue low-income housing and to "make all efforts necessary" to ensure the creation of at least 133 units

of low-income housing each year. The court also required the creation of a fair housing committee (FHC), responsible for implementing and monitoring its remedial plan, and an evaluation committee, composed of community members to review the deliberations of the FHC and report to the court with its recommendations. Finally, the court, against Parma's objections, created (as it had done in *Reed*) the position of a special master, with extensive authority to oversee the remedy and report to the court.[153]

The remedial process in *Parma* encountered a number of problems, and it was to occupy Judge Battisti's and the parties' attention for many years.[154] Once the appeals were concluded, Parma apparently took a number of steps to satisfy the remedial requirements. Eventually, however, disputes arose with respect to several remedial requirements, including the court-ordered advertising campaign, Parma's decision to create its own housing authority, and the city's efforts to secure adequate federal financial support. Judge Battisti had appointed local civil right attorney Avery Friedman as amicus curiae.[155] In March 1985, Friedman, at the court's request, issued a report critical of the city's general approach to implementation of the remedy, and that proposed a number of changes.[156] Parma did not react well. Its lawyers accused Friedman of "implacable hostility," prompting Judge Battisti to issue an order defending Friedman, finding Parma's attorneys in violation of Federal Rule 11, and threatening them with monetary sanctions.[157]

In August 1995—twenty-three years after the suit was filed, less than a year after Judge Battisti died, and fifteen months after the Cleveland school officials took a similar step in *Reed*—Parma filed a motion for relief from the remedial order. As in *Reed*, the parties entered into a detailed agreement that modified part of the original remedial order and provided benchmarks for the accomplishment of unfinished implementation obligations.[158] The agreement also established a mechanism for triggering a two-year process for determining compliance and obtaining a dismissal of the case.[159] Judge Kathleen O'Malley, to whom the case had been transferred,[160] approved the agreement.

Brown, the Court, and Frank Battisti

The two cases featured in this chapter, *Reed v. Rhodes* and *United States v. Parma*, may well represent the most significant and sustained efforts in the last quarter of the twentieth century to enlist the federal court system in the struggle for racial and social justice in the Cleveland area.[161] These cases arose in the context of a country and community still struggling with the profound changes brought about by the Supreme Court in *Brown v. Board of Education* and the civil rights movement to which it gave birth. But though *Brown* may have done much to change America's conception of itself, by the 1970s and 1980s its efficaciousness as a socially transformative event was still very much in doubt.[162] Cleveland was perhaps even more segregated than it had been in 1954. Its schools not only failed to provide quality education, they also helped create and maintain a community where racial isolation prevailed. And this racial isolation and alienation was not confined to the schools. It spilled out into the surrounding communities, fueled by private racial fears and, as in Parma, by the purposeful actions of public officials.

As in other communities throughout the country, prospects for change in Cleveland without judicial intervention seemed bleak. The pleas for meaningful change had for too long gone unanswered.[163] *Brown*, as subsequently clarified by the Supreme Court, required change "now."[164] But as Professor Klarman has noted, public enforcement of constitutional and civil rights generally depends upon widespread public support for those rights.[165] If the records in the *Parma* and *Reed* cases tell us anything, it is that many white citizens of Cleveland, including responsible public officials who themselves presumably took an oath to support the Constitution, clearly were not supportive of the rights of their black fellow citizens.

When the black citizens of Cleveland turned to the courts, the U.S. District Court for the Northern District of Ohio responded. It would be a mistake to think that the judges of the court adjudicated these cases with pleasure or enthusiasm. More than once, Chief Judge Battisti publicly lamented the fact the court was compelled to take control of the Cleveland school system in *Reed* or the Parma housing problem in *United States v. Parma*. In court and out,[166] he repeatedly denied the notion that he welcomed having any responsibility to run the Cleveland schools. For him, "the role of the court is to guarantee that the constitution is followed" and to "ensure equal protection of the law"—no more but also no less.[167]

In her fascinating historical account of the U.S. District Court for the Southern District of Ohio, Roberta Alexander referred to that court as "a place of recourse."[168] This is, of course, an apt way to describe the Northern District as well. Like all other federal courts, it is a place where "ordinary citizens" can go to hold the government accountable—"a place where the Constitution and all of our history come into being" and where "the Constitution continues to live . . . through the vigilance and courage of we the people."[169] But in the eyes of Judge Battisti, his court was something more: it was a "place where we reason together."[170] During the period covered by this chapter, the disputes about discrimination in the schools of Cleveland and the residential policies of Parma roiled the community amidst the din of often angry and even vitriolic recriminations.[171] In the words of a person who was involved in *Reed*, the desegregation controversy was perhaps the most "controversial, painful, difficult, unpopular source of conflict in the community." But even in that environment, the court served as a place where those opposing and defending the racial status quo could publicly air their disputes—to be sure, in often heated and contentious terms—and subject them to the language of reason.

It is, of course, fair to ask whether *Reed* and *Parma* achieved the goal of "bringing *Brown* to Cleveland."[172] This is a large and difficult question that cannot adequately be addressed here. The record is at best mixed. With respect to the Cleveland schools, even as Judge White declared that they had achieved unitary status, he felt compelled to concede he was not "convinced that the voluminous remedial orders issued in this case benefitted the students of the Cleveland Public Schools to the degree that all Parties and the Court would have hoped"[173]—a point dramatically emphasized in Judge Cole's dissent from the Sixth Circuit's affirmance of White's decision.[174] If the measure of success lies in the achievement of dramatic (or, for that matter, even measurable) changes in the racial composition of the Cleveland schools, the record is indeed a bleak one.[175] Similarly, if success is measured in terms of improvement in the actual quality of education received by minority, or indeed all, students, the record is no less problematic. In *Brown*, the Supreme Court had linked the "feeling of inferiority" experienced by black students as a result of racial separation and isolation with the failure of segregated schools to provide "equal educational opportunities."[176] But even when Judge Krupansky declared in 1996 that the system had achieved partial unitary status, he noted that twenty years of desegregation efforts had "not resulted in improved academic performance profiles" for Cleveland schoolchildren.[177] In fact, the chronically poor record of the Cleveland public schools was a primary factor in the city's school system becoming one of the first major systems in the country to seek alternatives to public schools, including the use of charter schools and school vouchers.[178]

There are, of course, other ways to assess the extent to which *Reed* and *Parma* succeeded in bringing *Brown* to Cleveland. In each case, the court's involvement led to the end, at least as a matter of public policy, of officially sponsored racial discrimination. That this was no small achievement can by gleaned from the testimony of people such as Peggy Shelby Gillespie, who graduated from a Cleveland high school in 1980. When asked in 2004 what effect the desegregation order had on her, she said that she "was able to become friends with some students from other backgrounds, despite the chaos that surrounded forced integration." Asked what she learned from the desegregation experience, her response was quite telling: "I learned the kids who came over were just people. They were just like me." She went on to say that she learned those kids "were victims of what society handed down to us."[179]

Justice William Rehnquist once sarcastically debunked the notion that *Brown*'s goal was the creation of an "'Emerald City' where all races, ethnic groups, and persons of various income levels live side by side in a large metropolitan area."[180] If this is the standard applicable to cases such as *Reed* and *Parma*, the record of these cases might well be judged a failure. Such a standard, however, would be profoundly unrealistic. If the modern history of our country is any guide, a vision that looks to our courts to solve all our problems or to realize all our aspirations is destined to disappoint.[181] But there is an alternative understanding of *Brown* that we might apply when judging these cases and the work of the court: that *Brown* forbids a legal system from "announcing, on a daily basis, that some children are not fit to be educated with others" or that some people are not fit to live in the same community with others.[182] As one Cleveland observer, reflecting on *Reed* fifty years after *Brown*, put it: "Brown did not give civil rights activists what it promised. But it did give hope, a beginning it is up to all of us who are Brown's children to continue."[183] By this standard, the court's work can well be judged a success.

Before closing, a final observation is appropriate. Reading the voluminous record in *Reed* and *Parma*, a record that includes hundreds of pages of judicial orders and opinions as well as decades of press coverage and other commentary, one is struck by the extent to which the story of bringing *Brown* to Cleveland has been the story of Frank Battisti. No single judge, of course, can be the sole bearer of the record of any court as distinguished and as large as the Northern District of Ohio. But it was Judge Battisti whose personal courage, intellect, stamina, and conviction were largely responsible for whatever racial progress Cleveland was able to achieve during that period.[184]

By all accounts, Battisti himself was a controversial figure, some say even polarizing. He commanded great admiration and loyalty among his friends, but often drew ferocious criticism from his detractors.[185] In the words of one observer, "It is hard to find anyone who is neutral" about him.[186] But in the tradition of such judges as Frank Johnson, John Minor Wisdom, and J. Skelly Wright,[187] Judge Battisti suffered the slings and arrows (and worse) of public disapprobation in the performance of his duty to enforce the rights secured to all by the Constitution.[188] In honoring Battisti's life, Judge Nathaniel Jones put it this way: "He did not flinch from the scorching condemnation heaped upon him" for performing that duty.[189] The Sixth Circuit's 1996 Annual Report included a memorial resolution for Judge Battisti. In that resolution, his appellate colleagues wrote that "the level of isolation that was visited upon him after his initial decision in *Reed v. Rhodes* . . . is almost unimaginable." They went on to note that "Judge Battisti was known as a person of compassion who nonetheless exacted from himself legal rigor in reaching each of his decisions" and that he "clearly understood the responsibility of his position and the weight of fairness and jurisprudence." Judge Battisti, his colleagues continued, "considered how the law would affect people, not just how a decision would fit neatly into a legal theory." And referring specifically to *Reed* and *Parma*, they praised him for finding "answers to very tough problems in very troubled times."[190] To the extent that the promise of *Brown* was in fact realized in Cleveland in the late twentieth century, it was largely due to the determination of this distinguished judge.

Notes

Richard Saphire is a professor of law at the University of Dayton School of Law. His thanks go to Maureen Andersen, Susan Elliot, and Kim Ballard for valuable research assistance. He extends special thanks to Daniel J. McMullen, James Hardiman, and Avery Friedman for providing vital information and insight into the litigation discussed in this essay and to Paul Moke and Michael Solimine for their thoughtful review of a previous draft. Research for this chapter was supported by a grant from the University of Dayton School of Law.

1. 347 U.S. 483 (1954).
2. Anthony Lewis, "What Has *Brown* Wrought?" in *"Brown" at 50: The Unfinished Legacy*, ed. D. Rhode and C. Ogletree (Chicago: American Bar Association, 2004), 114.
3. Plessy v. Ferguson, 163 U.S. 537 (1986).
4. Stephen G. Breyer, "Turning *Brown*'s Hope into Reality," in Rhode and Ogletree, *"Brown" at 50*, 145.
5. The scholarship on this issue is voluminous. For important examples, see *"Brown" at 50* (a collection of essays).
6. See, e.g., Charles T. Clotfelter, *After* Brown: *The Rise and Retreat of School Desegregation* (Princeton, N.J.: Princeton University Press, 2004); Charles J. Ogletree, *All Deliberate Speed: Reflections on the First Half Century of* Brown v. Board of Education (New

York; W.W. Norton., 2004); Robert A. Garda, "Coming Full Circle: The Journey from Separate but Equal to Separate and Unequal Schools," *Duke Journal of Constitutional Law and Public Policy* 2 (2007): 1.

7. After the Court held that segregated schools were unconstitutional, it restored the case to its docket for reargument on the issue of appropriate remedies. This case is commonly known as *Brown II*, 349 U.S. 294 (1995).

8. See, e.g., Michael J. Klarman, *From Jim Crow to Civil Rights: The Supreme Court and the Struggle for Racial Equality* (New York: Oxford University Press, 2004).

9. Cooper v. Aaron, 358 U.S. 1 (1958).

10. Green v. County School Board, 391 U.S. 430 (1968) (rejecting so-called freedom of choice plans).

11. Ibid.

12. Swann v. Charlotte-Mecklenburg Board of Education, 402 U.S. 1 (1971).

13. For a useful and general account of the cases, see Michael W. Combs, "The Federal Judiciary and Northern School Desegregation: Judicial Management in Perspective," *Journal of Law and Education* 13 (1984): 345.

14. Keyes v. School District No. 1, Denver, Colorado, 413 U.S. 189 (1973). The establishment of this principle was important because it relieved a plaintiff of the burden of proving, in order to obtain districtwide relief, that every school in the district was unconstitutionally segregated. The so-called Keyes' presumption became a central factor in the ultimate disposition of the Dayton and Columbus, Ohio, school desegregations—Dayton Board of Education v. Brinkman, 443 U.S. 526 (1979), and Columbus Board of Education v. Penick, 443 U.S. 449 (1979)—as well as in the Cleveland case, Reed v. Rhodes, to be discussed later in this chapter.

15. Milliken v. Bradley, 418 U.S. 717 (1974). To the extent that *Brown* and its progeny required racially *integrated* schools, *Milliken* made such a goal almost impossible. See Gary Orfield and Erica Frankenberg, "Reviving *Brown v. Board of Education*: How Courts and Enforcement Agencies Can Produce More Integrated Schools," in Rhode and Ogletree, *"Brown" at 50*, 194 (noting that *Milliken* makes stable integration-oriented plans almost impossible).

16. Christopher Wye, "Black Civil Rights," in *Cleveland: A Metropolitan Reader*, ed. D. Keating, N. Krumholz, and D. Perry (Kent, Ohio: Kent State University Press, 1995), 127.

17. See Christopher G. Wye, *Midwest Ghetto: Patterns of Change and Continuity in the Black Stucture, 1930–1945* (Kent, Ohio: Kent State University Press, 1974).

18. For a general account of the history of the Cleveland school system, including many of the difficulties and stresses it experienced at that time, see "Cleveland Public Schools," in *The Encyclopedia of Cleveland History*, available at http://ech.cwru.edu/ech-cgi/article .pl?id=CPS2 (accessed July 23, 2010). A useful account of the historical evolution of the system, viewed through the lens of race, can be found in John W. Wilson, "The Cleveland Case: Factors Contributing to the Racial Isolation and Desegregation of the Cleveland Public Schools" (Ph.D. diss., Kent State University, 1983), 69–1105.

19. Willard C. Richan, "Racial Isolation in the Cleveland Public Schools" (1967), 2, 4. See also 8–19. This study was sponsored by and prepared as a report for the U.S. Commission on Civil Rights.

20. Ibid., 38.

21. See "School Conflict Creates a Martyr," *Cleveland Plain Dealer*, April 25, 1999, D5 (discussing the events that led up to Rev. Klunder's death).

22. See Leonard N. Moore, "The School Desegregation Crisis of Cleveland, Ohio, 1963–1964," *Journal of Urban History* 28 (January 2002): 135, 151–54. According to Moore, the school board president at the time, McCallister, exacerbated matters by defending the

board's discriminatory policies "on the grounds that black students were 'educationally inferior' to white students," and racist statements by private citizens also inflamed the situation; see p. 145 (quoting a white parent as saying: "We are looking for education for our children, not for Negro sons and daughters-in-law. I don't want my grandchildren black. I am proud of my race. I want to stay white.").

23. The federal suit was preceded by unsuccessful efforts to get the state courts to enjoin further school construction, and it came after a common pleas judge had issued an injunction against various efforts of the community groups to protest at the school headquarters.

24. 234 F. Supp. 381 (N.D. Ohio 1964).

25. Judge Kalbfleisch was nominated to the U.S. District Court for the Northern District of Ohio on August 21, 1959, by President Dwight Eisenhower, to fill the seat vacated by Judge Paul C. Weick when he was nominated to the U.S. Court of Appeals for the Sixth Circuit. Judge Kalbfleisch served as chief judge from 1967 to 1969 and assumed senior status on September 30, 1970. He continued to serve until his death in 1990. Judge Kalbfleisch had presided over at least one other desegregation case in which he ruled against the plaintiffs, Lynch v. Kenston School District Board of Education, 229 F. Supp. 740 (N.D. Ohio 1964).

26. Klarman, *From Jim Crow to Civil Rights*, 23.

27. The evidence showed that the school zone in which the new schools were being constructed was 98 percent black at the time suit was filed; given the Board's neighborhood school policy, this assured that the new schools would have very few nonblack students. 234 F. Supp. at 386.

28. Ibid.

29. 338 F.2d 941 (6th Cir. 1964) (per curiam).

30. For an extended account of Briggs's tenure as superintendent of the Cleveland schools, see Kay Ellen Benjamin, "A Case Study of a Cleveland Superintendent: Paul W. Briggs, 1964–1978" (Ph.D. diss., Cleveland State University, 1995).

31. For a more extensive account of Briggs's early efforts to establish himself, see Richan, "Racial Isolation," 73–75. See also the editorial entitled "Now We Have Sound Leadership for Racial Progress," *Cleveland Press*, August 6, 1964, B6, and the editorial entitled "Superintendent Grows in Stature," *Cleveland Plain Dealer*, September 27, 1964, AA4.

32. "School Desegregation Pleas Began 150 Years Ago," *Cleveland Plain Dealer*, February 24, 1973, A8.

33. For an account of some of the measures that Briggs had undertaken that were designed to have an integrative effect, see Wilson, "Cleveland Case," 103–4.

34. "School Board Cites Progress," *Cleveland Plain Dealer*, April 24, 1973, D8.

35. See David L. Parham, "A Brief History of *Reed v. Rhodes*, the Cleveland School Desegregation Case," *Cleveland Bar Journal* 49 (February-March 1978): 49.

36. Frank J. Battisti, who at the time was a judge on the Common Pleas Court of Mahoning County, Ohio, was nominated to the federal bench by President John F. Kennedy in 1961 and was confirmed by the Senate on September 22 of that year. He was sworn in on his thirty-ninth birthday, making him the youngest federal judge in the country. He served as chief judge of the district court from 1969 to 1990 and took senior status in March 1994. See "In Memoriam: The Honorable Frank Joseph Battisti, October 4, 1922–October 19, 1994," *Cleveland State Law Review* 42 (1993–94): 367.

37. See Brent Larkin, "City's Own Top 10 for Last 100 Years," *Cleveland Plain Dealer*, December 26, 199, F1 (listing the Cleveland desegregation case as number 8 on a list of the top 10 "significant events" in the city's history).

38. See Scott Stephens and Ebony Reed, "For Blacks in Cleveland, There Were No 'Good Old Days,'" *Cleveland Plain Dealer*, May 16, 2004, A21. For an excellent account of the litigation in the Cleveland and Dayton cases, see Paul R. Dimond, *Beyond Busing* (Ann

Arbor: University of Michigan Press, 1985). School systems in Cincinnati, Youngstown, Lorain, Lima, and Chagrin Falls were also involved in litigation.

39. This is not to say that all of the other Ohio cases went smoothly. For example, in 1974 in Dayton, Dr. Charles Glatt, a court-appointed desegregation expert, was murdered in his office in the federal court building by a white parent of a Dayton public school student. Roberta Sue Alexander, *A Place of Recourse: A History of the U.S. District Court for the Southern District of Ohio, 1803–2003* (Athens: Ohio University Press, 2005), 166.

40. Reed v. Rhodes, 869 F. Supp. 1274, 1277 (N.D. Ohio 1994).

41. Reed v. Rhodes, 1992 WL 80626 (N.D. Ohio 1992).

42. An extensive account of the litigation through the early 1980s can be found in Wilson, "Cleveland Case." An overview of the case through mid-1991 can be found in section 4 of the July 1991 "Report of the Office of School and Community Relations." This report was submitted to Judge Battisti pursuant to the court's order of July 10, 1990. Thanks are due to Daniel J. McMullen for making a copy of this report available.

43. The case also generated well over five hundred orders by the court, most of which were not published. And though the defendants sought review of several unfavorable decisions of the Sixth Circuit in the U.S. Supreme Court, the Court never agreed to consider any aspect of the case on the merits. For a discussion of related cases, see David L Parham, "A Brief History of *Reed v. Rhodes*: The Cleveland School Desegregation Case," *Cleveland Bar Journal* 49 (February–March 1978): 104–6.

44. Judge Battisti died unexpectedly in 1994. See Zina Vishnevsky, "Battisti's Death Is the Result of Rare Conditions," *Cleveland Plain Dealer*, October 20, 1994, A18.

45. At the time of Battisti's death, Robert Krupansky was a senior judge on the Sixth Circuit Court of Appeals, to which he had been appointed by President Richard Nixon in 1970. Krupansky had been a member of the U.S. District Court for the Northern District of Ohio before being appointed to the Sixth Circuit. He was designated to take over part of Judge Battisti's docket, including the *Reed* case. He reviewed his initial involvement in the case in Reed v. Rhodes, 934 F. Supp. 1459, 1461 (N.D. Ohio 1996).

46. The case was transferred from Judge Krupansky to Judge White in December 1996. See Scott Stephens, "State Must Still Pay, Says Plaintiffs; Desegregation Battle Now about Lawyers' Fees," *Cleveland Plain Dealer*, September 18, 1998, B1.

47. Reed, 422 F. Supp. at 711 n.2.

48. Ibid., 712.

49. For an account of some of the highlights of the trial, see Wilson, "Cleveland Case," 106–17.

50. 422 F. Supp. at 718.

51. Ibid., 755; see also 746. An obvious irony in the broad-based objection that has been directed to the use of busing remedies in Cleveland, as well as other cities, lies in the fact that for years, school officials bused black students to predominantly black schools instead of dealing with conditions of overcrowding in ways that might have had integrative effects.

52. Intact busing was the pernicious practice of sending whole classes of black students, including their teachers, to underutilized and predominantly white schools, but refusing to allow these students to be integrated into the receiving schools.

53. 422 F. Supp. at 796. In addition to finding a violation by the Cleveland Board of Education, the court held that the Ohio Board of Education was legally responsible for the segregation in the Cleveland schools in light of its awareness of the segregation of the schools, its obligation under state law to take action to remedy that segregation, and its failure to act on that obligation.

54. 347 U.S. at 494, 563.

55. These excerpts from Flonnoy's testimony were included in the Sixth Circuit's opinion affirming the district court's liability and remedial determinations. Reed v. Rhodes, 607 F.2d 714, 732–733 (6th Cir. 1979).

56. Ibid., 733.

57. 422 F. Supp. at 722.

58. Ibid., 753. Elsewhere, the court referred to this practice of containment as "blatant." Ibid., 782.

59. Ibid., 769 (emphasis added).

60. Ibid., 783 (emphasis added), 745, 796.

61. Ibid., 779; see also 786.

62. See "Teachers Disavow Segregation Blame," *Cleveland Plain Dealer*, September 1, 1976, A11 (noting that the vote to appeal was unanimous); "School Board to Appeal Ruling," *Cleveland Plain Dealer*, September 1, 1976, A1. On his own motion, Judge Battisti facilitated the appeal by certifying the case for interlocutory appeal, 422 F. Supp. at 797. Sixth Circuit judge Weick issued a stay of the district court's injunction, 549 F.2d 1046 (6th Cir. 1976), but that stay was soon vacated by a three-judge panel, 549 F.2d 1050 (6th Cir. 1976).

63. Stephen Adams, et al., "Appellate Court Delays Start of Cleveland's Desegregation," *Cleveland Plain Dealer*, January 9, 1979, 1A; Richard G. Zimmerman, "2 Ohio Cases Vital in Desegregation Flight," *Cleveland Plain Dealer*, January 9, 1979, A14. On remand, Judge Battisti invited all parties to supplement the record with additional evidence, but none did.

64. In the Dayton school desegregation case, the Supreme Court further elaborated the principles applicable in determining when unconstitutional segregation in part of a school system could raise a presumption that the entire system was unconstitutional and thus subject to a systemwide remedy. Dayton Board of Education v. Brinkman, 433 U.S. 406 (1977). The Dayton case, as well as the Columbus desegregation case, would return to the Supreme Court two years later. See Dimond, *Beyond Busing*.

65. Reed v. Rhodes, 455 F. Supp. 546 (N.D. Ohio 1978). Judge Battisti once again pulled no punches in characterizing the conduct of the Cleveland school officials. See ibid., 563 (noting that defendants had "often converted such integrative opportunities to racially segregative nightmare [*sic*] for the children involved"), and ibid., 569.

66. 455 F. Supp. at 572.

67. For a more detailed account of the plans proposed by the school board and rejected by the court, see Wilson, "Cleveland Case," 181–209; see also "Desegregation Text from Judge Battisti," *Cleveland Plain Dealer*, May 28, 1977, A2 (describing Battisti's objections to the plans proposed by the Cleveland defendants).

68. Reed v. Rhodes, 1 F. Supp. 2d 705, 710 (N.D. Ohio 1998) (referring to the testimony of Dr. Christine Rossell).

69. For a complete list of the topics covered, see 455 F. Supp. at 572–73.

70. Ibid., 574–97.

71. Ibid., 597, 602–4, 608. The final requirement—that every school in the system have a racial composition (including faculty and administrators) that could vary no more than plus or minus 15 percent from the racial composition of the district as a whole—was generally (and pejoratively) described as a requirement of "racial balance," and it became one of the most inflammatory elements of the remedial order. It was the principal reason why three justices of the Supreme Court were later to refer to the remedy as "drastic." Cleveland Board of Education v. Reed, 445 U.S. 935 (1980) (Rehnquist, J., dissenting from the denial of certiorari).

72. 455 F. Supp. at 604–6. In recognition of the defendants' lack of financial and administrative skills and the fact that compliance with the order would entail considerable expense, Battisti ordered that the state defendants share jointly in the cost of implementation.

73. See Jean Dubail, "Judge and General: U.S. Circuit Judge Robert B. May Have Viewed the State Takeover of the Cleveland Schools as a Surgical Strike, but Now He Finds Himself Directing a Ground War," *Cleveland Plain Dealer*, November 12, 1995, C1 (describing the litigation as a "ground war").

74. John Wilson's characterization of the school board's reaction to Judge Battisti's remedial order is particularly apt: "Through numerous appeals in the media, the Board of Education demonstrated its resentment of the desegregation process as conceived by the court, it rejected busing as the solution to its problems, and it considered the court's constraints over its administration as a form of receivership." Wilson, "Cleveland Case," 231. See also Vishnevsky, "Battisti's Death" (describing the "rancor" with which Judge Battisti's ruling was received, especially with respect to the busing requirement).

75. Reed v. Rhodes, 607 F.2d 714 (6th Cir. 1979). The Supreme Court refused to review this decision, 445 U.S. 935 (1980) (denying certiorari), with three justices dissenting. The Sixth Circuit remanded for reconsideration of whether the record supported a finding of liability and remedial obligation by the Ohio Board of Education. On remand, Judge Battisti reaffirmed his conclusion that the state defendant was in part responsible for Cleveland's school segregation, 500 F. Supp. 404 (N.D. Ohio 1980), and the Sixth Circuit subsequently affirmed. 662 F.2d 1219 (6th Cir. 1981).

76. Reed v. Rhodes, 869 F. Supp. 1265 (N.D. Ohio 1994).

77. This order was published at 1992 WL 80626 (N.D. Ohio 1992).

78. Judge Battisti described the negotiation process as "protracted, arduous, uncertain, and at times, fragile." Reed v. Rhodes, 869 F. Supp. 1274, 1281 (N.D. Ohio 1994). He was profuse in his praise for McMullen, noting that without his "energy and commitment, there would not presently be a Settlement Agreement awaiting the Court's approval." Ibid., 1278. McMullen, currently a partner with Calfee, Halter & Griswold, LLP, in Cleveland, clerked for Battisti in 1982.

79. The full consent decree can be found at 869 F. Supp. at 1268–74.

80. Scott Stephens, "School District Seeks End to Court Control: Motion Filed in U.S. District Court," *Cleveland Plain Dealer*, July 2, 1997, B1.

81. "Finally," *Cleveland Plain Dealer*, February 25, 1994, B6. The *Plain Dealer* attributed the consent decree to the changeover in school board leadership that occurred in 1991, with the "reform slate of candidates" running on a "promise to resolve the desegregation suit through negotiations, rather than litigation." These previous boards, reportedly, "saw only enemies and conspiracies."

82. 869 F. Supp. at 1284.

83. Frank Battisti died on October 19, 1994, at the age of seventy-two. He died of an infection that was apparently related to an insect bite sustained while on a fishing trip to Wyoming. See Vishnevsky, "Battisti's Death."

84. Judge Krupansky recounted his taking over Battisti's docket—and the events that ensued in the months afterward—in an opinion in which he denied the plaintiffs' motion that he recuse himself from the case. Reed v. Rhodes, 934 F. Supp. 1459, 1462–63 (N.D. Ohio 1996).

85. Ibid., 1461.

86. See "It's Time to Break Glass," *Cleveland Plain Dealer*, November 17, 1994, A1, and Patricia M. Jones and Scott Stevens, "Parrish Not Invited to Meeting on Schools," *Cleveland Plain Dealer*, November 17, 1994, A1 (articles describing the political controversy between Parrish, Mayor White, and the school board).

87. Patrice M. Jones and Scott Stevens, "Parrish Quits to Return to North Carolina," *Cleveland Plain Dealer*, February 17, 1995, A1.

88. On March 3, Krupansky appointed former OSMCR director Daniel J. McMullen as special master. McMullen had left the OSMCR position at the end of September 1994.

89. 934 F. Supp. at 1463–64. See also Reed v. Rhodes, 934 F. Supp. 1533, 1537 n.1 (N.D. Ohio 1996).

90. At the time, Sanders was Ohio's superintendent of public instruction. The court's March 3 order included language making it clear that Judge Krupansky's goal was to "*expediently return the control of the schools to local authorities without supervision at the earliest practicable date, thereby making the Board accountable to the citizenry and the political elective process of the Cleveland School District.*" 934 F. Supp. at 1465n12 (emphasis in original).

91. 934 F. Supp. at 1539–40. He also noted that the local board leadership continued to find itself in turmoil and that the "self-promoting politicians and their collaborating commentators" continued to engage in "factually unsupported critical rhetoric" of the state leadership.

92. Reed v. Rhodes, 934 F. Supp. 1533 (N.D. Ohio 1996). The court applied standards that had been established in 1992 by the Supreme Court for modification of a consent decree.

93. Ibid., 1551; see also 1552.

94. Judge Krupansky's rather charitable characterization of the defendants' conduct also seemed to gloss over such events as Judge Battisti's initiation of contempt proceedings against the Cleveland Board of Education and a number of school officials. See Wilson, "Cleveland Case," 220–21. See also "Battisti Jails School Board Officials," *Cleveland Plain Dealer,* September 1, 1981, A4 (noting that Judge Battisti had jailed the school board treasurer and president for contempt).

95. In each of the previous appeals of Judge Battisti's decisions, the Sixth Circuit panel was unanimous. (Judge Weick, acting as a single judge, had issued decisions critical of Judge Battisti, but his actions were set aside by a three-judge panel.)

96. Reed v. Rhodes, 179 F.3d 453 (6th Cir. 1999). Judge Edmunds, a federal district court judge, sat by designation. The Sixth Circuit consolidated Judge Krupansky's decision modifying the consent decree and declaring unitary status with his earlier decisions denying plaintiffs' recusal motion and adjudicating the plaintiffs' application for an award of attorneys fees. The latter decision is reported at 934 F. Supp. 1492 (N.D. Ohio 1996).

97. But see William D. Henderson, "Demography and Desegregation in the Cleveland Public Schools: Toward a Comprehensive Theory of Educational Failure and Success," *Review of Law and Social Change* 26 (2001–2): 461 (where Henderson impressively argues that the demographic changes that Cleveland experienced and the "dismal condition in the Cleveland schools, [have] little if anything to do with the desegregation order").

98. 179 F. 3d at 463. The court referred to the 1988 testimony of an expert, Dr. Gordon Foster, that Cleveland was the only large, majority black school system in the country that was "totally desegregated."

99. Ibid., 465.

100. 503 U.S. 467 (1992).

101. 179 F.3d at 473 (Cole, J., dissenting).

102. Ibid., 475.

103. Ibid., 478, 484.

104. Krupansky continued to serve on the Sixth Circuit until his death on November 8, 2004.

105. The consent decree provided that on or after July 1, 1997, the parties could move the court to hold hearings to determine whether all requirements of the decree and any outstanding remedial orders had been complied with, and it set out three criteria to be applied in making that determination. 869 F. Supp. at 1273 ("Section 15—Compliance Hearing"). The provisions that were to continue until July 2000 included: the continuing oversight of the agreement by an individual to be appointed to cabinet rank by both the

Cleveland Board of Education and the Ohio Department of Education, the continuing financial support of the school district by the state, and the ongoing implementation of a facilities plan.

106. Reed v. Rhodes, 1 F. Supp. 3d 705 (N.D. Ohio 1998). Judge White's decision was handed down before the Sixth Circuit decided the appeal of Judge Krupansky's 1996 decision modifying the consent decree and declaring partial unitary status.

107. 215 F.3d 1327 (6th Cir. 2000) (per curiam).

108. Stephens and Reed, "For Blacks in Cleveland."

109. The decision to settle the case at an early stage may have been influenced by the recommendation to do so by Dr. G. Robert Bowers, the Ohio Assistant Superintendent of Public Instruction in the Ohio Department of Education. Dr. Bowers, who had also been involved in the Cleveland, Columbus, Dayton and Cincinnati desegregation cases, advised the Lorain school Superintendent to settle the case because he believed that the defendants would ultimately be found liable. See Lorain NAACP v. Lorain Board of Education, 768 F. Supp. 1224, 1238 (N.D. Ohio, 1991).

110. Ibid. Judge Dowd's decision was ultimately reversed by the Sixth Circuit. Lorain NAACP v. Lorain Board of Education, 979 F.2d 1141 (6th Cir. 1992). The fact that Judge Dowd's decision on this matter and the Sixth Circuit's decision reversing him were the only two published opinions in the entire Lorain litigation in itself provides a dramatic contrast with the Cleveland case, where the parties' ongoing and longstanding contentiousness led to multiple reported decisions.

111. While Judge Dowd found that the Lorain schools had fallen short of the minority recruitment goals established in the consent decree, he concluded that under recently decided Supreme Court and Sixth Circuit cases, those goals had proven unrealistic and constitutionally indefensible. Although the order effectively terminated the litigation, over the next eight months the parties continued to skirmish over the plaintiffs' application for attorneys fees.

112. 42 U.S.C. § 2000(a)–(e) (1964). The act specifically authorized the U.S. Justice Department to bring school desegregation actions.

113. Klarman, From Jim Crow to Civil Rights, 79–104.

114. Report of the National Advisory Commission on Civil Disorders, Report 225 (1968).

115. United States v. Parma, 494 F. Supp. 1049, 1057 (N.D. Ohio 1980).

116. Douglas S. Massey and Nancy Denton, "Hypersegregation in U.S. Metropolitan Areas: Black and Hispanic Segregation along Five Dimensions," Demography 26 (1989): 373, 382. For other studies addressing the migration of blacks to northern urban areas and the resultant racial segregation in housing, see A. Taeuber and K. Taeuber, Negroes in Cities: Residential Segregation and Neighborhood Change (Chicago: Aldine, 1965), and C. V. Woodward, The Strange Career of Jim Crow, 2nd ed. (New York: Oxford University Press,1966). For discussion of residential housing discrimination in the Cleveland area, see W. Dennis Keating, "Open Housing in Metropolitan Cleveland," in Keating, Krumholz, and Perry, Cleveland, 300.

117. See J. Kain and J. Quigley, Housing Markets and Racial Discrimination: A Microeconomic Analysis (New York: National Bureau of Economic Research, 1975), 84–85 (charting changes in population by race from 1950 to 1960 in Cleveland and nine other cities).

118. For a general discussion of these practices, see Stanley P. Stocker-Edwards, "Black Housing, 1860–1980: The Development, Perpetuation, and Attempts to Eradicate the Dual Housing Market in America," Harvard BlackLetter Law Journal 5 (1989): 50.

119. 341 F. Supp. 1175 (N.D. Ohio 1972), aff'd. and rev'd. in part, 473 F.2d 910 (6th Cir. 1973) (table).

120. The court enjoined the city from failing to issue the permits necessary for the construction of the public housing projects in question. Ibid., 1180. It also enjoined the CMHA from "planning any further public housing in Negro neighborhoods of the city of Cleveland." Ibid., 1185.

121. Ibid., at 1178, 1182.

122. 355 F. Supp. 1245 (N.D. Ohio 1973).

123. The assignment of a number of post-*Banks* housing discrimination cases was probably not fortuitous. Under the rules governing the Northern District of Ohio at the time, a plaintiff could designate a case as a "related case" (i.e., related to *Banks*), all but assuring the assignment of the new case to the same judge who had presided over the related case. Avery Friedman, interview with the author, June 23, 2010.

124. Besides the CMHA, plaintiffs named as defendants a number of Cleveland suburbs, including Euclid, Garfield Heights, Solon, and Parma, together with their mayors and council members.

125. 355 F. Supp. at 1250.

126. Ibid., 1255. Judge Lambros emphasized racial remarks made by one of the Parma defendants, the troubling racial demographics of Cuyahoga County, and the clear discriminatory effects of the local consent requirement.

127. Apparently, the case was remanded for consideration of the plaintiffs' claim under 42 U.S.C. § 1983, which the three-judge court had declined to consider, although this statute seemed to have provided the only basis for the claims that the court had actually decided.

128. Mahaley v. Cuyahoga Metropolitan Housing Authority, 355 F. Supp. 1257, 1266 (N.D. Ohio 1973), *rev'd*, 500 F.2d 1087 (6th Cir. 1974).

129. Ibid., 1269. In a move that only added to the unorthodoxy of the decision, the suburban defendants were urged to enter into negotiations with CMHA in an effort to reach an amicable resolution of their differences; failing that, a hearing would be held at which the defendants might have another chance to persuade the court that their actions were not illegal.

130. 500 F.2d 1087 (6th Cir. 1974). Among other things, the court criticized Judge Battisti's remedy for treating the case like a school desegregation case. It also concluded that the three-judge panel had correctly found the relevant statutes constitutional and constitutionally applied and that any discriminatory effect associated with the failure of the Cleveland suburbs to create low-income housing was not sufficient to establish a constitutional violation.

131. Ibid., 1094 (Edwards, J., dissenting). Three of the grounds for Edwards's dissent were based on procedural or jurisdictional considerations. The fourth posited that the plaintiffs should be allowed to pursue their substantive claims at trial.

132. As noted earlier, other cities within the jurisdictional bounds of the Northern District, including Lorain and Youngstown, were also involved in school desegregation suits. In a thoughtful letter to the author, Judge David Dowd emphasized that a full account of civil rights litigation in the district during the last quarter of the twentieth century should include the stories of these (and other) cases as well. Letter to author from Judge David D. Dowd, June 21, 2010. Although Judge Dowd is surely correct, space and time constraints preclude their inclusion here. It is also worth noting that *Banks*, *Mahaley*, and the *Parma* case were not the only housing discrimination cases brought during that period. See, e.g., Skillken v. City of Toledo, 380 F. Supp. 228 (N.D. Ohio 1974), *rev'd and remanded*, 528 F.2d 867 (6th Cir. 1975), *vacated*, 429 U.S. 1068 (1977), *on remand* 558 F.2d 350, *cert. denied*, 434 U.S. 985 (1977) (extended litigation challenging alleged racial discrimination in failure by Toledo, Ohio, zoning officials to rezone certain areas to permit construction of low-rent housing).

133. 341 F. Supp. at 1175. He went on to set out statistics that described the extent of this racial division.

134. 355 F. Supp. at 1260.

135. 500 F.2d at 1094.

136. 355 F. Supp. at 1253–55.

137. W. Dennis Keating, *The Suburban Racial Dilemma* (Philadelphia: Temple University Press, 1994), 14.

138. Demographic tables showing the black percentages of the population in Cleveland and many of its surrounding suburbs in 1970 can be found at United States v. Parma, 494 F. Supp. 1049, 1056 (N.D. Ohio 1980). By 1980, Parma's black population had increased only marginally, remaining under 1 percent of the total population. Keating, *Suburban Racial Dilemma*, 140. It is worth noting that many more blacks worked in Parma than lived there. 494 F. Supp. at 1057.

139. 494 F. Supp. at 1057.

140. Shortly before this suit was filed, the DOJ filed a similar suit against Parma. That suit focused on the city's refusal to issue a building permit to allow the construction of a federally assisted, low-income housing apartment development, as well as its enactment of ordinances regulating the height of new residential buildings and a local referendum on any involvement by the city in any federal rent subsidy program. The DOJ suit was consolidated with a suit brought by private plaintiffs, including the Cleveland branch of the NAACP, challenging Parma's housing policies as discriminatory. This suit, *Cornelius v. City of Parma*, 374 F. Supp. 730 (N.D. Ohio 1974), was assigned to Judge Battisti while the appeal in the *Mahaley* litigation was still pending. As noted earlier, Parma was also a defendant in *Mahaley*. Judge Battisti held that none of the plaintiffs in *Cornelius* had legal standing to sue. The Sixth Circuit ultimately remanded the case, and the Supreme Court refused to review, 506 F.2d 1401 (6th Cir. 1975), *cert. denied*, 424 U.S. 955 (1976). The *Cornelius* suit was eventually consolidated with *United States v. Parma* (which will be discussed).

While *Cornelius* was pending, Parma made the dramatic move of filing its own suit in federal court to enjoin the United States from seeking to enforce the Fair Housing Act against the city, claiming that the statute did not apply to it, and that if it did, the statute was unconstitutional. This suit was also assigned to Judge Battisti, who, in an unreported decision that was affirmed by the Sixth Circuit, dismissed it on procedural grounds. City of Parma v. Levi, 536 F.2d 133 (6th Cir. 1976).

141. See Philip J. Cooper, *Hard Judicial Choices: Federal District Court Judges and State and Local Officials* (New York: Oxford University Press, 1988), 47–84.

142. See Marv Silver, "A Taxing Decision in Parma," *Cleveland Plain Dealer*, November 29, 1996, B10.

143. 494 F. Supp. at 1065–66 (quoting from deposition of Cleveland mayor Carl Stokes). Among the statements made by Parma officials was Parma City Council president Kenneth Kuczma's remark, "I do not want Negroes to live in the City of Parma." Ibid., 1065. Kuczma had also stated that the "people of Parma" were "fearful" of Negroes coming into the city and that he himself had that fear. Ibid., 1079. Another council member asked a local HUD official whether he knew "that we don't want blacks in Parma." Ibid., 1080.

144. Ibid., 1097. The court held for the plaintiff on both its racial intent theory and its effects theory.

145. United States v. Parma, 471 F. Supp. 453, 454 (N.D. Ohio 1979).

146. Silver, "Taxing Decision."

147. 494 F. Supp. at 1099.

148. Cooper, *Hard Judicial Choices*, 64.

149. United States v. Parma, 504 F. Supp. 913 (N.D. Ohio 1980). Parma's appeal of the liability decision was dismissed. 633 F.2d 218 (6th Cir. 1980) (table).

150. 504 F. Supp. at 916.

151. "Parma Labels Battisti Housing Cure 'H-bomb,'" *Cleveland Plain Dealer*, October 16, 1980, B4.

152. To ensure the creation of low-income housing, Parma was required either to sign a cooperation agreement with CMHA or to establish its own housing authority. 504 F. Supp. at 922. Ultimately, it did the latter.

153. Parma appealed the liability decision and the remedial order. The Sixth Circuit initially granted a stay of the remedy pending deliberation on the merits. 644 F.2d 887 (6th Cir. 1981) (table). In its decision on the merits, the court affirmed the liability determination and most of the remedial order, with two exceptions — the specific requirement that Parma create at least 133 units of low-income housing per year, which it found premature, and the creation of a special master, which it reversed. 661 F.2d 562 (6th Cir. 1981), *cert. denied*, 456 U.S. 926 (1982). Interestingly, Sixth Circuit judge Weick, who had earlier found Parma's effort to obtain interlocutory relief meritorious, wrote an opinion dissenting from the denial of en banc review. 669 F.2d 1100 (6th Cir. 1981). Weick blasted Judge Battisti, in what surely was a curious and perhaps intemperate statement, for "tarring and feathering" the "entire population" of the communities, including Parma, in the several housing discrimination cases over which he had presided. Ibid., 1101. He also accused Battisti of issuing "extreme orders," and he felt moved to commiserate with Parma, claiming that it "had not met with much favor" in the Sixth Circuit either. Ibid., 1103. In Weick's mind, it was not the black citizens of the Cleveland area who had cause to complain but Parma, which had been inflicted with a "grievous wrong" by the federal government and the federal courts. Ibid., 1104.

154. Accounts of the remedial process can be found in Keating, *Suburban Racial Dilemma*, 143–48, and Cooper, *Hard Judicial Choices*, 73–80. Although a number of obstacles and disagreements arose, the remedial process was nowhere near as contentious as the one in *Reed* had been.

155. Judge Battisti's original plan to appoint a special master had been overturned by the Sixth Circuit. Friedman's position was unpaid, and he did not have the formal powers assignable to that position, but there were periods where he was functioning as in effect a quasi or de facto master. Friedman interview.

156. Friedman's proposals are summarized in Cooper, *Hard Judicial Choices*, 78.

157. Parma was successful in getting an emergency stay of the sanctions from the Sixth Circuit, but the appeal was ultimately dismissed. 774 F.2d 1164 (6th Cir. 1985).

158. Editorial entitled "A Welcoming Atmosphere; Hard Work Has Brought Parma within Sight of Discrimination Suit's End," *Cleveland Plain Dealer*, November 20, 1996, B10.

159. See Agreement and Dismissal in United States v. Parma, available at http://www .justice.gov/crt/housing/documents/parmasettle.php; editorial entitled "Parma's New Welcome Wagon," *Cleveland Plain Dealer*, April 5, 1997, B10.

160. See "Welcoming Atmosphere"; Tom Breckenridge, "Court OKs Parma Plan; City to Offset Housing Practices," *Cleveland Plain Dealer*, November 16, 1996, B1.

161. These were, of course, not the only cases in which social and racial justice was at stake. Some of their stories are told in other chapters in this volume

162. Indeed, one might argue that this doubt has still not been resolved.

163. See "School Desegregation Pleas Here Began."

164. Green v. County School Board, 391 U.S. 430 (1968) (holding that a school board's duty was to produce a plan "that promises realistically to work, and promises realistically to work now").

165. Klarman, *From Jim Crow to Civil Rights,* 224.

166. See, e.g., "Judge Battisti Denies He's Trying to Run Schools," *Cleveland Press,* May 15, 1980, A10; "Battisti Lashes Back at Critics: 'I Didn't Impoverish Schools,'" *Cleveland Plain Dealer,* February 8, 1978, A6.

167. 1992 WL 80626, at *5.

168. Alexander, *Place of Recourse.*

169. Ibid., 1 (citations omitted).

170. Editorial entitled "Battisti: They Praised Him, They Damned Him," *Cleveland Plain Dealer,* September 1, 1976, A11 (quoting Judge Battisti as saying, during the course of the *Reed* litigation, that "this is the place where we reason together").

171. At one point, Judge Battisti felt compelled to lament the "senseless anger" the desegregation controversy had generated in the community. 1992 WL 80626, at *1.

172. Nathaniel Jones, a lead lawyer for the plaintiffs in *Reed* and subsequently a distinguished judge on the U.S. Court of Appeals, once noted in a tribute to Judge Battisti that the desegregation decision "brought the Fourteenth Amendment to Cleveland, the notion that all children are equal." Vishnevsky, "Battisti's Death" (quoting Nathaniel Jones).

173. 1 F. Supp. 2d at 756.

174. 179 F.2d at 473.

175. See Diane Ravitch, "School Reform: Past, Present, and Future," *Case Western Law Review* 51 (2000): 187 (noting that the Cleveland school system continued to experience serious racial segregation). See also Byron F. Lutz, "Post *Brown vs. the Board of Education*: The Effects of the End of Court-Ordered Desegregation," 2005, staff working paper no. 2005–64, issued by Division of Research and Statistics and Monetary Affairs, Federal Reserve Board, Washington, D.C. (noting that the dismissal of court-ordered desegregation plans in general produce a gradual increase in racial segregation).

The record in Parma is also a mixed one. Recall that when *United States v. Parma* was filed, less than .04 percent of the residents of the city were black. According to press accounts, black residency had increased to around 1 percent by 1996, although a number of processes and significant resources were in place to assist black home buyers interested in living in the city. See Silver, "Taxing Decision," for discussion of modest progress in Parma into the early 1990s, and Keating, "Open Housing in Metropolitan Cleveland," 303.

176. 347 U.S. at 494.

177. 934 F. Supp. at 1555.

178. Ravitch, "School Reform," 190.

179. "Students in Class of '80 Recall Effect of Busing on Their Schools, Lives," *Cleveland Plain Dealer,* May 16, 2004, A21.

180. Cleveland Board of Education v. Reed, 445 U.S. at 1331 (Rehnquist, J., dissenting from the denial of certiorari).

181. Note Judge Krupansky's admonition that the "responsibility to address and correct the underlying sociological conditions that significantly undermine the Cleveland School District" could not be borne only by the courts or even the school system itself. 934 F. Supp. at 1556.

182. Cass Sunstein, "Did *Brown* Matter?" in Rhode and Ogletree, *"Brown"* at 50, 125 (proposing such a standard).

183. Chris Sheridan, "*Brown* Ruling Was Only a Beginning," *Cleveland Plain Dealer,* May 23, 2004, H2.

184. This is, of course, not to diminish the leadership and courage of many other Clevelanders whose civil rights activism was instrumental in helping to further the spirit and promise of the Fourteenth Amendment and *Brown.* The list of such persons is large, but it surely includes folks such as Bruce Klunder, Daisy and Charles Craggett, James Hardiman,

and the members and leaders of such organizations as the Cleveland Chapter of the NAACP, the Relay Parents March to Fill Empty Classrooms, and the United Freedom Movement.

185. See Vishnevsky, "Battisti's Death" (noting that Battisti "was called independent by some and dictatorial by others"). In interviews and communications with his former clerks and friends, Battisti was described to this author as deeply religious, warm, compassionate, and invariably gracious. These traits were a common theme in the many memorial comments made after his death. See, e.g., David F. Forte, "Lunch with Frank Battisti," *Cleveland State Law Review* 42 (1993–94): 371; Daniel J. McMullen, "On Heroes and Idealists," *Cleveland State Law Review* 42 (1993–94): 373; Harry Stainer, "Battisti Given Final Farewell; Friend Calls Him Martyr for Kids," *Cleveland Plain Dealer*, October 23, 1994, B1.

186. "Battisti: They Praised Him." According to this observer, Battisti was described as "opinionated" and "impatient" during the trial, as well as a judge "who never shied away from controversial cases."

187. See, e.g., J. W. Peltason, *Fifty Eight Lonely Men: Southern Federal Judges and School Desegregation* (New York: Harcourt, Brace and World, 1961); Jack Bass, *Taming the Storm: The Life and Times of Judge Frank Johnson, Jr., and the South's Fight over Civil Rights* (New York: Doubleday, 1993).

188. Editorial entitled "Judge Frank Battisti," *Cleveland Plain Dealer*, October 20, 1994 (noting that Judge Battisti endured "years of being vilified, of death threats directed at him and his family").

189. Nathaniel R. Jones, "Judge Frank Battisti and the Promises He Kept," *Cleveland State Law Review* 42 (1994): 367.

190. Memorial Resolution for Frank J. Battisti, 1996 Annual Report and Roster of Judges.

6

The Struggle for Gender Equality in the Northern District of Ohio

Tracy A. Thomas

T HE U.S. DISTRICT Court for the Northern District of Ohio, like many of its sister courts, was reluctantly drawn into the national debate over sex equality in the 1970s. The court's response mirrored the greater social response, initially showing a hostility to claims of gender discrimination that was slowly displaced by recognition and endorsement of sex equality rights. Three of the district's cases on women's rights that went to the U.S. Supreme Court, discussed in this chapter, helped navigate this shift toward gender equality.

The Northern District was goaded into action by the newly formed Women's Law Fund (WLF), one of the first nonprofit litigation organizations in the nation to bring sex discrimination claims. The WLF was led by Jane Picker, one of the first female law professors at Cleveland State University, and counseled by board member Ruth Bader Ginsburg, then head of the American Civil Liberties Union (ACLU) Women's Rights Project and later a U.S. Supreme Court justice. These leaders instigated the reforms needed through the judicial process, believing, like many social justice groups, that the courts were the best vehicles to bring about change. In 1971, the Fund's first case, *LaFleur v. Cleveland Board of Education*, challenged mandatory maternity leaves for pregnant teachers.[1] As this chapter will show, the lawyers encountered an incredulous court and resistance from the community as they took on deeply embedded notions of the proper role of women in the workplace and family.

The community backlash continued as advocates sought to protect a woman's right to bodily autonomy and abortion. In 1973, the Supreme Court legalized abortion in *Roe v. Wade*.[2] The *Roe* Court recognized a fundamental privacy right to choose abortion, free from governmental interference in the first trimester, but new regulations continued to circumscribe abortion. Two major abortion regulation cases came before the Northern District on their way to the Supreme Court: *Akron Center for Reproductive Health v. City of Akron* and *Akron Center for Reproductive Health v. Rosen*.[3] The Northern District wrestled with the legality of highly detailed regulations designed to discourage abortion, first upholding them in part but later invalidating the laws. The Supreme Court overruled the lower courts in both cases. Although the district courts had carefully tried to fit the cases within constitutional parameters, they had not predicted the Supreme Court's changing standards.

These three cases from Ohio together offer a snapshot of the larger societal change for women's rights. The nascent women's movement in the courts proceeded initially along dual fronts of employment and abortion. The Northern District cases show the tensions and commonalities between these approaches and exemplify the development of broad-scale gender litigation across the nation.

A Reluctant Agent of Change

In April 1971, the Northern District of Ohio was confronted with one of its earliest cases of sex discrimination. In *LaFleur v. Cleveland Board of Education*, Jo Carol LaFleur, a junior high teacher at an all-black inner-city school in Cleveland, challenged the board's policy of requiring unpaid maternity leave for all married female teachers who were more than four months pregnant. The rule also prohibited a teacher from returning to her job prior to the first school term after her child was three months old, and it did not guarantee her a position, but only a priority for any vacancy. These maternity policies were part of the long history of discrimination by schools against women, which forced married and then pregnant women to resign their jobs.[4]

The Cleveland maternity leave policy enacted in 1952 was passed because male administrators thought that it was inappropriate for schoolchildren to see a pregnant woman and confront the obvious implications of sexuality. As testimony would show, the policy was motivated by school officials' desire to save a noticeably pregnant woman from embarrassment in the form of giggling schoolchildren and their comments such as "my teacher swallowed a watermelon," and to protect students from the sight of a conspicuously pregnant woman.[5] But the board rationalized its policy during the *LaFleur* litigation as being important to protecting the health of the woman and baby and to providing continuity of instruction for the children. The school superintendent who drafted the original regulation believed that women should stay home with their children after giving birth: "I am a strong believer that young children ought to have the mother there to take tender care of the babies." Many of America's problems, he suggested, stemmed from working mothers who neglected their infants.[6]

LaFleur thought the policy was "archaic and silly" and refused to quit her job. She believed that since her baby was due in July, leaving at the end of the semester better served continuity of instruction rather than leaving abruptly in mid-March as the principal insisted. (LaFleur had refused to tell the principal her due date, so he was guessing as to the four-month point.) Furthermore, students who were pregnant were allowed to attend school throughout their pregnancies, and LaFleur taught some of these pregnant students in a transition class for girls who were at risk for dropping out of school. The idealistic LaFleur had wanted to teach these students out of her emerging sense of social justice, utilizing the specialized training she received in "ghetto teaching" in a master of teaching program she completed at John Carroll University. She thought that she could serve as a good role model for her students, being a married woman who was taking care of herself and her baby during pregnancy. The principal disagreed, and tempers flared as he forced LaFleur out by completing the leave forms for her.[7]

It was difficult for LaFleur to find a lawyer to take her case. She filed a grievance with the teacher's union, but the union representative told her to "just go home and have your baby." She tried the Cleveland branch of the ACLU, but it turned down her case, saying it was "a loser." The organization was instead focusing its litigation efforts on cases for male students challenging school bans on beards as a denial of fundamental rights.[8] Desperate, LaFleur called the library at the *Cleveland Plain Dealer* looking for the name of a "women's lib" group. The newspaper librarian gave her several numbers, including that for the Women's Equity Action League (WEAL), through which she reached volunteer attorney Jane Picker.[9]

WEAL was founded in Cleveland in 1968 and later headquartered in Washington, D.C., until it disbanded in 1989. It was formed as a small spin-off from the National Organization of Women (NOW) by more conservative feminists wishing to avoid issues of abortion and sexuality. Its founder, Dr. Elizabeth Boyer, explained: "There's a great difference between the women's liberation movement and the women's rights movement which WEAL represents."[10] WEAL believed that the abortion issue would discredit the emerging feminist movement and "feminist respectability." Instead, the group focused its agenda on the advancement of opportunities for women in education and employment, including monitoring implementation and enforcement of Title IX of the 1972 Education Act Amendments regarding equal opportunity for women in education and sports.[11]

Picker became a WEAL volunteer attorney when she moved to Cleveland in the fall of 1970. A Yale Law School graduate, she relocated to Cleveland when her husband, Sidney, was hired as a visiting professor at Case Western Reserve School of Law. When Sidney was offered a permanent position in December 1970, Picker began to look for a job but found it extraordinarily difficult to find a firm willing to hire a woman. Such resistance led her to conclude that Cleveland was "the most conservative city" she had ever seen. She had been raised in the East, lived abroad in Bangkok and Australia, and worked in Washington, D.C., and never before had she been aware of being discriminated against as a woman as she was in Cleveland. Squire, Sanders & Dempsey eventually hired her as the firm's first female lawyer to work as an attorney. (Two other female lawyers worked at the firm, one as a law librarian and one as a secretary.) However, the firm denied her the opportunity to litigate cases as she desired and instead relegated her to "public law" and backroom research. When the call came from LaFleur in early 1971, Picker was conflicted out of the case because the firm and her partner Charles Clarke represented the defendant, the Cleveland School Board.

Another WEAL volunteer, Carol Agin, tried the case. But Picker handled all of the research and wrote the briefs. It was her idea to plead the case under 42 U.S.C. § 1983 as a federal claim for constitutional violations of civil rights. Picker had been sent to the Cleveland law library on an assignment from the firm. While there, she began flipping through the federal employment reporters and read the many cases of successful race discrimination litigation under section 1983. She thought that the same approach should work for sex, and she used the general contours of the Fourteenth Amendment to frame the legal issues in *LaFleur.*[12]

The case was assigned to Judge James Connell, a crusty and conservative seventy-three-year-old former prosecutor who "was very unfriendly to the case." He was "very old school" and "believed a woman's place was in the home, and therefore, certainly, a pregnant woman's place was in the home." Judge Connell called a pretrial hearing immediately after the papers in the case were filed, just weeks after LaFleur was forced out of her job. He greeted the counsel for the school board, Charles Clarke, in a welcoming and gentlemanly manner. He then turned to Carol Agin and said, "Young woman, why do you waste the federal court's time with such frivolous matters?" Concerned that the court's apparent bias would prejudice the plaintiff, Picker asked her neighbor, Case Western law professor Lewis Katz, to serve as co-counsel in the case. As Katz explained, "You have to understand. Women were treated very shabbily in and by the profession at that time, and for some years after."[13] Indeed, it would be twenty years before judicial task forces on gender fairness would denounce this type of gender bias in the courts.[14]

The two-day hearing in the *LaFleur* case was, according to Katz, "extremely unpleasant." Judge Connell clearly thought this case was ridiculous, and he directed his wrath toward the plaintiffs, sustaining objections that had not been made and rephrasing many of attorney Agin's questions. Meanwhile, a second plaintiff had joined the case—Ann Nelson, the wife of one of Katz's law students. The student had come to Katz at midsemester in need of a scholarship when his pregnant wife lost her job as a Cleveland junior high school teacher. Teachers in their first year of teaching, as Ann Nelson was, were terminated if they became pregnant, rather than given leave and the opportunity to return.

Plaintiffs' counsel worked to debunk the proffered medical evidence that there was a risk to the woman and baby if the mother worked during pregnancy. Their own medical expert, Sarah Marcus, was a feisty, eighty-year-old obstetrician who mocked the school district's assumptions about women's frailty. She noted that most women engaged in strenuous work at home: "There is nothing that the teacher does as a teacher that is any more strenuous than what a pregnant mother does with housework; and her attentions to the other children, if she has any, are also strenuous."[15] Katz tried to cross-examine the defense's medical expert despite the judge's interruptions—Judge Connell believed he had a good understanding of the medical science, having grown up as the son of an Akron obstetrician—and Katz did get the defense expert to admit that work did not negatively impact a woman's pregnancy, a point that would be central on appeal. Defense counsel focused on the disabilities of the pregnant woman.

He asked LaFleur whether this was her first baby, to which the seven-month-pregnant woman responded, "Yes." Later, she realized that she would have answered differently had he asked her if this was her first pregnancy; she had been pregnant before but miscarried early while she was teaching first grade. That answer might have fueled the misconception that teaching was harmful to the baby.[16]

At the end of the trial, plaintiffs asked for an injunction to stay the board's decisions. Judge Connell coldly responded, "You'll get what you deserve and you don't deserve an injunction."[17] The court denied their request for preliminary and permanent injunctive relief, finding the school board policy to be reasonable and constitutionally permissible. Judge Connell determined that the mandatory maternity regulation was reasonable primarily because it minimized classroom distractions and disruptions when the "teachers suffered many indignities as a result of pregnancy which consisted of children pointing, giggling, laughing and making snide remarks causing interruption and interference with the classroom program of study." He also found that the problem of the teacher's health and safety was a valid concern for the school board in that "in an environment where the possibility of violence and accident exists, pregnancy greatly magnifies the probability of serious injury."[18] The plaintiffs urged the court to apply a more rigorous level of judicial scrutiny due to the fundamental nature of the interests involved. The district court, however, relied on the 1908 Supreme Court case of *Muller v. Oregon*, which upheld a maximum hours law to protect women. Judge Connell quoted: "The two sexes differ in structure of body, in the functions to be performed by each, in the amount of physical strength, in the capacity for long continued labor, particularly when done standing, the influence of vigorous health upon the future well-being of the race, the self-reliance which enables one to assert full rights, and in the capacity to maintain the struggle for subsistence."[19]

On appeal, the U.S. Court of Appeals for the Sixth Circuit reversed Judge Connell's decision, finding the maternity rule arbitrary and unreasonable in its overbreadth. In a 2-to-1 decision, the majority found that the school board's justifications were not reasonable and barely credible: "Basic rights such as those involved in the employment relationship cannot be made to yield to embarrassment." In rejecting the mandatory leave rule, the Sixth Circuit relied on *Reed v. Reed*, decided after the *LaFleur* trial court decision, in which the Supreme Court held for the first time that sex was a classification deserving of heightened scrutiny under the Equal Protection Clause.[20]

When the Supreme Court granted certiorari in the *LaFleur* case, Jane Picker took over as lead counsel. By then she had left her law firm and was one of three tenure-track female law professors at Cleveland State University. Picker created the Women's Law Fund in 1972 to finance precedent-setting litigation for women's rights.[21] Like other litigation advocacy groups of the times modeled after the National Association for the Advancement of Colored People and its success in the school desegregation cases, the WLF existed to fund rights litigation and bring about meaningful social change through the courts. Law professor Ruth Bader Ginsburg served on the board of the WLF, and Picker reciprocated, serving on Ginsburg's board at the ACLU Women's Rights Project, also organized in 1972. Ginsburg had taken pro bono referrals for the New Jersey ACLU since the late 1960s, cases that were referred to her, she said, because "sex discrimination cases were regarded as a woman's job." She accepted the cases because of her impression that the ACLU nationally and locally was not enthusiastic about taking on women's rights cases and that women were not adequately represented on the organization's governing board. The ACLU first focused its efforts on sex discrimination in the fall of 1971 when it declared women's rights an issue of great urgency and asked all affiliates to give it high priority in funding and litigation.[22] Feminist litigation began to take on a national agenda as attorneys in the sex discrimination cases shared information and coordinated efforts. As Justice Ginsburg reflected, "Progress does not occur automatically, but requires a concerted effort to change habitual modes of thinking and action."[23] Picker agreed: "It was no simple evolution. We made the change that happened."[24]

The WLF was initially funded by generous grants from the Ford Foundation. Spurred by tenacious female staff members, Ford was the earliest philanthropy to commit to the women's movement.[25] The foundation's first feminist pilot project was the *LaFleur* case. Ford began negotiations for a litigation grant with Jane Picker as a representative of WEAL. When Picker's WEAL colleagues objected to litigating a case dealing with pregnancy discrimination, she left the organization, taking with her Ford's money for a two-year start-up grant for the WLF. But in 1984, Ford's WLF funding ended: in the 1980s, a change in leadership at Ford shifted its emphasis to issues affecting women of color and poor and working-class women.[26] Picker turned elsewhere for financial support, moving her organization to the Cleveland-Marshall College of Law, where she established a sex discrimination clinic staffed by students and funded primarily by attorney fee awards.[27]

The *LaFleur* case was the WLF's first and perhaps biggest case. Picker argued the case before the U.S. Supreme Court in January 1974 in what was her first argument of any kind before a court. Amicus briefs flowed in on both sides. Delta Air Lines, which fired pregnant stewardesses, supported the school board. The Nixon administration, in the heat of the Watergate cover-up, sided with the teachers. Picker's sense was that the Court was not taking this case seriously. Just before the argument, she saw the justices passing around a journal article called "Love's Labors Lost: New Conceptions of Maternity Leaves," and she watched them chuckle like schoolboys.[28] She began her argument more angry than nervous. The first question from Justice Harry Blackmun asked her whether she really saw any difference between a man losing his job because he refused to shave his beard and a woman losing her job because she was pregnant. The tall and imposing Picker put her hands on her hips and said that such analogies between fashion and a child were "indeed ludicrous."[29]

The Supreme Court ruled for the women but rejected the equality analysis urged by Picker and the appellate court. Instead, the Court grounded its decision in due process privacy rights, harkening back to *Roe v. Wade* and the right to choose an abortion, decided just one year before. "This Court has long recognized that freedom of personal choice in matters of marriage and family life is one of the liberties protected by the Due Process Clause. By acting to penalize the pregnant teacher for deciding to bear a child, overly restrictive maternity leave regulations can constitute a heavy burden on the exercise of these protected freedoms." The opinion by Justice Potter Stewart emphasized the procedural aspects of due process in its concern over the school board's irrebuttable presumption that pregnant women were unable to continue working later in their pregnancies, rather than using a more individualized determination. The Court also rejected the board's purported reasons of continuity of instruction and maternal health, noting that the policy was originally inspired by "other, less weighty considerations" and the "outmoded taboos" of saving pregnant teachers from the embarrassment of giggling students and insulating children from the sight of a conspicuously pregnant woman.[30]

The Court's decision to abandon the equal protection claim and all of its promise for women's rights infuriated Picker.[31] Counsel for the school board had urged this approach, cautioning the Court in his rebuttal that the question of equal protection was "one of the most evasive issues that this Court has to determine" and that "with all due respect to my sisters at the bar, [it] does go somewhat beyond the narrow issue in this case."[32] The case as litigated, however, clearly presented the issue of equal protection, even if the Court was unwilling to go there. Justice Blackmun's conference papers and memorandum on *LaFleur* acknowledged that equal protection would have provided an "easier" and "cleaner" basis for the decision but indicated that none of the justices, except perhaps Justice Thurgood Marshall, thought pregnancy distinctions constituted discrimination on the basis of sex.[33] Conceptualized as due process, the case held little precedential power for the women's movement. Picker had hoped for an equal protection decision early in the women's rights litigation that would have accomplished the purposes of the then pending equal rights amendment (ERA), which Picker believed was redundant with the equality guarantees of the Fourteenth Amendment.[34] The due process decision narrowed the issue to procedural technicalities of irrebuttable presumptions and was useless in fighting other sex discrimination battles. As Jo Carol LaFleur later recounted, her case was a leading opinion in the constitutional law textbooks her class used when she was a law student in 1975—textbooks that her fellow students asked her to autograph—but it soon became just a footnote.[35]

Soon after *LaFleur*, the Court began to address sex discrimination claims under equal protection. Congress amended Title VII of the Equal Employment Opportunity Act to apply to public schools, and the Equal Employment Opportunity Commission adopted a guideline that prohibited special maternity leave rules as sex discrimination. In 1978, Congress passed the Pregnancy Discrimination Act defining pregnancy discrimination as "sex" discrimination.[36] But *LaFleur* was still a milestone in the legal status of women in the workplace and had the tangible effect of quickly invalidating the many mandatory maternity leave policies nationwide that had predominated since the 1950s. As LaFleur later reflected, "Sometimes it takes a trial lawyer to vindicate a person's rights; and . . . every now and then advocacy for one client ripples throughout the nation and aids thousands of persons, altering the cultural contours and drowning ugly stereotypes."[37]

In the end, LaFleur and Nelson were awarded back pay and attorneys fees. LaFleur refused the punitive reassignment position she was offered in the most violent Cleveland school and instead worked as a teacher in suburban Lakewood until she began law school in 1974, first at Cleveland State and then in Utah. She became a public defender, clinical law professor, private attorney, and mediator. Reflecting on the case, LaFleur (now Nessett-Sale) said, "I'm not quite sure why I started my case. . . . There must have been a lot of other women who were affected by this rule. . . . The fundamental unfairness of it seemed morally wrong, not just stupid but wrong; and that men were making the decisions didn't help, because they didn't know what it was to be pregnant. It wasn't fair, and it made me angry."[38]

She recalled how her young son, Michael, attended the Sixth Circuit argument in *LaFleur*, at her lawyer's suggestion. She and Michael rode up the elevator with an elderly man who remarked, "He's a cute little guy," and she replied, "He's a sweetheart." When she later saw that man, retired Supreme Court Justice Tom Clark, sitting on her panel, she was just glad the toddler had not been having a tantrum on the way to the courtroom. In a remembrance of the case, LaFleur poignantly acknowledged her children—her college-age daughter, who helped edit the article, and her son, "the baby at the center of the lawsuit, who died in his youth."[39]

Abortion as a Woman's Right

The *LaFleur* case reached the Supreme Court at the crest of the feminist wave. Congress adopted the ERA in 1972, and more than half the state legislatures ratified the amendment over the next few months. Congress also passed the Equal Pay Act in 1973. And in January 1973, the Supreme Court decided *Roe v. Wade*, recognizing a woman's right to choose an abortion.

Abortion had become a women's rights issue beginning in the late 1960s. The procedure was criminalized in the late nineteenth century, altering the common-law practice that had permitted abortion up until the time of quickening at four months. Efforts to reform the criminal laws began in the 1950s and 1960s, led by public health officials concerned about the injuries and deaths resulting from illegal abortions. They sought reforms such as those suggested by an American Law Institute proposal, first made in 1957, that gave doctors greater authority to decide when "therapeutic abortions" were justifiable for the physical or mental health of the mother. Feminists then began to connect their concern with the ability of women to participate fully in the economy with the ability of women to remove the burdens of childbearing by controlling their reproductive lives. An influential speech by Betty Friedan in February 1969 expanded this feminist argument by declaring that abortion was the right of women to control their own bodies, their own lives, and their own place in society. Four states—Alaska, Hawaii, New York, and Washington—legalized abortion in 1970, and courts in seven other states declared their criminal abortion statutes unconstitutional. In 1973, *Roe* then recognized a woman's fundamental privacy right to choose an abortion in consultation with her doctor. Immediately after *Roe*, legislatures continued to pass abortion restrictions, fueled by the growing right to life movement that expanded nationally in 1973 beyond its original sponsorship by the Catholic Church. But "the decision in *Roe v. Wade* neither started nor ended the debate over abortion."[40]

Akron Center for Reproductive Health v. City of Akron involved a challenge to one of these post-*Roe* regulations. The case came at the beginning of the public debate on abortion, an issue that had previously been relegated to private discussion and underground practice. After the Supreme Court legalized abortion in *Roe*, the issue became publicly visible in the Akron, Ohio, area when four abortion clinics began operating. Women traveled to Akron from all parts of Ohio and neighboring states for legal and affordable abortions. In August 1976, two leaders in the Greater Akron Right to Life organization, Jane Hubbard and Ann Marie Segedy, proposed that the city regulate abortion. The Akron City Council did not pass the proposed ordinance on the advice of the city's legal department, which concluded the law was unconstitutional, but instead passed a narrower law requiring only that abortions after the first three months of pregnancy had to be performed in hospitals.[41]

A second and more comprehensive abortion regulation was then proposed in October 1977, shortly before council elections. The regulation was drafted by Alan Segedy, a lawyer for the right to life group, in consultation with two law professors at the University of Notre Dame and the University of Texas.[42] The regulation was designed to be a model for national restrictions on abortion, and it was quickly adopted by twenty states. Similar municipal regulations had been passed (and declared unconstitutional) in Chicago and St. Louis.[43] The Akron regulation had seventeen provisions requiring, among other things: (1) the performance of second-trimester abortions in hospitals; (2) parental consent for minors under fifteen; (3) parental notification for minors between fifteen and eighteen; (4) informed consent for all women, pursuant to highly detailed disclosures by the physician on the risks and procedures of abortion, the possible dire physical and emotional consequences of abortion, and the fact that "the unborn child is a human life from the moment of conception"; (5) a twenty-four-hour waiting period following this counseling; and (6) the "humane disposal of the fetus."[44] Akron's chief trial attorney, Willard F. Spicer, advised the council that the law was unconstitutional, saying, "There's no question in my mind if the ordinance was passed it would be knocked out very quickly." He also detailed in a memo the city's exposure to significant attorneys fees and damages if it lost the case.[45] Just a year earlier, a three-judge panel on the Northern District had struck down a similar Ohio statute requiring parental consent.[46]

The proposed Akron ordinance triggered a series of heated public meetings before the City Council Health and Social Services Committee during the snowy winter of 1978, when Akron was hit by a blizzard dubbed the "storm of the century."[47] Each hearing was packed with 200 to 300 people. NOW led the organized opposition to the ordinance. The supporters were led by a national right to life leader from Cincinnati, Dr. J. C. Willke. With his wife, Willke had self-published a book in 1971 called the *Handbook of Abortion*, which soon became a bible for the right to life movement.[48] The county health director, Dr. William Keck, testified against the bill, arguing that professional ethics and existing regulations were sufficient assurances of quality health care.[49] Religious leaders came out strongly for the ordinance: the Catholic bishop lobbied parishes; a Catholic nun and principal contacted parents from her school; and an Orthodox Jew, Marvin Weinberger, was the driving force of the local movement. Both the national Catholic Church and the Orthodox Jewish leadership had spoken out against abortion and called for active repeal of state laws that liberalized grounds for the procedure. Weinberger, a law student who was described as "overzealous," talked about "little stunts" he used to manipulate the media and attract publicity. These included an all-night prayer vigil in frigid weather on the eve of the council vote, which was attended by 600 antiabortion protestors and was held at the Lutheran church across the street from council chambers. The vigil made the national nightly news on all three existing television channels. On the day of the vote, 150 people overflowed council chambers and the hallway to hear the final forty-five-minute debate. Thirty protestors paraded outside of chambers, wrapped in blankets against the cold.[50] In hindsight, it seems the feminist movement was surprised by and unprepared for the determination of the abortion opposition, perhaps naively assuming that *Roe* had settled the question of the availability of abortion.

The Akron abortion resolution passed by a vote of 7 to 6. The lone Republican on the council of thirteen, John Frank, voted against the regulation. Frank later said his own personal experience involving an unplanned pregnancy of his former girlfriend persuaded him that abortion was none of the council's business. He declared, "It's a woman decision whether or not to have a baby. Period."[51] The two women on the council split their vote. Kathleen Greissing, a nurse, voted for it as an assurance of "good quality healthcare for women." Elsie Reaven, who was ousted as chair of the Health and Social Services Committee in a move to shepherd the ordinance through, was outraged that the "dominant male faction in council had the arrogance to persist against all reason in burdening and possibly encumbering women." The ordinance became law when the mayor neither signed nor vetoed the bill.[52]

The ACLU brought suit on behalf of three abortion clinics and one doctor. No pregnant woman would agree to be a plaintiff because the trial judge, Leroy Contie, refused to allow the women (or the doctors) to proceed anonymously under pseudonyms, as was commonly done in abortion cases.[53] A putative plaintiff detailed her fear regarding the publicity entailed in participating in the case and the potential embarrassment, harassment, and personal attacks. The brief in support of the motion explained that "many citizens of Akron, Ohio, have had strong emotional reaction to the debate over the propriety of abortion," and it detailed the "manifestations of social strife" that had occurred including regular public demonstrations, threatening and harassing telephone calls and letters, and one act of arson. Even plaintiffs' lead counsel, Stephan Landsman, a professor at Cleveland-Marshall College of Law, initially turned down the case because he did not want abortion demonstrations in front of his house. His wife's incredulous reaction to his fears—"Are you kidding me?"—convinced him to take the case.

The case proceeded as a question of women's health. At trial, plaintiffs argued that the Akron abortion ordinance was a "straightjacket for doctors." Defendants argued that women's health concerns necessitated regulation. The case became a battle of the experts. Plaintiffs presented prestigious medical experts supported by the national ACLU, including one who had received a Nobel Prize in the Philosophy of Medicine. The right to life intervenors, who led the defense's case, proffered less impressive witnesses who were easily discredited on cross-examination. This litigation of abortion as a medical issue, however, rendered the women involved invisible. As Bonnie Bolitho, a witness and counselor at one of the abortion clinics, later said, "It was pretty clear to me that the vast majority of men involved in this were not interested in the lives of individual women."[54]

Justice Blackmun's medical analysis in *Roe*, derived from his experience as an attorney for the Mayo Clinic, seemed to call for this type of health care approach. *Roe* had framed abortion as an issue of doctors' paternalistic care and medical science, even while offering a seemingly objective ground for legalizing abortion. The emphasis on the medical nature of abortion affected the strategy of legislatures and litigants, including the parties in the Akron case. It was only on appeal to the Supreme Court that the Akron plaintiffs secondarily articulated the issue as the denial of women's autonomy and a portrayal of women as irrational and incapable decision makers. But "casting abortion as a medical decision shifts the focus away from women. . . . Protecting physicians' rights provided little or no foundation for according women rights. Indeed, it undermined women and their rights by denying them the respect necessary to support their right of choice."[55]

Judge Contie was a conservative, Catholic Italian American who by most accounts was considered a "great judge," respected for his hard work and known as a "pretty tough character."[56] A Nixon appointee, he was the first Northern District judge to sit in Akron (nominated to fill James Connell's seat just after the *LaFleur* case), and he was later appointed by President Ronald Reagan to the U.S. Court of Appeals for the Sixth Circuit. Contie had served as law director for the city of Canton and was well known for his aggressive attack on local Mafia crime and police corruption, which led to the bombing of his home.

Judge Contie made a particular effort in the case to distance himself from the national political controversy over abortion: "Analytically, . . . this case is no different than the numerous others that come before this Court. It is the duty of this Court to determine the controversy before it based upon the requirements of the Constitution as expounded by the Supreme Court and the Court of Appeals for the Sixth Circuit. In considering the present case, this Court has attempted to do just that, nothing more and nothing less." He added a footnote, quoting Justice Felix Frankfurter: "As a member of this Court, I am not justified in writing my private notions of policy into the Constitution, no matter how deeply I may cherish them or how mischievous I may deem their disregard. . . . It can never be emphasized too much that one's own opinion about the wisdom or evil of a law should be excluded altogether when one is doing one's duty on the bench."[57]

Judge Contie issued a compromise decision almost one year after the trial, and both sides claimed they had won. Antiabortion leaders called the ruling "terrific" and "a major victory for pro-life people," but the head of the Ohio ACLU retorted, "Another such victory and they [the right to life leaders] will be permanently undone."[58] The decision invalidated parental consent, parental notification, detailed informed consent, disposal restrictions, and clinic inspection. It upheld the twenty-four-hour waiting period, the doctor's explanation of risks and procedures, and reporting requirements. Contie's approach was careful and measured but frustrating to the plaintiffs, who wanted him to consider the underlying issues of council's improper use of religious motives in legislating abortion. The court seemed to be searching for a practical way to split the proverbial baby, constrained to follow the commands of *Roe* yet resistant to embracing the evolving precepts of gender equity reflected in the abortion issue.[59]

The Sixth Circuit, in a 2-to-1 decision, invalidated all of the provisions except for two: parental notification and the hospital requirement for second-term abortions. The appellate court criticized Judge Contie for employing a less demanding judicial review than that required by *Roe* for first-trimester restrictions. Contie had used a less exacting standard than strict scrutiny by asking whether the regulation was unduly burdensome and whether the government had a valid state interest.[60]

The U.S. Supreme Court forcefully struck down the Akron law, reaffirming its abortion rights jurisprudence ten years after *Roe*.[61] Justice Lewis Powell, writing for the majority in a 6-to-3 decision, found some of the provisions to be motivated by impermissible objectives: "It is fair to say that much of the information required is designed not to inform the woman's consent but rather to persuade her to withhold it altogether." The Court applied heightened scrutiny to invalidate the five provisions it considered, and it rejected a lower standard of inquiry that "would uphold virtually any abortion regulation under a rational-basis test." The solicitor general for the Reagan administration, Rex Lee, argued for the abandonment of the *Roe* strict scrutiny review in favor of the lesser "undue burden" standard. Justice Blackmun, author of *Roe*, asked him point-blank, "Mr. Solicitor General, are you asking that *Roe v. Wade* be overruled?" Lee responded no, saying that he was simply arguing for a standard that accommodated a deference to the legislature.[62]

Akron's law director, Robert Pritt, also saw the case as one involving legislative power and the principle of local home rule. He had initially defended the ordinance on legal, rather than moral, grounds, but he became troubled by abortion by the end of the case. Pritt was concerned about the "tremendous amount of money" allegedly being made by the clinics, as was Councilman Ray Kapper, who said, "I talked to a lot of people over those years and a lot of them don't know what kind of money those rip-off artists were making off teen-agers."[63]

The Supreme Court's decision in *City of Akron* was seen as an enormous symbolic victory for women's rights, with the practical effect of invalidating the abortion regulations of more than twenty-one states. Judge David Dowd, Contie's successor on the bench, awarded the plaintiffs attorneys fees of $368,710.[64] Councilman John Frank demanded that Willke and the national right to life organization pay the city's expenses, but they refused, politely thanking the city for its valiant antiabortion efforts.[65] The share of fees paid to Cleveland-Marshall College of Law was used for the Harry Blackmun Scholarship Fund, named for the author of the *Roe* decision. Justice Blackmun himself attended the dedication, lured to Cleveland by the promise of a much-beloved baseball game with Cleveland Hall of Fame pitcher Bob Feller.[66]

The invalidation of the abortion regulation in *City of Akron*, however, remained good law for only a short time. Less than a decade later, in *Planned Parenthood v. Casey*, the Supreme Court reversed course and upheld provisions requiring informed consent, twenty-four-hour waiting periods, and parental consent.[67] Today, Ohio, like many states, has reenacted the types of abortion restrictions that were previously struck down.[68] The decision in *City of Akron* is now usually cited, if it is cited at all, for the dissent by the newly appointed Justice Sandra Day O'Connor, which showed the first inkling that the Court's abortion jurisprudence was in doubt.

A Shifting Perspective

Just three years after the Supreme Court's decision in *City of Akron*, the Northern District once again considered the legality of parental notification. In *Akron Center for Reproductive Health v. Rosen*, the court considered a 1985 Ohio law that required a minor under the age of eighteen to notify one parent about a planned abortion.[69] Unlike the parent notification provision struck down in *City of Akron*, this law included a judicial bypass exception.

Judge Ann Aldrich was assigned the case and granted both the preliminary and the permanent injunctions invalidating the parental notification law. Considering the facial validity of the law, Aldrich found numerous constitutional defects with the bypass provision, including a lack of anonymity, no expedited process, confusing pleading forms, the clear and convincing standard, and the physician's duty to notify. Aldrich found that the law had potential for "violations of the constitutional rights of mature minors and minors for whom notification would not be in their best interests."[70] The sponsor of the bill, Representative Jerome Luebbers of Cincinnati, said, "I fully expected that the judge would do this. She's predictable."[71]

Judge Aldrich was predictable because she had distinguished herself as one of the most liberal members of the court, with a strong commitment to social justice. A framed needlepoint slogan hanging on the wall of her chambers read: "Women who seek to be equal with men lack ambition." Standing over six feet tall, Aldrich was a tough woman who had been on her own from the age of eight, when her mother died in a Rhode Island hurricane. She rebuilt railroad lines in Yugoslavia after World War II, raced Siberian huskies, and married a Central Intelligence Agency (CIA) agent as her first husband. She was the only woman in her class at New York University Law School, and she recounted how she was hated by most of her classmates, who thought she was taking space from a worthy veteran and was there just to get a husband. As an attorney and law professor, she focused her efforts on racial justice. She represented the United Church of Christ and sued the Federal Communications Commission to make it easier for minorities to own radio stations in the South. Aldrich arrived in Cleveland in 1968 as the first full-time female law professor at Cleveland-Marshall, where she was later joined by WLF founders Jane Picker and Lizabeth Moody. Women still constituted less than 1 percent of law professors nationwide at the time, even though the first woman had been appointed to a tenure-track position at Berkeley in 1919.[72] Aldrich was instrumental in founding the law school's diversity student recruitment program. She drove to Tupelo, Mississippi, seeking to find qualified future law students at the historically all-black teachers' colleges of the South. The students, among them the future Ohio appellate judge Patricia Blackmon, often came with nothing, and Professor Aldrich supported them, even inviting them to live in her home.[73]

Aldrich was the first woman judge in the Northern District, appointed in 1980 by President Jimmy Carter. She followed the legacy of Florence Allen, the first female judge elected to the state court in Ohio in 1921 and appointed to the U.S. Court of Appeals for the Sixth Circuit in 1934. Carter made a determined effort to increase the number of women and black federal judges; he would appoint forty-one women to the bench during his tenure. Yet like most federal and state courts, the Northern District would remain less than 20 percent female for the next twenty-five years.[74] When a new judicial position was created in the Northern District, the women's rights advocates went into high gear. Advocates such as Lana Moresky from NOW worked to vet female candidates. Most of those candidates were law professors, including three from Cleveland State, as there was a lack of senior women in corporations or law firms at that time.

Once appointed to the bench, Judge Aldrich encountered turmoil and collegial difficulties on the court when she accused the chief judge of influence peddling and when she herself was accused of lying for romantic gain. The scandal that ensued temporarily diminished the dignity of Cleveland's federal bench, leading one judge to say, "I wish this were all a bad dream and we could wake up and say it's over."[75]

With one woman on the court, the potential existed for litigants in gender cases to find a more receptive judicial audience. As empirical work has shown, there are significant differences in voting patterns among judges in sex discrimination cases, with male judges much less likely to decide in favor of the plaintiff.[76] One lawyer representing a defendant in an employment sex discrimination case before Judge Aldrich seemed concerned about this inclination and asked the judge to recuse herself. She refused. In *Akron II*, Aldrich showed an appreciation of the practical difficulties facing young women seeking abortions, even though she did not accept the plaintiffs' arguments completely. She found that the evidentiary standard in the bypass procedure created "an unacceptably high risk of erroneous determinations," since "the judge's decision will necessarily be based largely upon subjective standards without the benefit of any evidence other than a woman's testimony."[77] As Aldrich had suspected, many of these judicial bypass decisions turned out "to be at the whim of the judge." One judge denied a judicial exemption to a seventeen-year-old despite evidence of physical abuse by her father, another judge denied a bypass because a seventeen-year-old girl had not had enough "hard knocks," and a third judge denied the exception because the teenager refused to file a paternity suit against her partner.[78]

The law took effect after the Supreme Court overruled Judge Aldrich's decision in *Ohio v. Akron Center for Reproductive Health (Akron II)*. Though the Sixth Circuit Court of Appeals had affirmed the unconstitutionality of the statute, the Supreme Court found the judicial bypass procedure valid.[79] Justice Blackmun vigorously dissented, finding Ohio's bypass procedure to be a "tortuous maze" that deliberately placed a pattern of obstacles in the path of pregnant minors. He found the challenged provisions to be merely "poorly disguised elements of discouragement for the abortion decision."[80] Counsel for the plaintiffs, Linda Sogg, had tried to make these points at oral argument, explaining how the law "stacks the decks" against the minor. But Sogg was encumbered by a shrill voice and a lack of appreciation for the tenuousness of the abortion right among the justices. They were more persuaded by the legalistic arguments of Rita Eppler from the Ohio Attorney General's Office, who argued that the law balanced the rights of minor women against the rights and interests of their parents.[81]

In upholding the parental notification law, Justice Anthony Kennedy and two other justices applied a low level of judicial scrutiny, concluding that the regulation did not impose an undue burden and that it was a rational way to further the end of protecting the health of young women. This standard, suggested by Justice O'Connor's dissent in *City of Akron*, was subsequently adopted by the controlling plurality of the Court two years after *Akron II* in *Planned Parenthood v. Casey*.[82] The *Casey* decision identified an important government interest in protecting a minor's mental health from the psychological risk that she might later regret her abortion. This mental health rationale was later extended to all women by the Court's 2007 decision in *Gonzales v. Carhart*, which upheld the federal Partial-Birth Abortion Act banning a rarely used late-term abortion procedure. The *Carhart* Court held it was important to protect adult women from the alleged mental and emotional consequences of the decision to have an abortion. Scientific studies conducted after the decision, however, concluded that the evidence did not support the claim that abortion caused mental health problems in women.[83] A scathing dissent by Justice Ginsburg in *Carhart* emphasized that the rationale of protecting women "reflects ancient notions about women's place in the family and under the Constitution—ideas that have long since been discredited."[84] These abortion decisions reinforced stereotypes about women's primary role as mothers and the assumed irrationality of their decision making—normative concerns of gender that reached beyond the issue of abortion.[85]

THE Northern District of Ohio was drawn into the national debate over women's rights through a series of key cases that ultimately were resolved by the U.S. Supreme Court. These cases served as vehicles for meaningful social change for women, even while they also served to reinforce conventional gender norms. The cases were fueled by dedicated women advocates, parties, and judges who understood the need for social change to promote gender equality. Although the courts often operated out of a sense of the rule of law, they did address the claims of sex equality that came before them, ultimately acknowledging women's rights as they developed.

Notes

Special thanks go to Bill Rich for making important Akron connections and to Kristina Melomed for her enthusiasm and invaluable research assistance.
 1. 326 F. Supp. 1208 (N.D. Ohio 1971).

2. 410 U.S. 113 (1973).

3. 479 F. Supp. 1172 (N.D. Ohio 1979); 633 F. Supp. 1123 (N.D. Ohio 1986).

4. Transcript of Oral Argument, Cleveland School Board v. LaFleur, October 15, 1973, at 28 (citing Amicus Brief of National Education Association); see Greco v. Roper, 61 N.E.2d 307 (Ohio 1945) (upholding resignation rule for married female teachers).

5. Cleveland Board of Education v. LaFleur, 414 U.S. 632, 641 (1974).

6. Peter Irons, *The Courage of Their Convictions: 16 Americans Who Fought Their Way to the Supreme Court* (New York: Penguin Books, 1988), 307, 309–10.

7. LaFleur, 326 F. Supp. at 1209; Jo Carol Nesset-Sale, "From Sideline to Frontline: The Making of a Civil Rights Plaintiff—A Retrospective by the Plaintiff in *Cleveland Board of Education v. LaFleur*, a Landmark Pregnancy Discrimination Case," *Georgetown Journal of Gender and the Law* 7 (2006): 1, 10, 12–14; Jo Carol LaFleur, "Go Home and Have Your Baby," in Irons, *Courage of Their Convictions*, 317; Norman Milachak, "A Case Named Michael Toddles to the Supreme Court," *Cleveland Press*, April 27, 1973.

8. See, e.g., Gfell v. Rickelman, 313 F.Supp. 364 (N.D. Ohio 1970), aff'd, 441 F.2d 444 (6th Cir. 1971) (rejecting due process claim); Jackson v. Dorrier, 424 F.2d 213 (6th Cir. 1970) (rejecting due process claim), cert. denied, 400 U.S. 850 (1970); but see Breen v. Kahl, 296 Supp. 702 (W.D. Wis. 1969), aff'd, 419 F.2d 1034, 1036 (7th Cir.) (holding that "[t]he right to wear one's hair at any length or in any desired manner is an ingredient of personal freedom protected by" the Due Process Clause of the Fourteenth Amendment), cert. denied, 398 U.S. 937 (1970).

9. Nesset-Sale, "From Sideline to Frontline," 14–16; LaFleur, "Go Home," 321; Brian Williams, "Mother-to-Be Sues for Job," *Cleveland Plain Dealer*, March 27, 1971.

10. Sue Kincaid, "WEAL Works for Women's Opportunity," *Cleveland Press*, September 22, 1970.

11. Barbara Flicker, *Justice and School Systems: The Role of the Courts in Education Litigation* (Philadelphia: Temple University Press, 1990), 132–25.

12. Nesset-Sale, "From Sideline to Frontline," 16; LaFleur, "Go Home," 322; Jane M. Picker, interviews by the author, February 21, 2010, and October 18, 2010; see Deborah Dinner, "Recovering the *LaFleur* Doctrine," *Yale Journal of Law and Feminism* 22 (2010): 23–24.

13. Lewis Katz, interview by Kristina Melomed, January 29, 2010.

14. Ohio Joint Task Force on Gender Fairness: Final Report (1995). Executive Summary of Report available online at www.ohiobar.org/task_force. Full copies available for purchase from the Ohio State Bar Association.

15. Hearing Transcript, LaFleur v. Cleveland Board of Education, April 19, 1971, at 158, in Women's Law Fund Papers, Western Reserve Historical Society, Cleveland, Ohio (hereafter cited as WLF Papers).

16. Ibid.; Jo Carol Nesset-Sale, interview by the author, July 16, 2010; Katz interview; "2 Pregnant Teachers Fight Ouster in Court," *Cleveland Plain Dealer*, April 20, 1971.

17. Katz interview; LaFleur, "Go Home," 322.

18. LaFleur, 326 F. Supp. at 1213–14.

19. 208 U.S. 412 (1908).

20. 465 F.2d 1184 (6th Cir. 1972).

21. Women's Law Fund pamphlet, WLF Papers. The fund was officially incorporated in November 1972.

22. Amy Leigh Campbell, *Raising the Bar: Ruth Bader Ginsburg and the ACLU Women's Rights Project* (Xlibris, 2004), 27.

23. Justice Ruth Bader Ginsburg, "Foreword, Report of the Special Committee on Gender of the D.C. Circuit Task Force on Gender, Race, and Ethnic Bias," reprinted in *Georgetown Law Journal* 84 (1996): 1651.

24. Picker, February interview; Susan M. Hartmann, *The Other Feminists: Activists in the Liberal Establishment* (New Haven, Conn.: Yale University Press, 1998), 82.

25. Hartmann, *Other Feminists*, 135, 162, 174. In the 1970s alone, Ford-supported organizations sponsored or filed amicus briefs in more than twenty sex discrimination cases that reached the Supreme Court.

26. Ibid., 174; letter from Ford Foundation to Jane Picker, August 15, 1983, WLF Papers.

27. The WLF continued to handle employment sex discrimination cases, including charged claims against police and fire departments. See, e.g., Malone v. City of East Cleveland, 1978 WL 186 (N.D. Ohio 1978); Baker v. Portage County Sheriff's Dep't, C-75 661 (N.D. Ohio 1975); also see Jane M. Picker, "Sex Discrimination in Public Education and Local Government Employment," *Urban Lawyer* 5 (1973): 347, 355. It also handled cases of female student-athletes under the newly enacted Title IX, including the first decision in the United States allowing a girl to play football. Clinton v. Nagy, 411 F. Supp. 1396 (N.D. Ohio 1974). The fund dissolved in 2006, finding that its "mission had been accomplished" when it was no longer difficult for women plaintiffs to find lawyers to take their cases. Historical Sketch, WLF Papers.

28. Erica B. Grubb and Margarita C. McCoy, "Love's Labors Lost: New Conceptions of Maternity Leaves," *Harvard Civil Rights–Civil Liberties Law Review* 7 (1972): 260.

29. Picker, February interview; LaFleur, "Go Home," 325.

30. 414 U.S. at 639–42.

31. Picker, February interview.

32. Transcript of Oral Argument, Cleveland School Board v. LaFleur, 42.

33. Dinner, "Recovering the *LaFleur* Doctrine," 58 (quoting Harry A. Blackmun, Memorandum to the Conference, October 15, 1973, and Blackmun's notes on conference, October 19, 1973, in Harry A. Blackmun Papers, box 175, folder 1, on file with the Library of Congress, Washington, D.C.). Indeed, six months later, the Court dismissed in a footnote the contention that a pregnancy classification was discrimination on the basis of "sex." Geduldig v. Aiello, 417 U.S. 484, 496 n.20 (1974).

34. See Jane M. Picker, "Law and the Status of Women in the United States," *Columbia Human Rights Law Review* 8 (1976–77): 311.

35. See Donna Matthews, "Avoiding Gender Equality," *Women's Rights Law Reporter* (April 1998): 140–41; LaFleur, "Go Home," 329.

36. 42 U.S.C. § 2000e(k).

37. Nesset-Sale, "From Sideline to Frontline," 1.

38. LaFleur, "Go Home," 325.

39. Nesset-Sale, "From Sideline to Frontline," 1, 21; Irons, *Courage of Their Convictions*, 317. Michael committed suicide during his freshman year of college.

40. Linda Greenhouse and Reva Siegel, *Before Roe v. Wade: Voices That Shaped the Abortion Debate before the Supreme Court's Ruling* (New York: Kaplan Publishing, 2010), xii–xiii, 3, 24, 38–40, 81, 121–25; Nancy Ford, "The Evolution of a Constitutional Right to an Abortion: Fashioned in the 1970s and Secured in the 1980s," *Journal of Legal Medicine* 4 (1983): 271.

41. "Akron Council to Get 'Tough' Abortion Plan," *Akron Beacon Journal*, October 17, 1977.

42. William Hershey, "More Hearings Planned on Abortion," *Akron Beacon Journal*, December 21, 1977.

43. See Friendship Medical Center, Ltd. v. Chicago Bd. of Health, 367 F. Supp. 597, 608–21 (N.D. Ill. 1973); Ward v. Poelker, 495 F.2d 1349, 1352 (8th Cir. 1974).

44. Robert Sangeorge, "A New Abortion Controversy Faces High Court," *United Press International*, January 30, 1982.

45. Memorandum to John V. Frank from W. F. Spicer, "Council Liability," February 27, 1978 (on file with author); William Hershey, "Goehler Wants Abortion Vote This Month," *Akron Beacon Journal*, February 17, 1978; Hershey, "Legal Flaws Seen in Abortion Bill," *Akron Beacon Journal*, February 11, 1978.

46. Hoe v. Brown, 446 F. Supp. 329 (N.D. Ohio 1976).

47. Jean Peters, "Policing of Abortion Clinics Debates," *Akron Beacon Journal*, February 5, 1978.

48. Greenhouse and Siegel, *Before* Roe v. Wade, 99–112.

49. Statement by C. William Keck, M.D., M.P.H., to Akron City Council Health and Social Service Committee, February 4, 1978, in Joint Appendix to City of Akron v. Akron Center for Reproductive Health, U.S.S.Ct., 304a, 308a.

50. William Hershey, "Bishop Urges Council to OK Abortion Bill," *Akron Beacon Journal*, January 8, 1978; William Canterbury, "600 Abortion Foes Shun the Cold during Night-Long Candle Rally, *Akron Beacon Journal*, February 28, 1978; Abe Zaidan and William Hershey, "Weinberger Stunt 'Appalls' Kapper," *Akron Beacon Journal*, March 7, 1978; David B. Cooper, "'Little Stunts' for Big Issues: Manipulating the Press?" *Akron Beacon Journal*, March 9, 1978.

51. John Frank, interview by the author, June 21, 2010.

52. David Brinkley, *NBC News*, February 28, 1978; William Hershey, "Council Passes Abortion Control Bill; Opponents Vow Challenge in Court, *Akron Beacon Journal*, February 28, 1978; Hershey, "Abortion Debate Centers on Consent Provisions," *Akron Beacon Journal*, January 26, 1978; Hershey, "More Hearings Planned on Abortion," *Akron Beacon Journal*, December 21, 1977; Editorial, "Fast Ruling on Ordinance Would Serve Community," *Akron Beacon Journal*, March 9, 1978; Editorial, "The Abortion Issue . . . in Akron," *Washington Post*, September 11, 1982.

53. Affidavit of Linda Loe, May 3, 1978, in Joint App., 52a; Order Denying Motion, in Joint App., 58a; Brief in Support of Motion to Reconsider, in Joint App. 62a.

54. Bonnie Bolitho, interview by the author, June 29, 2010.

55. Elizabeth Reilly, "The 'Jurisprudence of Doubt': How the Premises of the Supreme Court's Abortion Jurisprudence Undermine Procreative Liberty," *Journal of Law and Politics* 14 (Fall 1998): 757, 779.

56. Stephan Landsman, interview by the author, June 8, 2010.

57. Akron Center for Reproductive Health, Inc. v. City of Akron, 479 F. Supp. 1172, 1180–81 (N.D. Ohio 1979).

58. Dennis McEaneney, "Who Won? . . . Both Sides Claim Victory after Contie Decision," *Akron Beacon Journal*, August 22, 1979; Editorial, "Ruling on Abortion Law Seems Logical and Wise," *Akron Beacon Journal*, August 23, 1979; Linda Greenhouse, "Court Reaffirms Right to Abortion and Bars Variety of Local Curbs," *New York Times*, June 16, 1983.

59. 479 F. Supp. at 1201–7, 1215.

60. 651 F.2d 1198, 1203–4 (6th Cir. 1981); see also 651 F.2d at 1215 (Kennedy, J., dissenting).

61. 462 U.S. 416 (1983).

62. 462 U.S. 420, 444; Transcript of Oral Argument, City of Akron v. Akron Center for Reproductive Health, November 30, 1982; Lincoln Caplan, *The Tenth Justice: The Solicitor General and the Rule of Law* (New York: Alfred A. Knopf, 1987), 105–663. Robert Pritt, interview by the author, June 18, 2010.

64. Virginia Wiegand, "ACLU Awarded $368,710 in Fees for Abortion Battle," *Akron Beacon Journal*, February 7, 1985; Wiegand, "Abortion Fight Will Cost Akron, 2 Taxpayers," *Akron Beacon Journal*, July 7, 1984.

65. Rick Reiff, "Life Group Asked to Pay ACLU," *Akron Beacon Journal*, June 18, 1983; David B. Cooper, "Who'll Pay for Abortion Appeal? Councilman Frank Has Unusual

Idea," *Akron Beacon Journal*, June 23, 1983; letter to Dr. Jack Wilke [*sic*], from John V. Frank, June 20, 1983 (on file with author).

66. Landsman, interview.

67. 505 U.S. 833 (1992). The Court struck down the provision requiring a married woman to notify her husband of her intent to abort.

68. Ohio Rev. Code § 2919.121 (parental consent, eff. 1998); Ohio Rev. Code § 2317.56 (informed consent, 24-hour waiting period, informed of medical risks and characteristics of fetus, alternatives, and adoption, eff. 2000); Ohio Rev. Code § 3701.79 (reporting, eff. 2006).

69. 633 F. Supp. 1123 (N.D. Ohio 1986).

70. Ibid., 1135–44.

71. M. R. Kropko, "Judge Strikes Down Abortion Notification Law," *Associated Press*, April 23, 1986.

72. Herma Hill Kay, "The Future of Women Law Professors," *Iowa Law Review* 77 (1991): 5, 8.

73. "Ann Aldrich Set Firsts as Lawyer, Professor and Federal District Judge," Obituary, *Cleveland Plain Dealer*, May 3, 2010.

74. "Women in Federal and State-Level Judgeships," Report of the Center for Women in Government and Civil Society, Rockefeller College of Public Affairs and Policy, University at Albany, State University of New York, Spring 2010.

75. "Ohio Judicial Inquiry Ends without Indictments," *New York Times*, August 31, 1984; Mary Thornton, "Powerful, Controversial U.S. Judge in Cleveland Target of Probe," *Washington Post*, July 11, 1983; "Law: A Bad Courthouse Soap Opera," *Time*, June 20, 1983.

76. Christina Boyd, Lee Epstein, and Andrew Martin, "Untangling the Causal Effects of Sex on Judging," *American Journal of Political Science* 54 (April 2010): 389; Boyd and Epstein, "When Women Rule, It Makes a Difference," *Washington Post*, May 3, 2009.

77. 633 F. Supp. at 1137.

78. In re Jane Doe, 566 N.E.2d 1181 (Ohio 1991); Rich Harris, "Abortion Law Faces New Challenge," *Cleveland Plain Dealer*, March 13, 1992.

79. Akron Center for Reproductive Health v. Slaby, 854 F.2d 852 (6th Cir. 1988), *rev'd sub nom.* Ohio v. Akron Center for Reproductive Health, 497 U.S. 502 (1990).

80. 497 U.S. at 525–27.

81. Transcript of Oral Argument, Ohio v. Akron Center for Reproductive Health, November 29, 1989.

82. 505 U.S. 833 (1992).

83. Brenda Major, Mark Applebaum, Linda Beckman, Mary Ann Dutton, Nancy Felipe Russo, and Carolyn West, "Abortion and Mental Health: Evaluating the Evidence," *American Psychologist* 64 (December 2009): 863; Jocelyn T. Warren, Marie Harvey, and Jillian T. Henderson, "Do Depression and Low Self-Esteem Follow Abortion among Adolescents? Evidence from a National Study," *Perspectives on Sexual and Reproductive Health* 42 (December 2010): 230–35.

84. 550 U.S. 124, 184 (2007).

85. Maya Manian, "Irrational Women: Informed Consent and Abortion Regret," in *Feminist Legal History: Essays on Women and Law*, ed. Tracy A. Thomas and Tracey Jean Boisseau (New York: New York University Press, 2011); Jill Elaine Hasday, "Protecting Them from Themselves: The Persistence of Mutual Benefits Arguments for Sex and Race Inequality," *New York University Law Review* 84 (2009): 1464, 1478.

7

Religion in the Public Sector

Martin H. Belsky

THE FIRST AMENDMENT to the U.S. Constitution provides that the government shall make "no law respecting an establishment of religion, or prohibiting the free exercise thereof."[1] The intent of both the "establishment" and the "free exercise" provisions has been to protect religious freedom, especially for those of minority religions.[2]

Beginning in the 1960s, the Supreme Court applied these limitations rigorously.[3] Since the mid-1980s, the standards have been changing and, to some degree, softening.[4] Cases applying these evolving principles come to the federal district courts as matters of law and are resolved on motions, often cross-motions, for summary judgment.[5] There is seldom any dispute on the facts. The only issue is whether the government, at some level, has committed or should be precluded from committing a constitutional violation. The factual contexts of these controversies are often highly politicized and certainly sensitive.[6]

Over the years, the judges of the U.S. District Court for the Northern District of Ohio in a number of religious freedom cases have had to decide how best to balance the opposing interests as well as to analyze the law. They have resolved conflicts between those in the majority, wanting more religion in the public sphere as expressed by their political leaders, and those in the minority, urging the separation of church and state. Can there, for example, ever be a public display of the Ten Commandments?[7] Can a board of education open its meetings with a prayer or a moment of silence?[8]

The judges have also had to choose between the desires of an individual to exercise his or her religious tenets and the needs and particular policies of governance. A prisoner's right to eat only certain foods might have to give way to the legitimate penological interest of cost control.[9] Similarly, prison requirements that prohibit certain religiously prescribed hairstyles must be accepted because of concerns of hygiene and security.[10] And sometimes, the judges have had to weigh competing constitutional and policy rights. Solicitation of funds by a religious group on public parks and streets might be undesirable, but a city cannot use the argument of potential harassment by that group as a basis to bar that religious practice.[11] A religious group must be allowed to rent a city-owned and city-run convention center for an event touted as "men only," despite public accommodation ordinances and laws that bar gender discrimination.[12] Similarly, since the Constitution proscribes any interference in church practice or law, absent compelling reasons, a church must be allowed to dismiss an individual from religious service even though its reasons might violate clear federal policies and laws against discrimination based on pregnancy[13] or disability.[14]

This chapter will discuss how judges of the Northern District have dealt with certain highly visible, highly politicized, and often very troubling religion cases that raise the issue of just how high the "wall of separation" between government and religion should be.[15] It will also demonstrate how, even in the most difficult and sensitive cases, their decisions must be premised on the limited and carefully prescribed role of a federal district court judge: "It is the duty of this Court to determine the controversy before it based upon the requirements of the Constitution as expounded by the Supreme Court and the Court of Appeals for the Sixth Circuit. . . . [The] Court [must attempt] to do just that, nothing more and nothing less."[16]

In the two areas highlighted in this chapter—religious symbols on public property and the funding of sectarian programs—this process of review and application of the "requirements" has not always been as straightforward as one might assume. Sometimes, the decisions of the higher courts did not give real guidance. As Judge Solomon Oliver Jr. explained: "Since its inception . . . the Establishment Clause has presented some of the most difficult questions of interpretation and application faced by the courts. As the Supreme Court has stated, 'in many of these decisions we have expressly or implicitly acknowledged that we can only dimly perceive the lines of demarcation in this extraordinarily sensitive area of constitutional law.'"[17]

In other cases, the legal standards, as articulated by a majority of the U.S. Supreme Court, are in the process of reconsideration, evolution, or even radical change.[18] A district court judge or a court of appeals judge can follow what he or she believes is the present articulated law as shown by decisions not yet explicitly overruled. But then, is it fair to the parties to disregard the clear trend of recent decisions? On this, at least, the Supreme Court seems to have spoken:

> We do not acknowledge, and we do not hold, that other courts should conclude our more recent cases have, by implication, overruled an earlier precedent. We reaffirm that "if a precedent to this Court has direct application in a case, yet appears to rest on reasons rejected in some other line of decisions, *the [lower courts] should follow the case which directly controls, leaving to this Court the prerogative of overruling its own decisions.*"[19]

Finally, in some of these highly politicized and highly publicized cases, a judge must be aware of the impact of a decision on the community. It is often appropriate to seek settlement of a dispute rather than a firestorm. The lawsuit itself, or the open and viable threat of a lawsuit, can "exacerbate the effect" of the constitutional violation.[20]

Applying the Principles

In 1963, the U.S. Supreme Court, in *Lemon v. Kurtzman*,[21] established a three-prong test to review any potential infringement of the establishment clause: (1) "the statute [or rule] had to have a secular legislative purpose," that is, a clear nonreligious reason; (2) the "principal or primary effect" of the law, rule, regulation, or practice had to be one that "neither advances nor inhibits religion," that is, it had to be neutral toward religion and religions; and (3) the statute or rule could not foster "an excessive government entanglement with religion," that is, it could not allow government at any level to become intertwined with religious institutions or principles.[22]

But these guidelines have not proven to be effective. Almost every rule, action, or policy can be justified by some secular purpose.[23] And in more recent cases, the third, or "excessive entanglement," prong has been collapsed into "an aspect of the inquiry into a statute's effect."[24] So effectively, the review is now more confined. If a government action is "neutral" and does not carry with it the "imprimatur of governmental endorsement," it is constitutional.[25]

Applying this standard, courts are required to analyze the impact on the majority of a religious activity or symbol that is sponsored, endorsed, or even promoted by the government.[26] As Justice Sandra Day O'Connor stressed in *Lynch v. Donnelly*: "The Establishment Clause prohibits government from making adherence to a religion relevant in any way to a person's standing in the political community. . . . The . . . more direct infringement is government endorsement or disapproval of religion. Endorsement sends a message to non-adherents that they are outsiders, not full members of the political community, and an accompanying message to adherents that they are insiders, favored members of the political community. Disapproval sends the opposite message."[27]

Symbols and Monuments

One obvious area where government can be seen as endorsing a certain sect of religion over another, or even religion over nonreligion, involves government promotion or acceptance of clearly religious symbols—such as a cross or a Ten Commandments display.

American Civil Liberties Union v. City of Stow

On June 23, 1966, the city council of Stow, Ohio, adopted a seal with four quadrants. One quadrant had a sketch of a factory; another had a home; and a third had a scroll with a quill, pen, and ink. The last quadrant, on the upper left, had "an open book, overlaid with a large cross."[28] For more than twenty years, this seal was used on city cars and city stationery. It was also displayed at city hall and on city tax forms.[29] After a federal court declared the use of a religious seal in Edmond, Oklahoma, to be in violation of the First Amendment,[30] the American Civil Liberties Union (ACLU), in July 1996, indicated to the Stow city law director that it would sue if the city did not change its seal to have the cross and Bible removed. In December 1996, the city council of Stow voted to keep the seal as it was, first in a 5-to-2 vote and then in a tie vote.[31]

For several months, the issue of the seal's content was a focus of city council meetings. A trust fund was established to pay for the costs of a lawsuit. Church groups organized prayer meetings. The law director and some council members talked about the small likelihood of success against a lawsuit and the costs involved.[32] On February 27, 1997, the city council voted 4 to 3 to change the seal.[33] This, however, did not end the debate. Opponents of the council's decision secured enough votes for a referendum. On November 4, 1997, 57 percent of the voters in the special Stow referendum chose to overturn the decision of the council. And on November 8, the city received official notice from the ACLU of its intent to sue.[34] The ACLU, in fact, filed suit on December 16, 1997.[35] In response, a Stow citizens' group, Concerned Citizens for Constitutional Freedom, which had campaigned for the referendum, sought aid from conservative religious organizations, finally accepting the assistance of the Virginia-based American Center for Law and Justice.[36]

The case was first assigned to Judge David D. Dowd Jr., but he recused himself. It then went to Judge Samuel H. Bell, but he retired before the issues could be resolved. Finally, the case was assigned to a brand-new federal judge, Dan Aaron Polster. All three judges had organized settlement conferences, but no settlement could be reached.[37] Judge Polster rendered his decision on December 16, 1998. It was almost anticlimactic. First, it was essential to get to the actual issue. The city of Stow had offered one witness, a person who had served on the original 1966 committee that developed the seal. That witness, who asked to remain anonymous, said the book was not a Bible and the thing others called a cross was just the letter T.[38] Moreover, the city stressed that even if it was a cross, it was "not necessarily a Christian cross because it is stylized and does not have nails."[39] Judge Polster found this argument "disingenuous." He noted that no reasonable person could deny the religious significance of the cross. Symbols should draw people together, he said. Yet the tension in the community that grew as a result of the challenge to the seal "could only exacerbate the effect of causing non-Christians in Stow to feel like outsiders."[40]

That concern — the rights of the "ins" against the rights of the "outs" — is the real significance to the Stow case and the Stow opinion. It is also the real conflict in the First Amendment itself.

The interplay between the establishment and free exercise clauses of the Constitution has vexed generations of courts and legal scholars. These two clauses can never be fully reconciled because they reflect a fundamental tension that has existed since the Pilgrims landed in the early seventeenth century. Simply put, this country was founded by profoundly religious people, who left England because they did not want anyone, particularly the government, telling them how to pray. Nearly four hundred years later, federal courts across the country are struggling on a daily basis to balance the right of each American, both as an individual and as part of a community, to engage in religious expression with the companion right of each American not to feel excluded or ostracized by a community's expression of religious sentiment if it conflicts with his or her own personal beliefs.[41] In other words, in a democratic society, ordinarily the majority controls. However, the U.S. Constitution decided that in certain areas, including religion, the majority should not be allowed to interfere with the rights or inclusiveness of a minority.[42]

Judge Polster indicated that the establishment law cases from the Supreme Court and the Sixth Circuit were particularly focused on whether the government action had the purpose or effect of either endorsing or disapproving of religion or a religion.[43] Particularly, as Justice O'Connor stressed in *Lynch v. Donnelly*:[44] "The Establishment Clause is violated when an objective and informed observer would conclude that the government action in question 'sends a message to non-adherents that they are outsiders, not full members of the political community, and an accompanying message to adherents that they are insiders, favored members of the political community.'"[45] Judge Polster insisted that by applying this test, it was clear "to any reasonable observer" that the seal was endorsing one particular religion—Christianity. Therefore, the seal was invalid. It was "unconstitutionally sectarian."[46]

The judge's opinion, of course, was not the end of the dispute. By a 5-to-2 margin, the city council voted to appeal the decision.[47] There were then extended discussions between the parties, and with the guiding hand of the district court and with the explicit decision by the insurance company for the city that it would not fund an appeal, the city agreed to withdraw its appeal and replace the cross with the motto "In God We Trust."[48]

The ruling might not have pleased either those who favored a broader inclusion of religion in the public sphere or those who wanted a more absolute separation of church and state. "In God We Trust" is still an explicit endorsement of God-based religions. But this did not seem to bother the court in *Stow*. It had noted the many instances of governmental practices, mottoes, statements, and even coins and stamps that referred to God. In fact, the court noted twice the fact that "our money says 'In God We Trust.'"[49] So, as the court indicated, maybe the First Amendment applied only to sectarian endorsements. Perhaps there was a "triviality exception" to the establishment clause.[50]

Judge Polster was told by counsel on behalf of the city of Stow that the law as to establishment was and continued to be changing.[51] As mentioned, prior to the *Stow* decision, the U.S. Supreme Court had considered the city seal for

Edmund, Oklahoma. In *Robinson v. City of Edmond,*[52] the U.S. District Court for the Western District of Oklahoma held the city of Edmond's seal with a cross in one quadrant to be constitutional. The Tenth Circuit disagreed, overruled the federal district court decision, and found that the seal was an explicit endorsement of Christianity and therefore in violation of the establishment clause. It is significant that three justices of the U.S. Supreme Court dissented in the denial of certiorari. The basis for their dissent was supposedly a desire to have the issue of standing addressed.[53] Still, the speculation suggested that the Supreme Court was one or two votes away from consideration of the issue of what was or was not endorsement in or by a symbol.[54] Judge Polster chose not to speculate. Unlike the district court judge in Oklahoma, he focused on the law at the time and did not try to predict the future.[55]

A similar choice had to be made by Northern District judges when they addressed cases involving the public display of the Ten Commandments.

The Ten Commandments Cases—*Ashbrook* and *Lucas*

In 1980, in *Stone v. Graham,* a per curiam opinion, the U.S. Supreme Court held that a statute that required the posting of a copy of the Ten Commandments (the Decalogue) on the wall of each public classroom violated the First Amendment.[56] Applying two *Lemon* prongs, the Court first stated that the supposedly secular legislative purpose to call attention to the roots of the "fundamental legal code of Western Civilization and the common law of the United States" was not legitimate. The "pre-eminent purpose for posting the Ten Commandments on schoolroom walls," the Court said, "is plainly religious in nature. The Ten Commandments are undeniably a sacred text in the Jewish and Christian faiths, and no legislative recitation of a supposed secular purpose can blind us to that fact." These Commandments were not limited to general moral principles but also specifically included the "religious duties of believers."[57]

Moreover, the effect of the posting was to "induce" the observers (here, the schoolchildren) to "read, meditate upon, perhaps to venerate and obey the Commandments."[58] Finally, the fact that the money for the display or distribution of the Decalogue came from private, nongovernmental sources was held to be irrelevant. The money was being used under the "auspices" of and therefore with the "official support" of the government.[59]

That decision, of course, did not end the debate. In 2000, an Ohio common pleas court judge in Mansfield (Richland County) put two framed posters in his courtroom. One poster featured the Bill of Rights and the other the Ten Commandments. On other walls in the courtroom were portraits with quotations from historical figures such as Thomas Jefferson, James Madison, Alexander Hamilton, and Abraham Lincoln. There were many other displays in the courthouse that contained photographic reproductions of historical documents and posters of other historical figures. There was an immediate challenge to the Ten Commandments display, which was heard by U.S. District Court Judge Kathleen McDonald O'Malley in *American Civil Liberties Union Foundation v. Ashbrook*.[60]

Following *Stone v. Graham*, Judge O'Malley applied the *Lemon* three-part test. She found that the clear purpose of the display was religious and not merely the promotion of general values: "The 'moral absolutes' the [state] Judge has chosen to display are those embraced by particular religious groups."[61] Moreover, even if the court had concluded that the purpose of the display was secular, in applying the endorsement test any reasonable observer would have believed that the government was endorsing a sacred text.[62]

The county and the state court judge argued that the display had to be seen in the context of all the displays in the courthouse. Judge O'Malley rejected that argument. The display here was not integrated into a secular display—it was "both prominent and relatively isolated."[63] Further, the language in the display was not like the use of the word *God* in the state motto, "With God, All Things Are Possible," nor was it like the "In God We Trust" on coins. Those were examples of how certain things, by "historical precedent," became "ceremonial deism," which no reasonable observer would accept as endorsement of any particular religion. This specific display simply was not in the historically or ceremonially justified category.[64]

On appeal, the majority of the judges of the Sixth Circuit agreed.[65] Adopting the reasoning of the district court, they found that there was no permissible secular purpose to the display and that it thus failed that prong of the *Lemon* test.[66] Although not needed for its holding, the court also found, like the district court, that a reasonable person would believe by the placement of the display that there was a government endorsement of religion and that the display was not merely acceptable ceremonial deism.[67]

Judge Alice Batchelder dissented. Citing cases in the previous decade, she minimized and distinguished the prior Supreme Court decision in *Stone v. Graham*. Judge Batchelder asserted that the state judge's articulated secular purpose—to educate community groups on moral principles—should have been given deference on a declaratory judgment motion.[68] Moreover, this display with barely readable text, in the context of other displays in the building, made it clear that "a reasonable observer would not deem the display to be an endorsement of religion."[69] Finally, Judge Batchelder argued that the courts should take into account "historical precedent." Certain religious usages had become part of the "fabric of our society."[70] And obviously, as indicated by numerous usages, "government acknowledgment of the important foundational role of the Ten Commandments is indeed part of the fabric of our society."[71]

This issue resurfaced almost immediately in dealing with a Ten Commandments display on the Lucas County Courthouse lawn, erected in 1957. On November 26, 2002, the American Civil Liberties Union filed suit to have it removed.[72] The case was assigned to Chief Judge James Carr. As there were two cases pending before the U.S. Supreme Court concerning displays of the Decalogue, he deferred his decision until the higher court ruled in those cases.[73]

The Supreme Court decided the two cases on June 27, 2005, in *Van Orden v. Perry* and *McCreary v. ACLU*.[74] These decisions, however, did not resolve definitively all issues relating to when, where, and how a display of the Ten Commandments was permissible. The constitutionality of each display had to be determined case by case, depending on the context and surroundings.[75]

In both cases, four justices found the two displays constitutional and four found them unconstitutional. Justice Stephen Breyer made the fifth and deciding vote in each instance. In *Van Orden v. Perry* , the challenge was to the placement of a six-foot-tall, three-foot-wide pink granite monument with the Ten Commandments, as well as other Jewish and Christian symbols, on the grounds of the Texas state capitol. The monument was one of seventeen monuments and twenty-one historical markers that decorated the twenty-two-acre park, and it had been in place for forty years. As a matter of context and history, Justice Breyer found the display a close case but not unconstitutional.[76]

In *McCreary v. ACLU*, the Commandments were inside two courthouses and a public school in Kentucky. In his majority opinion, Justice David Souter, joined by Justice Breyer, found the display to be a violation of the establishment clause. The Court emphasized the history of the courthouse displays. At first, the Ten Commandments comprised a solitary display; they became part of a broader display of historical documents only in the face of litigation. The Supreme Court accepted the lower court's determination that there was a "patently religious purpose" to displaying the Commandments and that this purpose was not hidden by "sandwiching them" between secular texts only after they had been challenged.[77]

In short, it was now up to Chief Judge Carr to decide "which of [these] two cases is most like the one in Lucas County."[78] His colleague had ruled just a few years earlier that a mounted poster in a courtroom, even though there were other displays in the courthouse, violated the establishment clause. Here, there was a monument that was very visible to pedestrians and nearby offices. There were other symbols adorning the monument. It was near a Catholic war memorial, and, as with the display in the *Ashbrook* case, there were numerous other memorials and displays close by.[79]

Again as with the *Ashbrook* case, the county argued that the monument had a clear secular purpose, for it represented "historical notions of law and commemorate[d] the role of the Decalogue in the enforcement of the rule of law."[80] Chief Judge Carr noted the difficulty the Supreme Court had in applying the establishment clause to Ten Commandments displays, and then he sought to "analyze the ACLU's claims" under the reasoning of the Supreme Court in *McCreary* and *Van Orden*.[81]

Judge Batchelder had suggested that the courts should defer to the government's stated secular purpose unless it was a sham, and Chief Judge Carr noted that the Supreme Court made the same suggestion in *McCreary*.[82] The "rather scant" record indicated that the monument had been put up by the Fraternal Order of Eagles in 1958 to "promote a moral code of conduct, rather than religious dogma, and they did so as part of a broad-reaching effort by that organization to reduce juvenile delinquency." The court would not second-guess the justification, especially as the Supreme Court had "specifically included combating juvenile delinquency by depicting a moral code of conduct as a legitimate secular purpose."[83]

As to whether the display would be considered by a reasonable observer to be government endorsement of religion, the judge looked at the context. The monument was not put up by the government but by a private entity, which had placed these types of monuments in other places as well. It was surrounded by other displays, and though the situation was not as clear-cut as that described in the *Van Orden* case, this fact negated the idea of endorsement by the state. He therefore determined that the "physical context of the monument would not cause an objective observer to conclude the County is using it to proclaim religious doctrine."[84] Further, deference meant that "while some who see it may read its text as a proclamation of faith, and give it a measure of devotion, the Lucas County Decalogue neither compels that interpretation nor commands that response on the part of an objective observer."[85]

Simply stated, in reviewing the most recent cases and particularly the opinion of Justice Breyer, the judge found that some of the factors that had not been relevant in 1980, the time of *Stone v. Graham*, were relevant in 2006. The avowed secular purpose was to be given credence and not viewed skeptically. The goal of the display was to have the passing public read and review the explicit God-given rules. This did not mean that "despite the sectarian antecedents of its test, [it] has the effect of endorsing religion in general or the specific tenets of any particular sectarian assembly." And the courts were now to take into account the source of the funding for the display.[86]

The changing standards that had to be applied by judges of the Northern District can also be illustrated by looking at how the court dealt with the constitutional issues involved with funding religious entities and activities.

Funding of Religious Activities or Entities—
Simmons-Harris v. Zelman

In 1973, in *Committee for Public Education v. Nyquist*,[87] the U.S. Supreme Court reviewed a New York state statute that provided various forms of aid to nonpublic elementary and secondary schools. Applying the *Lemon* three-part test, the Court found that the giving of money or other forms of aid to religious schools, whether directly or indirectly through tuition reimbursements, had the primary effect of advancing religion and was therefore in violation of the establishment clause.

In *Aguilar v. Felton* (1985), the U.S. Supreme Court considered a First Amendment challenge to a New York City program that sent public school teachers into parochial schools to provide remedial education. The program had been established pursuant to a 1965 federal statute providing funding to elementary and secondary schools. The Supreme Court, in a 5-to-4 decision, again applying the *Lemon* test, found that such a program provided an "excessive entanglement of church and state in the administration of those benefits."[88]

In 1985, Judge John Potter applied these standards in reviewing a policy in the Findley, Ohio, school system that allowed religion classes to be taught in public elementary schools before and after the school day. He found that the policy, under a *Lemon* review, gave the "symbolism of endorsement" and also meant "excessive entanglement" of the school with religious instruction. It was therefore unconstitutional.[89]

But in 1997, the U.S. Supreme Court, in *Agostini v. Felton*, began to rethink its previous decisions, and, again in a 5-to-4 decision, it specifically overruled *Aguilar*. Writing for the majority, Justice O'Connor talked about the trend of cases and the Court's changed understanding of the law and found that the use of government money for specific programs did not promote religion, entangle government with religion, or even "endorse" religion. It was therefore constitutional.[90]

In *Good News Club v. Milford Central School District* (2001), a religious club in New York State's Milford Central School District wanted to use elementary school classrooms for religious instruction before and after classes. The U.S. Supreme Court said allowing such use could not possibly be considered endorsement of religion.[91]

But what about the actual funding of sectarian schools? Did the trend of cases indicate that the law was changing in regard to public funding of programs in religious institutions? As long as laws and programs were neutral on religions and did not coerce participation or endorse any religious dogma, would they now be upheld?[92] Despite recent Supreme Court decisions, by the end of the 1990s the Justices had not overruled *Nyquist*. What should a federal judge do when considering a 1995 Ohio statute that provided money to students to attend sectarian schools through a voucher system?

In 1995, the Ohio legislature enacted a special program for all students in the Cleveland City School District. One component of the program allowed children to attend "alternative schools," including religious schools, through a voucher system. Another component provided a tutorial program for students in the Cleveland public schools.[93] The provision for vouchers to private—including sectarian—schools was challenged as being in violation of the establishment clause because it provided direct funding for religious education with public funds. The premise for the challenge was the holding in *Committee for Public Education v. Nyquist*.[94]

The case was assigned to Judge Solomon Oliver Jr. On August 24, he granted the plaintiffs' motion for the preliminary injunction and then a few days later entered a limited stay of the injunction to allow those students already enrolled to continue for one semester. He also scheduled an expedited process to consider motions for summary judgment made by both sides. On the day it was issued, Judge Oliver's order was appealed to the Sixth Circuit. While that appeal was being considered, the state filed a motion for a stay with the U.S. Supreme Court.[95]

On November 5, 1999, the Supreme Court granted the state's request for a stay, pending disposition of the appeal by the Sixth Circuit. The Sixth Circuit then put all appeals "in abeyance" because of the expedited schedule.[96] The stay of the injunction was decided by a 5-to-4 vote. The five justices who voted for the stay were the same five who had, two years before in *Agostini*, overruled an earlier precedent to allow government funding of teachers in private sectarian schools.[97] These five justices would also uphold the constitutionality of this Ohio voucher system in 2002.[98]

As Judge Oliver saw it, his role was not to be a predictor of what the Supreme Court might or might not do. His role was to analyze what the law was as of the time of his determination.[99] On the merits of the constitutional issue of separation of church and state, he did not accept the argument that this was a neutral voucher system. Specifically, he noted that "over 82% of the schools involved [in the voucher program] are church-affiliated" and "96% of the students are enrolled in sectarian schools." Further, he said, "a central part of each school's program is instruction in the theology or doctrine of a particular faith and the religion and religious doctrines are an integral part of the entire school experience." Judge Oliver described an example of a parent's handbook for one of the schools involved in the voucher program. There, the specific "objectives of education" were to "communicate the gospel message of Jesus," "provide an opportunity for growth in prayer," and "provide instruction in religious truths and values." Another school he described noted that it would be "highly inconsistent for any parent to send a child not a Christian and/or not interested in learning about Jesus Christ" and that the "primary focus" of all school activities and teachings was "on our Lord and Savior, Christ."[100]

In short, according to Judge Oliver, the voucher program resulted in "government-sponsored religious indoctrination."[101] And this was inconsistent with the mandate of the First Amendment that the government had to be "scrupulously neutral."[102]

After reviewing the history of the establishment clause and cases dealing specifically with aid to sectarian schools,[103] Judge Oliver indicated that the controlling "applicable standard" was *Lemon v. Kurtzman* and that the most recent decisions from the Supreme Court modified only one aspect of that test. Moreover, the case most directly on point, *Committee for Public Education v. Nyquist*, which had been based on the standards set out in *Lemon*, was still the precedent that had to be followed or distinguished.[104]

Nyquist dealt with a New York law that provided reimbursement to parents of children who attended private schools, including sectarian schools. In the case Judge Oliver was deciding, the Ohio law provided vouchers that parents could use to send their children to private schools, including sectarian schools. The Supreme Court had said that the New York grants had the "impermissible effect of advancing religion." And for his part, Judge Oliver held that the Ohio voucher law was "indistinguishable for Establishment Clause purposes from the tuition reimbursement program in *Nyquist*."[105]

The state of Ohio argued that the trend of cases indicated *Nyquist* was no longer good law. But Judge Oliver indicated that whatever his personal perspectives might be as to the value of the program, he was "constrained" by his role as a district court judge to follow specific precedent: it was "was not within the power of this court to declare that a case decided by the United States Supreme Court should be overruled."[106]

Reviewing cases after *Nyquist*, the court again stated that "[in] all pertinent respects, the voucher program [was] factually indistinguishable from the tuition reimbursement program" in *Nyquist* and was "unlike any case in which the Supreme Court has upheld programs providing aid to religious educational institutions." It was therefore "in violation of the Establishment Clause."[107]

The plaintiffs understood the implications of the Supreme Court's original stay and so consented to a stay of Judge Oliver's order, pending further judicial review.[108] A year later, the Sixth Circuit affirmed Oliver's decision.[109] A two-judge majority, reviewing the district court's summary judgment de novo, stressed that "the Supreme Court has not overturned or rescinded the *Lemon* test, even as it has used its framework to shape differing analysis."[110] Like the district court, the Sixth Circuit majority felt that *Nyquist* was "on point with the matter at hand."[111] And again like the district court, it cited the Supreme Court's admonition not to assume that a clear precedent has been overruled by implication and that lower federal courts should leave to the Supreme Court the prerogative of applying a new standard: "The Supreme Court has refrained from overruling *Nyquist*, and has instead distinguished various cases on the basis of their facts; this Court has accordingly followed that approach."[112] Since *Nyquist* governed the court's result, the Ohio voucher program violated the establishment clause.[113]

The dissenting opinion sought to distinguish the Ohio voucher plan from the New York plan in *Nyquist*.[114] But in any event, it said, "the rule of law upon which *Nyquist* was decided has changed,"[115] and the constitutionality of the Ohio voucher program had to be tested "against this background of changed Supreme Court Establishment Clause jurisprudence."[116] After reviewing the cases and the "changed jurisprudence," the dissent stated that a new review should give "careful consideration to the full panoply of Supreme Court Establishment Clause jurisprudence, and not just one, inapposite 1973 case [*Nyquist*]."[117]

In light of its decision on the original stay, it was quite predictable that the U.S. Supreme Court would reverse both the district court and the Sixth Circuit.[118] And, of course, it did.[119] Chief Justice William Rehnquist wrote the opinion for the five-justice majority. He pointed out that in a series of cases, the Court had had "consistent and unbroken" jurisprudence. Establishment clause challenges to "neutral government programs that provide aid directly to a broad class of individuals, who, in turn, direct the aid to religious schools or institutions of their own choosing" had been rejected.[120] The Ohio plan had no incentives to "skew" a choice toward religious schools. The law was neutral. Parents could freely choose to send their children to a private school, including a sectarian school, or to a public school with special financial assistance provided to that public school student.[121] The fact that an overwhelming majority of those in the program chose to go to a sectarian school was just not relevant. "No reasonable observer would think that a neutral program of private choice, where state aid reaches religious schools solely as a result of the numerous independent decisions of private individuals, carries with it the imprimatur of government endorsement."[122]

The lower courts had relied on the 1973 *Nyquist* decision. Over strong dissents, both the Chief Justice and Justice O'Connor in her concurrence argued that this decision did not mark "a dramatic break from the past."[123] However, the justices noted, "to the extent the scope of *Nyquist* has remained an open question in light of these later decisions, we now hold that *Nyquist* does not govern neutral educational assistance programs that, like the program here, offer aid directly to a broad class of individual recipients defined without regard to religion."[124]

Conclusion

The judges of the U.S. District Court for the Northern District of Ohio have been asked to be arbiters in the constitutional debate about the allowable scope of religion in the public sphere. Their impact has been significant. Sometimes,

as with the issue of a cross on the Stow city seal, they can be final decision makers. But more often, they must follow the precedent set by the appellate courts,
particularly the Supreme Court. In some cases, as in the Lucas County Ten
Commandments case, they can await guidance from the higher courts. On most
occasions, however, as in the school vouchers case, they must decide by trying
to discern what prior precedents mean. In those situations, it is important that
they develop a careful record to allow appellate courts to properly address the
issues.[125] In the future, as in the past, their job as federal district judges will
continue to require them to use all their skills to "determine the controversy."

Notes

1. U.S. Const. amend. I. This provision was later applied to state and local governments, through the Fourteenth Amendment. Everson v. United States, 330 U.S. 1, 8 (1947).
2. See Ezra Stiles, "The United States Elevated to Glory and Honor" 55 (1793), quoted
in John Witte Jr., "The Essential Rights and Liberties of Religion in the American Constitutional Experiment," *Notre Dame Law Review* 71 (1996): 371, 373. See, e.g., Church of the
Lukumi Babalu Aye, Inc. v. City of Hialeah, 508 U.S. 520 (1993); Everson, 330 U.S. at 16.
3. See John Sexton, "The Warren Court and the Religion Clauses of the First Amendment," in *The Warren Court: A Retrospective*, ed. Bernard Schwartz (New York: Oxford
University Press, 1996), 104, 111.
4. See Martin H. Belsky, "Antidisestablishmentarianism: The Religion Clauses at the
End of the Millennium," *Tulsa Law Journal* 33 (1997): 93.
5. See, e.g., American Civil Liberties Union v. Board of Commissioners of Lucas County,
444 F. Supp. 2d 805 (N.D. Ohio 2006) (cross-motions); Coles v. Cleveland Board of Education, 959 F. Supp. 1337 (N.D. Ohio 1996) (cross-motions), rev'd, 171 F.3d 369 (6th Cir. 1999);
Ford v. Manuel, 629 F. Supp. 771 (N.D. Ohio 1985) (cross-motions); Rosati v. Toledo, Ohio
Catholic Diocese, 233 F. Supp. 2d 917 (N.D. Ohio 2002) (Defendant's Motion).
6. See Kevin J. McCabe, "Note: Toward a Consensus on Religious Images in Civic
Seals under the Establishment Clause—*American Civil Liberties Union v. City of Stow*"
Villanova Law Review 46 (2001): 585.
7. Compare American Civil Liberties Union v. Board of Commissioners of Lucas County,
444 F. Supp. 2d 805 (N.D. Ohio 2006) with American Civil Liberties Union Foundation v.
Ashbrook, 211 F. Supp. 873 (N.D. Ohio 2002), aff'd, 375 F.3d 484 (6th Cir. 2004).
8. Coles, 959 F. Supp. 1337. In *Coles*, the Cleveland Board of Education opened its
board meetings with a prayer or a moment of silence. A former student and a schoolteacher
challenged this practice. Judge David D. Dowd Jr. ruled that the prayer of a public delibera-
tive body in an adult situation, such as a school board meeting, was similar to having a
prayer at the beginning of a legislative session. It was not similar to having a prayer in a
school setting. It therefore did not violate the establishment clause. On appeal, in a 2-to-1
decision, the Sixth Circuit noted that the case was "squarely between the proverbial rock"
of impermissible opening prayers at graduation ceremonies "and the hard place" of allowable prayers at legislative sessions. Though noting that "reasonable minds can differ," the
majority found the case closer to the prayers at graduation—"the proverbial rock." Coles,
171 F.3d at 371.

9. Yaacov v. Collins, 649 F. Supp. 2d 679 (N.D. Ohio 2009). See also Abdulah v. Fard, 974 F. Supp. 1112 (N.D. Ohio 1997), *aff'd*, 1999 U.S. App. LEXIS 1466, 173 F.3d 854 (6th Cir. 1999).

10. See Wellmaker v. Duhill, 836 F. Supp. 1375 (N.D. Ohio 1993); Johnson v. Collins, 2009 U.S. Dist. LEXIS 47844 (N.D. Ohio 2009).

11. McMurdie v. Doubt, 467 F. Supp. 766 (N.D. Ohio 1979).

12. City of Cleveland v. Nation of Islam, 922 F. Supp. 56 (N.D. Ohio 1995). The court did note that those precluded might be able to sue the conveners for discrimination.

13. See Cline v. Catholic Diocese, Case No. 3:97CV7472 (N.D. Ohio 1999), *rev'd*, 206 F.3d 651 (6th Cir. 1999).

14. Rosati, 233 F. Supp. 2d at 917.

15. The phrase *wall of separation* was used by Thomas Jefferson to describe the theory of the separation of church and state established by the First Amendment. See Everson, 330 U.S. at 1, 16.

16. Akron Center for Reproductive Health v. City of Akron, 479 F. Supp. 1172 (N.D. Ohio 1979), *aff'd in part and rev'd in part*, 651 F.2d 1198 (6th Cir. 1981), *aff'd in part and rev'd in part*, 462 U.S. 416 (1983).

17. Simmons-Harris v. Zelman, 72 F. Supp. 834, 850 (N.D. Ohio 1999), *aff'd*, 234 F.3d 945 (6th Cir. 2000), *rev'd sub nom.* Zelman v. Simmons-Harris, 536 U.S. 639 (2002), *citing* Mueller v. Allen, 463 U.S. 388, 393 (1983).

18. See Belsky, "Antidisestablishmentarianism," 33.

19. Simmons-Harris, 72 F. Supp. at 850, *quoting* Agostini v. Felton, 521 U.S. 203, 237 (1997), which in turn was quoting Rodriguez de Qujas v. Shearson/American Express, Inc. 490 U.S. 477 (1989) (emphasis and indentation in District Court Opinion).

20. American Civil Liberties Union v. City of Stow, 29 F. Supp. 2d 845, 852 (N.D. Ohio 1998) (hereafter cited as City of Stow).

21. Lemon v. Kurtzman, 403 U.S. 602 (1993).

22. This analysis, with cites to the *Lemon* case itself, comes from Martin H. Belsky, "The Religion Clauses and the 'Really New Federalism,'" *Tulsa Law Review* 42 (2007): 537, 543.

23. See School Dist. of Grand Rapids v. Ball, 473 U.S. 373, 383 (1985).

24. Agostini, 521 U.S. at 203, 234.

25. See Belsky, "Religion Clauses," 543.

26. See, e.g., Rusk v. Crestview, 220 F. Supp. 854, 857 (N.D. Ohio 2002), *rev'd*, 379 F.3d 418 (6th Cir. 2004); City of Stow, 29 F. Supp. 2d at 853.

27. Lynch v. Donnelly, 465 U.S. 668, 687 (1984) (O'Connor, J., concurring).

28. City of Stow, 29 F. Supp. 2d at 847.

29. Ibid.

30. See Robinson v. City of Edmond, 68 F.3d 1226 (10th Cir. 1995), *cert. denied*, 517 U.S. 1201 (1996).

31. "Stow Council Members Decide to Do Nothing about City Seal," *Akron Beacon Journal*, Metro Edition, December 20, 1996, D1; "Stow Votes to Retain Seal's Icons," *Akron Beacon Journal*, December 20, 1996, D5.

32. See Steve Hoffman, "Stow Gears Up for Seal Battle," *Akron Beacon Journal*, January 24, 1997, D1; Hoffman, "Pastors Plan Fight with ACLU over Seal," *Akron Beacon Journal*, February 5, 1998, D1; Hoffman, "Stow Remains Split over Seal," *Akron Beacon Journal*, February 11, 1997, B6.

33. There would be a two-year phaseout of the seal. Steve Hoffman, "City Officials in Stow Look to Seal Up Issue," *Akron Beacon Journal*, March 1, 1997, B1.

34. Jim Quinn, "Stow Votes to Reinstate Controversial Seal," *Akron Beacon Journal*, November 5, 1997, D5; Jim Quinn, "Clock Ticking on Lawsuit over Stow Seal," *Akron Beacon Journal*, November 8, 1997, C1.

35. William Canterbury, "ACLU Files Promised Lawsuit on Stow Seal," *Akron Beacon Journal*, December 17, 1997, D6.

36. Jim Quinn, "Stow Seal Legal Fight Might Cost Taxpayers," *Akron Beacon Journal*, November 28, 1997, B1; Quinn, "Stow Citizens May Join Suit," *Akron Beacon Journal*, January 21, 1998, B1.

37. Betty Lin-Fisher, "Judge Calls for Meeting on Stow Seal," *Akron Beacon Journal*, September 12, 1998, B1.

38. Motion of Defendant, City of Stow, for Summary Judgment, Case No. 5:97CV3271, May 15, 1998 (N.D. Ohio).

39. City of Stow, 29 F. Supp. 2d at 851.

40. Ibid., 851–52.

41. Ibid., 847.

42. Honorable Dan Aaron Polster, interview by Martin H. Belsky (Author), July 19, 2010.

43. City of Stow, 29 F. Supp. 2d at 847.

44. Lynch, 465 U.S. at 668, 690.

45. City of Stow, 29 F. Supp. 2d at 848–49.

46. Ibid., 852–53.

47. Betty Lin-Fisher, "City Council Votes to Appeal Ruling," *Akron Beacon Journal*, January 15, 1999, C2.

48. Karen Farkas, *Cleveland Plain Dealer*, April 16, 1999, B1.

49. City of Stow, 29 F. Supp. 2d at 850, 852.

50. *Compare* Martin H. Belsky, "Taking the Pledge," in *Law and Theology*, ed. Martin H. Belsky and Joseph Bessler-Northcutt (Durham, N.C.: Carolina Academic Press, 2005), 139, *with* Steven G. Gey, "'Under God': The Pledge of Allegiance and Other Constitutional Trivia," *North Carolina Law Review* 81 (2003): 1865.

51. Polster, interview.

52. Robinson v. City of Edmond, 68 F.3d 1226 (10th Cir. 1995), *cert. denied*, 517 U.S. 1201 (1996).

53. Robinson, 517 U.S. at 1201.

54. See McCabe, "Note," 585, 594–95.

55. See Salazar v. Buono, 559 U.S.__, 130 S. Ct. 1803 (2010) (considering the acceptability of a Latin cross on public land).

56. Stone .v Graham, 449 U.S. 39 (1980).

57. Ibid., 41.

58. Ibid., 42.

59. Ibid.

60. American Civil Liberties Union v. Ashbrook, 211 F. Supp. 2d 873, 875–77 (N.D. Ohio 2002), *aff'd*, 375 F.3d 484 (6th Cir. 2004), *cert. denied*, DeWeese v. ACLU of Ohio Found., Inc., 545 U.S. 115 (2005).

61. American Civil Liberties Union, 211 F. Supp. 2d at 888.

62. Ibid., 890.

63. Ibid., 892.

64. Ibid., 893.

65. American Civil Liberties Union v. Ashbrook, 375 F.3d 484 (6th Cir. 2004), *cert. denied*, DeWeese, 545 U.S. 115 (2005).

66. American Civil Liberties Union, 375 F.3d at 491–92.

67. Ibid., 494–95.
68. Ibid., 501–3.
69. Ibid., 503–6.
70. Ibid., 506 (citing Marsh v. Chambers, 463 U.S. 783, 792 [1983]).
71. Ibid.
72. Dale Emch, "Ohio's ACLU Sues to Bring Down Lucas County Ten Command-ments," *Toledo Blade,* December 13, 2002, A1.
73. Dale Emch, "Ten Commandments Case—Fate of Monument Downtown Hinges on U.S. Top Court," *Toledo Blade,* March 4, 2005, B1.
74. Van Orden v. Perry, 545 U.S. 677 (2005); McCreary County v. ACLU, 545 U.S. 844.
75. Robin Erb, "Rulings Throw Marker's Fate into Question—U.S. High Court Says Displays to Be Weighed Case by Case," *Toledo Blade,* June 28, 2005, A1.
76. Van Orden, 545 U.S. at 677, 698, 704 (Breyer, J., concurring).
77. Martin H. Belsky and Joseph Bessler-Northcutt, eds., *Law and Theology* (Durham, N.C.: Carolina Academic Press, 2005), 150. See McCreary County, 545 U.S. at 844. See also American Civil Liberties Union v. Board of Comm'rs, 444 F. Supp. 2d 805, 814 (N.D. Ohio 2006).
78. Erb, "Rulings Throw Marker's Fate into Question.—U.S. High Court Says Displays to be Weighed Case by Case," *Toledo Blade,* June 28, 2005 at A1.
79. American Civil Liberties Union v. Board of Comm'rs, of Lucas County, 444 F. Supp. 2d 805, 806–7 (N.D. Ohio 2006).
80. Ibid., 808.
81. Ibid., 809–10.
82. Ibid., 811.
83. Ibid., 812.
84. Ibid., 813.
85. Ibid., 813–14.
86. Ibid., 815–16.
87. Committee for Public Education v. Nyquist, 413 U.S. 756 (1973).
88. Aguilar v. Felton, 473 U.S. 402 (1985).
89. Ford, 629 F. Supp. at 771.
90. Agostini, 521 U.S. at 203.
91. Good News Club v. Milford Cent. Sch. District, 533 U.S. 98 (2001).
92. Belsky, "Antidisestablishmentarianism," 93, 100.
93. Simmons-Harris v. Zelman, 72 F. Supp. 2d 834, 836 (N.D. Ohio 1999), *aff'd,* 234 F.3d 945 (6th Cir. 2000), *rev'd sub nom.* Zelman v. Simmons-Harris, 536 U.S. 639 (2002). The original law was declared invalid under the Ohio constitution by the Ohio Supreme Court. It was "re-enacted in all pertinent parts" in 1999. Ibid.
94. Simmons-Harris, 72 F. Supp. 2d at 844.
95. Ibid., 840.
96. Ibid., 841.
97. Zelman v. Simmons-Harris, 528 U.S. 983 (1999).
98. Zelman, 536 U.S. at 639.
99. Honorable Solomon Oliver Jr., interview by author, July 19, 2010.
100. Simmons-Harris, 72 F. Supp. 2d at 837–38.
101. Ibid., 849.
102. Ibid., 863.
103. Simmons-Harris, 72 F. Supp. 2d at 842–44.
104. Ibid., 844–45.
105. Ibid., 845–49.

106. Ibid., 850.

107. Ibid., 864, 865.

108. Solomon, interview. See Simmons-Harris, 72 F. Supp. 2d at 865.

109. Simmons-Harris v. Zelman, 234 F.3d 945 (6th Cir. 2000), *rev'd sub nom.* Zelman v. Simmons-Harris, 536 U.S. 639 (2002).

110. Simmons-Harris, 234 F.3d at 952.

111. Ibid., 953.

112. Ibid., 955–56.

113. Ibid., 958, 961.

114. Ibid., 963–64.

115. Ibid., 965.

116. Ibid., 967.

117. Ibid., 974 (bracketed detail added).

118. See, e.g., "Comment: What Wall? Government Neutrality and the Cleveland Voucher Program," *Cumberland Law Review* 31 (2000): 709, 717–18; Mark Chadsey, "State Aid to Religious Schools: From Everson to Zelman," *Santa Clara Law Review* 44 (2004): 699, 748, 760.

119. Zelman, 536 U.S. at 639.

120. Ibid., 649.

121. Ibid., 653–54, 655–56.

122. Ibid., 655.

123. Ibid., 663 (concurring opinion of O'Connor). See ibid., 649.

124. Ibid., 662.

125. Solomon, interview.

8

From *Euclid* to the Development of Federal Environmental Law

*The U.S. District Court for the Northern District of Ohio
and the Regulation of Physical Space*

Keith H. Hirokawa

IN 1969, THE federal district court for the Northern District of Ohio occupied a position of potentially profound influence, for the Cuyahoga River was burning. Although the blaze on the river would illuminate the Ohio sky for only twenty-four minutes[1] — not even long enough for the local papers to snap a single photograph — the flames would be reflected on the hearts and homes of an entire embattled nation for decades through the flurry of federal environmental laws that followed. The Cuyahoga River became the symbol of a past that the nation would resolve to remedy.

The U.S. District Court for the Northern District of Ohio was not called upon to adjudicate the liabilities resulting from this pivotal event. But in the years preceding the Cuyahoga fire, the district court was asked to navigate conflicting jurisprudential approaches to the use of land, air, and water. This chapter explores a handful of these cases, bringing them to light in order to illustrate the nation's struggle over suspicious conceptions of economic advantage and fairness, flexible distinctions of private and public property, and evolving ideas of nature and health. The chapter begins with the 1924 decision in *Ambler Realty Corporation v. Village of Euclid,* which remains the most famous challenge to the constitutionality of zoning regulations. It then turns to the 1930 decision in *Swetland v. Curtiss Airports Corporation,* where the district court addressed the inevitable limitations in property rights above land following the advancement of powered human flight. Finally, it considers an opinion released on the eve of the Cuyahoga River fire, when the court was asked to choose between saving a town and protecting railroad operations in *Biechelle v. Norfolk & Western Railway Company.* Although the district court's decisions in these controversies do not bear the indelible character that we often attribute to law (the *Euclid* and *Swetland* opinions were overturned, and the decision in *Biechelle* might be considered unfortunate), the federal district courts for the Northern District of Ohio contributed to a legal framework in which the fire could occur and, perhaps more significantly, in which the fire could be perceived as an important event.

Nature and Nuisance in the Northern District of Ohio

It is often said that the exercise of property rights by any one owner must be limited in order to provide such property rights to many. In this regard, nuisance law has been an essential platform for determining when a person's actions fall outside the protective shelter of property rights. Typically expressed as an unreasonable interference with another individual's property interests or with the needs of the general public welfare—*sic utere tuo ut alienum non laedus* ("One should use his own property in such a manner as not to injure that of another")[2]—nuisance acts serve as a limitation on the freedom to control captured water, air, and land. Although the advent of administrative agencies has been the impetus for developing a deeper understanding of how and when land uses cause impacts to others and the environment, nuisance doctrine continues to serve as the foremost catalog of limitations on property rights.[3]

For the purposes of this chapter, nuisance law is historically relevant because Ohio was particularly industrious in developing its natural resources long before local, state, or federal governments were actively regulating natural resource production. Ohio's access to commerce via waterways and railroads, as well as its forests and mineral and oil deposits, have allowed the state to host a competitive marketplace. The state claims the first discovery of oil from a drilled well, in 1814, and it was one of the nation's most productive coal-mining states during the Industrial Revolution.[4] With an active industry, of course, came the inevitability that nuisance law—especially in conflicts over domestic and industrial pollution, vast landscape transformations, and controversies among competing property claims—would help characterize the geopolitical circumstances of the region. Three preliminary points are salient to understanding the influence of nuisance law on the controversies that loomed in the Northern District.

First, nuisance law requires courts to define the scope of property rights, and as such, nuisance is governed by state law. Ohio's development of nuisance law illustrates the manner in which law balances the economic and industrial needs of the time. For instance, although courts in Ohio employed nuisance to limit activities that directly interfered with the enjoyment of property by others (such as noise, smoke, and odors),[5] the courts were reluctant to enjoin normal railroad operations due to the immense public interest involved in freight transportation.[6] Nuisance was also invoked to regulate the means of social change. Because nuisance is a tidy tool for keeping public ways clear of obstruction, it was invoked to curtail the aggressive behaviors of labor advocates during strikes.[7] The flexibility inherent in the law of nuisance led to property dispute resolutions that reflected the "felt necessities of the time."[8]

Second, in Ohio as elsewhere, state and local governments have traditionally relied on nuisance as a justification for the governmental regulation of land use impacts. Because legislative prohibitions of nuisances are justified under the police power for the protection of the public health, safety, and welfare, courts were initially deferential to the local determination of public welfare needs, a rule that was punctuated in 1887 in *Mugler v. Kansas*.[9] Rejecting a challenge to the prohibition on liquor manufacture despite the devastating economic effect on the plaintiff's facility, the *Mugler* Court stressed that because property owners were not entitled to cause nuisances, prohibiting owners from causing nuisances did not impair property rights.[10]

Third, as state and local governments adapted the police power to an expanding array of public objectives, courts were called upon to tether the use of nuisance to a justification for regulating property use. In 1922, the U.S. Supreme Court changed the landscape by holding that a coal-mining regulation violated the property protections of the takings clause. In *Pennsylvania Coal Company v. Mahon*, Justice Oliver Wendell Holmes Jr. echoed the *Mugler* decision by noting that "government hardly could go on if to some extent values incident to property could not be diminished without paying for every such change in the general law," yet he cautioned that a regulation of property use might so fundamentally alter the benefits of ownership as to act as a physical invasion.[11] Simply because the regulatory goal served a public purpose, Holmes reasoned, did not justify allotting the burden of the public welfare to a few. Although "property may be regulated to a certain extent, if regulation goes too far it will be recognized as a taking."[12]

Land: Pigs in the Parlor of the Village of Euclid

The *Pennsylvania Coal* decision was cause for concern in local governments. In the time between the *Mugler* Court's reluctance to recognize the property effects of land use regulations and Justice Holmes's "too far" calculus in *Pennsylvania Coal*, so many local governments had adopted zoning regulations that the Court's resolution of the legitimacy of zoning was unavoidable. Zoning, a new concept at the dawn of twentieth century, was largely a consequence of the failure of nuisance to control the negative effects of urbanization: urban blight seemed immune to nuisance for a variety of reasons, not the least of which was the inability of plaintiffs to identify a suitable defendant. Zoning embodied the idea that the form of a city could be intentional, rather than subjected to the private, unrestricted, and often chaotic process of land use as an incident of property rights.

New York is typically credited for adopting the first comprehensive zoning ordinance, in 1916. Ohio adopted enabling legislation in 1920 that authorized local governments to enact zoning ordinances.[13] In 1922, an advisory commission appointed by Herbert Hoover, the secretary of commerce at that time, produced the Standard Zoning Enabling Act (SZEA), a model act that was widely followed in the early zoning jurisdictions.[14] By 1926, hundreds of municipal governments had implemented comprehensive zoning schemes. However, of all the dates on which zoning regulations were enacted in this period, the most important was November 13, 1922, the date on which the village of Euclid, Ohio, concluded its six-month investigation of zoning laws and adopted its own zoning ordinance.[15]

The zoning scheme in Euclid was specifically intended to halt an industrial development trend spreading into the village from the city of Cleveland. In the preamble to the ordinance, the public needs for building regulations were specified: that as a "residential suburb" of Cleveland, the village was largely residential or restricted to residential uses; that the village had made available sufficient land for manufacturing, industrial, and commercial purposes; that the public water and sewer systems lacked capacity to accommodate "more congested use"; and that the regulations were necessary to preserve the character of the village for the public "health, safety, convenience, comfort, prosperity, and general welfare."[16] To accomplish this feat, the village established use, height, and building area regulations to apply throughout its jurisdiction. Those who objected to the regulations were especially opposed to the use restrictions. Use districts identified the most appropriate locations for industrial, commercial, and multifamily and single-family residential development, and the districts were intended to exclude all land uses that were considered incompatible with the primary use. Industry, therefore, would not be located next to affluent, single-family neighborhoods.

Ambler Realty, which held acreage in the village for its investment possibilities, objected strongly. When it decided to bring the first federal court challenge to comprehensive zoning against the village of Euclid, several cases were pending or had been decided in various state courts. The decisions (and the causes raised to the courts) showed no common thread from which an understanding of the zoning application of the police power could be stitched.[17] Yet there was enough concern raised by the challenge for the village to amend its zoning ordinance by adding several permitted uses to several districts and altering the zoning map to make Ambler Realty's speculative holdings more adaptable to commercial and industrial development.[18] The offer did not appease Ambler Realty, and the matter proceeded to trial before District Court Judge David C. Westenhaver of the Northern District of Ohio.

At the outset of the decision, Judge Westenhaver acknowledged the importance of the dispute. The court presaged, "This case is obviously destined to go higher."[19] But the magnitude of the case was undermined by Judge Westenhaver's impression of the evidence submitted at trial. "Much of the evidence is immaterial; still more of it is without substantial weight," he opined, speaking specifically about the volume of evidence regarding the lack of capacity in the village's water and sewer supply to the stated purpose of preventing potential congestion from unrestricted development. Westenhaver agreed that such problems were of public concern, but he held to the belief that such concerns involved the village's failure or refusal to perform its duty to provide public services and should not fall onto the shoulders of vacant property owners.

The village claimed that the police power authorized local governments to avoid urban evils through prevention. Judge Westenhaver dismissed the village's reasoning as mere rhetorical device. To him, the deference requested by the village to its political machine was the injury, as it would eventually subject private property "to temporary and passing phases of public opinion" in a way that cut at the heart of the notion of property itself.[20] Property value, asserted the judge, was only a consequence of property use; there could be no property without the right to control and use.[21] He ruled that whatever the village's purpose might be, zoning's restrictive effect on an owner's land use choices resulted in a transfer of property rights from a private to a public owner, a trick that could be accomplished only when the owner was compensated.

The U.S. Supreme Court was not so suspicious of zoning. In an opinion authored by Justice George Sutherland, zoning found its justification in the police power. In the first place, wrote Sutherland, where the legislative scheme was "fairly debatable," it was not for the court to interfere and scrutinize the judgment of the community.[22] As to the substance of zoning, the Court found that the public welfare would be served by separating incompatible land uses and identifying areas in which an industrial, commercial, or other more intensive use would be "like a pig in the parlor instead of the barnyard."[23] Residential neighborhoods, which were most sensitive, could be protected by restricting the location of incompatible land uses without running afoul of property. Nuisance, which may have been a poor tool for avoiding the evils of urbanization, would be the platform on which municipalities would create order in the city and design urban life. Yet with the expansion of nuisance in the form of zoning, the Northern District Court's effort to protect private property and the preferences of owners was futile.

What remained troubling (and continues to taint zoning to this day) was the type of order envisioned in the zoning scheme. Beyond the property conflicts at issue in *Euclid*, the divide between Westenhaver's and Sutherland's understandings of the zoning power raised concerns about the social effects of separating land uses. Judge Westenhaver feared the manner in which zoning promised greater property protections for the affluent. Noting that the U.S. Supreme Court had rejected an effort to establish race districts in the city of Louisville,[24] Judge Westenhaver cast zoning as an indirect means of legalized segregation. From the bench, zoning reflected on the welfare of the few and not the public: "The purpose to be accomplished is really to regulate the mode of living of persons who may hereafter inhabit it. In the last analysis, the result to be accomplished is to classify the population and segregate them according to their income or situation in life."[25] Whether Westenhaver's concern was inescapable remained a matter of some debate, but the weight of experience seemed to suggest zoning was a means to ensure that "rich people can see other rich people on the far side of their large suburban lots, and the poor live snugly next door to the poor."[26] Nevertheless, Justice Sutherland addressed this concern, focusing not on the potential abuse of zoning but on the proper use of this power. The police power, Sutherland argued, enabled governments to adapt to social and economic changes to preserve the public welfare.[27]

Air: Property into the Heavens

Nuisance law played a more doctrinal role in determining the propriety of other land uses, and as a second instance of the Northern District Court's jurisprudential influence, this chapter considers the advent of human flight. In *Swetland v. Curtiss Airports Corporation*,[28] the federal district court enjoined the operation of an airport to protect adjacent properties from dust, dropped circulars, and low flights during takeoffs and landings. However, to reach this result, the district court tangled with one of the common law's most elusive doctrinal canons—*ad coelum*—and, in the process, attempted to resolve the conflict to protect property despite the inevitable future of human flight.

The idea of ownership of airspace—*cuius est solum, eius est usque ad coelum et ad inferos* ("for whoever owns the soil, it is theirs up to Heaven and down to Hell")—has ancient origins.[29] William Blackstone opined: "Land in its legal signification has an indefinite extent, upwards as well as downwards; whoever owns the land possess all the space upwards to an indefinite extent; such is the maxim of the law."[30] Coined before any feasible expectation of human flight, the canon developed over centuries of controversies that involved intruding tree limbs, overhanging scaffolding, and unwanted projectiles entering the space above neighboring properties.[31] Arguably, however, the resilience of *ad coelum* was illusory. The doctrine applied reasonably well to tree limbs and bullets: the role of *ad coelum* in such disputes was not particularly problematic. But then, on the morning of December 17, 1903, amid a world of skepticism about the possibility, the Wright brothers of Dayton, Ohio, accomplished a herculean feat and guaranteed a collision between innovation and the *ad coelum* doctrine. The brothers launched a human into the air, sustained by a machine, for a distance of 120 feet.[32] Their marvelous invention would soon change methods of warfare, travel, and communication, and it ultimately would make the world seem much smaller.

The primary question raised by the airplane was one of unoccupied space: how far into the heavens did the property boundary reach? The importance of this question cannot be overstated. By 1930, humans had flown across the globe and navigated the airspace over both poles. Aviation securities were traded on the New York Stock Exchange. People and mail traveled the air. Innovation and interest in flight had not yet peaked, and the aviation industry found itself prepared to outlast the stock market crash of 1929.[33] Yet there was no clear indication that pilots were entitled to fly over private property.

Two doctrines—nuisance and trespass—might have settled the matter. The difference between the two approaches revolved around burden of proof. Trespass, as an exclusionary doctrine, protected boundaries: an injury was proven where an intrusion was shown. In contrast, nuisance required a plaintiff to show injury from some other, nonboundary incident of property, resulting in an interference with the enjoyment of property.[34] A resolution of *ad coelum* would require the court to take a position on boundaries. If property boundaries actually reached into the heavens above, any passing projectile might pierce the boundary and be considered a trespass, and as such, a finding that overhead flights could constitute a trespass would hobble flight. Each flight could subject the pilot to hundreds, if not thousands, of trespass actions.

To the extent that the intrusion of airspace resulted in touching the land or improvements, the injury might be presumed a trespass.[35] A similar argument might be made for low airspace intrusions, particularly at heights where the landowner might be expected to use the space.[36] Yet even the lowest elevations of most flights (at launching and landing, for instance) would occur at heights reachable only by unusually tall structures, and it might not be reasonable to think that every owner had plans to erect another Eiffel Tower. *Ad coelum* was soon tested in Ohio. When subsidiaries of the Curtiss-Wright Corporation opened an airport and flight school in a rural residential area, the Northern District was given the opportunity to shape the direction and content of property rights in airspace.[37]

The Wright brothers were Ohio boys, and Ohio claimed flight as their invention: the federal district court for the Northern District of Ohio could have proven an expedient venue for the evolution of airspace rights. As such, when Judge George Phillip Hahn was asked to enjoin the airport in 1930, the court's resolution bore the undertones of industry and invention. *Swetland v. Curtiss Airports Corporation* concerned the impacts of an airport and flying school on land adjacent to existing residential uses. The airport was designed to direct flights over the residences, often below 500 feet.[38] Even at such heights, airplanes were alleged to cause trespass and nuisance injuries. Judge Hahn wasted no time in recognizing the parochial importance of the issue in the case: "Because of the inventions and activities of the Wright Brothers, at Dayton, Ohio, Ohio regards itself as the mother state of aviation."[39] In addition, because aviation at that time remained largely experimental, Judge Hahn was not hesitant to secure the future of flight, asserting that "it is indispensable to the safety of the nation that airports and flying schools such as contemplated by the defendants be encouraged in every reasonable respect."[40]

The federal involvement in flight was an influential moment for Judge Hahn. Congress had defined "navigable airspace" and declared that such space "shall be subject to a public right of freedom of interstate and foreign air navigation."[41] The federal regulations also established elevations below which "aircraft shall not be flown": a safe distance or 1,000 feet above congested areas and "elsewhere at a height less than 500 feet, except where indispensable to an industrial flying operation."[42] Judge Hahn deferred to the expertise of the secretary of commerce in the area of aeronautics and identified the altitude of 500 feet as the upper limit of the effective possession of property, opining that the rights of the property owners above that elevation were impractical. The court concluded that the federal laws constitutionally curbed nuisance and trespass actions against reasonable flights and that *ad coelum* had no precedent extending property rights to "air space normally traversed by the aviator."[43]

Although Judge Hahn rejected the application of *ad coelum* into the heavens, he fractured his skepticism on the more challenging factual issue in the case—what rights did property owners have against lower flight elevations, such as during takeoffs and landings? Such impacts could be considered significant and pervasive, and as such, he said, "until the progress of aerial navigation has reached a point of development where airplanes can readily reach an altitude of 500 feet before crossing the property of an adjoining owner, or such crossing involves an unreasonable interference with property rights or with effective possession," courts could require larger airports to facilitate flying at such heights.[44] Specifically, Judge Hahn found that *ad coelum* could apply to flights at heights lower than 500 feet, and he portrayed such injury as optionally actionable in nuisance or trespass.

Judge Hahn's appeal to boundaries and trespass was overturned by the Sixth Circuit Court of Appeals. The Sixth Circuit agreed that an airport could not be established "where its normal operation will deprive a plaintiff of the use and enjoyment of [another's] property."[45] Moreover, the Sixth Circuit agreed that a landowner "has a dominant right of occupancy for purposes incident to his use and enjoyment of the surface," which might include a reasonable expectation of occupancy in the space in the "lower stratum."[46] However, in the "upper stratum," the landowner was not entitled to exclude or prevent use by others, except where such use interfered with his or her enjoyment of the surface. The appellate court held that the appropriate remedy for the latter was in nuisance and "not trespass." As the landowner had no right of exclusivity in the upper stratum, overhead flights did not impair a property right.[47]

Eventually, the U.S. Supreme Court would acquiesce in a limited applicability of *ad coelum* to flight by restricting the importance of boundaries at heights above where one could reasonably expect to use space. As noted by the Court, given the importance of flight, *ad coelum* "has no place in the modern world. The air is a public highway, as Congress has declared. Were that not true, every transcontinental flight would subject the operator to countless trespass suits. Common sense revolts at the idea."[48] Nuisance, not trespass, would provide the basis for navigating between competing land uses and setting the limitations of property rights in air. *Swetland* and the controversies that followed represent a second instance in which law whittled away at the boundaries of property over the objections of the Northern District courts.

Water: Keeping Our Feet out of the Fire

Like the controversies over zoning and airspace, geopolitical circumstances served as significant factors in the ability of the Northern District of Ohio to exert influence over the direction of pollution control laws. In 1969, District Court Judge Don Young faced growing tensions between industry and public health as he sifted through the trial records from a class action suit brought by residents of Sandusky against the Norfolk & Western Railway Company.[49] Sounding in nuisance, *Biechelle v. Norfolk & Western Railway Co.* concerned the health and environmental impacts of uncontained, airborne coal dust from the railroad's storage of fine industrial coals. The "black, greasy, dirt, which was difficult to wash or clean off" silted the waters of Lake Erie and "ruined the paint on [the plaintiffs'] homes, drifted inside and damaged rugs, draperies and other furnishings" in the town of Sandusky.[50] The plaintiffs offered evidence regarding their deteriorating health during windier seasons or more active markets, which led to the "inescapable" conclusion of the seriousness of plaintiffs' injuries.

The railroad offered evidence relating the degree of care taken in its operations. As argued by the railroad, the dust did not take flight *as a result* of the railroad's actions, and indeed, the railroad had taken every necessary and otherwise standard precaution. The railroad argued that its containment efforts should absolve it of any possible liability. The district court was unmoved: "Assuming this to be true, which plaintiffs strenuously deny, this argument may be answered by reference to an old case, citation unknown, dealing with the action of a man whose house was being shaken to pieces by blasting in a neighbor's quarry. The court held that it was no comfort to the plaintiff to know that his house was being demolished by the defendant in the most careful manner possible."[51] The court was clearly impressed with the defendant's effort to take advantage of precedential imprecision in distinguishing nuisance from negligence.[52] However, because the general public should not be required to suffer for the profits of the few, the law of nuisance would deliver industry into a new age: "We are, happily, departing from the era in which it was considered proper for any commercial enterprise, in the name of those profits which are not a dirty word in Ohio, to pollute the atmosphere, earth, and water beyond the endurance of the general public."[53] Whether Judge Young intended this statement as a warning to industry or as a personal commitment, his message was clear: the public had tolerated the indiscriminate mistreatment of the commons, but commercial enterprise had abused the privilege. As such, Judge Young chose to harken in the new era by shifting the burden of pollution onto commerce.

Young's disposition was far from radical. By 1969, citizens had witnessed as many environmental disasters (as that term might have been understood in 1969) as they had seen failures by the state and federal legislatures to control pollution. No state or federal agency exerted control over the location, design, or operation of solid waste facilities; the disposal of hazardous wastes; or waste disposal enforcement. Local agencies struggled to manage waste disposal and regulate air quality as part of their health programs.[54] Water remained as much a resource for drinking as for waste disposal. Nuisance had been unable to cast these circumstances as injuries in a manner that the court could redress. Yet at that time, the public demands for a clean and healthy environment were no longer met with contempt or reticence or even mere tolerance. Environmental quality was becoming a common call, reflecting on the reach of the message.

The final dilemma facing Judge Young was how to fashion a remedy to relieve the plaintiffs of their injuries. He recognized that a nuisance suit involved two competing property rights, not just a single offending use: "Just as the defendant has no right to destroy the property of the plaintiffs by its operations," he reasoned, "it is questionable whether plaintiffs have a right to relief which would destroy the legitimate activities of defendant."[55] Because of Young's sympathetic perspective on nuisance as a competition among rights, rather than as a mere infringement of an injured party, the array of options read like a bad dream: "It is possible that this Court has the burden of deciding whether the plaintiffs must continue to suffer in defendant's filth, or become citizens of a ghost town on an abandoned railway line and a silted-up harbor."[56]

Ultimately, Judge Young was guided by prudence, recognizing that "the present difficulty is certain, but the future disasters are uncertain."[57] Because the plaintiffs could choose to avoid further injury by relocating, staying clear of the silted waters, or simply ducking through the dust clouds, the court bet on the plaintiffs to lessen future injuries. Judge Young ordered the defendant "to continue the various methods of dust control it has been employing," based on the belief that "it should be possible to work out economically feasible methods of controlling the emission of coal dust without inhibiting the operations of defendant's facilities, and even permitting defendant to expand the operations should it desire to do so."[58] The judge described his reasoning in a manner that, in retrospect, projects a tragic irony. "It may well be," he said, "that the citizens of Sandusky can jump out of the frying pan and still avoid falling into the fire."[59] Three days later, on June 22, 1969, the Cuyahoga River was ablaze. Although the citizens of Sandusky may have been clear of the flames, the nation would not recover so quickly.

The federal courts of the Northern District of Ohio were not called upon to adjudicate the rights or liabilities from the 1969 fire. Nevertheless, the Northern District played a pivotal role in the controversy by essentially compelling the conclusion that the pollution problem could be solved only by appeal to the legislative branch, rather than the judiciary. Indeed, given Judge Young's resolution of *Biechelle*, it could easily be concluded that the judicial branch was willing but ill equipped to employ common-law nuisance remedies to transform pollution practices. Other limitations in Ohio's nuisance law suggest the judiciary's deficiency was more pronounced in the Northern District of Ohio, where many of the problems exemplified by the Cuyahoga River fire were not even actionable under the state's nuisance doctrine.

The first hurdle to consider was the preclusive effect that long-standing pollution practices had on private nuisance claims. For instance, in 1860, the city of Cleveland began to discharge raw sewage into a tributary stream known as Kingsbury Run. Approximately forty years later, the city's discharges had increased dramatically and combined with a variety of other domestic and industrial discharges to eventually overwhelm the stream. The stream was no longer able to absorb or carry the waste away. On appeal from an award of damages, the Ohio Supreme Court reversed, finding that "Kingsbury run is not within the rules of law for the protection of streams devoted to their primary uses."[60] By its continuous and public use of the run for over twenty-one years, the city had acquired prescriptive rights to the continuing discharge of waste against any competing riparian rights to the contrary, and the stream would be considered devoted to this use.[61] In addition to the typically onerous challenges faced by private nuisance plaintiffs, prescription was a gargantuan hurdle: prescription would block private nuisance claims, and given how common it was at the time to use streams, rivers, and lakes for sewage disposal, prescription was a blow to the Cuyahoga.[62]

Second, although the defense of prescription had little effect on the protection of the public welfare through public nuisance litigation, Ohio law raised other obstructions to public nuisance claims in environmental matters. In the 1940s and 1950s, the state and its municipalities began to assert some semblance of control over pollution. In 1951, the state adopted its first comprehensive water pollution statute.[63] The so-called Deddens Act provided that "no person shall cause pollution . . . of any waters of the state, or place or cause to be placed any sewage, industrial waste, or other wastes in a location where they cause pollution of any waters of the state."[64] The Water Pollution Control Board was given vast authority to gather evidence, issue enforcement orders, and grant permits. The general recollection, however, is that although Ohio's water quality law appeared far-reaching, it was inadequately (if ever) enforced by the state. As recounted by Jonathan Adler, the permits issued by the board did not indicate that the board was particularly visionary in its role. Permit conditions and discharge limits were not stringent, and the board adopted "a relatively hands off approach" to enforcement of permit limits.[65] The problem was that the statute also prevented cities and citizens from protecting themselves in the courts. Even though the legislature declared pollution into Ohio's waters to be a public nuisance, the law did not apply "in cases where the water pollution control board has issued a valid and unexpired permit."[66] Arguably, Ohio's first comprehensive pollution control laws merely legalized pollution and protected pollution practices from judicial scrutiny.

In addition, dedicating flowing waters to the benefit of industrial uses was not only practical (where else would wastes go?), it was also legitimized in the court's approval of zoning. In some cases, local governments would use the zoning power to attack the manner in which land uses impacted environmental quality, such as in the adoption of zoning regulations to control urban sediment transportation, to set minimum lot sizes for the purposes of aquifer protection, and to establish environmental quality districts that prevented erosion and landslides.[67] However, the Supreme Court's decision in *Euclid* also authorized local governments to regulate the impacts of land uses by locating offensive uses where the impacts could be minimized. More specifically, *Euclid* authorized local governments to concentrate the major sources of industrial pollution to the most appropriate areas of a city as a way of *avoiding* the creation of nuisances. In Cleveland and Akron, the most appropriate areas were on the Cuyahoga River.[68] The river served as a waste depository for these developing cities.

Just what sparked the 1969 Cuyahoga fire remains a matter of speculation, and given the limited damage it caused, many continue to wonder why we even remember this fire.[69] Most likely, its lasting significance stems from the monumental effort that ensued in the administrative and legislative bodies of the state of Ohio and the federal government.[70] Five months later, Senator Walter Hickel brought four steel companies—U.S. Steel, Republic Steel, Jones and Laughlin Steel, and Interlake Steel—to answer for pollution in the Cuyahoga River and Lake Erie.[71] Ten months after the fire, the Ohio Water Pollution Control Board imposed a building moratorium in the Cleveland area pending the development of a plan to control the regional sewer system.[72] The state of Ohio soon adopted its own host of environmental laws. The federal government also began its occupation of what has become a comprehensive field of environmental law by adopting regulatory programs governing air, water, and land pollution. Congress would even establish the Cuyahoga Valley National Park "for the purpose of preserving and protecting for public use and enjoyment, the historic, scenic, natural, and recreational values of the Cuyahoga River."[73]

The legacy of the Northern District of Ohio on the development of environmental law certainly includes the 1969 fire on the Cuyahoga River. But the flurry of environmental laws emerging from the embers of the fire had obvious implications for environments suffering historical practices of unscrupulous pollution. The courts of the Northern District of Ohio preside over many such areas and have been instrumental in facilitating the transition to modern environmental law due in part to the intensity of industrial operations pervading the region. Early in this transition, the Northern District courts were heavily tasked with enjoining industrial pollution activities and enforcing civil penalties under federal water pollution statute.[74] The mere presence of the court may have influenced the speedy resolution of regulatory enforcement actions, such as the enforcement action filed by the Department of Justice against U.S. Steel that immediately resulted in a settlement for a civil penalty of $6.45 million and a commitment to spend approximately $60 million to clean up air pollution from its mill in Lorain, Ohio.[75] Because of EPA's dissatisfaction with regulatory efforts of the state of Ohio,[76] the Northern District was also asked to enforce the rigid "new stationary source" emission standards under the Clean Air Act against the city of Painesville, despite a determination by Ohio EPA that the city's coal-burning facility could not be regulated as a new source.[77] The Northern District courts thereafter maintained their prominent role in developing environmental law over the course of several decades by ruling that a scienter is not required for an assessment of an administrative penalty for violation of environmental laws,[78] by offering loose constructions of statutory provisions intended to preclude duplicative enforcement of environmental laws,[79] by preserving the fullest range of cost recovery options for the United States in hazardous waste cleanup actions,[80] and by protecting the investigative function of the EPA.[81] As such, the story of the Northern District of Ohio confirms that, although "there is no question that modern environmental law finds its roots in common law nuisance,"[82] modern environmental law resulted from the legislative empowerment of courts to participate in the transformation of pollution practices, freed from the confines of the law of nuisance.

Conclusion

Over time, social and economic changes demanded that law concede significant claims of ownership in physical space. Property owners had been increasingly left to rely on the law of nuisance. Ultimately, however, nuisance failed to ensure those rights that were challenged by new circumstances and technologies. As portrayed in this chapter, the Northern District Court was situated—but perhaps unable—to influence the substance and direction of such rights and responsibilities in the use of land, air, and water resources.

By 1969, the Cuyahoga River had burned on at least nine separate occasions.[83] *Time* magazine ran an article on August 1, 1969, identifying the Cuyahoga as "among the worst" of all of the severely polluted rivers of the nation. The description of the Cuyahoga in the article was laden with shock and horror: "No Visible Life. Some River! Chocolate-brown, oily, bubbling with subsurface gases, it oozes rather than flows. 'Anyone who falls into the Cuyahoga does not drown,' Cleveland's citizens joke grimly, 'he decays.' The Federal Water Pollution Control Administration dryly notes: 'The lower Cuyahoga has no visible life, not even low forms such as leeches and sludge worms that usually thrive on wastes.' It is also—literally—a fire hazard."[84]

A combustible Cuyahoga would be only the first of many projects that lay ahead for the Northern District and the nation. Today, however, the circumstances causing the Cuyahoga River to ooze rather than flow have largely been resolved. The unabated disposal of waste into land, water, and air has been tempered by a mix of heavy-handed federalism and collaborative governance. Importantly, the array of pollution legislation enacted after the 1969 Cuyahoga River fire conceded the limitations of nuisance as a tool for achieving environmental quality, a result compelled in light of the evolution of nuisance and rights to physical space in the federal district for the Northern District of Ohio.[85]

Notes

Keith Hirokawa is an associate professor of law, Albany Law School. The author wishes to thank Luke Sledge and Andrew Wilson for their insightful research.

1. "Oil Slick Fire Damages 2 River Spans," *Cleveland Plain Dealer*, June 23, 1969, C11, as cited in Jonathan H. Adler, "Fables of the Cuyahoga: Reconstructing a History of Environmental Protection," *Fordham Environmental Law Journal* 14 (Fall 2002): 89, 95.

2. *Black's Law Dictionary*, 6th ed. (St. Paul, Minn.: West Publishing, 1990), 1380.

3. State v. Schweda, 736 N.W.2d 49, 56 (Wisc. 2007).

4. Ohio Oil and Gas Association, "Our Industry," available at http://www.ooga.org/history/our-industry; Ohio Air Quality Development Authority, "The Ohio Coal Story," available at http://www.ohioairquality.org/acdo/ohio_coal_story.asp.

5. See, e.g., Kepler v. Industrial Disposal Co., 85 N.E.2d 308 (Ohio App. 1948) (emissions from burning waste); Weber v. Butler County Bd. of Health, 74 N.E.2d 331 (Ohio 1947) (garbage accumulation and piggery odors).

6. Ohio courts adopted both the rule that railroad companies were legally entitled to operate their engines and the common knowledge that rail engines caused injuries from their noise, odors, and smoke. See, e.g., City of Hamilton v. Hausenbein, 139 N.E.2d 459, 461 (Ohio App. 1956) (reversing conviction of train engineer under ordinance prohibiting "loud and great annoying noise" in residential areas, on grounds that "the normal necessary noises incident to the operation of a railroad [cannot] be said legally to unreasonably disturb

any one"). See also Metzger v. Pennsylvania, O & D R. Co., 66 N.E.2d 203, 206 (Ohio 1946) (finding that the emission of black smoke from rail engines is not a nuisance); City of Niles v. Drummond, 232 N.E.2d 830 (Ohio App. 1967) (finding that local ordinance prohibiting running and idling of railroad engines for longer than ten minutes was arbitrary and capricious and an unreasonable exercise of the police power).

7. A court, sympathetic to labor, enjoined the leaders of a strike from obstructing replacement laborers from reaching the plaintiff's mill, noting: "Even 'scabs' and those who employ 'scabs' in a time of strike have rights which the strikers are bound by the law to respect. . . . It is just as much a nuisance to block up the street and impair the right by the continual presence of bodies . . . who obstruct the ingress and egress, as it would be to build barricades and embankments in the street." American Steel & Wire Co. v. Wire Drawers & Die Makers' Unions, 90 F. 608, 612, 614 (N.D. Ohio 1898).

8. Oliver Wendell Holmes Jr., *The Common Law* (John Harvard Library) (1881; Massachusetts: Belknap Press of Harvard University Press, 2009), 3–4.

9. See, e.g., Mutual Film Co. v. Industrial Comm'n of Ohio, 215 F. 138 (N.D. Ohio 1914) (upholding the state delegation to a board of censors the power to license moving pictures to determine "moral, educational or amusing and harmless character" of the film); Mugler v. Kansas, 123 U.S. 623 (1887).

10. Mugler, 123 U.S. at 623.

11. Pennsylvania Coal v. Mahon, 260 U.S. 393, 413 (1922).

12. Ibid., 415.

13. Ohio Gen. Code para. 4366–7–11.

14. For a brief but interesting history of the Standard Zoning Enabling Act and its contemporary model acts relating to land use controls, see Ruth Knack, Stuart Meck, and Israel Stollman, "The Real Story behind the Standard Planning and Zoning Acts of the 1920s," *Land Use Law & Zoning Digest* 48, no. 2 (February 1996): 3–9, 3.

15. Village of Euclid, Ohio, Ordinance No. 2812 (adopted November 13, 1922).

16. Ibid.

17. Michael Allan Wolf, *The Zoning of America*: Euclid v. Ambler (Lawrence: University Press of Kansas, 2008).

18. Village of Euclid, Ohio, Ordinance Nos. 3366, 3367, and 3368 (adopted June 11, 1923).

19. Amber Realty Co. v. Village of Euclid, 297 F. 307, 308 (N.D. Ohio 1924).

20. Ibid., 314.

21. Ibid., 313.

22. Village of Euclid v. Amber Realty, 272 U.S. 365,388 (1926). A few months after the U.S. Supreme Court reversed his decision in *Euclid*, Judge Westenhaver was again called upon to rule on the validity of a local land use regulation. By the time *Weiss v. Guion* reached the Northern District in 1926, Westenhaver had been reversed on direct appeal to the U.S. Supreme Court twice in two years. See United States v. Hubbard, 266 U.S. 474 (1925) (decided on January 5, 1925, in which the U.S. Supreme Court reversed Judge Westenhaver's determination that the Interstate Commerce Commission exceeded its authority in finding that passenger fare arrangements for certain interurban electric railroads had a discriminatory effect on interstate commerce; the U.S. Supreme Court's reversal of Judge Westenhaver's *Euclid* decision occurred late in 1926). Hence, it might not be surprising that in *Weiss*, which concerned a challenge to building setbacks from a public roadway, Judge Westenhaver attempted to distance himself from his own opinion in the *Euclid* controversy. Ruling that the establishment of building setbacks was well within the scope of the police power, Westenhaver reminded the parties that "no opinion to the contrary has ever been entertained or expressed by me." Weiss v. Guion, 17 F. 202, 204 (N.D. Ohio 1926). This ap-

pears to be the final significant judicial opinion on the matter of the police power from Judge Westenhaver, who only a few years later was one of the first of the important *Euclid* players to pass away.

23. Euclid, 272 U.S. at 388.

24. Buchanon v. Warley, 245 U.S. 60 (1917).

25. Euclid, 297 F. at 316.

26. David Ray Papke, "Keeping the Underclass in Its Place: Zoning, the Poor, and Residential Segregation," *Urban Lawyer* 41 (October 2009): 787, 788.

27. In the more unfortunate but perhaps telling portion of the opinion, Sutherland opined that apartments often posed such a challenge, causing a parasitic, nuisance effect on single-family neighborhoods. Euclid, 272 U.S. at 394.

28. Swetland v. Curtiss, 41 F.2d 929 (N.D. Ohio 1930), *modified in* 55 F.2d 201 (6th Cir. 1932).

29. See John G. Sprankling, "Owning the Center of the Earth," *UCLA Law Review* 55 (April 2008): 979, 981.

30. Herrin v. Sutherland, 241 P. 328, 332 (1925) (Sup. Ct. Mont. 1925).

31. Courts have found it a trespass to "thrust one's arm into the space over a neighbor's land" or to shoot over another's land; overhanging branches and projecting eaves have been found to be either trespass or nuisance; and "a board attached to defendant's building and overhanging plaintiff's land" has been determined to "constitutes a trespass," as have other overhangs. See Hannabalson v. Sessions, 90 N.W. 93 (Iowa 1902); Whittaker v. Stangvick, 111 N.W. 295 (Minn. 1907); e.g., Grandona v. Lovdal, 70 Cal. 161 (Cal. 1886); Harrington v. McCarthy, 48 N.E. 278 (Mass. 1897); Puerto v. Chieppa, 62 A. 664 (Conn. 1905).

32. For an account of the Wright brothers' first flight at the beginning of "a turbulent and flamboyant era of aviation development," see Roger E. Bilstein, *Flight in America: From the Wrights to the Astronauts*, rev. ed. (Baltimore, Md.: Johns Hopkins University Press, 1994), 12–17. For a description of the Wright family and its series of firsts, see T. A. Heppenheimer, *First Flight: The Wright Brothers and the Invention of the Airplane* (Hoboken, N.J.: Wiley, 2003), 1–2.

33. See Heppenheimer, *First Flight*, 74–96.

34. See Henry E. Smith, "Exclusion and Property Rights in the Law of Nuisance," *Virginia Law Review* 90 (June 2004): 965.

35. See, e.g., Herrin v. Sutherland, 241 P. 328 (Mont. 1925) (shot from a rifle landed on the plaintiff's house and cattle).

36. Butler v. Frontier Telephone, 19 N.Y.Ann.Cas. 315 (N.Y. 1906) ("'Usque ad coelum' is upper boundary").

37. A few months before, the Supreme Judicial Court of Massachusetts had recognized that "aerial navigation, as important as it may be, has no inherent superiority over the land-owner where the rights and claims are in actual conflict." It then established a line between airspace that could possibly be built into, using the Eiffel Tower as an example, and what was feasibly used: "property which can be seized, touched, occupied, handled, cultivated, built upon and utilized in its every feature." Smith v. New England Aircraft Co., 170 N.E. 385 (Mass. 1930).

38. Swetland, 41 F.2d 929, 931 (N.D. Ohio 1930).

39. Ibid., 932 (holding that the mere existence and operation of an airport was determined not to be a nuisance per se under Ohio law).

40. Ibid.

41. Ibid., 938; Air Commerce Act, 344 Stat. 574 (1926). Soon thereafter, in 1929, the legislature of the state of Ohio passed its own laws "relative to aeronautics," which appeared to defer to federal control.

42. Swetland, 41 F.2d at 939.

43. Ibid., 938–39.

44. Ibid., 942.

45. Swetland v. Curtiss, 55 F.2d 201 (6th Cir. 1932).

46. Ibid., 203.

47. Ibid., 204. Interestingly, the airport was later acquired by the municipality under eminent domain and operated as an airport. Suit was brought, and it was determined that the previous injunction did not apply to the town. However, the ruling left open the possibility of a similar action being successful against the municipality; still, no further cases were decided. See Swetland v. Curry, 188 F.2d 841 (6th Cir. 1951).

48. U.S. v. Causby, 328 U.S. 256 (1946); Laird v. Nelms, 406 U.S. 797 (1972) (referring to the Air Commerce Act of 1926 enacted in recognition of the dangers of countless trespass suits). Currently, the U.S. Code states that "a citizen of the United States has a public right of transit through the navigable airspace." 49 U.S.C. § 40103 (1994).

49. Biechelle v. Norfolk & Western Railway Co., 309 F. Supp. 354 (N.D. Ohio 1969). Norfolk & Western was a successor corporation to the Pennsylvania Railroad Company.

50. Ibid., 357.

51. Ibid., 358.

52. The railroad's argument, in which the absence of negligence constituted a defense in a nuisance action, found authority in Ohio law. See, e.g., Metzger, 66 N.E.2d at 203, 206 (holding that the defendant railroad was entitled to a directed verdict where plaintiff did not allege or prove negligence in stopping under a bridge and emitting black smoke onto plaintiff, who was then injured falling down stairs that she could not see). Even before the *Biechelle* case, however, the Sixth Circuit had questioned the notion of limiting nuisance in such a manner and provided a brief review of Ohio court cases, suggesting that negligence was not such a limitation on nuisance claims. See E. Rauh & Sons Fertilizer Co. v. Shreffler, 139 F.2d 38, 41 (6th Cir. 1943).

53. Biechelle, 309 F. Supp. at 358.

54. See U.S. EPA, "State Activities in Solid Waste Management," report, EPA SW-158, 1974 (1975); U.S. Department of Health, Education, and Welfare, "Report for Consultation on the Greater Metropolitan Cleveland Intrastate Air Quality Control Region" (February 1969), 35–37.

55. Biechelle, 309 F. Supp. at 359. Notably, the *Biechelle* controversy preceded the influential opinion in *Boomer v. Atlantic Cement Co.* by a single year, and thus, it may not be surprising that Judge Young so seriously questioned the efficacy of enjoining railroad operations. In *Boomer*, the New York court diverged from the general rule that injunctive relief should follow a finding that a nuisance exists. Boomer v. Atlantic Cement Co., 26 N.Y.2d 219 (1970). The *Boomer* decision is notable both for the manner in which the court balanced the costs and benefits of injunctive relief and for endorsing a resolution of payment of permanent damages to the plaintiff as an alternative to injunctive relief. The *Boomer* decision has been criticized for its effect of allowing defendants to pay for the right to pollute. Of course, the question of judicial hesitancy in enjoining major industries did not originally arise with the *Boomer* case. In 1886, for instance, the Pennsylvania Supreme Court held that claims of injury from coal-mining discharges that resulted in significant stream pollution "must yield to the necessities of a great public industry [the coal industry]." Pennsylvania Coal Co. v. Sanderson, 6 A. 453, 459 (Pa. 1886).

56. Biechelle, 309 F. Supp. at 358.

57. Ibid.

58. Ibid., at 359.

59. Ibid., at 358.

60. Standard Bag & Paper Co. v. City of Cleveland , 15 Ohio C.D. 380, 1903 WL 590, at*9 (Ohio 1903) (noting that it is certain there are contributions, but uncertainty as to the amounts, discharged by "slaughter houses, oil refineries, rolling mills, foundries and other manufacturing establishments, some twenty-one in number and about one hundred private water closets, all located near Kingsbury run and emptying into it").

61. Standard Bag & Paper Co., 74 N.E. 206 (Ohio 1905).

62. Although Ohio courts would eventually limit prescription as a defense to pollution, the reign of such rules was consistent with judicial resolutions in other pollution contexts. See, e.g., Industrial Fibre Co. v. State, 166 N.E. 418 (Ohio Ct. App. 1928) (dismissal of a suit against a rayon plant because the plant was located in the neighborhood first, a defense known as "coming to the nuisance").

63. Many states had previously adopted piecemeal, nuisance-based legislation making it unlawful to dispose of rubbish or contaminate a drinking supply. However, approximately thirty states adopted "comprehensive" water quality legislation between 1942 and 1955 that sought to both regulate and abate the sources of pollution. See W. B. Smith, "Statutory Treatment of Industrial Stream Pollution," *George Washington Law Review* 24 (January 1956): 302, 310 n.59 . By 1966, all states had adopted some form of water pollution control legislation. See N. William Hines, "Nor Any Drop to Drink: Public Regulation of Water Quality; Part I: State Pollution Control Programs," *Iowa Law Review* 51 (October 1966): 186, 215.

64. Ohio Water Pollution Control Act, 124 Ohio Laws 855 (1951).

65. Adler, "Fables of the Cuyahoga," 117.

66. Ohio Rev. Code Ann. § 6111.04 (West 2000). Ironically, the statute contained a savings clause that preserved common-law rights and presumably applied to private nuisance. Ohio Rev. Code Ann. § 6111.08 (West 2000). The statute also specifically exempted industrial discharges and acid mine drainage until the board was able to identify practical treatment methodologies. Ohio Rev. Code Ann. § 6111.04 (West 2000).

67. Meisz v. Village of Mayfield Heights, 111 N.E.2d 20 (Ohio Ct. App. 1952); Ketchel v. Bainbridge, 557 N.E.2d 779 (Ohio 1990); Cash v. Cincinnati Zoning Board of Appeals, 690 N.E.2d 593 (Ohio Ct. App. 1996).

68. The Cuyahoga has provided waste removal service to some of the more prominent stalwarts of Cleveland's economic circumstances: Republic Steel, U.S. Steel, and Jones and Laughlin discharged solids, iron, oil, sulfates, ammonia, acids, and other hazardous materials; discharges from operations at Lamson and Sessions and Sonoco Products caused some sort of reddish tinge; and Firestone, B. F. Goodrich, Goodyear Tire Division, Goodyear Aerospace Division, and Diamond Salt contributed discharges of heavy metals, high temperatures, oils, color, and other hazardous materials. U.S. Department of the Interior, "Lake Erie Report: A Plan for Water Pollution Control," (August 1968), 47. Available at: http://nepis.epa.gov.

69. Damon Sims, "Cuyahoga River Fire 40 Years Ago Ignited an Ongoing Cleanup Campaign," *Science and Technology News*, June 22, 2009, available at http://cleveland.com/science/index.ssf/2009/06/cuyahoga_river_fire_40_years_a.html ("Even after 40 years, maybe the most surprising thing about the June 22, 1969 fire is that it is remembered at all").

70. Just one year prior to the 1969 fire, Joe G. Moore, commissioner of the Federal Water Pollution Control Administration, wryly noted: "Man is destroying Lake Erie. Although the accelerating destruction process has been inadvertent, it is as positive as if he had put all his energies into devising and implementing the means. After two generations the process has gained in momentum which now requires a monumental effort to retard." U.S. Department of the Interior, "Lake Erie Report," Foreword.

71. *New York Times*, October 8, 1969 (abstracts) 94, 1969 WLNR 59999.

72. See Adler, "Fables of the Cuyahoga," 118.

73. 16 U.S.C. §§ 46off (2000).

74. United States v. Detrex Chemical Industries, 393 F. Supp. 735 (N.D. Ohio 1975) (allowing EPA to pursue both injunctive remedies and civil penalties under the Federal Water Pollution Control Act).

75. "U.S. Steel to Cut Ohio-Pollution," *Toledo Blade*, September 5, 1980, 5.

76. The state's inactive regulatory enforcement was the subject of an unsuccessful citizen suit early in this history. See Pinkey et al. v. Ohio Environmental Protection Agency, 375 F. Supp. 305 (N.D. Ohio 1974).

77. United States v. City of Painesville, 431 F. Supp. 496 (N.D. Ohio 1979).

78. U.S. v. Liviola, 605 F. Supp. 96 (N.D. Ohio 1985).

79. In 2000, Judge David D. Dowd Jr. denied a motion by the city of Youngstown to dismiss a Clean Water Act enforcement action brought by the EPA on grounds that the state of Ohio was also prosecuting the alleged CWA violations. Judge Dowd preserved the EPA's authority to pursue enforcement action despite the EPA's grant of authority to Ohio to administer the CWA. United States v. City of Youngstown, 109 F. Supp. 2d 739 (N.D. Ohio 2000). See also Natural Resources Defense Council v. Vygen Corporation, 803 F. Supp. 97 (N.D. Ohio 1992) (finding that enforcement action under state pollution control law did not preclude citizens suit under the Clean Water Act, which precluded citizen enforcement where agency was "diligently prosecuting" CWA).

80. In United States v. Chrysler Corporation, 157 F. Supp. 2d 849 (N.D. Ohio 2001), Judge Dowd performed a surgical analysis of the statutory framework and Sixth Circuit precedent to allow the United States to recover hazardous waste response costs under the cost recovery provisions in section 107 of Comprehensive Environmental Response, Compensation, and Liability Act, rather than the contribution provisions in section 113, despite also finding that the United States could not claim the status of innocent landowner. Specifically, when the federal government acquired the contaminated property, it was aware of the contamination. Nevertheless, the federal government's acquisition was mandated by congressional decree, and the acquisition was made with the intention of remediating the site and establishing a park.

81. United States v. Cleveland Electric Illuminating Company, 510 F. Supp. 51, 53 (N.D. Ohio 1981) (ordering compliance with a subpoena *duces tecum* upon finding that "there is no doubt that energy, the environment, and unemployment are all matters of great concern in this society as it enters this new decade. Given the intent of Congress to have the EPA monitor the interrelationships of these factors, this Court is of the opinion that CEI's motion to quash the subpoena should be overruled.").

82. Schweda, 736 N.W.2d at 49, 56.

83. See Adler, "Fables of the Cuyahoga."

84. "Environment: The Cities—The Price of Optimism," *Time*, August 1, 1969, available at http://www.time.com/time/magazine/article/0,9171,901182–1,00.html.

85. Of course, nuisance law has never been completely removed from the scene. Following the adoption of federal and state environmental laws through the 1970s and 1980s, nuisance has retaken a hold in the process of securing environmental quality. See, e.g., Village of Wilsonville v. SCA Services, 426 N.E.2d 824 (Ill. 1981) (finding nuisance and enjoining chemical waste disposal facility despite facility's permits to operate). More recently, nuisance has drawn a great deal of attention in the climate change arena for its adaptive potential in tracking developments in the natural sciences. See J. B. Ruhl, "Making Nuisance Ecological," *Case Western Reserve Law Review* 58 (Spring 2008): 753, 756.

9

Preserving Trust in Government

Public Corruption and the Court

Nancy E. Marion

POLITICAL CORRUPTION BY public officials is not a new phenomenon. Corrupt behavior has been part of government for many years, and unfortunately, no level of leadership is immune from the questionable behavior of politicians. Generally speaking, corruption involves the abuse of public office for private benefit or personal gain. It is the manipulation of power or public trust by those elected or appointed to office.[1] It occurs when politicians use the power of their office for their own advantage, for example, to raise money for a campaign or increase their income.[2] Corrupt behavior can involve requiring subordinates to perform certain tasks that enhance the officeholder personally rather than to carry out the duties of the office. It can also be breaking rules or laws concerning the proper exercise of public duties for personal or private gain. In the end, the corrupt behavior undermines the standards of integrity associated with public office.

Today, those accused of political corruption are often charged with federal offenses. The cases are heard in district courts around the country, which are the trial-level courts for the federal judicial system.

Federal Role Increased

Until the twentieth century, cases concerning political corruption were prosecuted in state courts after the accused were indicted for theft or other similar charges. However, in more recent times, individuals charged with acts of political corruption have increasingly been indicted at the federal level, with their cases being heard in a federal district court. The charges are usually for crimes such as racketeering, mail fraud, bribery, contempt, or theft of office. Such changes have altered the role of the court, and beyond that, they have altered the way people view the role of the federal court in dealing with public corruption. In the past, people did not expect the federal courts to weed out corruption by politicians, but today, they see the federal courts as being responsible for determining the truth behind allegations of corruption by their elected officials.

There are many arguments for a more active federal role in prosecuting political corruption, as opposed to the state prosecution. One is simply that, in many situations, state and local prosecutors are too close to those accused of wrongdoing, making a full investigation of the alleged illegal acts difficult. And local law enforcement may be reluctant to handle high-profile crimes or crimes committed by famous people. In these situations, federal officials can more easily investigate criminal charges because they do not have personal or professional relationships with those involved. Second, federal officials have more money and other resources than state officials to investigate and prosecute allegations against elected officials. Most states are limited in regard to how many individuals and how much money they have available to investigate criminal charges. The federal government does not face those same resource limitations. Third, many local jurisdictions are less capable of handling technically sophisticated or prolonged investigations, such as complex financial or electronic investigations. Fourth, federal judges are appointed for life, giving them more independence than state judges, who must seek election and reelection. Consequently, federal judges have more independence to prosecute political wrongdoers.

A fifth reason for having the federal government prosecute corruption is that a more active federal involvement can lead to more consistency and equality from one state to the next. Some states have more resources than others and are therefore more apt to pursue criminal allegations than those with more limited resources. Increased federal involvement would help guarantee that all public officials accused of crimes would be investigated to the fullest extent possible. Sixth, increased federal responsibility can be a complement to state law enforcement, allowing local officials to enhance their resources.[3] Finally, federal involvement in corruption cases is sometimes needed because many offenders cross state lines or political boundaries.

At the same time, arguments can be made against the expanded role of the federal court. Federal involvement may mean that the states have less power to decide issues in their own territories.[4] When the right or ability of state and local officials to make policy decisions affecting their neighborhoods shifts to the federal government, federal power is increased and the ability of the states to respond to problems as they see fit is decreased. The states are smaller and closer to the people and can make better judgments than the larger and more remote federal government. Another argument against increased federal action in corruption cases is simply that a greater volume of cases in the federal courts makes more funding demands on the system,[5] so that more federal investigators, police, prosecutors, and prisons will be needed. There may be more court backlogs and more offenders in correctional facilities. In fact, a report by Supreme Court Chief Justice William Rehnquist noted that the trend of having more federal cases led to a double-digit increase in the number of criminal cases in federal courts.[6] Some also complain that federal prosecutors are politically motivated because U.S. attorneys are political appointees who can use their power to harass members of other parties at the direction of officials in Washington. This happened in 2006, when the Bush administration allegedly encouraged some U.S. attorneys to investigate Democratic politicians for voter fraud. When they failed to do so, citing the traditional nonpartisan role of their position, these individuals were dismissed from their jobs as federal prosecutors.[7]

In all likelihood, the changed role of the federal court in prosecuting corruption is primarily due to new federal statutes passed by Congress in the 1970s under the Racketeer Influenced and Corrupt Organization (RICO) Act, also known as the RICO statute. The new law was designed to strengthen the federal attack on large-scale organized crime syndicates, and it was used successfully to battle those involved in organized crime. RICO allowed federal personnel to step in to investigate and prosecute illegal behavior that was once the domain of state courts, and it helped establish the trend for more federal prosecution of corruption charges.

RICO Statute

During Prohibition, a culture of underground organized crime units, or families, was able to thrive in many American cities, largely because local criminal justice systems did not have the resources to investigate and prosecute these families. At that time, law enforcement did not fully understand the true nature of organized crime families, what they did, and how they operated. Law enforcement officials were also hindered in their attempts to thwart organized crime because policies banned the use of wiretaps and other technology to collect evidence that could be used in court against criminal defendants.

This situation changed during the 1950s when a series of congressional hearings brought the activities of organized crime to light. As a result of the expanded knowledge of underworld organizations, Congress passed new legislation to help law enforcement and the courts become more effective in their fight against organized crime. Most important was the Organized Crime Control Act of 1970. Section 901(a) of that law gave federal investigators and law enforcement personnel new powers to collect evidence that could be admitted into courtroom proceedings to convict alleged offenders. Key provisions of the law gave more power to federal agencies by changing the way law enforcement could gather evidence and by allowing that evidence to be included in a trial.

Title IX of the RICO statute made it a crime for anyone to use the income or profits derived from thirty-two "predicate offenses" to establish, acquire, or operate a legitimate business that was involved in interstate or foreign commerce. Some of the predicate offenses, as defined by Congress, were white slavery (prostitution), kidnapping, drug trafficking, sports bribery, arson, extortion, obstruction of justice, counterfeiting, wire fraud, bankruptcy fraud, trafficking in contraband cigarettes, and embezzlement of union funds. The law stipulated that one of the crimes had to have been committed within the previous five years, but the second could have been committed within the prior ten years. This provision essentially gave prosecutors fifteen years to prosecute crimes under RICO. If a person was convicted of violating the new law, he or she could be punished by a fine of up to $20,000 and twenty years in prison. In addition, the government could seize any assets acquired from the illegal activity.[8]

In general, RICO made it a federal offense for members of a criminal group to follow a pattern or sequence of criminal acts that traditionally would have been considered state or local offenses in order to further their group's objectives. In other words, the new law made it a federal crime to be involved in or be part of a criminal "enterprise" such as an organized crime family if members of the enterprise conducted their business through an established "pattern of racketeering" or by committing a series of already defined state or federal crimes. If it could be proven that a person was a knowing and active member of the enterprise, he or she would be guilty of the crime, even if the racketeering acts were committed by others in the group. Because of the RICO statute, membership in an organized crime group was now a federal offense.[9] The law also made running an organized crime group illegal under federal law.

One important change that resulted from RICO was a shift in power from the state to federal agencies in investigating and prosecuting what had traditionally been state offenses. Now, instead of state officials prosecuting each individual crime committed by each individual member separately, the federal government could prosecute the members as one organization. Consequently, even today, the federal courts, rather than the states, have the responsibility to investigate and prosecute corruption cases. The federal courts responsible for that task are the federal district courts, including the U.S. District Court for the Northern District of Ohio.

Impact of RICO: Four Cases

Four recent corruption cases in Ohio clearly demonstrate the expanded role of the federal courts in prosecuting corruption cases, particularly by the U.S. District Court for the Northern District of Ohio. Each of the cases involved illegal behavior by politicians and subsequent investigation and prosecution by the federal court system instead of a state system.

Gray and Jackson

Nathaniel Gray and Gilbert Jackson developed a scheme to provide cash and gifts to public officials in Cleveland and other cities in exchange for political influence in bidding for municipal contracts for their clients and for financial gain for themselves. One Cleveland official involved in the scheme was the mayor of East Cleveland, Emmanuel Onunwor. Onunwor and Gray proposed that East Cleveland water and sewer rates be raised by more than 40 percent.

Despite reports that showed the rates did not need to be raised by that amount, the two men were able to convince city council members to support a contract that forced the city to pay an outside company $3.9 million a year to manage the Water Department, even though it had been managed by the city for $1.4 million. Onunwor also failed to disclose cash payments he received from Gray. In August 2008, city officials in Cleveland filed a multimillion-dollar racketeering suit against Onunwor and Gray to recover losses surrounding the Water Department contract, seeking $14 million in damages.[10] A federal jury later found Onunwor guilty of taking cash bribes from Gray and of racketeering conspiracy, as well as a variety of other charges.[11] He was sentenced to 108 months in prison and ordered to pay restitution to the city of East Cleveland of over $5.1 million.[12]

Later, a grand jury presented a forty-five-count indictment that alleged Gray and Jackson violated the RICO statute, the Hobbs Act, and mail and wire fraud statutes. Gray was also charged with one count of tax evasion.[13] In the end, both men were convicted of multiple charges. After their verdict was announced, Gray and Jackson asked for a new trial.

The presiding judge, James S. Gwin, nominated to the federal bench by President Bill Clinton in 1997, had served as a Stark County Common Pleas Court judge for more than seven years prior to serving on the federal court.[14] Thus, he had significant experience dealing with criminal cases. Judge Gwin denied both defendants' requests for a new trial.[15] Telling Gray that he "had immense talents but you squandered them,"[16] he sentenced him to 240 months in prison and ordered him to pay $1,587,000 in restitution to the Internal Revenue Service (IRS) and $3,700 in special assessments. He sentenced Jackson to 142 months in prison and ordered him to pay $800 in costs and $100,000 in restitution to the city of Cleveland.[17] Both men appealed their verdicts.

Sixth Circuit Court of Appeals Judges Ronald Gilman, Julia Gibbons, and Allen Griffen,[18] after reviewing the defendants' arguments, unanimously decided that they "lack merit and do not warrant further review." The judges, one a Democratic appointee and two Republican appointees, all agreed that "the district court was thorough in its analysis and correct in its conclusions that none of these stated grounds mandate suppression of the surveillance evidence obtained under Title III or the video recordings." They therefore affirmed the district court's orders denying defendants' motions to suppress and upheld the convictions and sentences on all other counts.[19]

Strollo

Lenine "Lenny" Strollo, an alleged head of the criminal organization in Youngstown, Ohio, was convicted of a racketeering charge for running an illegal gambling operation in 1990 and sentenced to fourteen months in prison.[20] After leaving prison, it is believed that Strollo oversaw organized crime in the region alongside Joseph "Little Joey" Naples Jr. They controlled illicit gambling in the Youngstown area, with each man maintaining his own area of Mahoning County.[21] When Naples was killed in 1991,[22] Strollo became the boss of the family, and Ernie Biondillo, a Naples protégé, took over Naples's vending machine business and gambling operations. But Biondillo, angry that he was not appointed boss, refused to support Strollo. This angered Strollo, so he decided to have Biondillo killed.[23]

Biondillo was murdered in June 1996. Federal Bureau of Investigation (FBI) agents immediately implicated Strollo in that murder.[24] That same year, Strollo directed two men to kill Mahoning County prosecutor-elect Paul Gains. Gains was shot on Christmas Eve as he returned home. The killers left him for dead on his kitchen floor, but the gun of the would-be assassin had jammed and Gains survived the shooting. When he became the county prosecutor in January 1997,[25] he began investigating the shootings but was able to make little progress until March 26, 1997, when a woman called him and gave information not only about his shooting but also about Biondillo.[26] Eventually, five men with ties to organized crime were accused of shooting Gains. The assassination attempt led to a massive federal undercover probe into public corruption in Youngstown government, leading to the indictment of prosecutors, a former assistant U.S. attorney, judges, attorneys, the sheriff, a police chief, a county engineer, and politicians.[27]

In addition to his involvement in these murders, Strollo, according to federal authorities, ran illegal gambling operations. Federal investigators alleged that he was part owner of a hotel and gambling casino in Puerto Rico, was involved with Internet gambling on the island of St. Kitts, ran a numbers lottery on the island of St. Martin,[28] and along with his brother was involved in gambling operations at the Rincon Indian Reservation Casino near San Diego.

In December 1997, federal authorities arrested Strollo for the murder of Biondillo, the attempted murder of Gains, and his relationship to several gambling operations. RICO charges against him stemmed from allegations that he directed a criminal enterprise that engaged in murder, gambling, and other violent acts. There were also charges related to obstruction of justice, fraud, extortion, gambling, and bribery of public officials.[29]

In February 1999, Strollo agreed to become a government witness in exchange for pleading guilty and receiving a reduced sentence. As part of the plea bargain agreement, he confessed in a federal court hearing to numerous crimes, including racketeering and tax evasion. He also admitted that he and others were responsible for Biondillo's death. Finally, he pleaded guilty to bribing former Mahoning County officials and to giving money to Sheriff Philip Chance during his campaign for office.[30] He then went on to talk with FBI agents and federal prosecutors about organized crime in Youngstown and elsewhere, even testifying at trials for the government. He gave testimony about unsolved murders and provided information that led to the convictions of multiple other men involved in organized crime. He also described political corruption in Mahoning County, including his relationship with U.S. Representative James Traficant.

Judge Kathleen O'Malley, a Bill Clinton nominee, had been on the bench for only five years before she was assigned this case. But as a former chief council of the Ohio State Attorney General's Office, she had extensive experience with criminal law and criminal proceedings.[31] She agreed to delay Strollo's sentencing until 2004 so that he could fulfill his cooperation agreement with the government. When the time for sentencing arrived, Judge O'Malley sentenced him to twelve years and eight months in prison, with three years of supervised release and 250 hours of community service upon release.[32] She agreed that his federal prison sentence would include safety considerations aimed at protecting him from others against whom he testified. She also agreed that his federal prison term could run concurrently with a state prison term resulting from criminal charges on the state level.[33] Strollo was sent to prison and was released in 2008.

Traficant

Jim Traficant was elected sheriff of the Youngstown area in 1980. In this position, he refused to sign foreclosure deeds and seize houses from laid-off steelworkers. Although he was sent to jail for this refusal, voters viewed him as fighting for the "little guy."[34] In 1983, Traficant was caught on tape taking a bribe from members of organized crime, who hoped that he would overlook prostitution, gambling, and drug trafficking in the area. He represented himself at trial despite not having a law degree and said that he took the money from organized crime because he was running a sting operation that only he knew about.[35] A federal jury acquitted him on all charges.

Not long after, in 1984, Traficant ran for Congress and went on to spend seventeen years in Washington representing the people of Youngstown as a Democrat. There, he was known for his one-minute speeches, often denouncing the IRS and calling it the "Internal Rectal Service." He was famous for arm-waving theatrics and expressions such as "beam me up" and for his odd wardrobe, fluffy hairdo, and coarse language.

In September 1987, Traficant lost a federal tax court case. A U.S. tax court ruled that he owed between $100,000 and $1 million in back taxes for the bribes he took and failed to report as income when he was sheriff. Traficant argued that he accepted the money but did not keep it.

In 2002, Traficant was once again accused of accepting gifts and favors from businesspeople in exchange for lobbying federal agencies on their behalf. This charge stemmed from Traficant's demands that his employees return part of their salaries to him or perform manual labor on his horse farm. He was also accused of asking contractors to perform free work in exchange for political favors.[36] Local contractors and businesspeople provided thousands of dollars in free goods to Traficant (including cash, meals, power tools, and work on his home and farm) in return for his help.

As a result of the allegations, Traficant faced a ten-count felony indictment in federal court. Prosecutors charged him with obstructing justice by attempting to destroy evidence and filing false tax returns. He denied the charges and claimed that the government had been out to get him for more than twenty years, from the time he had successfully defended himself against racketeering charges.[37]

Once again, Traficant chose to represent himself despite offers of help from attorneys and other supporters. He sought to show jurors that he was still the "little guy" working for the average person.[38] He wanted to portray himself as a man being unjustly punished by the government.

Traficant and the judge in the case often wrangled. U.S. District Judge Lesley Wells was an experienced federal jurist, having been nominated to serve on the court by President Clinton and being seated on February 11, 1994. Her experience allowed her to maintain order throughout the proceedings. Early in the trial, Traficant lost a motion to delay his trial. He then filed a lawsuit accusing the government of violating his civil rights. The judge ordered that Traficant could not claim he was a victim of a vendetta or misconduct by federal prosecutors.[39] Traficant and the judge also disagreed about the jury. Traficant wanted the jury to include people from his congressional district, but the judge ruled the jury would be made up of citizens from the Cleveland area because it was the court's standard procedure in trials of this nature to draw jurors from nine counties surrounding Cleveland.[40] Because of the rulings, Traficant accused the judge of favoring government prosecutors.[41]

During the trial, Traficant sometimes struggled to get witnesses who were to testify in his behalf to appear in the courtroom in a timely manner. Wells scolded him and warned him repeatedly that it was his responsibility to get his witnesses to court on time. When his witnesses finally did appear, they rarely contradicted the prosecution witnesses, and some even helped the prosecutors. In addition, the judge was often forced to interrupt the trial to keep Traficant from violating rules of evidence. Toward the end of the trial, he seemed to be unable to question his witnesses coherently, and he often repeated questions or jumped from one topic to the next. He appeared tired, disorganized, and overwhelmed.

As the trial wore on, Judge Wells frequently had to stop the proceedings to discuss proper courtroom procedure with the defendant.[42] She scolded Traficant for his tardiness, his unpreparedness, and his unlawyerly behavior. She told him, "These men and women [of the jury] will not be permitted to sit here idly while you dillydally and delay."[43] Further, Wells did not allow Traficant to present witnesses and evidence he sought to use in his defense when she considered them to be irrelevant[44] or when the evidence had not been properly submitted.[45]

At the same time, Wells showed a great deal of patience by overlooking Traficant's outbursts and insults. She gave him wide latitude. And she never cited him for contempt, even when the prosecutors begged her to do so.

When Traficant finally rested his defense, he told the jury that the government did not prove its case. He pointed out that prosecutors had no evidence or tapes to prove the charges, and he explained to the jurors that some of the witnesses against him acknowledged they were also charged with various crimes and had made deals with prosecutors in exchange for lighter sentences.[46]

Traficant then made a motion to have the charges against him dropped, claiming that his Fifth and Sixth Amendment rights were violated. He argued that he was not permitted to present a defense and repeated that the whole case was part of a government conspiracy and vendetta against him. Judge Wells denied the motion. Traficant responded by telling the judge that she was one-sided, that she did not conduct a fair and just trial,[47] and that she mishandled the case by not allowing him to present witnesses. He also claimed that the court made unfair remarks to the jury and that he had discovered new evidence since the original trial that would result in a different verdict.

In the end, the jury convicted Traficant of all ten federal charges against him, including bribery, obstruction of justice, conspiracy to defraud the United States, filing a false tax return, and RICO offenses. Traficant said it was a very unfair process, but he accepted the verdict.[48]

The Ethics Committee of the House of Representatives also investigated the allegations made against Traficant. It held a public hearing to determine if the charges were true. During the hearing, Traficant told the ethics panel that the Justice Department had targeted him for years and that the FBI had been after him since 1983. In the end, the members of the House Ethics Committee decided that Traficant was guilty and voted to expel him from the their chamber. The panel's recommendation then went to the full House, which also voted that he be expelled.[49]

After he was forced out of the House, Traficant filed a motion with the district court, arguing that if the federal court sentenced him to prison, it would be a second punishment and therefore a violation of the double jeopardy provision. He argued that his expulsion from the House of Representatives should be the sole punishment for his conviction. Judge Wells rejected the double jeopardy argument, agreeing with prosecutors that expulsion "was not criminal punishment." Upon handing down the sentence, she told Traficant he had no respect for the government and used lies to distract attention from the charges against him.[50] She went on to say,

> You've been a congressman in the United States, and because of that position you had extraordinary power and authority. That power and that authority were granted to you as a public trust. That power and authority that you were granted was not on your behalf, but on the behalf of the people of your 17th Congressional District of Ohio. You cast yourself the way you apparently want the world to see you, and much of the world does, as a kind of folk hero, a champion of the people, and as a voice for the average guy, but you were also a United States Congressman. You've done a lot of good in your years in Congress. . . . [But] you know perfectly well that the good that you have done does not excuse the crimes that you were convicted of. Your office didn't belong

to you. The privileges and the powers of your office were not yours to trade for some kind of personal gain. . . . You had the American people paying for members of your congressional staff to spend their days, as they put it, going south; going out on your farm and doing chores. . . . You ran your office, your congressional office, as what we call a racketeering enterprise. You sought bribes from businessmen, you sought that in exchange for government favors that you owed people as a matter of your position. And then when inquiries started, you added a new kind of role as the investigation became apparent to you, and you cast yourself as the number one victim of persecution in America. To deflect attention from what was going on and what you assumed was going to be revealed, you took on this role and tried to use it as a cover for your own self-serving and really flagrant abuses of an office of public trust. . . . It was our responsibility, the jury's responsibility, and my responsibility, to provide you a full and fair trial, and that exactly is what you got. . . . You attacked all federal judges as mere tools of the prosecution and law enforcement agencies, and you never for a moment took responsibility for yourself or your actions. You apparently think you are above the law. . . . You have descended into ranting and raving and bullying and spewing your venom against the government and all the men and women who serve it, and that's all at the people's expense.[51]

Judge Wells sentenced Traficant to eight years in prison and fined him $150,000. He was sent to Allenwood Federal Correctional Institute in Pennsylvania,[52] where he appealed his conviction, arguing again that his sentence violated his Fifth Amendment protection against double jeopardy. Traficant, who chose to hire an attorney for the appeal,[53] also claimed that the trial was not fair because the process used to select the jury violated his constitutional rights. In the end, the Sixth Circuit Court of Appeals affirmed Traficant's conviction and sentence. In considering his argument about double jeopardy, Sixth Circuit Judge R. Guy Cole Jr., writing for a unanimous three-judge panel, concluded: "Because it would thwart the constitutional separation of powers if Congress could shield its members from criminal prosecution by the Executive Branch, we cannot read the Double Jeopardy Clause to include Congress's disciplining its own members."[54] In other words, if Traficant were correct, then allowing Congress to punish one of its members would prevent that member from facing criminal charges, which would be unjust. When it came to Traficant's argument concerning the jury selection process, Judge Cole explained that Traficant had had eight months to challenge the process. He was even reminded of deadlines by the court during that time. Therefore, the judge wrote that the district court's "denial of Traficant's tardy motion was neither unlawful nor unfair."[55]

Traficant served seventeen months at Allenwood and then spent three years at the Federal Medical Center in Rochester. He was released in September 2009. In May 2010, he filed petitions to run as an independent for Congress, but many of the signatures on his petitions were determined to be invalid. On appeal, the signatures were approved, and his name appeared on the ballot to represent the Seventeenth District of Ohio in the House of Representatives.[56] He finished in third place with 16 percent of the vote.

Corruption in Cuyahoga County: Dimora and Russo

Since 2008, the U.S. District Court for the Northern District of Ohio has heard numerous cases of public corruption as a result of an ongoing federal probe of corruption in Cuyahoga County. The probe involves multiple individuals, both elected and nonelected, from a variety of offices and businesses. Ann Rowland, the lead prosecutor for the case, has a thirty-year career as a federal prosecutor and is known for convicting crooked government officials and underworld crime figures.[57] As of March 2012, more than fifty guilty pleas have been filed with the court by government employees and private contractors who have admitted to wrongdoing.[58]

The probe, investigating what has been described as one of the worst corruption cases in Ohio's history, revolves around two primary figures: Jimmy Dimora and Frank Russo. Dimora is a former five-term mayor of Bedford Heights, a suburb of Cleveland. In 1994, he was elected as chairman of the Cuyahoga County Democratic Party and then was elected to be a member of the city council, being reelected twice to that position. Despite the allegations against him, many members of the Democratic Party continue to support him because he has been so successful in maintaining and expanding Democratic control over county offices. The second primary person involved in the probe, Frank Russo, is the Cuyahoga County auditor. As auditor, he is responsible for appraising properties and assessing values of homes and businesses across the county and, based on that, setting the tax rate for those properties.

Together, Dimora and Russo are accused of accepting gifts from business owners in exchange for political favors. Specifically, it is alleged that they received thousands of dollars of improvements to their homes and other properties, vacations, and cash from business owners. In exchange for those gifts, Dimora and Russo arranged for jobs for friends, gave lucrative contracts to businesses, and lowered the property values (and thus tax levels) of homes and businesses owned by friends and companies.[59] Dimora was arrested in September 2010 and pleaded not guilty to twenty-six counts of bribery, mail fraud, and conspiracy to obstruct a federal investigation.[60] That same week, Frank Russo pleaded guilty to accepting more than $1 million in bribes and kickbacks after being charged in a twenty-one-count federal indictment. He agreed to a plea deal with federal investigators whereby he would serve twenty-one years in prison and pay restitution. The agreement also stipulated that Russo would not have to testify against any others in the probe. His son, Vince, also pleaded guilty to four counts of conspiracy and bribery in exchange for serving an eighteen-month prison sentence and paying restitution.[61]

More than thirty others have been charged or have pleaded guilty in the investigation of corruption in Cleveland's city government. They include prominent business owners, school board members, a judge, and one of Dimora's fellow city council members. Some have been sentenced to time in prison or forced to pay fines for their misdeeds. The investigation has caused long-term changes in the way the city is run and the public's perception of city officials.

Impact on Federal Corruption Cases in the Community

Public reaction to political scandal varies depending on many factors, such as the severity of the charges, the number of people involved, and even the extent of media coverage given to the events. There has been a strong public outcry against those involved in the corruption case in Cuyahoga County, and many citizens have demanded some kind of action against them. One citizens' group sought to form a citizen review panel to examine records from Russo's office to determine if tax dollars were being used properly.[62] Others in and around Cuyahoga County demanded that Dimora and Russo resign.[63] A stronger response to the corruption probe was a proposal to change the structure of local government in order to "get money out of politics."[64] Issue 6, passed by voters, will replace the existing system of three elected commissioners with an elected county executive and an elected eleven-member council. The plan would also eliminate many other elected officials, including the auditor, recorder, and treasurer, whose responsibilities would be performed by a chief financial officer, appointed by the council. Under the plan, the prosecutor would remain an elected position.[65] Citizens across Cuyahoga County voted for the plan, choosing to restructure the government.

The Cleveland corruption probe has had other lasting effects on the public and the government. The investigation has made people pay more attention to county government and encouraged them to get more involved in local politics. Another long-term change is the "new and improved" ethics policy for city workers, introduced by Cleveland's mayor, Frank Jackson. The new policy has improved upon the previous one by stripping out the legalese and making the policy specifics clear to city workers.[66]

Public reaction to the Traficant trial was largely one of disgust. People wanted to see him punished and sent to prison for his corrupt and sometimes disrespectful behavior. Some wanted the court to send a message to politicians that they are elected to serve the people, not profit from their terms in office.[67] At the same time, there were those who continued to support Traficant regardless of the evidence of his wrongdoing as a public official or his antics during trial.[68]

These cases have had impacts on the citizens in other ways, as well. When the federal district courts began hearing corruption cases that had previously been heard in state and local courts, it changed public expectations in regard to the federal government and the courts. Corruption cases like Traficant's spawned cynicism among the citizens and promoted a lack of trust in government. If a politician has broken the rules and has been caught behaving unethically, the relationship between the voter and the government is threatened. As a result, many people lose their confidence in public institutions in the wake of public corruption and may decide to stop participating in elections.[69]

For many, the underlying issue of public corruption is ethics: the honesty of politicians and their ability to make appropriate judgments about what is right and wrong. The issue relates to the moral values (or lack thereof) of those involved in the scandal, their integrity to do what is right,[70] and the ability of the elected official to make the proper choices. Most people consider the use of a public position to pursue a personal agenda unacceptable ethically and politically. Moreover, many people think that politicians ought to serve as examples of ethical behavior and morality, and therefore, they hold elected officials to higher standards than the average person. Scandalous, inappropriate, or illegal behavior on the part of politicians points to their flawed personalities and a general lack of suitable ethics or morals. When cases involving such transgressions are heard in the courts, the public is made aware of the lack of honesty among their elected officials. And when allegations of corruption occur, people often lose trust in their officials, resulting in a decline in public confidence.[71] Very simply, corrupt acts erode the public's trust in the political system.[72] When people lose trust in their public institutions and elected officials, the whole system can begin to crumble, and the proper functioning of a democratic government begins to collapse.[73]

Conclusion

Many theoretical issues remain regarding the question of whether corruption should be a federal or state issue.[74] It has been suggested that the federal government should get involved in such cases to ensure that the civil and criminal rights of the affected parties are protected. It should also get involved to provide financial or technical assistance to states, especially if the case is "too big" for states to handle or if the states become overwhelmed. The federal courts may be the more appropriate venues in which to hear corruption cases if there are dangerous suspects or if there is a chance that the suspects will flee. Finally, federal personnel should get involved if there are crimes committed by major local government officials or major local industries.

In any event, federal court involvement in corruption cases has become a staple in today's system, and the district courts now bear the responsibility for hearing such charges. Obviously, many types of corruption cases have been heard by the U.S. District Court for the Northern District of Ohio in recent years; although these cases would have been the jurisdiction of the state courts in the past, the primary responsibility for corruption cases like those described in this chapter has been given to the federal courts. As a result, the public now expects the federal courts to determine if public officials are involved in criminal behavior and to sentence them accordingly. These cases illustrate that federal investigators are willing to punish the wrongdoers and that the Department of Justice places great importance on combating all forms of public corruption because of the harm caused to communities. They also clearly demonstrate the scope of the federal government's commitment to confronting allegations of corruption at all levels of government.[75] In the future, the U.S. District Court for the Northern District of Ohio will continue to hear cases of political corruption and punish those who take advantage of their elected positions in an effort to protect the public from political wrongdoing.

Notes

1. Randy Scherer, *Political Scandals* (Detroit, Mich.: Greenhaven Press, 2008), 7.

2. Nancy Marion, *The Politics of Disgrace* (Durham, N.C.: Carolina Academic Press, 2010), 13–14.

3. David Masci, "Crossing State Lines: Criminal Law and the Federal Government," *Congressional Quarterly Weekly Report* (November 21, 1992): 3676–78.

4. Ibid.

5. Franklin E. Zimring and Gordon Hawkins, "Toward a Principled Basis for Federal Criminal Legislation," *Annals of the American Academy of Political and Social Science* 543 (January 1996): 15–26.

6. Laurie Asseo, "Rehnquist Says Too Many Crimes Are Federalized," *Cleveland Plain Dealer*, January 1, 1999, A18.

7. Dan Eggen and Amy Goldstein, "Voter-Fraud Complaints by GOP Drove Dismissals," *Washington Post*, May 14, 2007, available at www.washingtonpost.com/wp-dyn/content/article/2007/05/13 (accessed October 8, 2010).

8. Joe Griffin, *Mob Nemesis: How the FBI Crippled Organized Crime* (New York: Prometheus Books, 2002), 69; Stephen Fox, *Blood and Power* (New York: William Morrow, 1989), 397; Federal Bureau of Investigation, *An Introduction to Organized Crime in the United States* (Washington, D.C.: U.S. Department of Justice, 1993), 5; Sellwyn Raab, *Five Families: The Rise, Decline and Resurgence of America's Most Powerful Mafia Enterprise* (New York: St. Martin's Press, 2005), 178.

9. Ernest Volkman, *Gangbusters* (New York: Avon Books, 1998), 165; Rick Porello, *To Kill the Irishman* (Cleveland: Next Hat Press, 1998), 97; Fox, *Blood and Power*, 397.

10. Damon Sims, "East Cleveland Files Racketeering Suit against Onunwor, Gray," *Cleveland Plain Dealer*, August 29, 2008, available at http://blog.cleveland.com/metro/2008/08/east_cleveland_files_racketeer.html (accessed January 22, 2010).

11. U.S. Department of Justice, "Defendant Pleads Guilty to Tax Evasion in Multi-district Public Corruption Probe," January 4, 2006, available at http://www.justice/gov/ops/pr/2006/January/06_crm_003.html; U.S. Department of Justice, "Six Defendants Charged in Wide-Ranging Racketeering and Extortion Scheme," January 18, 2005, available at http://www.fbi.gov/dojpressrel/pressrel05/011805a.htm (accessed April 16, 2010).

12. Mary Ann Whitley, "Jimmy Dimora's Claims in Cuyahoga County Corruption Investigation Raise the Question: When Does a Goodwill Gesture Become a Bribe?" *Cleveland Plain Dealer*, July 11, 2009, available at http://blog.cleveland.com/metro//print.html (accessed May 3, 2010).

13. U.S. Department of Justice, "Six Defendants Charged in Wide-Ranging Racketeering and Extortion Scheme," January 18, 2005, available at http://www.fbi.gov/news/pressrel/press-releases/six-defendants-charged-in-wide-ranging-racketeering-and-extortion-scheme.

14. "Judge James S. Gwin (Northern District of Ohio) Discusses Life in the Federal Courts," available at www.acslaw.org/node/7865 (accessed September 27, 2010).

15. Nathaniel Gray, Petitioner v. United States No. 08–792, Supreme Court of the United States 129 S. Ct. 2824; 174 L. Ed. 2d 552; 2009 U.S. LEXIS 4625; 77 U.S.L.W. 3690.

16. Phillip Morris, "The Pirates of the Cuyahoga Are Thieves without Honor" *Cleveland Plain Dealer*, September 14, 2010, available at www.cleveland.com/morris/index.ssf/2010/07/bribe_case_with.php (accessed September 27, 2010).

17. U.S. District Court, Northern District of Ohio (Cleveland) Criminal Docket for Case #: 1:04-cr-00580-JG-2; Case Title: United States of America v. Jones et al.; available at https://ecf.ohnd.uscourts.gov/cgi-bin/DkRpt.pl?26910021718595-L (accessed April 30, 2010).

18. "History of the Sixth Circuit," available at http://www.ca6.uscourts.gov/ . . . /circuit/ judges/ (accessed September 27, 2010).

19. United States Court of Appeals for the Sixth Circuit; United States of America v. Nathaniel Gray (2008; 521 F.3d 514; 05-4482; 06-3209) and United States of America v. Gilbert Jackson (06-3086).

20. Mark Rollenhagen, "Agents Investigate Mob in Mahoning Valley Area," *Cleveland Plain Dealer*, October 26, 1997, A1.

21. Ibid.

22. Ibid.

23. "Breaking the Mob: Gunfire, Corruption Bring Crack-Down in Youngstown," *Columbus Dispatch*, April 25, 1999, B1.

24. Rollenhagen, "Agents Investigate Mob."

25. Mark Rollenhagen, "FBI Agent Links Strollo to Shooting; Says Aide Ordered Attack on Official," *Cleveland Plain Dealer*, February 4, 1998, B1.

26. "Breaking the Mob."

27. Bill Heltzel, "Some Intent on Fighting Organized Crime in Youngstown," *Pittsburgh Post-Gazette*, December 31, 2000, available at www.post-gazette.com/regionstate/20001231youngstown15.asp (accessed October 8, 2010).

28. Rollenhagen, "Agents Investigate Mob."

29. Mark Rollenhagen, "Canfield Man Faces Rackets Charges; Officials Say He Ran Youngstown Gambling," *Cleveland Plain Dealer*, December 12, 1997, A1; Andrew Welsh-Huggins, "Trial May Expose Mafia Links with Public Officials, Street Crime," *Associated Press State and Local Wire*, November 28, 1998.

30. Amy Beth Graves, "Youngstown Mob Leader Testifies against Alleged Accomplices," *Cleveland Plain Dealer*, March 3, 1999.

31. Matt Osenga, "Kathleen O'Malley Officially Nominated to Federal Court?" March 11, 2010, available at inventivestep.net/2010/03/11/Kathleen-omalley-officially (accessed October 8, 2010).

32. "Strollo to Leave Prison in 2008; His Testimony Put End to Valley Mob," December 9, 2007, available at www4.vindy.com/content/local_regional/321053353202604.php (accessed September 29, 2010).

33. Ibid.

34. Alan L. Adler, "Controversial Sheriff Defends Himself in Court," *Associated Press*, March 6, 1983.

35. Alan L. Adler, "Sheriff Bases Defense on Documents' Validity," *Associated Press*, January 23, 1983.

36. John Caniglia, "Traficant Got Kickbacks, U.S. Says," *Cleveland Plain Dealer*, January 9, 2002, B3.

37. John Caniglia, "Traficant Will Face Jury of Strangers in New Trial," *Cleveland Plain Dealer*, February 4, 2002, A1.

38. Milan Simonich, "Traficant Tackles Corruption Charges Head-On; This Week Flamboyant Ohio Lawmaker Will Defend Himself in Court," *Pittsburgh Post Gazette*, February 3, 2002, A1.

39. Paul Singer, "Judge Says Traficant Cannot Claim Government Vendetta as a Defense," *Associated Press State and Local Wire*, January 29, 2002.

40. Paul Singer, "Traficant Hires Lawyers to Challenge Jury Selection," May 23, 2002, *Enquirer*, available at Cincinnati.com, www.enquirer.com/editions/2002/05/23/loc_traficant_hires (accessed September 27, 2010).

41. Paul Singer, "Judge, Traficant Clash over Evidence," *Associated Press State and Local Wire*, February 14, 2002.

42. Mark Gillispie, "Traficant's Legal Strategy Seems to Be Faltering," *Cleveland Plain Dealer*, March 4, 2002, A1.

43. Patricia Meade, "Judge to Jury: Case Nears End," April 3, 2002, available at www .vindy.com/news/2002/apr/03/judge-to-jury-case-nears-end (accessed September 27, 2010).

44. Sabrina Eaton, Mark Naymik, and Tom Diemer, "Traficant to Seek Re-election, Appeal Verdict," *Cleveland Plain Dealer*, April 13, 2002, A1.

45. Singer, "Judge, Traficant Clash."

46. Mark Gillispie, "Traficant Conviction Not a Done Deal, Trial Observers Say," *Cleveland Plain Dealer*, April 7, 2002, A1.

47. Damon Chappie and Amy Keller, "Traficant Case Heads to Jury," *Roll Call*, April 8, 2002.

48. Paul Singer, "Ohio Congressman James Traficant Convicted of All Counts in Federal Corruption Case," *Associated Press*, April 11, 2002.

49. Jesse J. Holland, "House Panel Votes to Expel Traficant," *Associated Press*, July 18, 2002.

50. "Ex-Congressman Is Sent to Jail but Says He'll Be Re-elected," *New York Times*, July 31, 2002, available at query.nytimes.com/gst/fullpage.html?res=9594EEDE1E38F932 (accessed September 27, 2010).

51. "Judge Wells: 'You've been a congressman in the United States,'" August 31, 2002, available at www.vindy.com/news/2002/aug/31/judge-wells-you've-been-a (accessed September 27, 2010).

52. John Caniglia, "Traficant Gets 8 Years; Defiant Ex-congressman Screams at Judge, Lawyers," *Cleveland Plain Dealer*, July 31, 2002, A1.

53. United States of America v. James A. Traficant, 368 F.3d 646 (2004).

54. Ibid.

55. Ibid.

56. Alex Isenstadt, "Jim Traficant Lands on Ohio Ballot," *Politico*, August 30, 2010, available at http://www.politico.com/news/stories/0810/41605.html (accessed October 8, 2010).

57. Damon Sims, "County Probe Prosecutor Ann Rowland Experienced in Public Corruption Trials," *Cleveland Plain Dealer*, August 1, 2008, available at http://blog.cleveland .com/metro//print.html (accessed June 13, 2010).

58. "No Verdict Yet in Dimora Trial," *Ideastream*, March 2, 2012, available at http:// www.ideastream.org/news/feature/45530 (accessed March 8, 2012).

59. Damon Sims, "The Cuyahoga County Raids: Things You Should Know," *Cleveland Plain Dealer*, August 1, 2008, available at http://blog.cleveland.com/pdextra/2008/08/ the_cuyohoga_county_raids_five.html (accessed May 6, 2010).

60. Jay Miller, "Jimmy Dimora, Others Charged in Cuyahoga County Corruption Investigation," *Crain's Cleveland Business*, September 27, 2010, available at http://www .crainscleveland.com/apps/pbcs.dll/article?AID=/20100915/FREE/100919917 (accessed May 6, 2010).

61. Danielle Frizzi, "Frank Russo's Son Pleads Guilty to Bribery," *Chicago Tribune*, September 27, 2010, available at http://www.chicagotribune.com/topic.wjw-news-cleveland-frank (accessed September 27, 2010).

62. Felipe Nieves, "Court OKs Rob Frost's Request for Citizen Review Panel to Check Cuyahoga County Contracts," *Cleveland Plain Dealer*, June 19, 2009, http://blog.cleveland .com/metro//print.html (accessed May 6, 2010).

63. Mark Naymik, "Pals, Politicians Leave Cuyahoga County Auditor Frank Russo's Side as Troubles Mount," *Cleveland Plain Dealer*, September 15, 2009, available at crainscleveland .com/article/20100915/FREE/100919917 (accessed September 27, 2010); http://blog.cleveland .com/metro/2009/09/pals_politicians_leave_cuyahog.html (accessed May 6, 2010).

64. Mark Puente, "Prosecutor Bill Mason Pledges to Reform Campaign Finance and Return Campaign Contributions from Employees," *Cleveland Plain Dealer*, October 10, 2009, available at http://blog.cleveland.com/metro/2009/10/prosecutor_bill_mason_pleges_t.html (accessed May 3, 2010).

65. Mark Naymik, "Where Do Democrats Go from Here? Its Leadership Divided, Its Clout Diminished, the Party Has Been Hit Hard by the Triumph of Issue 6," *Cleveland Plain Dealer*, November 8, 2009, available at http://blog.cleveland.com/metro/2009/11/where_do_democrats_go_from_her.html (accessed May 3, 2010).

66. Felipe Nieves, "Cleveland Mayor Frank Jackson Unveils 'New and Improved' Ethics Policy," *Cleveland Plain Dealer*, June 19, 2009, available at http://blog.cleveland.com/metro//print.html (accessed May 6, 2010).

67. "How to Punish a Convicted Congressman?" *Cleveland Plain Dealer*, April 20, 2002, A11.

68. Martin Stolz, "Rep. Traficant Still Looms Large over Primary," *Cleveland Plain Dealer*, April 28, 2002.

69. Paul J. Quirk, "Scandal Time: The Clinton Impeachment and the Distraction of American Politics," in *The Clinton Scandal*, ed. Mark J. Rozell and Clyde Wilcox (Washington, D.C.: Georgetown University Press, 2000), 119–41.

70. Carol W. Lewis, *The Ethics Challenge in Public Service* (San Francisco: Jossey-Bass Publishers, 1991).

71. Ari Adut, *On Scandal: Moral Disturbances in Society, Politics and Art* (New York: Cambridge University Press, 2008), 4; Sheldon S. Steinberg and David T. Austern, *Government, Ethics and Managers* (New York: Quorum Books, 1990).

72. Sebastian Mallaby, "Political Scandals Erode the Public's Trust in the Political System," in Scherer, *Political Scandals*, 10–13.

73. Scherer, *Political Scandals*, 7.

74. Asseo, "Rehnquist Says"; Masci, "Crossing State Lines"; James Q. Wilson, "What, If Anything, Can the Federal Government Do about Crime?" *Perspectives on Crime and Criminal Justice: 1996–97 Lecture Series* (Washington, D.C.: National Institute of Justice, 1997), 1–22; Zimring and Hawkins, "Toward a Principled Basis."

75. U.S. Department of Justice, "Six Defendants Charged."

10

The U.S. District Court for the Northern District of Ohio and the May 4, 1970 Shootings at Kent State University

Thomas R. Hensley

O N MAY 4, 1970, members of the Ohio National Guard—called to Kent State University (KSU) in response to riotous activity in downtown Kent, Ohio, three days earlier—fired into a crowd of unarmed students, killing four and wounding nine. This event received worldwide attention. Kent State was closed for almost two months, and a nationwide student strike was held. In the ten-year period following the shootings, numerous attempts were made in both state and federal courts to determine who was legally responsible for the tragic events. The U.S. District Court for the Northern District of Ohio played a critical role throughout the decade of litigation. This chapter seeks to present and analyze the events surrounding the shootings at Kent State, the legal aftermath of the shootings, and the activities of the district court in seeking to determine legal responsibility for the events of May 4.[1]

The Vietnam War and May 4, 1970 at Kent State

College students nationwide had protested against the Vietnam War through-out Democrat Lyndon Johnson's presidency from 1964 to 1968, but the election of Republican president Richard Nixon in 1968 promised a scaling down of the conflict and eventual U.S. withdrawal from Vietnam. However, on Thursday, April 30, 1970, this promise seemed to disappear when Nixon went on national television to announce an expansion of the war into Cambodia, which he claimed the Viet Cong were using as a sanctuary.

This surprise announcement triggered student protests on numerous college campuses throughout the United States, including Kent State University. On Friday, May 1, a rally was held on the Commons, the traditional gathering place in the middle of the KSU campus for such events. Approximately five hundred students attended the rally, which featured several speakers opposing the expanded war and the burying of the American flag to protest the "killing" of the Constitution by Nixon. The leaders stated that another rally would be held on the Commons on Monday, May 4, at noon.

Also on May 1, serious problems arose in downtown Kent, a popular place for college students from all over northeast Ohio to drink and hang out. Although the exact details remain uncertain, a variety of people began protesting the Nixon announcement on the war. They stopped cars and asked drivers if they opposed the war. They also built a bonfire in the middle of the downtown area. Police who rushed to the scene were met with antiwar chants as well as bottles and rocks. The mayor of Kent ordered all the bars closed. The angry patrons who had to leave the bars then joined the already sizable crowd. Local and area law enforcement personnel attempted to move the crowd back to the campus, just a few blocks away. Many windows of downtown merchants were broken, some law enforcement personnel were injured, and numerous protestors were arrested.

Saturday, May 2, was an equally eventful day. Citizens of Kent were shocked to find their downtown area trashed. Rumors spread like wildfire, including claims that the city was under siege by radicals seeking to destroy America. Officials received threats against themselves and their families as well as against government office buildings. The mayor of Kent, while preparing for another possible night of trouble, determined that he did not have enough personnel to assure the safety of his city and its citizens. He therefore called the governor's office, seeking a deployment of the National Guard to Kent. The governor agreed and ordered a group of approximately one hundred guardsmen to go to Kent that night.

While these developments were unfolding, protestors began to gather people from the dormitories in the early evening for a protest demonstration at the Reserve Officers' Training Corps (ROTC) building, a wooden structure from the World War II era that the protestors saw as a symbol of U.S. involvement in the Vietnam War. After several failed attempts, the students succeeded in setting fire to the building, which then began to burn furiously. When firefighters tried to put the blaze out, protestors cut their hoses and otherwise disrupted their work, thus leading to their retreat from the scene. At about this time, the Ohio National Guard began to roll into Kent. The guardsmen observed the skyline aglow from the burning ROTC building. They also experienced their first confrontation with student protestors, some of whom threw rocks and yelled profanities at them. The Guard went straight to the campus, although a contingent was assigned to police the downtown area. In this first confrontation between the Guard and student protestors, the guardsmen used tear gas to move the protestors into campus dormitories, including dormitories in which they did not live. Arrests occurred, some students were injured, and Guard members were on the receiving end of hurled rocks and obscenities.

Sunday, May 3, was a beautiful day in Kent, and many guardsmen and students fraternized with one another, but as night came, the mood of the campus changed dramatically. Ohio governor James Rhodes played a significant role on that day. He arrived in Kent in the morning to meet with Guard leaders and officials from the university and the city. When the meeting was opened to reporters, Rhodes pounded on the table while stating that the demonstrators were "worse than the brown shirts and the communist element and also the brown shirts and the vigilantes. They are the worst type of people that we harbor in America. And I want to say this—they are not going to take over the campus and the campus is now going to be part of the county and the state of Ohio. It is no sanctuary for these people to burn buildings down of private citizens, of businesses in the community, then run into a sanctuary."[2]

It is difficult to evaluate the impact of Rhodes's speech, but it certainly did not contribute to improving the relationship between demonstrators and guardsmen. That evening, protestors gathered at the corner of Main and Summit streets, the entrance to the university. Confronting the Guard, demonstration leaders demanded to speak with KSU president Robert White and Kent's mayor, Leroy Satrom. Protestors were initially told that the meeting could be arranged, but it failed to materialize. Demonstrators were warned to leave the area, but they refused to do so until the guardsmen advanced on them, using tear gas and displaying powerful rifles with attached bayonets. Numerous arrests occurred, guardsmen reported injuries, and tensions between guardsmen and students escalated further.

The three days of turmoil from May 1 to May 3 set the stage for the tragic events of May 4. University officials attempted to spread the word around campus that the noon rally scheduled for May 4 was prohibited because of the threat of violence, but many students did not know about the ban, and others decided to attend the rally nonetheless. By shortly after noon, approximately a hundred guardsmen had assembled at one end of the Commons, and perhaps five hundred protestors had gathered across the Commons at the Victory Bell. Several thousand other people watched from nearby hills and dormitories. A Guard jeep carrying a Kent State police officer approached the demonstrators, who were warned to disband because the rally had been prohibited. The jeep and its passengers were met by verbal abuse and thrown objects. Guard commander Robert Canterbury then ordered his troops to move forward to break up the demonstration. Guardsmen fired tear gas as they moved toward the students, who dispersed up a large hill by Taylor Hall and then down the back side of the hill onto a practice football field and the Taylor Hall parking lot. The guardsmen followed the demonstrators until they found themselves on the football field, where they had little room to maneuver because of fences on two parts of the field. Vulnerable to attack there, the guardsmen were hit by various objects, including rocks and bricks as well as tear gas canisters that demonstrators threw back at them. After approximately ten minutes, the troops retreated back up the hill. Once they reached the top, a group of guardsmen turned suddenly and fired into the crowd of demonstrators on the practice football field and in the Taylor Hall parking lot. The shooting lasted thirteen seconds. Approximately sixty-seven shots were fired, killing four and wounding nine Kent State students.[3]

The Search for Responsibility

Among the many questions arising from the shootings, none was more predominant than the issue of who was responsible for the shootings. Ultimately, the task of answering this question fell to the American courts, and no court loomed larger in the search for responsibility than the U.S. District Court for the Northern District of Ohio. Before turning to this topic, however, it is first necessary to describe briefly the reports of the nonjudicial agencies that examined the shootings. Although numerous organizations conducted studies, the Ohio State Highway Patrol, the Federal Bureau of Investigation (FBI), and the

President's Commission on Campus Unrest completed the most authoritative and influential reports.[4]

The Ohio State Highway Patrol was the first organization to complete a report. A massive piece, three thousand pages in length, the document was given to Portage County prosecutor Ronald Kane for use by a state grand jury. Although this document has never been formally released, it seems clear from subsequent developments that the Highway Patrol identified numerous student demonstrators who might be indicted and tried on criminal charges.

The FBI's report, based on the investigation it began immediately after the shootings, was submitted to the U.S. Department of Justice (DOJ). This report has never been made public, but the Justice Department did make available a summary.[5] The summary does not specifically state that any members of the Guard were responsible for the shootings; however, it does suggest that the Guard was responsible for the deaths and injuries.

The President's Commission on Campus Unrest, more commonly known as the Scranton Commission, after its director, William Scranton, the former governor of Pennsylvania, undertook the final major investigation.[6] The commission was charged with analyzing campus unrest throughout the United States, with a special emphasis on the May shootings at Kent State and Jackson State universities. The Scranton Commission report found fault all around in the Kent State case. In its conclusions, the commission stated: "The actions of some students were violent and criminal and those of some others were dangerous, reckless, and irresponsible."[7] But overall the commission concluded that the Guard was responsible: "The indiscriminate firing of rifles into a crowd of students and the deaths that followed were unnecessary, unwarranted, and inexcusable."[8]

State and Federal Criminal Cases

Although these analyses of the May 4 shootings were insightful, they were not authoritative, and they left many critical legal issues unanswered. It would ultimately fall to the American court system to determine who was legally responsible. This process would take ten years, during which federal and state courts heard both civil and criminal cases in trying to determine legal culpability for the Kent State shootings.

This chapter will first consider the state and federal criminal cases before turning to the federal civil trials. As we will see, the decisions of the U.S. District Court for the Northern District of Ohio played a major role in these criminal cases.

State Criminal Activities

The initial legal development was the convening of a special state grand jury investigation. Because Portage County did not have the resources to handle such a massive undertaking, the state assumed responsibility for conducting the grand jury investigation. Apparently relying heavily on the Ohio State Highway Patrol report, the grand jury returned indictments against twenty-five individuals, primarily Kent State students but also a few nonstudents and one faculty member. Interestingly, the indictments all involved activities on the days leading up to the May 4 shootings rather than on May 4 itself.

The grand jury also produced a lengthy report on the events of May 4 at Kent State.[9] The report exonerated the National Guard, accepting the argument that the guardsmen fired in self-defense, although it did strongly criticize the Guard leadership. The grand jury report was quite critical of the demonstrators, arguing that they were guilty of creating a riot on May 4 and on the previous three days as well. On May 4, the report stated, as the guardsmen retreated from the practice football field, they were "under a constant barrage of rocks and other flying objects accompanied by a constant flow of obscenities and chants such as 'KILL, KILL, KILL.'"[10] The report ultimately put blame on the Kent State administration officials, although no indictments were issued against any university officers.

Before the state criminal trials could begin, attorneys for the "Kent 25" asked the U.S. District Court for the Northern District of Ohio to overturn all of the indictments and to order that the grand jury report be destroyed. Judge William K. Thomas heard the case. On January 28, 1971, he declined to invalidate the charges against any of the Kent 25, but he did order that the report be expunged and destroyed because, he argued, "[it] irreparably injures, and as long as it remains in effect, the Report will continually injure . . . the rights of the indicted plaintiffs and of other persons similarly situated."[11] This was the Northern District Court's first involvement in the legal aftermath of May 4, 1970, but it certainly was not to be the last. And this decision by Judge Thomas was to establish a foundation that would eventually lead him to craft a final resolution after the decade of litigation.

Attorneys for the state had a difficult time from the very beginning of the trials of the Kent 25. A Portage County jury convicted the first defendant of one count of interfering with a fireman on May 2, but it found him not guilty on three other charges of arson, assaulting a fireman at the ROTC building fire, and first-degree riot. In the second trial, state attorneys, after calling four witnesses, moved for the charges to be dismissed. The third and fourth defendants pleaded guilty to first-degree riot, but the common pleas court judge, Edwin Jones, acquitted the fifth defendant because of a lack of evidence as well as "a great possibility that some of the defendant's rights under the Fourteenth Amendment were not necessarily observed."[12] At this point in the trials, on December 7, 1971, sixteen days into the proceedings, Special State Prosecutor John Hayward moved to dismiss charges against the remaining twenty members of the Kent 25 because of insufficient evidence. Predictably, reactions to the state criminal trials were mixed, with students generally supporting the outcome and Kent and Portage County residents typically upset with the results. U.S. senator Stephen Young of Ohio called the indictments "a fakery and a fraud from the outset" whose real purpose "was to whitewash Rhodes."[13]

Federal Criminal Cases

The attempt of the state of Ohio to find criminal activity around the May 4 shootings was now completed, but that did not mean that criminal charges were necessarily finished. The wounded students and the parents of the dead students thought that they had a much better chance to gain a legal victory at the federal level because the climate of opinion was much less intense at the national level as compared with the state level. Thus, they put forth great effort to promote a Justice Department grand jury to determine if anyone was guilty of violating federal criminal law. It was not until August 13, 1971, that Attorney General John Mitchell announced the decision not to convene a federal grand jury. Substantial speculation arose as to the reasons behind this decision, with some people arguing that it was a purely legal set of considerations and others believing it was a political decision.

For those offering a legal perspective, the argument was made that federal law did not provide any basis for indictments against Guard officers or enlisted men. Federal law required proof beyond a reasonable doubt that there was a specific intention to deprive students of their civil rights. This had always been a tough standard for federal prosecutors to meet, and little evidence could be found in the FBI report that would support prosecutors in bringing federal criminal indictments.

Those who believed political considerations motivated the decision not to convene a federal grand jury contended that the Guard was responsible for the shootings but that those at the highest levels of the federal government were trying to bury this "fact." The document that provided the strongest support for this political model was an "eyes only" memo that NBC News revealed on May 4, 1978. John Ehrlichman, a close adviser to President Nixon, sent the 1970 memo to Attorney General Mitchell. In it, Ehrlichman stated in no uncertain manner that the president did not want a grand jury investigation into the May 4 shootings at Kent State. We can only speculate what factors were behind Nixon's decision not to convene a federal grand jury. Charles Thomas, a historian with the National Archives, argued that the president took this position to conceal the presence of undercover federal agents on the Kent State campus before the shootings. Alternatively, Nixon might have wanted to give the incident as little attention as possible because it symbolized the agony of the ongoing Vietnam War. Whatever the reason for Nixon's position, Attorney General Mitchell complied with the order that no federal grand jury should be convened to examine the Kent State shootings.

Despite continuing efforts by the parents, students, and their supporters, the Justice Department did not alter its position against convening a federal grand jury for almost three years. When the DOJ ultimately did change its stance, the decision was closely related to the Watergate affair. Both Attorney General Mitchell and his successor, Richard Kleindienst, were linked to the expanding Watergate scandal, and a new attorney general, Elliot Richardson, was named to the position in August 1973. Richardson was free of the baggage of the past, and Watergate was consuming most of Nixon's time. Richardson and the Justice Department did feel a sense of independence from the White House, and on August 3, 1973, J. Stanley Pottinger, assistant attorney general in charge of the Civil Rights Division, announced that the investigation into the Kent State shootings was being reopened.

This decision seems to have been based on several factors. One element was the continuing growth of interest in the May 4 shootings. Another factor was the lobbying efforts by the parents and wounded students who wanted the truth regarding the shootings to be determined by the legal system. Finally, the Watergate affair served to free the Justice Department from the tight reins it had operated under during the pre-Watergate era.

In December 1973, after several months of investigation, the Justice Department announced that a federal grand jury would be convened to reexamine the May 4 shootings. Frank Battisti, chief judge of the U.S. District Court for the Northern District of Ohio, oversaw the lengthy and complicated grand jury investigation, which took thirty-nine sessions lasting three and a half months and had 173 witnesses, including most of the guardsmen who fired weapons. Finally, on March 29, 1974, the grand jury indicted eight members of the Ohio National Guard. Five of them were charged with violation of the students' civil rights, a felony crime. The indictment claimed that their actions "did thereby willfully deprive [the students] of the right secured and protected by the Constitution and laws of the United States not to be deprived of liberty without due process of law."[14] These five men faced possible life prison terms. The grand jury indicted the other three guardsmen on misdemeanor counts carrying one-year jail sentences.

The trial was delayed several months by appeals regarding the grand jury investigation, but it finally started in October 1974. Federal prosecutor Robert Murphy began the trial with an opening statement to the jury in which he admitted that the government had not been successful in linking the guardsmen to the bullets fired on May 4. But Murphy told the jury that he would prove the case through the Guard's statements to the FBI and the Ohio State Highway Patrol, through observing the locations of various actors by way of photographs, and through seeing in person the area of the confrontation.

Murphy's team called thirty-three witnesses over a ten-day period, but the prosecutor's case in chief was still insufficient. Responding to a routine motion by the defendants to end the trial before the defense presented it case, Battisti granted the motion, arguing that the government had not produced enough evidence to prove the guilt of the guardsmen beyond a reasonable doubt. He issued a written opinion in which he not only explained his decision more fully but also assigned blame to several parties. Battisti argued that the statute under which the guardsmen were being tried was a very difficult test for the government because of the requirement of establishing a *specific intent* to deny students their constitutional rights. This specific intent standard was hard to meet because the government had to elicit either explicit testimony from the guardsmen or present extremely obvious evidence of intent. The federal government had not been able to do either.

Although Battisti ruled in favor of the Guard, his written opinion stressed the narrow limits of his decision. "It must be clearly understood that the conduct of both the Guardsmen who fired and of the Guard and state officials who placed these guardsmen in this position . . . is neither approved nor vindicated by this opinion."[15] Battisti also stated: "The events at Kent State University were made up of a series of tragic blunders and mistakes of judgment. It is vital that state and National Guard officials not regard this decision as authorizing and approving the use of force against unarmed demonstrators, whatever the occasion or the issues involved. Such use of force is, and was, deplorable."[16]

Civil Cases in the Northern District Court

The U.S. District Court for the Northern District of Ohio obviously played a pivotal role in the criminal case that arose from the May 4 shootings at Kent State, with Chief Judge Battisti being the most important figure. The Northern District court was also to play a major role in the federal civil trial that followed the 1974 criminal case. Judges Donald Young and William K. Thomas were key figures during the four years it took to reach a decision.

In the immediate aftermath of the shootings, the wounded students and the parents of the slain students began pursuing the possibility of filing civil suits at both the state and federal levels. The Ohio Supreme Court ultimately rejected the efforts of the parents' and wounded students' attorneys to bring a state civil suit against the various Ohio officials, ruling that the doctrine of sovereign immunity prevented public officials from being sued for their actions.[17] A final attempt to pursue this avenue ended when the U.S. Supreme Court refused to hear the case in *Krause v. Ohio*.[18]

Despite the unsuccessful efforts to pursue a state civil trial, the parents and the wounded students pressed ahead with efforts to sue in federal district court. Just as with their efforts for a state trial, however, their attempts to initiate a civil suit in federal court ran head-on into the doctrine of sovereignty immunity. District Judge James C. Connell held that sovereign immunity prevented the potential plaintiffs from suing the state without its consent. An appeal to the Sixth Circuit Court of Appeals in Cincinnati was unsuccessful.[19] But on April

17, 1974, the U.S. Supreme Court surprised both courts when it ruled that sovereign immunity was not absolute and that the federal district court could hear this case. Speaking for a unanimous Court in *Scheuer v. Rhodes* (1973), Chief Justice Warren Burger wrote that "damages against individual defendants are a permissible remedy in some circumstances notwithstanding that they hold public office."[20]

The size and the complexity of the civil trial were enormous. Each of thirteen plaintiffs (the four sets of parents and the nine wounded students) sued over fifty defendants (Governor Rhodes, Kent State president Robert White, Guard officers, and Guard enlisted men), seeking $46 million in damages. The trial lasted fifteen weeks throughout the summer of 1975, making it one of the longest courtroom dramas in the history of American law. The twelve-person jury faced an astonishing amount of material; over a hundred witnesses were called to the stand, the trial transcript ran over twelve thousand pages, the jury instructions covered seventy-six pages, and a choice of at least five hundred verdicts had to be considered.

Judge Donald Young of Toledo was assigned the case in July 1974, and it took one year of preparation before the trial began the following May. Part of the delay was caused by the need to complete the federal criminal case of earlier 1974, and part of the delay was to allow attorneys for both sides to prepare. During that period, Young made several vital decisions, including the decision that all suits would be heard in one trial and that the trial would be conducted in two parts, the first to determine legal liability and, if liability were found, the second to determine the damages to be awarded.

Perhaps the most significant development that occurred before the trial began was the sudden resignation of Ramsey Clark, the former U.S. attorney general who was head of the legal team for the parents and students. The plaintiffs selected Joseph Kelner to replace Clark, but this last-minute change may have substantially weakened the effectiveness of the presentation by the plaintiffs' attorneys.

Throughout the trial, the parents and wounded students viewed Judge Young with hostility, believing him to be biased toward the defendants. As evidence, they pointed to Young's reference to Governor Rhodes as "your Excellency" when Rhodes took the witness stand. The plaintiffs and their attorneys also thought that the judge was much more receptive to the testimony by the defendants' witnesses, as evidenced by Young's tendency to overrule the objections of the plaintiffs' attorney and to uphold those made by defense counsel.

259

In their closing arguments, lead attorneys for both sides stressed the importance of the case. Kelner, chief counsel for the parents and wounded students, stated: "I dare say that the case, perhaps, has no rival in its importance in the history of American justice."[21] Charles Brown, lead attorney for the defendants, also claimed that the jury "in this historic case" was "not only the conscience of the community" but also "the conscience of the United States of America."[22]

After a long, hard summer, the jury reached its decision on August 25, 1975: "We the jury, on the issues joined, find in favor of all the defendants and against the plaintiffs."[23] The jury unanimously agreed that none of the defendants — Governor Rhodes, KSU president Robert White, Guard officers, and the Guard enlisted men — bore any legal responsibility regarding the events of May 4, 1970.

Although most of the jury members did not speak with reporters, two jurors did grant interviews. These interviews suggest that several factors featured prominently in the jury's decision. At the outset of the discussion by the jury, a consensus existed that Governor Rhodes could not be held liable. A somewhat blurry home movie taken by a student from his dormitory room gave the jury some foundation to believe that the Guard was in serious danger. In addition, the jury weighed heavily a tape recording of students yelling, "Charge! Charge! Lay down your guns, you're surrounded!"[24] which many jurors saw as threatening. Additional evidence mentioned by the jurors involved the actions of some protestors who were alleged to have taken gas masks and rocks to the noon rally. Finally, it was suggested that the jurors might have ruled somewhat differently if they could have considered defendants on an individual basis rather than as a group, as Judge Young had ordered.

Reaction to the decision was intense and emotional. The father of Allison Krause, one of the students who was killed, seemed to speak for all the parents and wounded students when he stated, "They don't understand what the Constitution is about. They have just destroyed the most wonderful document ever made by man. Thanks to them, murder by the state is correct. The Constitution does not protect anyone against armed barbarians."[25]

Although state and federal courts had exonerated the Guard leaders and enlisted men as well as Governor Rhodes and President White, the parents and wounded students were not finished, choosing to appeal the jury's decision in the federal civil case to the Sixth Circuit Court of Appeals in Cincinnati. Little doubt existed in their minds about pursuing an appeal. Their determination was strong and unanimous. At the same time, they knew they faced a difficult challenge. They would need to assemble a team of attorneys, and these attorneys would have to review thousands of pages of testimony to determine the precise issues upon which to appeal. In addition, circuit courts are generally deferential to district courts, and this looked to be especially true in the federal district case, where a decision in favor of the parents and students would negate the long and costly trial and require that a new trial be held.

The parents and students selected Sanford Rosen, a San Francisco attorney with long-standing ties to the American Civil Liberties Union (ACLU), to head their appellate team. Other members of the team were Nicholas Waranoff and Amitai Schwartz of San Francisco; Nelson Karl, Michael Geltner, and Clyde Ellis, all of whom were associated with the ACLU of Ohio; and David Engdahl of the University of Colorado. Preparing the brief to the Sixth Circuit took almost a year and a half.

The appellants' brief raised six major issues, but at oral argument, which began on June 21, 1977, the issue that seemed to capture the interest of the three-judge circuit panel was Judge Young's handling of a threat to a juror late in the trial. This matter began when one of the jurors reported to Young that another juror had been physically assaulted, threatened, and told to vote the right way. When the judge learned of this situation, he got the attorneys and jurors together, informing them of the developments.[26] He did not, however, question either the threatened juror or the other members of the jury about the effects this situation had on them. Instead, he sequestered the jury for the remainder of the trial.

On September 12, 1975, the three-judge panel announced its decision, ruling in favor of the parents and students on the basis of Judge Young's improper handling of the threat to the juror and ordering a new trial. The panel explained: "The intrusion in this case represents an attempt to pervert our system of justice at its very heart. No litigant should be required to accept the verdict of a jury which has been subjected to such an intrusion in the absence of a hearing and determination that no probability exists that the jury's deliberations or verdict would be affected. Although we are reluctant to do so, particularly in the face of the obvious good faith efforts of the trial judge to deal with a most difficult problem which arose near the end of an exhausting trial, we conclude that reversal for a new trial is required."[27] In addition to this critical reversal, the circuit court rendered several other crucial decisions. It ordered Kent State president White to be dropped from the list of defendants; it ruled that protestors' First Amendment rights were not violated; and it allowed grand jury testimony, which had been forbidden in the 1975 civil trial, to be used in the new trial.

The new case was assigned to the same judge who had presided at the original trial, Donald Young. The defendants strongly supported this assignment, but the parents and wounded students were angry and dismayed. Young, however, now focused on achieving an out-of-court settlement rather than holding a new trial. This is the most common method of resolving a civil case, requiring careful negotiation of the terms of the settlement, with both sides compromising to achieve a partial victory.

This case, however, involved some especially difficult problems beyond those found in routine out-of-court settlement negotiations. One complicating factor was the number of parties involved, with thirteen plaintiffs and twenty-eight defendants.[28] Another complicating element was the challenge of determining the amount of money to be awarded. Yet another issue was the wording of a statement that all defendants would sign. Finally, the key question of who should pay for the trial had to be answered.

Judge Young pushed hard for a settlement, but he was unsuccessful. The plaintiffs and their attorneys vividly remembered the 1975 civil trial over which he had presided, and the dislike and distrust stemming from that trial prevented the achievement of a settlement. Realizing that he was not going to be successful, Young stepped down from the case in September 1978. He stated that the plaintiffs should settle for $380,000, the approximate cost for Ohio to try the case, and he took a parting shot at the parents and wounded students: "I realize that settlement for so small a sum would not be very palatable to the plaintiffs, but something is better than nothing. I do not believe that the plaintiffs can ever win these cases, no matter how often they are tried or retried."[29]

The prospects for achieving a settlement seemed to improve dramatically with the naming of Judge William K. Thomas to preside over the case. Both sides respected Thomas. The parents and students favorably remembered his decision to expunge the report of the state grand jury, and the defendants were positively disposed to favor a settlement that would cost them no money because the state of Ohio would pay all the costs, allow them to escape any liability for the shootings, and end the ten-year legal battle.

As the time scheduled for the start of a new trial loomed over the negotiations, Thomas worked diligently to put together terms for a settlement but to no avail. The most difficult aspect of the settlement was achieving agreement on the joint statement about who was at fault, but it was the financial dimension that took the most time. In terms of the amount of money involved, Judge Young had suggested $380,000, but under Thomas's negotiations, the total rose to $675,000 to be paid by the state of Ohio, based on a new estimate of the costs to the state to try the case. Given the amount of money involved, Ohio law required that the State Controlling Board approve the expenditure. The board members had a variety of concerns, including whether they could legally take this action; the type of precedent this could set; and, of course, the political ramifications. Given these uncertainties, the board voted to postpone action indefinitely.

The board's failure to approve the financial settlement meant the trial had to begin. Both sides presented their opening statements. Then, on December 21, 1978, after the plaintiffs had called two witnesses, Judge Thomas announced a recess until January 1979. This break allowed him to finalize the precise terms of a settlement. Thomas was helped by the decision of Ohio secretary of state William J. Brown that the board had the authority to support a settlement. In another critical development, all of Ohio's major newspapers announced their support for the settlement, thus reducing dramatically any voter fallout.

On January 4, 1979, with all the pieces now in place, Judge Thomas was able to announce the terms of the settlement. The plaintiffs were to receive a total of $675,000 from the state of Ohio. Additionally, $75,000 went for attorneys fees and expenses. The parents of the slain students received $15,000 each, and the awards given to the wounded students ranged from $15,000 to $42,500, with the exception of Dean Kahler, who received $350,000, since he was by far the most seriously injured.

Twenty-eight defendants signed the following statement:

> In retrospect, the tragedy of May 4, 1970 should not have occurred. The students may have believed that they were right in continuing their mass protest in regard to the Cambodian invasion, even though this protest followed the posting and reading by the University of an order to ban rallies and an order to disperse. These orders have since been determined by the Sixth Circuit Court of Appeals to have been lawful.
>
> Some of the Guardsmen on Blanket Hill, fearful and anxious from prior events, may have believed in their own minds that their lives were in danger. Hindsight suggests that another method would have resolved the confrontation. Better ways must be found to deal with such confrontations.
>
> We devoutly wish that a means had been found to avoid the May 4 events culminating in the Guard shootings and the irreversible deaths and injuries. We deeply regret those events and are profoundly saddened by the deaths of four students and the wounding of nine others which resulted. We hope that the agreement to end this litigation will help to assuage the tragic memories regarding that sad day.[30]

The third component of the settlement involved the plaintiffs' agreeing to end all litigation against the defendants regarding the May 4 shootings.

Strong reasons existed for both sides to agree to the terms of the settlement. For the defendants, the settlement absolved them of legal responsibility, they had no personal monetary penalties, and the decade-long process was finally at an end. The settlement also made sense for the wounded students and parents. The Guard expressed its regret over the shootings even if it failed to admit any legal responsibility, and they themselves received a significant amount of money, distributed based upon the severity of the students' wounds; moreover, had the matter gone to trial, they had serious doubts about winning because they had no additional evidence to introduce, and a victory would probably have meant a further appeal.

Conclusion

The U.S. District Court for the Northern District of Ohio played an enormous role in dealing with the legal aftermath of the May 4, 1970, shootings on the campus of Kent State University. Judge Frank Battisti presided over the major criminal trial, in which none of the National Guard troops were found to have violated federal criminal law. Judge William Thomas was the key figure in reaching an out-of-court settlement in the civil case, which involved a statement of regret by the defendants, a financial award to the plaintiffs, and an agreement to terminate the ten-year legal battle.

However, the central question of who was legally responsible for the shootings was never answered. Nobody was ever found liable for any events on May 4, 1970, at Kent State University, despite the rioting, the wounding of nine students, and the death of four more. Does this mean we should be criticizing the district court judges? The proper answer seems to be no. The settlement in 1979 is probably as close to justice as the plaintiffs could hope to come in a complex legal world.

Notes

1. This chapter draws heavily from Thomas R. Hensley, "The May 4th Trials," in *Kent State and May 4th: A Social Science Perspective*, ed. Thomas R. Hensley and Jerry M. Lewis (Kent, Ohio: Kent State University Press, 2010), 64–86.

2. *Report of the President's Commission on Campus Unrest* (Washington, D.C.: U.S. Government Printing Office, 1970), 254.

3. The four students who died were Allison Krause, Jeffrey Miller, Sandra Scheuer, and William Schroeder. The nine wounded students were Alan Canfora, John Cleary, Thomas Grace, Dean Kahler, Joseph Lewis, Donald MacKenzie, James Russell, Robert Stamps, and Douglas Wrentmore.

4. Among the most important investigations were those done by the *Akron Beacon Journal*, the Ohio National Guard's Inspector General's Office, the Special Kent State University Commission on Campus Violence, the Ohio American Civil Liberties Union, the Ohio Council of Churches, the American Association of Colleges and Universities, and the Ohio Bureau of Investigation.

5. The full summary appears in *Congressional Record*, 93rd Cong., 1st sess., 1113–19 (January 3–16, 1973).

6. President's Commission on Campus Unrest, *The Kent State Tragedy* (Washington, D.C.: U.S. Government Printing Office, 1970).

7. Ibid., 90.

8. Ibid., 89.

9. "Report of the Special Grand Jury," "Supplemental Order, Portage County Court of Common Pleas," October 15, 1970.

10. Ibid., 10–11.

11. Hammond v. Brown, 323 F. Supp. 326 (1971), 357.

12. *Akron Beacon Journal*, December 8, 1971, A1.

13. Ibid.

14. U.S. v. Shafer, Indictment, C1.

15. U.S. v. Shafer, 384 F. Supp. 496 (1974), 503.

16. Ibid.

17. Krause v. The State of Ohio, 31 Ohio St. 2d 132 (1972).

18. Krause v. The State of Ohio, 41 U.S.L.W. 3329 (1973).

19. Krause v. Rhodes, 471 F.2d 430 (6th Cir. 1972).

20. Scheuer v. Rhodes, 416 U.S. 232, 237–38 (1974).

21. Trial Transcript, Krause v. Rhodes, 390 F. Supp. 1072, 12,189 (N.D. Ohio 1975).

22. Ibid., 12,361.

23. *Akron Beacon Journal*, August 29, 1975, A1.

24. *Cleveland Plain Dealer*, August 28, 1975, A16.

25. Ibid., A17.

26. Brief for Appellants at 1, 2, Krause v. Rhodes, 390 F. Supp. 1072 (N.D. Ohio 1975), on appeal.

27. Krause v. Rhodes, 570 F. Supp. 563, 567 (6th Cir. 1977).

28. Several defendants had been dropped from the case.

29. *Akron Beacon Journal*, September 22, 1978, A1.

30. Statement issued in Cleveland, Ohio, January 4, 1979, by the defendants in the federal civic trial. This statement was printed in many of the major newspapers in the northeast Ohio area.

11

When Law and Conscience Conflict

The Draft Nonregistration Case of
United States v. Mark Arden Schmucker

Elizabeth Reilly

IT WAS HIGH summer. The stone halls of the old District Courthouse in Cleveland seemed a world apart—light, heat, and sound muted. Mark Schmucker, a soft-spoken Mennonite college student, had been indicted for failing to register for the Selective Service and was being arraigned in Case CR 82–133A. Outside on the steps, sympathizers gathered and the media clustered; this was big news on a national scale. But inside, a quieter, more intense drama was unfolding.[1]

Only weeks before, the chief prosecutor in the case, Assistant U.S. Attorney Gary Arbeznik, had requested permission from the Department of Justice to decline prosecution in the case, due to Mark's sincere religious objections to registration itself. Echoing that reluctance, during trial District Judge Ann Aldrich stated, "Presiding over this case is not a task I would have chosen"; she would later describe the case as her "own personal hell." And Mark, though adamant about adhering to his religious convictions and not registering, candidly expressed that not only was he "tired of being Mr. Non-Registrant" but also that he had acted with respect for the government and the law and dreaded prison following conviction. So how is it that the "case nobody wanted" came to trial in the Northern District of Ohio courthouse?[2]

This is the story of what brought Mark Schmucker and the government to the courthouse and what happened once their worldviews collided.

Mark Schmucker's odyssey to indictment began in January 1980 when President Jimmy Carter expressed an interest in reinstituting registration after the Soviet Union began military action in Afghanistan. Mark, a lifelong Mennonite, was a student at Goshen College, a Mennonite school in Indiana. He had personally adopted the Mennonite beliefs, especially as they related to war, peace, and Christian love.

In response to the potential reinstitution of registration, the Mennonite Central Committee's U.S. Peace Section held an Assembly on the Draft and National Service on March 27–29, 1980, at Goshen. The assembly explored responses to registration consistent with the Mennonites' historical stance toward peace. One of the options presented was "conscientious resistance" or "noncooperation" through nonregistration, which proved to be an alternative that many of the young men facing registration were contemplating.[3] Many Goshen students determined that their religious beliefs required nonregistration, especially because there was no opportunity to be sequestered from the pool of potential draftees by seeking or obtaining conscientious objector (CO) status.[4]

Mark joined a group of concerned students to discuss how they would respond if registration were indeed reinstituted. The young men in his group met weekly and explored the religious underpinnings of opposition to military participation, the place of registration in the military system, and what their own personal religious responses to registration would be.[5]

While Mark was soul-searching, President Carter reinstituted registration with the Selective Service System, issuing Presidential Proclamation 4771 on July 2, 1980. At the signing of the proclamation, the president remarked: "I would ask the support of all Americans for this move: Americans in the age that will be registered and Americans of all ages . . . who believe in maintaining peace through strength." The proclamation required males born in 1960 to register for military service between the dates of July 21, 1980, and July 26, 1980, unless precluded by a condition beyond their control.[6] Mark had been born on October 4, 1960.

Despite reinstituting registration, Congress chose not to reinstitute a draft. In addition, the government chose not to engage in the usual follow-up to registration—classification in accord with the congressional system. As a result, potential conscientious objectors could not seek CO status and hence removal from the pool of combat-eligible registrants.[7]

The government itself identified the registration requirement as militaristic policy. President Carter declared that registration was a "military step" taken "to convince the Soviet Union that their action in Afghanistan is ill-advised." "The inauguration of registration by the President and Congress was not merely a prelude to possible future conscription. It was an act of independent foreign policy significance—a deliberate response to developments overseas." Its purpose was "to prepare for a draft of combat troops" and "to develop a pool of potential combat troops."[8]

Requiring Mark to register, therefore, required him to participate in a military activity that was repugnant to his deeply held religious convictions. Confronted with the need to make a decision, he realized that he could not register and remain true to his beliefs. Instead, on August 10, 1980, he wrote this letter to Selective Service.

> To Whom It May Concern:
> I am writing to inform you that I have violated the Military Selective Service Act by not registering. I feel that I must refuse to comply with this law because registering would force me to compromise my Christian faith.
> I believe that war in any form is wrong. Christ meant for Christians to love each other and to love their enemies. War is an expression of hatred and an institution that has legalized and encouraged types of violent conduct that no civilized country would allow within its borders during peacetime. The use of force to resolve disputes has created an atmosphere of coercion which directly conflicts with the message of love preached by Christ. A Christian must use truth, love, understanding, and equality to resolve any disputes in which he is involved. As a Christian, I feel that I must avoid participation in the conscription process by not registering because conscription is an inherant [*sic*] part of the war process.
> At this point, I feel that I should emphasize that I am not anti-American. I consider myself privileged to live in a country where basic human rights, self-government, and religious freedom are granted to the citizens. I am not opposed to serving this great land of ours by working in a hospital, teaching, or by working at some other type of public service job. However, I can not participate, in any manner, with the armed forces.
> Sincerely,
> *Mark Schmucker*[9]

On August 19, 1981, the Selective Service System sent a certified letter to Mark at the home address he supplied with his letter. The letter advised him to register or be subject to criminal prosecution and penalty. Mark refused, adhering to his conscientious decision that registration violated his religious tenets.

His file was referred to the Department of Justice on October 21, 1981. Three weeks later, David Kline, the department's senior legal adviser for crimes against government operations, referred the case to the Federal Bureau of Investigation (FBI). After a period of dormancy triggered by President Ronald Reagan's decision to grant a grace period to register, the government proceeded further on June 8, 1982, by sending a letter to the local U.S. attorney in Mark's district. All local U.S. attorneys were advised to handle nonregistration prosecutions on a priority basis.[10]

The FBI contacted Mark Schmucker in Goshen on June 22, 1982. Mark again explained that his religious beliefs precluded him from registering. Agent Patrick Quigley recounted the conversation at trial. After conversing with Mark, Quigley had no doubt that the young man sincerely believed that registration was wrong.[11]

Assistant U.S. Attorney Gary Arbeznik telephoned Mark a week later and, in his words, "practically pleaded with him to register." Once again, Mark explained that registration was impossible due to his religious convictions. Arbeznik called Kline at the Department of Justice to request authority to decline prosecution because Mark sincerely objected to the act of registration itself. Kline refused, opining that religion was no basis upon which to institute or decline prosecution.[12]

This process of identifying and pursuing nonregistrants was known as the "passive enforcement system"; it was the only enforcement mechanism in use. It relied entirely upon self-reporting (as in Mark's case) or on reports from third parties of noncompliance (primarily of vocal opponents of registration), rather than upon active government investigation of what was estimated to be more than six hundred thousand nonregistrants. Once singled out, these young men were pursued according to the "beg policy," as the government dubbed it: the repeated series of government demands to register, escalating from a Selective Service form letter to FBI contact to a local U.S. attorney's contact informing the target of the intent to prosecute unless he registered. If the person registered at any time prior to indictment, the case was dropped. If he registered any time after indictment, prosecution was deferred.[13]

In practice, the policy singled out the young men who had written to the Selective Service to express their objections to registration, along with a few highly vocal antiregistration activists reported by others. As the government acknowledged, "With the present univers[e] of hundreds of thousands of nonregistrants, the chances that a quiet non-registrant will be prosecuted is probably about the same as the chances that he will be struck by lightning."

From the government's perspective, the system resulted in pursuing only the "most adamant" nonregistrants. From the nonregistrants' perspective, the policy resulted in pursuing only those whose deeply held principles compelled them to refuse to register. For instance, of the other five nonregistration cases initially referred to Arbeznik, four of the young men registered and one was not eligible to register.[14]

Consistent with the government's expectation, the indicted men were all principled objectors to registration. Seventeen had written to the government. One was a vocal opponent whose position was exceptionally well publicized.[15] From those eighteen indictments, nine reported cases, including Schmucker's, resulted. Seven of the indicted men based their decision not to register on religious grounds.[16]

Interestingly, not all U.S. attorneys acted expeditiously to indict the young men whose names were referred to them. Jerome Frese, the U.S. attorney in South Bend, Indiana, with jurisdiction over Goshen College, had three non-registrants from the college—Craig Miller, Greg Smucker, and Byron Becker—referred to him before Mark Schmucker was referred to the Northern District of Ohio. Frese met with them, expressing sympathy for their religiously motivated positions. Then, despite the fact that the three had received monthly letters threatening indictment for almost a year and thus believed they would be charged at any time, Frese simply failed to bring the cases to indictment. In May 1982, the letters stopped. Not until April 1985 were they contacted again, this time by the FBI. The cases had been transferred to Fort Wayne, where the U.S. attorney had no reluctance to prosecute. Because of their changed personal circumstances, they each registered.[17]

Unlike Frese, Arbeznik faithfully adhered to the Department of Justice's directions "that non-registration matters be . . . handled on a priority basis."[18] At that point, Mark sought legal representation from William Whitaker of Akron, who became lead trial counsel. I was Whitaker's partner, and I participated throughout the case and was lead counsel for the appeal. After indictment, two additional attorneys joined the defense team, John Lawson and Dale Baich of Cleveland.

Bill Whitaker was known for his commitment to the peace movement for a number of reasons. He had been an antiwar activist and a leader of the Students for a Democratic Society (SDS) at Kent State University during the Vietnam War; as a law student, he had participated in defending the protestors who were arrested surrounding the events of May 4, 1970.[19] Before May 4, the Kent State

Reserve Officers' Training Corps (ROTC) building had been burned, and general campus unrest accompanying the Nixon administration's incursion into Cambodia had led to protestors gathering on campus. The protests ended with the now infamous National Guard shooting of students, which left four dead and nine wounded. Years later, Kent State proposed building a new gymnasium partially on Blanket Hill, the site of the May 4 shootings. Whitaker represented the protestors arrested for sitting in to block construction. I, as a law student at that time, assisted in those defenses. John Lawson also worked with the gymnasium protest, and he spearheaded a federal court action seeking to enjoin the construction. Later, Lawson served as a member of the Cleveland City Council. Dale Baich had just begun practice with Lawson in 1982; he was also a former judicial clerk for Judge Aldrich.

In addition to supporting Mark's conscientious objection to war, Whitaker also expressed concern that the rule of law had been suspended in choosing to prosecute Mark and other self-reported resisters: "I find it offensive that those they have been putting in jail are the ones with the courage and integrity to address the Selective Service System and their problems with complying with the law. Those who are truly trying to evade their responsibility, the Justice Department won't get to until they run out of funds for prosecution."[20]

Mark Schmucker was indicted by the grand jury for the Northern District of Ohio, Eastern Division, on July 22, 1982, for knowingly and willfully failing, evading, and refusing to register as required by the Military Selective Service Act, Rules and Regulations, and Presidential Proclamation 4771 of July 2, 1980, in violation of 50 U.S.C. §§ 453 and 462(a) (Appx. 1980).

The case was assigned to District Judge Ann Aldrich. Judge Aldrich brought a complex set of experiences to this case. As a lawyer, she had tried cases on Okinawa for the U.S. Marines and had represented the United Church of Christ in Connecticut, among many other legal roles. She was also the first woman to serve as a federal district court judge in the Northern District of Ohio. President Carter appointed her to the bench in 1980, from her position as a professor of law at Cleveland-Marshall College of Law, where she was the first woman to earn tenure. Her practice and teaching had proven her to be a trailblazer for environmental law and for racial equality in the legal profession.[21] Leaving her chambers, attorneys passed a sign that she had posted by the side of her door — something that she saw each time she left as well. As a young attorney back then, I loved that sign: it read, "A woman who aspires to be like a man lacks ambition." Ann Aldrich did not lack ambition.

Judge Aldrich's personal life also made this case a difficult one for her professionally. During the Vietnam War, she had counseled her son and other protestors and draft resisters. Her son resisted being drafted and eventually received conscientious objector status. She believed her experiences with her son and others enabled her to understand "what Schmucker was going through."[22]

At his arraignment before Magistrate Jack Streepy on July 29, 1982, Mark pleaded not guilty. He did so, he said, because "pleading guilty doesn't give us a chance to challenge the constitutionality of the law—can the government force religious, conscientious resistors to register?"[23] Most of the other indicted nonregistrants chose to plead not guilty as well and to challenge the government process of registration and selection for prosecution. One religious objector, Enten Eller, chose to plead guilty, and Kendall Warkentine, another religious objector, refused to enter any plea at all. The judge ultimately entered a guilty plea on his behalf.[24] After arraignment, Mark explained, "If this country had a nonviolent resisters force against evil, I would register for that. . . . I'm not trying to get out of anything. As a Mennonite, I'd like to speak out against war as a way of settling disputes between nations. Registration is the first step of the mobilization process."[25]

After indictment, Mark's case progressed swiftly toward trial. In the period leading up to the trial, a series of defense motions challenged the registration process and the passive enforcement process. As Mark indicated after indictment, his main defenses relied upon the First Amendment right to the free exercise of religion. The defense filed three primary motions to dismiss, one on grounds of selective prosecution, the second alleging denial of equal protection, and the third contending that continuing to require registration infringed upon Mark's free exercise of religion.

The selective prosecution argument was two-pronged. First, the defense argued that by the passive enforcement system and the beg policy, Mark had been singled out because of his religious beliefs and his courage in reporting his nonregistration to the government. As the second part of its selective prosecution argument, the defense contended that Mark had been denied prosecutorial discretion when Kline refused to permit Arbeznik to decline prosecution.

To support its equal protection argument, the defense noted that in the underlying Selective Service legislation, Congress had designated as noncombatants those who, like Mark, were conscientious objectors to all war. However, for the 1980 registration-only scheme, the government insisted there was no reason to classify registrants unless the draft itself were reinstituted. Thus, no objector could remove himself from the pool of potential combatants that was formed, in Carter's words, to send a military signal of strength and readiness to fight. Nonetheless, the government had chosen to exempt several classes of non-combatants from registration, notably, females and males with serious mental conditions. Women were exempted by the congressional authorization bill and presidential proclamation. The government adamantly defended the male-only scheme before the Supreme Court in *Rotsker v. Goldberg*.[26] Individuals in the second group—males with serious mental conditions—were exempted by Selective Service practice developed during the operation of the passive enforcement system. The service recognized that these persons were required under the law to register and seek exemption through classification later.[27]

During an in-chambers examination, Edward Frankle, the architect of the passive enforcement policy, explained the exemptions. Frankle testified that the proclamation was designed to exempt persons suffering from temporary physical incapacity, such as hospitalization. Once the incapacity ceased, the person was required to register. Mentally incapacitated persons sometimes requested an exemption from registration. Although the law required them to register, the Selective Service unilaterally exempted them from this requirement. From the defense's perspective, this proved that exemption was easily accommodated within the registration process when the critical facts of noncombatant status were known, and because Mark's critical facts were known, exemption did not undermine registration.[28] The defense insisted that by recognizing exemptions, the Selective Service had (1) adopted an administrative mechanism to accommodate valid reasons for exempting noncombatants from registration, and (2) singled out a class of noncombatants (conscientious objectors to registration) for different adverse treatment. Thus, these exemptions, together with the absolute refusal to exempt Mark from either registration or prosecution, denied Mark equal protection. The defense further questioned this refusal because both the presidential proclamation and Justice Department guidelines provided for individual exemptions from registration.

Independently—and underlying the other substantive motions—the defense argued that the First Amendment free exercise clause required accommodation of sincerely held religious beliefs when possible, even in the face of a compelling government interest.[29] Noting that exemptions had been used to accommodate others whose circumstances came to the attention of the government, such as individuals with severe mental conditions, the defense urged that the government's knowledge of Mark's sincere religious conviction and its acceptance of his sincerity provided authorities with the easy opportunity to accommodate his beliefs by declining prosecution, rather than by insisting upon it. That declination was especially plausible when it had been sought by the U.S. attorney responsible for the case and when it mediated the absence of any mechanism for declaring conscientious objection because of the lack of a classification process and active draft.[30]

Legally, although Mark acknowledged his failure to register, he maintained that his religious beliefs constitutionally entitled him to an accommodation. That accommodation could be reached without further action by the government: the government could accept the information he had already provided and exempt him from formal registration in light of his conscientious objection. Indisputably, the government authorities knew and agreed that his beliefs were sincere, as a result of their own administrative mechanism developed to pursue the nonregistrants who self-identified. Therefore, the government was in a position to accommodate him, just as it had accommodated others technically required to register but acknowledged not to be subject to any eventual draft.

In fact, in several later prosecutions the government ultimately accepted nonregistration or accommodated religious objectors by deviating from its system. During Charles Epp's trial, for instance, the trial judge brokered a solution in chambers. Given Epp's conscientious objection to registering and his letter that had provided the precise information necessary, the judge had the government accept the information (also repeated on a piece of paper in chambers) as a form of "constructive registration," and the government then withdrew the case. Similarly, Steven Schlossberg was spared trial and placed in ninety-day pretrial diversion after the government agreed to have the Selective Service issue him a letter granting him "Conscientious Objector" status, despite the government's general refusal to classify any registrant.[31]

The government supported its prosecution policy by arguing that the First Amendment exercise of sending the letter was not the cause of the prosecution but simply strong proof of willful failure to register, making the prosecution "in spite of" rather than "because of" the exercise of rights. Ultimately, the Supreme Court agreed with this position in *Wayte v. United States*.[32] But *Wayte* did not address Mark's additional arguments that the government withheld prosecutorial discretion when it was sought and that it had failed to afford an available and easy free exercise accommodation. The government supported its opposition to Mark's equal protection argument by invoking deference to the military and noting the necessity for narrowing the class of people required to register. It explained the choice to exempt women as easing the administrative burden and costs of the scheme. And finally, the government argued that having Mark register was as strong a compelling interest as could be—the need to provide for the national defense—and thus, the simple and "mere" requirement that he register was insufficient to require them to accommodate him. This last argument was a theme heard throughout the trial and appeal. The defense urged that either (1) registration was the single available act that declared a young man's readiness to serve in combat—as claimed by the government—and hence a significant burden on Mark's religious conviction that he could not participate in sending such a message, or (2) registration was not a very compelling need for the government to enforce against Mark when an easy accommodation existed, as it did by the time the question of bringing an indictment arose. The government insisted that registration was tantamount to a full-blown interest in national security but that asking Mark to register was an innocuous and simple request not deserving of accommodation. Neither the prosecutor nor the court saw an asymmetry at work—registration of every eligible male was vital to the government but not very much to ask of Mark. The defense, by contrast, urged that, at the very least, the same weight should be given to the requirement to register from the perspective of the defendant as from the perspective of the government.[33]

The pretrial motions required Judge Aldrich, a relatively new appointee to the bench, to grapple with the realities of the judicial role. From a fierce advocate for causes in which she personally believed, Aldrich had become a neutral arbiter dedicated to upholding the rule of law and faithfully applying higher court precedent. She responded by adhering to the integrity of the judicial role she had assumed. Describing her rulings on defense motions to dismiss the prosecution for selective prosecution and failure to accommodate Mark Schmucker's religious exercise, Judge Aldrich later told a reporter: "I wanted to find the law unconstitutional, I wanted to find for selective prosecution, but I couldn't. I couldn't and maintain my own intellectual integrity. I took an oath to enforce all the laws, not just certain ones. I was left with my own personal hell."[34]

Like Aldrich, Arbeznik was sympathetic to Mark, but he perceived his responsibility to uphold the rule of law as more important. A sincere assistant U.S. attorney and a career prosecutor, he had been and continues to be responsible for prosecuting some of the largest and most critical cases in the Northern District. Ultimately, Arbeznik is a lawyer in the classic mode—dedicated to the rule of law. That dedication was apparent in his conduct of the Schmucker prosecution and trial.

When he asked the Justice Department for authority not to prosecute, he later reported that he said, "'Are you sure you want to go through with this case?' . . . I preferred not to go on the guy, but we cannot use religion as a criterion to accept or decline a case." Despite having "sympathy for [Mark's] position," what ultimately mattered to Arbeznik was that "the law really is very clear." "A person cannot decide what laws he will obey and what laws he won't."[35]

As the Associated Press (AP) report put it: "Neither the government lawyer nor the federal judge wanted Mennonite college student Mark Schmucker to be tried for failing to register for the draft."[36] But inexorably, the strongly held principles of Schmucker and of the government, the prosecutor, and the judge propelled this historic case to trial in Cleveland.

Trial commenced on September 30, 1982. A jury of eight men and four women was impaneled the first day, and proceedings began on October 1. In contrast to the din caused by the throng of media and supporters outside the courthouse, an atmosphere of peacefulness prevailed in the room where the trial took place. The benches in the small visitor's gallery of the courtroom held Mennonites from Mark's hometown and from Goshen. Five were young men who had not registered, come to witness to the profession of religious fidelity to peace. The others, including Mark's parents, members of his community, and several pastors in historically pacifist churches, came in silent and loving support.[37] These people exuded an aura of serenity and acceptance that pervaded the courtroom. The more common trial environment, centered on a mere clash of positions and personalities, was supplanted by a solemn conflict between opposing sides arguing on behalf of deeply held principles.

Outside the courtroom, the defendant's supporters were anxious to explain the religious commitment to peace. Although "public protest is not a way of life among Mennonites," many felt a need to support Mark's stance publicly. "When is it wrong to practice your religion in America?" one young woman plaintively queried. Another Goshen College nonregistrant, Paul Reimer, explained that "because there is no C.O. [conscientious objector] status, there is no effective appeals procedure for people with sincere religious beliefs. Since there are no other alternatives, I'd go to jail." Several sympathizers passed out information and responded to questions from passersby, as their way of witnessing for peace. They readily answered questions from members of the media and other spectators, seeking to explain how their religious faith led them to this difficult choice. Gene Wenger, pastor from Hartville Church of the Brethren, explained, "The freedom of religion is being tested in this case because the conscience of many is being disregarded. Young men like Mark, who are many in number, are led in good faith not to comply."[38]

The Goshen students were especially articulate. Byron Becker noted to a reporter that the case was about law and religious belief but that only law was allowed to be argued in court. The young men explained that Mennonites traditionally have a positive attitude of cooperation with government but not the military: "We generally agree that the government is good and that it has a role in society." Jon Nofziger put it quite simply, "None of us are out looking for laws to break and we don't find any pleasure in it." Rather, adherence to their deeply held religious beliefs motivated them to take a stand. Don Blosser, a Mennonite theologian professor at Goshen, crystallized the conflict: "It's not that they don't want to follow the law, it's that they can't."[39]

Supporters questioned the position taken by the judge and prosecution that "we need to obey the law and not ask questions," noting that unquestioning obedience has led to horrors such as the atrocities committed by the Nazis who were tried at Nuremberg. "Where do the moral aspects of a law get heard if we just say 'Obey the law'?" Greg Smucker asked a reporter.[40]

Back inside the other world of the courthouse, the trial began. During his opening statement, Arbeznik focused upon the requirements of the registration law and the fact that Mark "indefinitely refused to obey the law" despite being "given many opportunities." The government called six witnesses in its case, to prove the repeated opportunities Mark had been provided to register and his consistent refusal to do so. The prosecutor and witnesses emphasized Mark's opposition to what they termed "mere" registration, and they noted that Mark's father had registered during World War II and had served in civilian alternative service. Mark's younger brother had also registered after adding "conscientious objector" on the form, despite the designation having no significance to the government.[41]

In the defense case, Mennonite theologian Don Blosser explained these different choices of individual conscience. He testified that Mark's choice of total noncooperation — nonregistration — was officially recognized by the Mennonite

Church as a means of putting into practice the church's long-standing opposition to war in any form. The choice was one of personal faith and conscience. Mark's conscience chose nonregistration.[42]

Presiding during trial, Judge Aldrich exuded an open, professional judicial demeanor. She acted decisively and without fanfare, maintaining masterful control over the courtroom. She transformed the conflict of principles she herself experienced into a detached and balanced empathy.

Thus, despite her belief that the law and the Constitution provided Mark with no refuge for his decision not to register, Judge Aldrich permitted him to testify to his reasons for refusing to register. In his testimony, Mark Schmucker identified the specific biblical passages upon which he based his beliefs in opposition to militarism. He explained that President Carter's desire to send a message of "hostile intent" to the Soviet Union conflicted with these beliefs. To Mark, an important quality of Christ was that, in addition to being peaceful, he had actively opposed the wrongs in life: "He did not sit back and just allow the evil in the world to go on." Mark believed that quietly fitting in by registering would condone and facilitate militarism. His refusal to register followed Christ's example of both avoiding wrongdoing and opposing the evil of using military force to solve problems. His letter explained these convictions to the government and reflected his respect for law.[43]

After this testimony, the judge questioned Mark:

Q. If there would have been a space available on the registration form where you could have checked "conscientious objector," would you then have registered?
A. No.[44]

The judge then instructed the jury that motive was not a defense.

On cross-examination, the prosecution emphasized three points. First, Mark knew of the registration requirement and decided not to comply with it. Second, this decision was one of free will, which he would not have changed even if the government had provided him an opportunity to identify his conscientious objection to war. Third, one reason for not registering was to delay military mobilization, and he understood that the government's decision to prosecute him would divert time and resources away from militarization. Earlier, Mark had recognized that his prosecution was part of the government effort to induce others to register. In an interview with the *Akron Beacon Journal* before trial, he noted, "The government has to prove its point."[45]

Arbeznik gave Schmucker one more opportunity to sign a registration card during cross-examination. Stating his religious objections, Mark refused. Later, Arbeznik noted that had he signed even then, he would probably have ended the prosecution.[46]

In closing, Arbeznik again focused on the rule of law: "It's just a matter of fairness. . . . He owes a duty . . . just like everyone else. We can't pick and choose the laws we follow because eventually we have no law. And without law, we have no liberty."[47] Alluding to his earlier request not to prosecute, he said, "The evidence may show the government did not want to prosecute Mark Schmucker, but then the evidence may also show that Mark Schmucker wanted the government to prosecute him."[48] Ultimately, Arbeznik relied upon the simplicity of the facts and Schmucker's having admitted to knowingly and willfully failing to register despite being required to do so by law. He asked the jurors to put aside any sympathy they might feel.

After the trial, he characterized the defense as playing to sympathy, stating that the verdict for the prosecution was simply a matter of having won legally and having the jury enforce the law. But he acknowledged that it was Mark's honesty and forthrightness that made the conviction straightforward and "easy to win," as the defendant had admitted to each of the elements of the crime with which he was charged. "We had three things to prove and he corroborated each of them for us on the stand."[49]

But even if the victory was "easy" on the law, it appeared that the case took a toll on Prosecutor Arbeznik. During closing, observers characterized him as "very emotional . . . pausing several times to collect himself, drinking water and clearing his throat before he could proceed."[50]

In the defense's argument to the jury, Bill Whitaker emphasized the "values conflict" that Mark had faced when determining not to register. Indeed, the more adamant the government was in insisting that registration was so vital to national security that Mark could not be accommodated, the more clear it became that registration was in fact acquiescing to military participation. What Mark had done, Whitaker argued, was find and adhere to his deep religious convictions. He had demonstrated the courage and sincerity of those convictions by being willing to act upon his values. Yet he found a way to demonstrate respect for the law by informing authorities about why he could not follow the registration requirement. "Are these the kind of values that we want to punish?" Whitaker asked. "Every parent should be proud to say 'My son follows the teachings of his church.' These are values that should be rewarded." U.S. Attorney

Arbeznik characterized this argument as an appeal to sympathy. Whitaker, however, felt it was a strong legal and factual argument based upon the claim that the free exercise clause required the government to accommodate Mark's beliefs by not making him register when they had all the information the registration law required, knew he objected based upon religious beliefs, and agreed that those beliefs were genuine and sincerely held: "I think that we presented that there was a conflict between the law and his conscience and I think the conflict could have been accommodated."[51]

The judge agreed with Arbeznik, denying defense motions for acquittal on the bases of violation of free exercise and selective prosecution, commenting only that "presiding over this trial is not a task I would particularly have chosen" and that "motive, however pure, is not a defense when the act is a crime." Aldrich believed that the registration law and the Constitution were not in conflict: "Keep in mind here, we are dealing with resistance to registration, not with resistance to the draft."[52] Presumably, a draft would have required accommodation, whereas registration did not. She also instructed the jury, as she had several times during the trial, that the religious reasons for refusing to register were irrelevant to the question of guilt or innocence:

> Intent and motive should never be confused. Motive is what prompts a person to act. Intent refers only to the state of mind with which the act is done. Good motive of the accused is immaterial except insofar as evidence of motive may aid determination of state of mind or intent. One may not commit a crime and be excused from criminal liability because he desired or expected that ultimate good would result from his criminal act. Moreover, if one commits a crime under the belief, however sincere, that his conduct was religiously, politically or morally required, that is no defense to the commission of a crime. A person may not decide for himself whether a law is good or bad, and whether he is free to disobey it.[53]

After sixty-four minutes of deliberation, the jury of eight men and four women returned a verdict of guilty on October 5, 1982, one day after Mark's twenty-second birthday.[54]

Mark left the courthouse to encounter a swarm of sympathizers and media. In response to questions, he told the media, "I expected this to happen. But it doesn't change my mind at all. I have broken the law and I have admitted doing it. I did what I had to do. I'm proud to live in a country with religious freedom." Yet, he confessed to having "a lot of fears. I don't want to go to jail, but I'll go," if that was the price of living out his convictions. Despite those fears, he was careful to note, "I bear them [the jurors] no ill will. I did what I felt I had to do. The verdict occurred as I expected it to."[55]

Mark was sentenced on October 19, 1982, as a crowd of supporters, estimated to number between 125 and 300, gathered on the courthouse steps.[56] Arbeznik was not present at sentencing, for he was vacationing in New York. The U.S. attorney, William Petro, recommended some form of incarceration. Mark and his parents feared that he would be sentenced to prison, a fate that had just been decreed in San Diego for Benjamin Sasway, who was convicted of failing to register. Mark also anticipated that the court might require him to register, which had happened to religious resister Enten Eller after his conviction in Virginia.[57]

Although resigned to serving a prison term if necessary, Mark was determined to stay true to the religious beliefs and principles upon which he had acted from the very beginning. At the sentencing hearing, he spoke candidly and respectfully to the court: "I made this decision based on deeply held moral beliefs. . . . I do not plan on changing that. . . . I did what I had to do. My decision not to register . . . is based on my decision to follow the teachings of Christ. I think you should know that I will not register. Not out of disrespect for the law, but because of my beliefs."[58]

He need not have worried on that account. Just as he had convinced both Agent Quigley of the FBI and Assistant U.S. Attorney Arbeznik, Mark had left no doubt in Judge Aldrich's mind that he had acted sincerely, forthrightly, and from strong religious conviction. After reading her sentence, Aldrich addressed Mark personally: "This Court specifically does not make your registering for the draft a condition of your probation. This Court believes that such a condition would insult what this Court believes to be an honest religious conviction on your part."[59]

Although she believed that her hands were tied on the law with respect to the substantive determination on the requirement to accommodate Mark's religious beliefs, the law did provide Aldrich with the opportunity to bring creativity and discretion into sentencing. As she explained it, "Motive is a point worth considering at sentencing."[60] Because she did not want him to carry a lifelong felony conviction with him, she chose to impose sentence under the Youth Corrections Act, which permitted eventual expungement of his record. "Based upon observation of you throughout the trial, and upon the material provided in the presentence report, this Court comes to the conclusion that not only are you very young chronologically, but that you are also very young in terms of real experience. You have led a very sheltered life and you are not street-wise," Aldrich said in passing sentence. "Consequently, serving time in a federal penitentiary will not only not benefit you; it might do you a great deal of harm."[61] She sentenced Mark to three years' probation, conditioned upon fulfilling two years of confined community service at Emmaus House, a Missouri home for severely and profoundly mentally disabled adults. Mark was confined to the premises, unless he received permission from both the probation office and the court to leave. During his service, the court neither permitted Mark to join the staff on excursions nor allowed him to visit the library. He was also fined $4,000.[62] The judge closed sentencing by saying, "The prayers of many of us are with you."[63]

After sentencing, Mark responded to media questions. "I'm relieved that I do not have to go to jail. I'm glad I will be given a chance to help other people," he said. He also alluded to the courage it took to remain steadfast to his principles: "I prepared for the worst. I think in terms of financial impact, this sentence will tell non-registrants to either put up or shut up."[64]

Reflecting later on her sentence, the judge stated, "I was shocked that it pleased everyone. I expected to hear from the American Legion . . . that he got off too easy. I thought all the people on the other side would not like me not finding the law unconstitutional." Instead, Mark's parents sent a letter thanking her for not sending him to prison.[65]

Although Mark appealed his conviction, he specifically refused to authorize his counsel to file for a suspension of his sentence pending appeal.

Schmucker appealed the conviction on the basis of its infringement of his free exercise rights, including the manner in which they undergirded his particular selective prosecution claim. I served as his lead appellate counsel. During oral argument, Judge S. Arthur Spiegel asked which claim on appeal was most important. "The free exercise of religion," I answered. "Isn't selective prosecution your best claim?" the judge inquired. "You cannot understand our selective prosecution claim without its basis in free exercise," I replied.

On November 25, 1983, the Sixth Circuit reversed the case and sent it back to the district court for further hearing on the selective prosecution claim. Three days later, Judge William Thomas of the district court suspended the remainder of Mark's alternative sentence until the case could be decided again. Mark was released from Emmaus House. The government petitioned the United States Supreme Court for a writ of certiorari to review the Sixth Circuit decision. At the time, the *Wayte* case was pending in the Supreme Court. After rejecting *Wayte's* selective prosecution claim based on free speech, the Supreme Court summarily returned Mark's case to the Sixth Circuit to decide in light of the *Wayte* opinion. The Sixth Circuit returned the case again to the district court, where Judge Aldrich again denied Mark's motions, determining that she was bound by the Supreme Court's decision and its implications.

On reappeal, the Sixth Circuit echoed Judge Aldrich and insisted that registration was a "minimal" burden on Mark. The court opined that registration was less intrusive, physically and "arguably morally," than training or combat. But this "minimal" act for Mark became a vital "need" for national security when the court assessed the government's interest.[66] Ultimately, the court affirmed Mark's conviction, on April 3, 1987.

Again exhibiting discretion and compassion consistent with upholding the law, on August 20, 1987, Aldrich granted the defense motion to modify sentence and reduced Mark's alternative service to the time already served at Emmaus House. He completed payment of the $4,000 fine on September 11, 1987. On October 19, 1987, Aldrich discharged Mark from probation and filed a certificate vacating his conviction pursuant to the Youth Corrections Act. When Judge Aldrich died in May 2010, the *Cleveland Plain Dealer* noted the many notable cases over which she presided, naming four of the highest-profile cases; Mark Schmucker's case (identified as involving a "conscientious objector") was one of the four. [67]

Mark's trial convinced him of the fairness of the justice system. "If you really believe in something," he stated, "you should stand up for that belief, even if following that belief demands that you go against the dictates of the government's law. . . . The court system is amazingly fair. It's true that you are presumed innocent until proven guilty."[68] Ironically, the government's refusal to accommodate his religious values resulted in his becoming more philosophical and political during his term of alternative service. The staunch consistency of his position altered somewhat in light of his reflections on his experiences at trial and at Emmaus House. In an interview conducted after ten months of service, Mark noted that he had gone "from having other people tell me what is right and wrong to what I believe is right and wrong. . . . You have the conflict between the ideal and the practical. I've become more practical." However, his adherence to principle remained steadfast: "If I had it to do all over again, I'd come to the same conclusion. I just would arrive there from a different route."[69]

Mark was troubled by the severity of his punishment given that there was no active draft and no national security threat. His disillusionment also stemmed from the extreme limits placed upon him. The judge, stating he was serving a sentence, refused him permission to accompany friends and others from Emmaus House on weekend outings, including to a Major League baseball game; he was unable to go home for Thanksgiving; and he missed completing his senior year in college.[70] Yet Mark remained an exemplary individual driven by principle. The administrator of the home stated, "If all my employees worked as hard as he did, it would be fantastic."[71]

The case of the *United States v. Mark Arden Schmucker* required every participant to confront fundamental questions of principle, courage, and integrity. Perhaps inspired by Mark's example, the defense attorneys, prosecutor, and judge all reflected deeply upon precisely what it means to be committed to law, liberty, and conscientious action. The U.S. District Court for the Northern District of Ohio, Eastern Division, witnessed that those answers are neither easy nor sure.

Notes

1. "He Won't Be a Soldier," *Elyria (Ohio) Chronicle-Telegram*, July 30, 1982, C1. The indictment was returned on July 22, 1982; the arraignment was held July 29, 1982, before Magistrate Jack Streepy. Mark Schmucker was the third nonregistrant to be indicted. All references to the record in the district court—motions, transcripts, exhibits, jury instructions, orders—are to U.S. District Court Criminal Docket, United States v. Mark Arden Schmucker, CR82–00133–A.

2. Affidavit of David Kline, Government Exhibit 4, para. 23 (Arbeznik request to decline prosecution); "Conviction of Schmucker Leaves U.S. Prosecutors Batting 1.000," *Akron Beacon Journal*, October 10, 1982, G1, G2 ("presiding" quotation); "Ohio Draft-Resister Case Pains Judge Whose Son Had Been an Objector," *Philadelphia Inquirer*, March 20, 1983, C05, 1983 WLNR 147432 ("personal hell" quotation); "Draft Resister Resigns Himself to Conviction and Prison Term," *Marysville (Ohio) Journal-Tribune*, September 15, 1982, 3 (Mr. Non-registrant quotation and story); "The Schmucker Case: One Nobody Wanted," *Marysville (Ohio) Journal-Tribune*, October 7, 1982, 5.

3. Mark Becker, "Men and Women Who Dare to Say No: Mennonite Resistance to Draft Registration, 1980–1985," unpublished paper from Bethel College, North Newton, Kans., July 1985, available at http://www.yachana.org/research/writings/draft/ (accessed August 5, 2010).

4. "Anti-war Trial Gets a Crowd," *Akron Beacon Journal*, October 4, 1982, D1 and D2 (asserting up to a thousand Goshen students refused to register); "He Won't Be a Soldier"; "God vs. the State: Goshen Students Obey Their Consciences First," *Elyria (Ohio) Chronicle-Telegram*, October 10, 1982, D1 (quoting Goshen provost John Lapp asserting that the vast majority of the twelve hundred Goshen students were conscientious objectors to war).

5. Information about Mark Schmucker's belief system and the path he followed in reaching his decision not to register is drawn from his trial testimony. Testimony of Mark Schmucker, Trial Transcript of 10–4–82, pp. 223–33.

6. Proclamation No. 4771, 3 C.F.R. 82 (1981), especially §§ 1-101, 1-102, and 1-109; Remarks on Signing Proclamation 4771, 16 WEEKLY COMP. OF PRES. DOC. 1274, 1274–75 (July 2, 1980) (quotation).

7. Wayte v. United States, 470 U.S. 598, 600 n.1 (1985); Rotsker v. Goldberg, 453 U.S. 57, 60–61 esp. n. 1, and 75–76 (1981); United States v. Schmucker II, 815 F.2d 413, 417, 419 (6th Cir. 1987). See Becker, "Men and Women," text accompanying note 25.

8. 16 WEEKLY COMP. PRES. DOC. 1274 (July 2, 1980) (first two quotations); Rotsker v. Goldberg, 448 U.S. 1306, 1309–10 (1980) (Brennan, J., granting stay pending appeal) (third quotation); Rotsker, 453 U.S. at 57, 75 (fourth quotation); ibid., 76 (emphasis original) (fifth quotation); ibid., 79 (sixth quotation).

9. Government Exhibit 1. As Mark later explained during trial, "I thought if I was going to break the law, I thought I should at least inform them that I was doing so." "Schmucker Case Goes to Jury," *Marysville (Ohio) Journal-Tribune*, October 5, 1982, 2.

10. Affidavit of Edward Frankle, Government Exhibit 3; Affidavit of David Kline, Government Exhibit 4.

11. Testimony of Patrick Quigley, Trial Transcript of 10–1–82, pp. 164–65.

12. Affidavit of David Kline, Government Exhibit 4; "Draft Trial Begins for Alliance Man," *Akron Beacon Journal*, September 30, 1982, B1; "He Won't Be a Soldier"; "'Prosecutor Wanted to Drop Draft Charges,'" *Elyria (Ohio) Chronicle-Telegram*, September 30, 1982, D1.

13. Affidavit of Edward Frankle, Government Exhibit 3, paras. 1–4 (government's opposition to the defense motion to dismiss for selective prosecution), and Testimony of Edward Frankle, Trial Transcript of 10–1–82, pp. 103–22 (Frankle was the architect of the passive enforcement system); Affidavit of David Kline, Government Exhibit 4, Attachment A: Memorandum from D. Lowell Jensen, Assistant Attorney General, Criminal Division, to All United States Attorneys (August 17, 1981); Memorandum from D. Lowell Jensen to United States Attorneys (July 9, 1982), Defendant Exhibit 1 in support of the motion to dismiss for selective prosecution ("[We] have asked that non-registration matters be assigned to experienced Assistant U.S. Attorneys and handled on a priority basis.").

14. Wayte, 470 U.S. at 598, 627–28 (Marshall, J., dissenting) ("struck by lightning" quoting Kline); Memorandum from D. Lowell Jensen to the Attorney General (June 28, 1982), p. 2, Defendant Exhibit 7 to the motion to dismiss for selective prosecution ("most adamant" quotation); "Schmucker Case: One Nobody Wanted" (other referred nonregistrants information).

15. "The first prosecutions are liable to consist of a large sample of (1) persons who object on religious and moral grounds and (2) persons who publicly refuse to register." Memorandum from D. Lowell Jensen to the Attorney General (June 20, 1982), Defendant Exhibit 2 in support of the motion to dismiss for selective prosecution; "A number of Mennonites, who historically have been reluctant to comply with Selective Service requirements, and others with religious or moral objections are represented in the 'self-reported' referrals." Memorandum from Lawrence Lippe to D. Lowell Jensen (March 19, 1982), Defendant Exhibit 12.

16. The persons indicted under "passive enforcement" were Mark Schmucker, Gary Eklund, Enten Eller, Charles Epp, Russell Ford, Jon Harshbarger, Edward Hasbrouck, Paul Jacob, Gillam Kerley, Michael McMillan, Andrew Mager, Russell Martin, Samuel Matthews, Daniel Rutt, Benjamin Sasway, Stephen Schlossberg, Kendall Warkentine, and David Wayte. The "active" enforcement system, initiated much later, resulted in two indictments by the end of 1987. Both were eventually dismissed. The first was against Phetsamay Maokhamphio, a philosophical resister. Becker, "Men and Women." The reported cases from those prosecutions are: United States v. Schmucker I, 721 F.2d 1046, 1049 (6th Cir. 1983), *rehearing denied*, 729 F.2d 1040 (6th Cir. 1984), *cert. granted and judg. vacated*, 471

U.S. 1001 (1985), *remanded*, 766 F.2d 1582 (6th Cir. 1985), *on reappeal*, 815 F.2d 413 (6th Cir. 1987); United States v. Eklund, 733 F.2d 1287 (8th Cir. 1984) (en banc), *cert. denied*, 471 U.S. 1003 (1985); United States v. Epp, 587 F. Supp. 383 (D. Kan. 1984); United States v. Ford, No. 82–1059 (D. Conn., unpub., April 11, 1983); United States v. Jacob, 608 F. Supp. 485 (E.D. Ark. 1985), *aff'd*, 781 F.2d 643 (8th Cir. 1986); United States v. Kerley, 787 F.2d 1147 (7th Cir. 1986); United States v. Martin, 557 F. Supp. 681 (N.D. Iowa 1982), *rev'd in part*, 733 F.2d 1309 (8th Cir. 1984); United States v. Rutt, 818 F.2d 867 (6th Cir. 1987); United States v. Sasway, 730 F.2d 771 (9th Cir., unpub., 1984); United States v. Wayte, 710 F.2d 1385 (9th Cir. 1984), *rev'd*, Wayte, 470 U.S. at 598 (1985).

17. Becker, "Men and Women"; see "Anti-war Trial Gets a Crowd."

18. Memorandum from D. Lowell Jensen to United States Attorneys (July 9, 1982).

19. See chapter 10.

20. "Conviction of Schmucker Leaves U.S. Prosecutors."

21. "Ann Aldrich, U.S. Judge, Dies at 82," *Cleveland Plain Dealer*, May 4, 2010, A1, 2010 WLNR 9266556.

22. "Ohio Draft-Resister Case Pains Judge."

23. "Schmucker Trial Nears," *Record*, September 24, 1982, 3, as cited in Becker, "Men and Women," n. 196.

24. Becker, "Men and Women."

25. Associated Press, "Man Pleads Innocent of Failing to Register," *Gettysburg (Pa.) Times*, July 30, 1982, 3.

26. Rotsker, 453 U.S. 57 (1981); "Congressional Watchdog," *Reporter*, 4, and *Semiannual Report: April 1, 1980 — Sept. 30, 1980*, 19, cited in Becker, "Men and Women," n. 32.

27. The so-called beg policy resulted in the Selective Service determining to exempt some persons from registration. During trial, Edward Frankle, the architect of the passive system, testified that several letters demanding registration had been sent to persons whose parents or guardians called or wrote to say they were mentally retarded. The Selective Service decided to exempt some of these individuals from registration and further pursuit under the passive policy. Testimony of Edward Frankle, Trial Transcript of 10–1–82, pp. 102–22. *Cf.* Schmucker II, 815 F.2d at 419.

28. Testimony of Edward Frankle, Trial Transcript of 10–1–82, pp. 103–22.

29. At the time, free exercise doctrine required a tripartite analysis: (1) Did the government obligation conflict with, and thus burden, sincere religious conviction? (2) Did the government have a compelling interest for imposing the obligation? (3) If so, could the government accommodate the religious conviction without unduly interfering with accomplishing the governmental interest? Thomas v. Review Board, 450 U.S. 707 (1981); Wisconsin v. Yoder, 406 U.S. 205 (1972); Sherbert v. Verner, 374 U.S. 398 (1963). Current free exercise doctrine permits neutral laws to impinge upon religious conduct without mandating accommodation. Employment Div. v. Smith, 494 U.S. 872 (1990).

30. Proclamation No. 4771, § 1–101 and § 1–109, 3 C.F.R. 82 (1981) (conditions beyond control); Testimony of Edward Frankle, Trial Transcript of 10–1–82, pp. 103–22; Affidavit of David Kline, Attachment A ("compelling reasons"). In *Rotsker v. Goldberg*, 453 U.S. 57 (1981), the Supreme Court upheld the draft registration scheme against a claim that it violated equal protection by exempting females from registration. The Court relied upon the government's claim that the registration was solely to create a pool of potential combatants and that because females were not eligible for combatant roles, their registration would hinder the process.

31. Becker, "Men and Women."

32. Wayte, 470 U.S. at 598.

33. In addition to the motions and responses to those motions filed in the district court, many of these arguments are encapsulated in the appellate record of the *Schmucker* case and in my earlier article explicating the arguments. United States v. Schmucker I, 721 F.2d 1046, 1049 (6th Cir. 1983), *rehearing denied*, 729 F.2d 1040 (6th Cir. 1984), *cert. granted and judg. vacated*, 471 U.S. 1001 (1985), *remanded*, 766 F.2d 1582 (6th Cir. 1985), *on reappeal*, 815 F.2d 413 (6th Cir. 1987); Elizabeth Reilly, "'Secure the Blessings of Liberty': A Free Exercise Analysis Inspired by Selective Service Non-registrants," *Northern Kentucky Law Review* 16, no. 1 (1988): 79. See also Becker, "Men and Women," at text accompanying note 28: "Even the Selective Service itself had, previous to Carter's State of the Union address, declared peacetime registration to be 'redundant and unnecessary.'"

34. "Ohio Draft-Resister Case Pains Judge" (quotation); "Bench Can Be a Lonely Place," *Tyrone (Ind.) Daily Herald*, March 14, 1983, A1 (noting how Aldrich had to resign from the ACLU and other advocacy groups because they might appear before her as litigants).

35. "Schmucker Case: One Nobody Wanted."

36. Ibid.

37. "Anti-war Trial Gets a Crowd."

38. Ibid. (all quotations).

39. "God vs. the State" (all quotations).

40. "Defense Begins in Resister's Trial," *Elyria (Ohio) Chronicle-Telegram*, October 4, 1982, B1.

41. "Draft Resister Charges Again Are Disputed," *Akron Beacon Journal*, October 2, 1982, A16 (quotation).

42. Testimony of Don Blosser, Trial Transcript of 10–4–82, pp. 258–60.

43. Testimony of Mark Schmucker, pp. 223–43.

44. Ibid., pp. 232–33.

45. "Draft Resister Resigns Himself to Conviction and Prison Term," *Marysville (Ohio) Journal-Tribune*, September 15, 1982, 3.

46. "Draft Resister Charges Again Are Disputed."

47. "Schmucker Guilty of Draft Sign-Up Charge," *Akron Beacon Journal*, October 6, 1982, A1, A16.

48. "Schmucker Case Goes to Jury," *Marysville (Ohio) Journal-Tribune*, October 5, 1982, 2.

49. "'Honesty Lost Case for Mennonite,'" *Elyria (Ohio) Chronicle-Telegram*, October 6, 1982, D1.

50. "Jury Weighs Case of Registration Foe," *Akron Beacon Journal*, October 5, 1982, C1, C4.

51. "Schmucker Case Goes to Jury" (first quotation); "'Honesty Lost Case for Mennonite,'" (second quotation).

52. "Schmucker Case: One Nobody Wanted"; "Jury Weighs Case of Registration Foe," C1.

53. Jury Instructions, p. 24.

54. "Third Draft Resister Convicted, Sentenced," *Hutchinson (Ind.) News*, October 6, 1982, 29.

55. "3d Draft Sign-Up Foe Sentenced," *Boston Globe*, October 20, 1982, 1982 WLNR 84191; "Mennonite Third Man Convicted as Resister," *Logansport (Ind.) Pharos-Tribune*, October 6, 1982, 3 (first quotation); "Schmucker Guilty of Draft Sign-Up Charge," A1 (second quotation); "'Honesty Lost Case for Mennonite,'" (third quotation).

56. "No Jail Term for Draft-Resister Schmucker," *Akron Beacon Journal*, October 20, 1982, A1, A14 (numbering the crowd at 300); "Draft Resister Escapes Prison Term; Sentence

Is Work," *Hutchinson (Ind.) News*, October 20, 1982, 24 (125 people remained at end of sentencing).

57. Becker, "Men and Women"; "'Honesty Lost Case for Mennonite'"; "No Jail Term for Draft-Resister Schmucker."

58. U.S. v. Schmucker, Transcript of Sentencing Proceedings, 10–19–82; "Draft Resister Escapes Prison Term."

59. Transcript of Sentencing Proceedings, 10–19–82.

60. "Schmucker Case: One Nobody Wanted."

61. Transcript of Sentencing Proceedings, 10–19–82.

62. Ibid. and Sentencing Order; "Stark Mennonite's Draft Evasion Conviction Overturned," *Akron Beacon Journal*, November 26, 1983, C1 (examples of refusals to permit leaving premises of Emmaus House during term of service).

63. Transcript of Sentencing Proceedings, 10–19–82.

64. "Draft Resister Escapes Prison Term" (first quotation); "Schmucker Sentenced to Work with Retarded," *Elyria (Ohio) Chronicle-Telegram*, October 20, 1982, A7 (second quotation).

65. "Bench Can Be a Lonely Place."

66. Schmucker II, 815 F.2d at 417–18.

67. All references to motions, transcripts, exhibits, orders, and decisions are to the U.S. District Court Criminal Docket record in United States v. Schmucker, CR-82–00133-A; "Ann Aldrich, U.S. Judge, Dies at 82."

68. "Convicted Resister Says Trial Was Fair," *Logansport (Ind.) Pharos-Tribune*, October 12, 1982, 8.

69. "Alliance Draft Resister Dejected over Public Service 'Sentence,'" *Akron Beacon Journal*, August 22, 1983, B1, B4; "I'm Less Idealistic Now, but Don't Regret Ignoring Draft Signup, Protester Says," *Miami (Fla.) Herald*, August 23, 1983, 8A, 1983 WLNR 249309.

70. "Stark Mennonite's Draft Evasion Conviction Overturned."

71. "Alliance Draft Resister Dejected"; "I'm Less Idealistic Now."

12

The Trials of John Demjanjuk

Renee C. Redman

PROMINENT AMONG THE duties of federal district courts in American society is the enforcement of citizenship and extradition laws. In the first type of case, the court must determine whether the citizenship of a naturalized U.S. citizen should be taken away. In the second type, the court is called on to certify to the secretary of state the veracity of the underlying facts in an extradition request made by another country. In both types of cases, the district courts play an important role in fact-finding and in interpreting complicated U.S. immigration and treaty law. The high-profile trials of John Demjanjuk in the U.S. District Court for the Northern District of Ohio demonstrate how courts perform these roles, as well as the challenges they confront in weighing forty-year-old witness testimony and foreign documentary evidence.

From 1977 to 2002, John Demjanjuk, a Ukrainian immigrant living in Seven Hills, Ohio, faced five legal proceedings brought by the U.S. government before two district court judges and two federal immigration judges: two denaturalization cases, an extradition proceeding, and two deportation proceedings. The first two cases were later reexamined in detail by a third district court judge acting as a special master, and Demjanjuk filed a motion to reopen the second denaturalization case in July 2011 before a fourth district court judge. All of these complicated proceedings centered on Demjanjuk's whereabouts and activities between May 1942, when he was captured by the German army in Poland, and June 1945. The government alleged that he was working in Nazi concentration camps. Over the years, Demjanjuk made numerous claims about his whereabouts but denied ever working in a concentration camp. In between the U.S. trials, he spent seven years in prison in Israel, where he was convicted but later acquitted of war crimes.

This chapter focuses on Demjanjuk's three trials in the U.S. District Court for the Northern District of Ohio. The legal proceedings, particularly the first denaturalization trial, were avidly followed in the Cleveland area and nationally. The government's effort to denaturalize and remove him from the United States and Demjanjuk's efforts to prevent this outcome would have symbolic importance for countless individuals and groups, especially Jews and Ukrainians, who share historical animosity. Indeed, it could be said that Demjanjuk chose to make himself a symbol. Self-described as a Ukrainian hero,[1] he opted to put himself through more than thirty years of litigation and imprisonment even as other accused Nazi collaborators simply left the United States to live peacefully elsewhere.

John Demjanjuk

John Demjanjuk was born Iwan Demjanjuk in the village of Dub Macharenzi, Ukraine, on April 3, 1920. He completed four grades in school and survived the famine in the early 1930s, becoming a collective farmer and tractor driver before being conscripted into the Russian army in 1940. Wounded in the back by shrapnel in September 1941, which left a scar, he returned to his artillery unit on the Crimean front after a brief stay in a hospital. In 1942, he was one of the more than one hundred thousand Soviet prisoners of war (POWs) captured by the Germans during the battle of Kerch.[2] Demjanjuk testified at his first denaturalization trial that after his capture, the Germans transported him to POW camps in Rovno in the Ukraine and later Chelm, Poland. He did not recall the exact dates but suggested that he might have been transferred to Chelm as late as 1943 or 1944.[3] He then claimed that in 1944, the Germans transported him to Graz, Austria, where he joined the Ukrainian National Army, an organization formed by the Germans to fight the Soviets. He stated that in Graz, he received a blood-type tattoo on the inside of his upper left arm, which he later cut out, leaving a scar. Soon afterward, he asserted, the Germans transferred him to a place he knew as Oelberg, Austria, where he remained from about November 1944 until May 1945 while assigned to guard a captured Soviet general.[4]

All sides agreed that after Germany surrendered in May 1945, Demjanjuk spent years in displaced persons (DP) camps in Europe before landing a job with the U.S. Army's transportation corps in Regensburg, Germany.[5] He married his wife, Vera, and had three children, one born in Europe and two born in the United States.[6] In 1950, the DP Commission granted Demjanjuk a certificate of displaced person status. This documentation enabled him to apply for a non-quota immigrant visa at the American consulate in Stuttgart, Germany, which he did in December 1951.[7] In his visa application, Demjanjuk wrote that he had been a farmer in Sobibor, Poland, from 1934 to 1943; in Pilau/Danzig, Germany, from 1943 to September 1944; and in Munich from September 1944 to May 1945. He also wrote that he was born in Kiev, USSR, and that his nationality was Polish/Ukrainian. Pursuant to the DP Act of 1948, Demjanjuk and his family immigrated to the United States on February 9, 1952.[8]

The Demjanjuks initially settled on a farm near Decatur, Indiana, but Ukrainian friends from the DP camps helped them move to Cleveland, where Demjanjuk soon found a job at a Ford Motor Company factory; he worked there for almost thirty years.[9] He and his family eventually settled in the Cleveland suburb of Seven Hills, became active members of the Ukrainian St. Vladimir Church, and reportedly led quiet lives.[10]

Demjanjuk filed a petition to become a naturalized U.S. citizen on August 12, 1958, swearing that the information he provided in the petition was true. Three months later, the U.S. District Court for the Northern District of Ohio granted him citizenship. He legally changed his name from Iwan Demjanjuk to John Demjanjuk the same day.[11]

Prosecution of War Criminals by the Department of Justice

In August 1977, the U.S. Department of Justice (DOJ) created the Special Litigation Unit within the Immigration and Naturalization Service (INS) to pursue Nazi collaborators who were living in the United States. Before the year was out, the unit began bringing denaturalization proceedings against suspected collaborators.[12] In 1979, the unit was transferred to the Criminal Division of the Justice

Department, and its name was changed to Office of Special Investigations (OSI). In July 2002, the *Cleveland Plain Dealer* reported that OSI had sought to denaturalize or deport from the United States 118 people. Of them, 68 were denaturalized and 56 were removed, including 3 who were extradited for trials in other countries. Additionally, 17 cases were in litigation at the time.[13]

The First Denaturalization Case against John Demjanjuk (1977–82)

The DOJ began investigating Demjanjuk's alleged service at Sobibor in 1976.[14] It was also investigating allegations against Feodor Fedorenko, a Ukrainian immigrant suspected of serving as a guard at the Treblinka extermination camp in Poland. In the course of the Fedorenko investigation, Treblinka survivors identified Demjanjuk as the sadistic guard known as Ivan the Terrible.[15]

The camps near Treblinka and Sobibor were created by the German government for the express purpose of exterminating Jews in occupied eastern Europe. Because the German Schutzstaffel (SS) lacked sufficient manpower to carry out the extermination program, it recruited Soviet POWs from camps in eastern Poland, including Rovno and Chelm, to round up and transport Jews as well as to staff the camp facilities. It trained the prisoners at a camp near Trawniki, gave them uniforms, and provided them with weapons. The POWs took oaths of service to the SS and were subject to its rules.[16] The few survivors of the extermination camps reported that Soviet POWs performed most of the extermination tasks. At Treblinka, there were about 30 German SS members and about 150 Soviet—mostly Ukrainian—guards.[17] Among the most feared of the Ukrainians was Ivan the Terrible. He was one of the operators of the gas chambers, and he stood out for his gratuitous cruelty.[18]

On August 25, 1977, the DOJ, in one of its first denaturalization cases against an alleged Nazi collaborator, filed a complaint in the U.S. District Court for the Northern District of Ohio alleging that Demjanjuk had lied on his visa and naturalization applications about his service as an SS guard in Treblinka.[19] The complaint alleged that he obtained his U.S. citizenship illegally because his service in Treblinka precluded him from qualifying as an "eligible displaced person" under the DP Act, which in turn precluded him from obtaining a valid visa. It further alleged that the visa was invalid because Demjanjuk willfully misrepresented his whereabouts during World War II. The government amended the complaint shortly before trial began to allege that in 1942–43, Demjanjuk served in the SS training camp in Trawniki and the extermination camps in Treblinka and Sobibor. The amended complaint also alleged that in 1944–45, he served in a German military unit made up of Ukrainians.[20] Pursuant to the Immigration and Naturalization Act (INA), all allegations, if true, were grounds for revocation of citizenship.[21] Denaturalization proceedings, like all immigration proceedings, are civil matters. Therefore, the defendant has no right to a jury or to free legal representation. The government, however, must prove its allegations by "clear unequivocal and convincing evidence."[22]

The denaturalization trial began on February 10, 1981, before Chief U.S. District Judge Frank J. Battisti and continued on fourteen days into March.[23] Appointed to the bench by President John F. Kennedy in 1961,[24] Battisti, at the time of this trial, was already well known in the Cleveland area for his rulings in several other controversial cases.[25] To accommodate the large number of spectators, the trial was held in the ceremonial courtroom of the federal courthouse in Cleveland, which had seating for sixty-four spectators. The press sat in the jury box, and the court provided about two dozen extra chairs for other observers. Demjanjuk's family members were seated in the front row. Throughout the proceedings, they generally sat impassively, except when his wife collapsed after listening to survivor testimony and was treated for hysteria. Security was tight, and on most days, there were lines of people seeking entry to the courtroom.[26] Spectators included Ukrainians in traditional embroidered dresses, Jewish school students, Holocaust survivors, and other members of the Cleveland community. During the first two weeks, Ukrainian spectators far outnumbered Jewish spectators. However, perhaps due to the testimony of Holocaust survivors, more Jews attended during the later weeks.[27] Throughout the trial, Demjanjuk sat next to an interpreter and displayed no emotion.[28] The interpreter on the first day, Bohdan A. Futey, a local lawyer and president of the United Ukrainian Organization of Greater Cleveland, explained that Demjanjuk spoke only "shop" or "street" English.[29]

At trial, John Martin and Spiros Gonakis represented Demjanjuk. OSI attorney Norman Moskowitz and Assistant U.S. Attorney John Horrigan presented the government's case, including the testimony of two expert witnesses and six fact witnesses (five Jewish survivors and one German guard from Treblinka). All six fact witnesses identified Demjanjuk as the man they knew as Ivan the Terrible, the operator of the Treblinka gas chamber.[30] The government's principal piece of evidence that Demjanjuk was at Trawniki was an identification card stating that "Iwan Demjanjuk is employed as a guard in the Guard Units of the Reich Leader of the SS for the Establishment of SS and Police Headquarters in the New Eastern Territory." The heading on the card read: "HEADQUARTERS LUBLIN, TRAINING CAMP TRAWNIKI, I.D. No. 1393." The other side of the card contained a photograph of Iwan Demjanjuk, his name, his date of birth (April 3, 1920), his father's name (Nikolai), his birthplace (Dub Macharenzi), and his nationality. Under "special features," the card listed "Scar on back." The card had been found in a Soviet archive of German war documents. At trial, the Soviet government provided the original document for inspection by the court and defense counsel.[31]

On the stand, Demjanjuk denied that the signature on the card was his, but when asked whether the photograph was of him, he testified, "I cannot say. Possibly it is me." He denied ever being in Trawniki or Treblinka or that he had been a guard in any German concentration camp. He argued in the alternative that even if he had worked at a concentration camp, he lied about it on his immigration application to avoid being returned to the Soviet Union, where he would have been executed for treason.[32] Although the survivors' testimony was riveting, parts of the trial were less captivating. Judge Battisti reportedly questioned the relevance of Martin's expert on Soviet/Ukrainian history and deemed all but two pieces of evidence offered by the defense to be irrelevant. During Martin's closing argument, the judge reportedly stopped him with many questions, including why he had not asked his client whether he was Ivan the Terrible.[33]

In June 1981, Battisti issued a forty-four-page opinion revoking Demjanjuk's citizenship. The judge concluded that the photograph on the Trawniki identification card was of Demjanjuk, that the card belonged to him, and that therefore he was at Trawniki.[34] The court noted that the Ukrainian name Iwan, as used on the card, was the Ukrainian analogue of the Russian name Ivan and that both were common names; further, although the card did not have a date, there was sufficient circumstantial evidence to conclude that it was issued sometime during the summer of 1942 and before July 19, 1942.[35] The court also found that Demjanjuk had not presented any evidence supporting his claims that the card was not authentic or that it was a Soviet forgery.[36] In response to his alternative defense—that he had lied about his whereabouts out of fear that he would be returned to the Soviet Union—the court noted that by the time Demjanjuk applied to enter the United States, he had no reason to be concerned, as Soviet citizens were not being repatriated.[37]

The court concluded that the government had met its burden to show that Demjanjuk had willfully concealed that he had trained as an armed guard at Trawniki and later served as a guard in Treblinka.[38] Relying on the Supreme Court's recent decision in *Fedorenko v. United States*,[39] Battisti found that Demjanjuk's naturalization had been procured by willful misrepresentation of material facts. He noted that none of the questions on the naturalization application at the time required Demjanjuk to disclose his service at the camps but that the application did ask whether he had "given false testimony for the purpose of obtaining any benefits under the immigration and nationality laws." An applicant who answered yes was required to elaborate. Thus, the court reasoned, if Demjanjuk had answered yes and disclosed his guard service, his naturalization application would have been denied, as it would have indicated he lacked good moral character—a statutory requirement for naturalization.[40] The court did not reach the issue of whether Demjanjuk had been in Sobibor.[41]

Before Battisti issued his ruling, the government sent Demjanjuk's counsel a letter disclosing that it had received five witness statements from the Soviet Union.[42] The witnesses were all at Trawniki in 1942, but only one, Nicolai Dorofeev, identified Demjanjuk as being there as well. The letter explained that the statements had arrived just before the trial began and that it had not been possible to obtain live or deposition testimony.[43] Battisti denied Demjanjuk's motion for a new trial based on the letter, holding that although the government should have disclosed the identity of Dorofeev, its failure did not entitle Demjanjuk to a new trial because the government's allegations regarding Trawniki were based on documentary evidence and not eyewitnesses.[44] In June 1982, the Court of Appeals for the Sixth Circuit dismissed Demjanjuk's appeal in two pages, concluding that the district court's findings of fact were not clearly erroneous and that the court did not abuse its discretion in denying Demjanjuk's motion for a new trial.[45] The Supreme Court denied review.[46]

On October 26, 1983, Demjanjuk's new attorneys—Mark J. O'Conner from Buffalo, New York, and John J. Gill of Cleveland—moved to vacate the district court's ruling on the grounds that government attorneys committed fraud on the court.[47] Judge Battisti ruled that (1) the DOJ and the Soviet government had not conspired to deceive the court as to the trustworthiness of the evidence, (2) there was no evidence that the government's witnesses' alleged perjury was not discoverable within one year after judgment, and (3) the recently filed affidavits of government witnesses did not materially differ from their trial testimony.[48]

Deportation and Extradition Proceedings (1982–85)

The INS put Demjanjuk in deportation proceedings on December 6, 1982.[49] O'Conner and Gill represented Demjanjuk, who testified that he lied on his immigration applications because he was afraid of being repatriated to the Soviet Union.[50] Relying on Battisti's findings, Immigration Judge Adolph F. Angelilli, on May 23, 1984, ordered Demjanjuk deported to the USSR but issued a discretionary grant of voluntary departure. A grant of voluntary departure allows a noncitizen who has been found deportable to leave the United States at his or her own expense and within a designated time period.[51] But Demjanjuk, instead of voluntarily leaving the country, chose to appeal. The Board of Immigration Appeals (BIA) affirmed the deportability ruling and reversed the grant of voluntary departure.[52] The Sixth Circuit affirmed the decision.[53]

The Soviet Union reportedly did not want Demjanjuk.[54] On November 18, 1983, while deportation proceedings were pending and pursuant to a request by Israel, the government filed a request with the district court for Demjanjuk's extradition to Israel.[55] At the time, Judge Battisti had before him Demjanjuk's motion to vacate the denaturalization order, and therefore, under the local rules of the court, the extradition case was assigned to him as well.[56] O'Conner and Gill moved for Judge Battisti's recusal on the grounds that he was biased against Demjanjuk and his new lawyers.[57] Demjanjuk's affidavit in support of the motion alleged that Battisti was colluding with OSI and the Soviet government.[58] In March 1984, the court denied the motion.[59]

A year later, on March 12, 1985, the district court held an extradition hearing.[60] As an extradition proceeding, this was not a trial on the merits but rather a limited inquiry into whether the respondent was the person named in the extradition complaint, whether the crimes for which the other country sought extradition were offenses "within the treaty," and whether there was "competent and adequate evidence" or "probable cause" to believe the respondent committed the act charged in the extradition request.[61] The next month, Battisti certified to the secretary of state that Demjanjuk was the person named in Israel's extradition request and that he was extraditable. He also revoked Demjanjuk's bond and ordered that he be taken into custody; however, he also ordered that his surrender to Israel be stayed until May 1 so that he could seek relief if he chose.[62]

Ten days later, Demjanjuk's attorneys filed a petition for a writ of habeas corpus with the Northern District of Ohio challenging the certificate of extraditability. Pursuant to the district's local rule, the petition was assigned to Judge

Battisti. On May 17, Battisti again denied counsel's request that he recuse himself, ruled that there was no need for the government to respond to the petition as the facts were already in the record, found that Demjanjuk had not presented any new evidence or arguments, and denied the petition.[63] Demjanjuk's attorneys appealed the denial to the Sixth Circuit. A panel composed of Judges Pierce Lively, Damon Keith, and Gilbert S. Merritt noted that there was no right to appeal a district court's extradition certification and that the scope of habeas review was narrow. The panel then dealt with what it termed Demjanjuk's "confused mélange of arguments" and affirmed Battisti's ruling.[64] It held that the validity of the Trawniki card was not before it and that there was no evidence that the government had purposefully offered a forged document into evidence, that Battisti was not required to recuse himself, and that he did not err in denying Demjanjuk's habeas petition.[65] Demjanjuk was flown to Israel on February 28, 1986, where he was tried for war crimes.

Reopening of Denaturalization Proceedings (1988–98)

On April 8, 1988, while Demjanjuk was awaiting the Israeli criminal court's verdict, his American lawyers filed a new complaint in the U.S. District Court for the Northern District of Ohio seeking injunctive and declaratory relief from the court's prior rulings, based on allegations that prosecutors had fraudulently withheld evidence during the denaturalization and extradition proceedings.[66] Later that month, an Israeli court ruled that Demjanjuk was the gas chamber operator at Treblinka known as Ivan the Terrible, convicted him of war crimes, and sentenced him to hang.[67] In February 1990, the U.S. television program 60 *Minutes* aired a segment in which villagers living near the Treblinka site told a reporter that Ivan the Terrible was a man named Ivan Marchenko.[68] The Israeli Supreme Court kept the appeal open to allow the admission of additional evidence relating to the identification of Ivan the Terrible.[69]

On June 5, 1992, the Sixth Circuit panel that had affirmed the district court's denial of a writ of habeas corpus in 1985 stated that its review of the record as well as "numerous recent press reports and articles in the United States indicate that the extradition warrant may have been improvidently issued because it was based on erroneous information," and *sua sponte*, reopened its prior ruling. The panel ordered the government to submit a brief describing all evidence of which it had knowledge "tending to show" that Demjanjuk was not Ivan the Terrible;

further, Demjanjuk was to file a brief describing all evidence in his knowledge "which tend[ed] to show that a man known as Ivan Marchenko was . . . 'Ivan the Terrible.'" The panel set a hearing for August 11.[70]

The *Cleveland Plain Dealer* reported that the Sixth Circuit came to this conclusion after Chief Judge Merritt read an article about new evidence indicating that Demjanjuk was a victim of mistaken identity. A former prosecutor appointed to the bench by President Jimmy Carter, Merritt had requested, in writing, a copy of an internal DOJ memo on Soviet witness statements identifying Ivan the Terrible as Marchenko. After the government twice ignored his request, he reportedly convinced the other two panel members to reopen the ruling.[71]

The Cleveland press reported on documents as they were filed with the Sixth Circuit panel over the following two months. Days before the hearing, the *Cleveland Plain Dealer* published an editorial cautiously approving of the panel's reopening.[72] On August 11, 1992, the panel heard oral argument on whether government attorneys had engaged in prosecutorial misconduct during the denaturalization case. The case was now so widely followed that the court issued tickets for seats in the courtroom and wired a second courtroom for closed-circuit television viewing of the proceedings.[73] Michael E. Tigar, at the time a well-known professor at the University of Texas School of Law, and Edward F. Marek, the Cleveland federal public defender, represented Demjanjuk for free.[74]

When a government attorney admitted that government lawyers had withheld potential evidence from Demjanjuk's attorneys during the 1980s proceedings, the judges on the panel were visibly angry. Judge Keith proclaimed: "It's frightening to think of the power a government possesses when it decides to go after someone."[75]

On August 17, the panel issued a short opinion finding it "undisputed" that the government had in its "possession prior to extradition proceedings statements and documents indicating that John Demjanjuk was not 'Ivan the Terrible,'" but it concluded that it required more information before deciding whether the government attorneys failed to produce any of the information during the denaturalization, deportation, and extradition proceedings. The panel relied on its "inherent power to grant relief, for 'after-discovered fraud,' from an earlier judgment," stating that a federal court had the power to "'vacate its own judgment upon proof that a fraud has been perpetrated upon the court.'"[76] Rather than send the case back to the district court where Demjanjuk's motion was pending, the panel appointed Judge Thomas A. Wiseman Jr. of the U.S. District Court for the Middle District of Tennessee as a special master to receive evidence and file a report on a possible cover-up of evidence favorable to Demjanjuk.[77] The order explained that appointment of a special master would be more efficient than sending the case back to Battisti.[78]

The reopened case proceeded in parallel with the Israeli criminal appeal. The special master began his investigation in September and held public hearings throughout the fall and winter that were avidly followed by the Cleveland press.[79] Over three hundred exhibits were introduced, six witnesses testified, and the deposition testimony of other witnesses was submitted.[80] Judge Wiseman filed his 210-page report on June 30, 1993.[81] After comparing the testimony of the attorneys who had been involved over the years, the special master found that the government's failure to produce information in response to Demjanjuk's interrogatories beginning in November 18, 1977, was "neglectful."[82] He observed that "the government was playing hardball" in seeking to provide the defense with as "little information and evidence as possible" but found that the government attorneys acted in good faith.[83] Regarding the seven basic allegations made by Demjanjuk, he found that five were without merit and that in the other two, the attorney acted in good faith. Therefore, the special master concluded that Demjanjuk had not met his burden to show that the government had committed fraud on the court.[84]

The special master agreed with Demjanjuk's attorneys that the *Brady* rule that applies in criminal proceedings—that due process requires prosecutors to disclose all exculpatory evidence to defendants—should apply in extradition proceedings, but he declined to apply it in this situation because such a rule would be "novel" and, in any case, the prosecutors did not believe they possessed or withheld exculpatory material.[85] He noted that extradition proceedings are civil in nature and that the utility of the discovery rules in civil proceedings is "defined by the advocate's skill and diligence; the burden is on the litigant to make proper discovery requests."[86]

Although the special master recommended that the government attorneys not be punished, he had some strong words for the lawyers on both sides, as well as for Demjanjuk. He reprimanded the government attorneys for failing to "challenge the evidence they possessed which led to their failure to follow up on leads that contradicted their version of events."[87] In 1980, for example, one of the OSI attorneys wrote and distributed an internal memo in which he expressed doubts that Demjanjuk was Ivan the Terrible, and he resigned shortly thereafter.[88] The special master blamed defense counsel for not adequately pursuing every lead they received through discovery.[89] He also placed some of the blame on

Demjanjuk, reasoning that his alibi as to his whereabouts during the war was "so incredible as to legitimately raise the suspicions of his prosecutors that he lied about everything—including his denial that he was Ivan the Terrible."[90]

Wiseman concluded his report by observing that the new evidence cast "substantial doubt" on the claim that Demjanjuk was Ivan the Terrible.[91] But he found that nothing uncovered in the proceedings or since the original denaturalization opinion "cast any substantial doubt on [Judge Battisti's] finding that Mr. Demjanjuk served in the German SS at the Trawniki training camp."[92] He therefore concluded that the decision to denaturalize and deport Demjanjuk was "a sound one."[93]

On July 29, 1993, a month after the special master filed his report, the Israeli Supreme Court overturned Demjanjuk's guilty verdict, finding that the prosecution had not proven he was Ivan the Terrible. Days later, on August 3, after oral argument and ten minutes of deliberation, the Sixth Circuit panel ordered that Demjanjuk be returned to the United States so that he could participate in the panel's reopened proceedings.[94]

Demjanjuk was back in the United States by late September 1993.[95] Although he was not seen publicly for weeks, his return was controversial in the Cleveland area.[96] The *Plain Dealer* editorialized that the United States should not forget that there was ample evidence that he was a concentration camp guard, even if he was not Ivan the Terrible.[97] Members of the Jewish community demonstrated in front of his home and in downtown Cleveland in an effort to make the same point.[98] Demjanjuk supporters hung yellow ribbons, flowers, and a sign on the snow fence in front of his house and demonstrated with chants of "The Holocaust is over" and "Let it rest."[99] Members of the Ku Klux Klan, dressed in their traditional regalia, carried signs reading "Support Your Local Police" and "Ivan Was Freed."[100] The city of Seven Hills passed an ordinance that essentially barred all demonstrations in residential neighborhoods.[101] However, an Ohio state court issued an order permitting limited demonstrations in front of Demjanjuk's home.[102]

Meanwhile, in a lengthy opinion issued on November 17, 1993, the Sixth Circuit panel found that the extradition order had been obtained through prosecutorial misconduct that rose to the level of fraud on the court. The panel applied the higher *Brady* disclosure standard from criminal proceedings, noting that "the consequences of denaturalization and extradition equal or exceed those of most criminal convictions," and it vacated the extradition order.[103] The government petitioned for a rehearing by the full Sixth Circuit Court of Appeals, a request that was denied later that month.[104]

Soon after, Battisti granted the government's motion to reopen the deportation case, but he stayed proceedings pending the Supreme Court's decision on whether it would review the Sixth Circuit's order.[105] But then, Battisti died suddenly, on October 19, from a tick bite suffered while on a fishing trip.[106] The same month, the Supreme Court declined review of the Sixth Circuit's order.

Two years later, in September 1996, Demjanjuk's public defender moved to dismiss the denaturalization case that had been assigned to Judge Paul R. Matia.[107] On February 21, 1998, Matia found that DOJ lawyers had "acted with reckless disregard for their duty to the court" in failing to disclose evidence, and he vacated the 1981 denaturalization order. Although this restored Demjanjuk's citizenship, Matia denied Demjanjuk's request that the government be precluded from filing a second denaturalization case. He explained that "just as the government should not be able to profit from its misbehavior, neither should a defendant be insulated from the consequences of his alleged moral turpitude because he becomes the inadvertent beneficiary of sanctions against the government."[108]

Second Denaturalization Proceeding (1999–2004)

More than a year later, on May 19, 1999, the DOJ filed a second complaint seeking to denaturalize Demjanjuk.[109] The grounds this time were that he had served as a guard in several Nazi training and concentration camps during World War II. The complaint alleged that Demjanjuk persecuted civilians at the Trawniki, L. G. Obskow, Majdanek, Sobibor, and Flossenburg camps.[110] Over the course of the next two years, the court denied Demjanjuk's motion to dismiss, his counterclaim seeking $5 million in damages from OSI for allegedly torturing him and his family, and other motions to postpone the trial, stating that it was time to bring the case to a conclusion.[111]

Demjanjuk's second denaturalization trial began on May 29, 2001, eight years after the Israeli Supreme Court had acquitted him. Although the *Cleveland Plain Dealer* and the *Cleveland Jewish News* reported daily on the seven days of proceedings, the atmosphere was less charged than that at the first trial. The government's case rested solely on documents rather than eyewitness testimony, making the proceedings much less interesting to non-lawyers. Few if any Holocaust survivors or members of the Ukrainian community attended.[112] Although reporters were present, as well as lawyers and law students drawn to watch defense attorney Michael Tigar at work, there were few spectators.[113] The *Plain Dealer* reported that generally, aside from reporters, there were only three spectators, one of whom was the mother of a federal attorney.[114] Demjanjuk's son and son-in-law sat at the defense table, but Demjanjuk himself did not attend or testify in the civil proceeding.[115]

On February 21, 2002, Matia issued his "findings of fact and conclusions of law," as well as a "supplemental opinion" that addressed Demjanjuk's defenses. The court painstakingly and meticulously evaluated the evidence and concluded that Demjanjuk had served in the SS at Trawniki and the concentration camps and that this service constituted assistance in the persecution of a civilian population, making him ineligible for a visa under the DP Act, and ordered that his naturalization be revoked.[116] The court relied on documents, many of which came from archives in the former Soviet Union that had not been available in the 1980s. It held that Demjanjuk had misrepresented and concealed his wartime residence and employment. Matia concluded that Demjanjuk had served in five concentration camps and that, in the last of which, Flossenburg, he was a member of the SS Death's Head Battalion. Demjanjuk had received the blood-type tattoo while at Flossenburg. The court held that his service with the SS was "willing," as he was paid, was eligible for benefits, and did not seek to leave or escape.[117]

Demjanjuk had, of course, previously admitted that the residences and occupations on his visa application were not true.[118] The court noted, however, that he still had "not given any credible evidence of where he was during most of World War II after the prisoner-of-war camp at Rovno." Moreover, Demjanjuk's testimony had changed over the years. The court further noted that his testimony as to why he wrote that he was a farmer in Sobibor on his immigration application had changed and was not credible.[119]

In its supplemental opinion, the court noted that the case was about documentary evidence; even if eyewitnesses were available, any testimony they gave about events sixty years earlier would be inherently unreliable.[120] The court found that Demjanjuk's efforts to challenge the authenticity of the documents, particularly that of the identification card, failed, and it concluded that the evidence "clearly, convincingly and unequivocally shows that" this was not a case of mistaken identity. It acknowledged that no evidence was introduced proving that the photograph on the identification card was of Demjanjuk but noted that he himself had admitted that it resembled him. Matia found that the evidence introduced by Demjanjuk—the report of a physical anthropologist and witness statements by men who claimed to have been guards at the camps—did not weaken the government's identification evidence.[121] Demjanjuk's lawyers had argued that the government failed to make its case because no evidence was introduced indicating that a Sobibor survivor could identify him. The court found that Demjanjuk "overstated" the statements by survivors and guards.[122]

Demjanjuk appealed to the Sixth Circuit, arguing that the opinion should be overruled because it was not based on witness testimony.[123] In 2004, the circuit court denied the appeal and affirmed the district court's denaturalization order.[124] The Supreme Court denied review.[125]

Second Deportation Proceeding (2004–9)

Deportation proceedings began anew on December 17, 2004. Judge Michael Creppy, chief immigration judge, whose office was in Falls Church, Virginia, assigned the case to himself. In three separate opinions issued on June 16, 2005, he denied Demjanjuk's motion to reassign the case to a different judge based on a law review article Judge Creppy had written about pursuing Nazi war criminals using immigration law;[126] granted the government's motion for application of collateral estoppel as a matter of law; and denied Demjanjuk's application for deferral of removal under the Convention Against Torture, finding no evidence that he would be tortured in the Ukraine.[127] Relying on the district court's order, Creppy found Demjanjuk removable by clear, convincing, and unequivocal evidence that he had served as a guard in Nazi concentration camps. On December 28, 2005, the judge ordered Demjanjuk removed to Ukraine or, in the alternative, Germany or Poland.[128]

The BIA dismissed Demjanjuk's appeals from the motion rulings and the removal order.[129] The Sixth Circuit upheld Demjanjuk's removal order in January 2008,[130] and the Supreme Court denied review the following May.[131] Although Poland, Ukraine, and Germany initially refused to accept Demjanjuk, Germany eventually agreed to do so.[132] Accordingly, the United States deported him to Germany on May 11, 2009, where he was immediately arrested and later charged with war crimes.[133]

On May 12, 2011, a court in Munich found ninety-one-year-old Demjanjuk guilty of being an accessory to the murders of about twenty-eight thousand people in Sobibor and sentenced him to five years' imprisonment, including the two years he had already spent in prison.[134] Reasoning that Demjanjuk did not have a passport and was therefore not a flight risk, the court released him while his appeal was pending. He lived in a nursing home in Bavaria, Germany.[135]

In April 2011, before the German court issued its verdict, Demjanjuk's American lawyers filed with the district court a request that counsel be appointed on his behalf in the denaturalization case. As Judge Matia had retired from the bench in 2005, Judge Dan Aaron Polster granted the motion on May 10.[136] In July 2011, Demjanjuk's lawyers filed a motion to set aside the denaturalization order on the grounds that prosecutors had not turned over all possible evidence, particularly a March 4, 1985, FBI memorandum about the identification card. The memorandum, written by then-Special Agent Thomas Martin, suggested that the Soviets might be using OSI to target anti-Soviet dissidents in the United States.[137] Polster denied the motion on December 21, 2011, without a hearing. He found that the FBI documents were merely suppositions without investigation and reasoned that the agent's "theory is no match, quantitatively or qualitatively, for the considerable documentary evidence presented by the Government and supported by expert authentication in the 2001 trial." He also noted that Demjanjuk had never provided a "single, consistent accounting of his whereabouts during the war years."[138] On January 20, 2012, he denied Demjanjuk's motion for reconsideration,[139] and Demjanjuk's attorneys appealed to the Sixth Circuit. Demjanjuk died of natural causes in Germany on March 17, 2012, at the age of ninety-one.[140]

Conclusion

The U.S. government's effort to remove Demjanjuk from the United States remains perhaps the longest and most convoluted of the Nazi collaborator cases. Two district court judges examined and weighed a mountain of evidence during denaturalization trials that took place twenty years apart, a third judge conducted an exhaustive review of the first proceeding, and a fourth judge revisited his denaturalization order months before Demjanjuk's death. The Sixth Circuit Court of Appeals reviewed all the judges' opinions except for the last. Demjanjuk's appeal became moot upon his death. However, in Cleveland and elsewhere the impact of the second denaturalization trial was quite different from that of the first.

Demjanjuk's 1981 denaturalization proceeding was one of the first brought in the United States, and the Jewish and Ukrainian communities were riveted by the testimony given by Demjanjuk and Jewish concentration camp survivors. Jews and Ukrainians have historically had a tense relationship. Jews mourn the many Jews who were killed by Ukrainians during the pogroms of 1648–49. Yet Bogdan Chelmenitzky, the Ukrainian leader considered responsible for the murders, is deemed a freedom fighter by many Ukrainians.[141] Ninety percent of Ukrainian Jews were murdered in the Holocaust.[142]

Two days before the first trial began, about 450 members of Demjanjuk's church met in Parma, Ohio, to pray, rally against the Justice Department, and raise funds for his defense.[143] On the opening day of trial, about 100 Demjanjuk supporters burned a Soviet flag in Cleveland's Public Square and rallied in front of the courthouse, chanting against the Soviet Union.[144] Some carried signs proclaiming "Holocaust Is a Hoax" and "Battisti Is Ivan the Terrible."[145] A small group of Jews, mostly students, also demonstrated with an Israeli flag.[146] The demonstrations continued throughout the trial, and Jews and Ukrainians stood in line for seats in the courtroom.

Over the years, members of both communities attempted to use Demjanjuk's trials to redress old grievances and educate the public.[147] During the first trial, the *Cleveland Jewish News* editorialized that Jews needed to attend to remind the court, the government, and the general public that the Holocaust should not be forgotten.[148] The Cleveland Jewish community almost unanimously approved of the first denaturalization ruling, which was largely based on eyewitness testimony. Many felt it was important to understand that seemingly normal people like Demjanjuk carried out the Nazis' goals and that survivor testimony was vital to educating Jews as well as others on the horrors of the Holocaust.[149]

Many Ukrainian Americans saw the proceedings as part of an effort to incriminate all Ukrainians by going after one symbolic man.[150] Members of the relatively small Ukrainian American community in Cleveland held vigils and rallies, and they wrote letters to politicians and newspaper editors in support of Demjanjuk. They were convinced that the Soviet Union had sent forged documents to OSI as part of the "Soviet treachery against the Ukrainian nation" that had begun with the 1932–33 famine. Some sought to use the trial to educate the world about the famine, which they considered "a grossly understudied genocide."[151] Some also blamed Jews, who they believed considered all Ukrainians to be Nazi collaborators, and the U.S. government, in the form of OSI, for targeting eastern European immigrants under pressure from "the Jewish lobby."[152] Others went so far as to excuse those who collaborated with the Nazis because, the argument went, they did so to save their own lives.[153]

In contrast, although the local press covered the second trial in 2002, few people attended the proceedings. By that time, the fall of the Soviet Union had made many more documents available, and the community had witnessed several denaturalization proceedings of alleged Nazi collaborators. The lack of interest was also attributable to the facts that Demjanjuk was accused of being a Nazi-trained guard and not Ivan the Terrible and that the proceedings were drier than the first trial, as the government's case in the second trial was based on documents and not eyewitnesses.[154] The Cleveland community generally placed its confidence in the fairness of the American judicial system and accepted the district court's conclusion that Demjanjuk should be stripped of his citizenship.

Notes

1. After his acquittal in Israel, Demjanjuk told Israeli television that he was a "hero" for holding out through what was then a sixteen-year legal battle, and he denied serving as a Nazi concentration camp guard. He boasted to the reporter, "I not Nazi. I'm pure Ukrainian." *Cleveland Plain Dealer*, August 1, 1993.

2. United States v. Demjanjuk, 518 F. Supp. 1362, 1363–64 (N.D. Ohio 1981).

3. Ibid., 1364.

4. Ibid., 1377. Neither he nor government prosecutors were ever able to locate an "Oelberg" in Austria.

5. Ibid., 1378.

6. Ibid.; Tom Teicholz, *The Trial of Ivan the Terrible: State of Israel v. John Demjanjuk* (New York: St. Martin's Press, 1990), 43.

7. United States v. Demjanjuk, 2002 WL 544622, at *19 (N.D. Ohio February 21, 2002).

8. Demjanjuk, 518 F. Supp. at 1379–80.

9. Teicholz, *Trial of Ivan the Terrible*, 46–47. Donald Coulter, an Indiana farmer, had filed an application stating that he would employ war refugees.

10. Ibid., 48–49.

11. Demjanjuk, 2002 WL 544622, at *20.

12. Report of the Special Master (1993) filed in Demjanjuk v. Petrovsky, No. 85–3435 (6th Cir.), at 27.

13. *Cleveland Plain Dealer*, July 28, 2002.

14. Report of the Special Master, 22. Demjanjuk did not agree to meet with INS investigators. The first time he answered questions about his whereabouts during the war was when he was deposed by Assistant U.S. Attorney Joseph Cippolene in April 1979. Teicholz, *Trial of Ivan the Terrible*, 52.

15. Report of the Special Master, 22–25; Teicholz, *Trial of Ivan the Terrible*, 27–31.

16. Demjanjuk, 518 F. Supp. at 1365.

17. United States v. Fedorenko, 455 F. Supp. 893, 902 n.12 (S.D. Fla. 1978), reversed on other grounds by 597 F.2d 946 (5th Cir. 1979). For an additional description of Treblinka, see also Teicholz, *Trial of Ivan the Terrible*, 5–16.

18. Teicholz, *Trial of Ivan the Terrible*, 11–12.

19. Report of the Special Master, 25–26. The government began denaturalization proceedings against Fedorenko ten days before. Charles R. Allen Jr., *Nazi War Criminals in America: Facts, Action—The Basic Handbook* (New York: Highgate House, 1985), 12.

20. Demjanjuk, 518 F. Supp. at 1363.

21. Immigration and Naturalization Act § 340(a), 8 U.S.C. § 1451(a).

22. Schneiderman v. United States, 320 U.S. 118, 125 (1943); Fedorenko v. United States, 449 U.S. 490 (1981).

23. Report of the Special Master, 124.

24. *Cleveland Plain Dealer*, March 24, 1994.

25. See chapters 5 and 10.

26. *Cleveland Jewish News*, February 27, 1981, and January 1, 1982.

27. *Cleveland Jewish News*, February 20 and 27, 1981.

28. *Cleveland Plain Dealer*, November 13, 1994; Alan A. Ryan Jr., *Quiet Neighbors: Prosecuting Nazi War Criminals in America* (New York: Harcourt Brace Jovanovich, 1984), 40–41.

29. *Cleveland Jewish News*, February 13, 1981.

30. Demjanjuk, 518 F. Supp. at 1369.

31. Ibid., 1366–68.

32. Ibid., 1368.

33. *Cleveland Jewish News*, January 1, 1982.

34. Demjanjuk, 518 F. Supp. at 1368.

35. Ibid., 1369.

36. Ibid., 1366.

37. Ibid., 1382 n.44.

38. Ibid., 1381.

39. Fedorenko, 449 U.S. at 509–23. In the only denaturalization case of a Nazi collaborator to reach the Supreme Court, the justices ruled that Fedorenko's failure to disclose his service in Treblinka made him ineligible for a visa as a matter of law. Fedorenko was deported to the Soviet Union in 1984. Matter of Fedorenko, 19 I&N Dec. 57, 60 (BIA 1984). He was tried as a war criminal, found guilty, and executed. *Los Angeles Times*, July 27, 1987.

40. Demjanjuk, 518 F. Supp. at 1383.

41. Ibid., 1386.

42. Report of the Special Master, 125.

43. Demjanjuk, 518 F. Supp. at 1384.

44. Ibid., 1386.

45. United States v. Demjanjuk, 680 F.2d 32 (6th Cir. 1982).

46. Demjanjuk v. United States, 459 U.S. 1036 (1982).

47. United States v. Demjanjuk, 103 F.R.D. 1, 2 (N.D. Ohio 1983). Mark O'Conner's father, Edward M. O'Conner, wrote the 1948 DP Act. Glenn R. Sharfman, "The Jewish Community's Reactions to the John Demjanjuk Trials," *Historian* 63, no. 1 (2000): 22. Edward was friends with one of Demjanjuk's staunchest supporters, Jerome Brentar, who had worked as a screening officer for the International Refugee Organization. Brentar owned a travel agency in Cleveland. Edward recommended his son even though he had no immigration experience and little trial or appellate experience. Teicholz, *Trial of Ivan the Terrible*, 74.

48. Demjanjuk, 103 F.R.D. at 2.

49. Matter of Extradition of John Demjanjuk, 612 F. Supp. 544, 547 (N.D. Ohio 1984).

50. Teicholz, *Trial of Ivan the Terrible*, 74–76.

51. Immigration and Naturalization Act § 240(b).

52. Matter of Demjanjuk, 612 F. Supp. at 547.

53. United States v. Demjanjuk, 767 F.2d 922 (6th Cir. 1985).

54. *Cleveland Plain Dealer*, November 13, 1994.

55. Matter of Demjanjuk, 612 F. Supp. at 547.

56. Demjanjuk v. Petrovsky, 612 F. Supp. 571, 573 n.2 (N.D. Ohio 1984).

57. Matter of Demjanjuk, 584 F. Supp. 1321 (N.D. Ohio 1984).
58. Ibid., 1334.
59. Ibid., 1321.
60. Matter of Demjanjuk, 612 F. Supp. at 544.
61. Ibid., 547.
62. Ibid., 572. Demjanjuk was taken into custody and imprisoned in federal prison in Springfield, Missouri.
63. Demjanjuk v. Petrovsky, 612 F. Supp. 571. Local Civil Rule 7.09(3) provided that "subsequent proceedings in civil cases and in criminal cases (including petitions under 28 U.S.C. Section 2255) shall be assigned to the judge who heard the original case."
64. Demjanjuk v. Petrovsky, 776 F.2d 571, 576 (6th Cir. 1985).
65. Ibid., at 584. A habeas petition on Demjanjuk's behalf with the U.S. Court of Appeals for the District of Columbia, seeking an immediate hearing and a stay of execution of the extradition warrant on the grounds that the International Convention on the Prevention and Punishment of the Crime of Genocide "has, or will soon" amend the U.S.-Israel extradition treaty, was denied on February 27, 1986. Demjanjuk v. Meese, 784 F.2d 1114 (D.C. Cir. 1986).
66. Demjanjuk v. United States, No. 88–0864 (N.D. Ohio April 8, 1988). See, e.g., Deborah Roy, "The Sixth Circuit's Unprecedented Reopening of *Demjanjuk v. Petrovsky*," *Cleveland State Law Review* 42 (1994): 737n21. The case was referred to a magistrate judge on January 28, 1992. Upon a joint motion by Demjanjuk and the government, the case was closed in 1992 after the Sixth Circuit *sua sponte* reopened the habeas mandate.
67. *Cleveland Plain Dealer*, November 13, 1994.
68. *Cleveland Plain Dealer*, February 26, 1990.
69. *Cleveland Plain Dealer*, November 13, 1994; Yoram Sheftel, *Defending "Ivan the Terrible": The Conspiracy to Convict John Demjanjuk* (Washington, D.C.: Regnery, 1996), 402.
70. Demjanjuk v. Petrovsky, 10 F.3d 338, 356–57 (6th Cir. 1994).
71. *Cleveland Plain Dealer*, November 13, 1994. In 1993, the World Jewish Congress opposed White House consideration of Judge Merritt for the Supreme Court due to his reopening of the Demjanjuk case and his handling of another accused concentration camp guard, Leonid Petkiewytsch. *Cleveland Plain Dealer*, June 9, 1993. President Bill Clinton nominated Ruth Bader Ginsburg.
72. *Cleveland Plain Dealer*, August 7, 1992.
73. *Cleveland Plain Dealer*, August 11, 1992.
74. Demjanjuk, 10 F.3d at 339.
75. *Cleveland Plain Dealer*, November 13, 1994.
76. Demjanjuk, 10 F.3d at 358, quoting Chambers v. NASCO, Inc., 501 U.S. 32 (1991).
77. Ibid., 358–59. Judge Wiseman, a former Tennessee state treasurer, was appointed by President Jimmy Carter.
78. *Cleveland Plain Dealer*, August 18, 1992.
79. *Cleveland Plain Dealer*, November 13, 1992.
80. Report of the Special Master, 6–16.
81. Demjanjuk, 10 F.3d at 339.
82. Report of the Special Master, 167.
83. Ibid., 172.
84. Ibid., 199–201.
85. Ibid., 182.
86. Ibid., 178–88.
87. Ibid., 201.

88. Ibid., 13, 34–35, 99–103; *Cleveland Plain Dealer*, June 20, 1992. For a copy of the memo, see Demjanjuk, 10 F.3d at 369–73.

89. Report of the Special Master, 204.

90. Ibid., 204 n.598.

91. Ibid., 207.

92. Ibid., 209.

93. Ibid., 210.

94. Demjanjuk v. Petrovsky, No. 85-3435, 1993 WL 394773 (6th Cir. August 3, 1993).

95. *Cleveland Plain Dealer*, November 13, 1994.

96. *Cleveland Plain Dealer*, October 8 and 12, 1993.

97. *Cleveland Plain Dealer*, July 30, 1993.

98. *Cleveland Plain Dealer*, September 28, 1993; Sharfman, "Jewish Community's Reaction," 31.

99. *Cleveland Plain Dealer*, September 24, 1993; Seven Hills v. Aryan Nations, 667 N.E.2d 942, 304 (Ohio 1996).

100. *Cleveland Plain Dealer*, September 26, 1993.

101. City of Seven Hills v. Aryan Nations, No. 66754, 1995 WL 66679 (Ohio App. 8 Dist. February 16, 1995).

102. Seven Hills, 667 N.E.2d 942.

103. Demjanjuk, 10 F.3d at 354.

104. Demjanjuk, 10 F.3d at 338; Rison v. Demjanjuk, 513 U.S. 914 (1994).

105. *Cleveland Plain Dealer*, February 5, 1994.

106. *Cleveland Plain Dealer*, October 20, 1994.

107. *Cleveland Plain Dealer*, September 11, 1996. Born in 1937 and a Harvard Law School graduate, Judge Matia was appointed by President George H. W. Bush in 1991 and was chief judge of the district from 1999 to 2004. See History of the Sixth Circuit, available at http://www.ca6.uscourts.gov/lib_hist/Courts/district%20court/OH/NDOH/judges/prm-bio.html.

108. *Cleveland Plain Dealer*, February 21, 1998.

109. United States v. Demjanjuk, 367 F.3d 623, 626 (6th Cir. 2004).

110. Ibid., 628.

111. Ibid., 627; *Cleveland Plain Dealer*, March 14, 2000, and May 22, 2001.

112. *Cleveland Jewish News*, June 4, 2001.

113. *Cleveland Jewish News*, May 31 and June 4, 2001.

114. *Cleveland Plain Dealer*, June 8, 2001.

115. *Cleveland Jewish News*, May 31, 2001; *Cleveland Plain Dealer*, May 30, 2001.

116. United States v. Demjanjuk, No. 1:99CV1193, 2002 WL 544622, at *31 (N.D. Ohio February 21, 2002).

117. Ibid., 10–11.

118. Ibid., 20.

119. United States v. Demjanjuk, No. 1:99CV1193, 2002 WL 544623, at *4 (N.D. Ohio February 21, 2002).

120. Ibid.

121. Ibid., 2.

122. Ibid., 4.

123. *Cleveland Plain Dealer*, April 22, 2002.

124. Demjanjuk, 367 F.3d.

125. Demjanjuk v. United States, 543 U.S. 970 (2004). Eli Rosenbaum, the director of OSI, warned: "The government will not waiver in its determination to find you, prosecute you and remove you from the U.S." *Cleveland Plain Dealer*, May 1, 2004.

126. *Cleveland Plain Dealer*, June 21, 2005. The article had been published in 1998. See Michael J. Creppy, "Nazi War Criminals in Immigration Law," *Georgetown Immigration Law Journal* 12 (Spring 1998): 443.

127. Matter of Demjanjuk, No. A08 237 417, 2006 WL 3922265, at *1–2 (BIA, December 21, 2006).

128. *Cleveland Plain Dealer*, December 29, 2005.

129. Matter of Demjanjuk, 2006 WL 3922265.

130. Demjanjuk v. Mukasey, 514 F.3d 616 (6th Cir. 2008).

131. Demjanjuk v. Mukasey, 553 U.S. 1061 (2008).

132. *Cleveland Plain Dealer*, June 20, 2008.

133. *New York Times*, May 12, 2009.

134. *Cleveland Plain Dealer*, May 12, 2011.

135. See *Spiegel Online International*, June 17, 2011.

136. Judge Polster was born in 1951, graduated from Harvard Law School, and was a federal prosecutor before being nominated by President William J. Clinton in 1997. See http://www.ohnd.uscourts.gov/home/judges/judge-dan-aaron-polster/.

137. United States v. Demjanjuk, No. 1:99CV1193, 2012 WL 6371801, at *6–7 (N.D. Ohio, December 20, 2011).

138. United States v. Demjanjuk, No. 1:99CV1193, 2012 WL 6371801, at *13 (N.D. Ohio, December 20, 2011).

139. United States v. Demjanjuk, No. 1:99CV1193, 2012 WL 175400 (N.D. Ohio, January 20, 2012).

140. See Robert D. McFadden, "John Demjanjuk, Accused of Atrocities as a Nazi Camp Guard, Is Dead at 91," *New York Times*, March 18, 2012.

141. Sharfman, "Jewish Community's Reactions," 24. Glenn Sharfman has published detailed summaries of the reactions of the Jewish and Ukrainian communities to Demjanjuk's litigations. See ibid., 47; Sharfman, "The Quest for Justice: The Reaction of the Ukrainian-American Community to the John Demjanjuk Trials," *Journal of Genocide Research* 2, no. 1 (2000): 65–87.

142. Sharfman, "Jewish Community's Reactions," 21.

143. Ryan, *Quiet Neighbors*, 108–9.

144. Ibid.; *Cleveland Jewish News*, February 13, 1981.

145. *Cleveland Jewish News*, February 13, 1981. Although the Demjanjuk family consistently denounced anti-Semitism and acknowledged the horrors of the Holocaust, Demjanjuk attracted the support of anti-Semites and Holocaust deniers. Sharfman, "Quest for Justice," 77.

146. *Cleveland Jewish News*, February 13, 1981.

147. Sharfman, "Jewish Community's Reactions," 33.

148. *Cleveland Jewish News*, February 27, 1981.

149. Sharfman, "Jewish Community's Reactions," 30.

150. Sharfman, "Quest for Justice," 67.

151. Ibid., 68–70; *Cleveland Jewish News*, February 27, 1981.

152. *Cleveland Plain Dealer*, June 11, 1992.

153. *Cleveland Plain Dealer*, March 6, 1987.

154. *Cleveland Plain Dealer*, June 8, 2001.

13

Capital Litigation in the Northern District

Alison K. Guernsey

T HE HISTORY OF death penalty litigation in the Northern District of
Ohio is both long and short. Situated in one of the most prolific capital-
sentencing states in the nation, the district has grappled with the cases of over
one hundred defendants sentenced to death under state law since the establishment of Ohio's modern death penalty statute in 1981. Despite the frequency of the litigation of cases originating at the state level, however, to date
there have been only two *federal* capital cases tried in the Northern District,
both initiated in 2006 and tried in 2007, and neither resulting in a sentence of
death. In a third capital case, the potential for a death sentence was eliminated pretrial as a result of the defendant's cognitive and behavioral impair-
ment. This chapter looks at the history of both types of death penalty litigation
in the district—those three cases initiated at the federal level as well as litigation originating from state capital convictions and reviewed through petitions
for a writ of habeas corpus.

History of Federal Death Penalty Statutes

To understand capital litigation in the Northern District of Ohio, it is necessary to understand the authority from which it stems. Although not explicitly authorized by the U.S. Constitution, there were clear indications in the text of the Bill of Rights that the drafters envisioned—and perhaps simply assumed—the existence of a criminal justice system able to impose the ultimate penalty.[1] With this backdrop, in 1790 the first Congress enacted the Act for the Punishment of Certain Crimes against the United States, which mandated death for those convicted of one of several enumerated crimes.[2] As opposition to the mandatory imposition of death grew, however, Congress reduced the number of death-eligible offenses to five in 1897, and instead of requiring a death sentence for certain offenses, it provided the jury absolute and unguided discretion to impose such a punishment.[3]

Although Congress amended the federal death penalty provisions several times at the beginning of the twentieth century, as the 1960s civil rights era progressed citizens and legislators increasingly raised concerns over the disparate impact that the imposition of the death penalty had on various poor and minority populations. These concerns resulted in several challenges to capital punishment's use and administration before the U.S. Supreme Court. The landmark case of *Furman v. Georgia*,[4] for example, involved an appeal on behalf of three defendants who had been sentenced to death by state juries. All three argued that capital sentencing was arbitrary and capricious and that its imposition and administration violated the Eighth and Fourteenth Amendments to the U.S. Constitution. In nine separate opinions, by a vote of 5 to 4, a majority of the Supreme Court held that all capital punishment statutes that provided juries with complete and unguided sentencing discretion to decide which individuals should live or die could result in arbitrary sentencing and amounted to cruel and unusual punishment. *Furman* not only invalidated scores of state death penalty statutes but also rendered unconstitutional Congress's 1897 act.

Importantly, *Furman* did not declare the use of the death penalty per se unconstitutional; instead, the Supreme Court focused on the problem of unfettered jury discretion. Responsive to the Court's concerns, several states and Congress began immediately amending their now invalid statutes in an attempt to strike the appropriate balance in a discretionary sentencing regime. Four years later, in *Gregg v. Georgia*,[5] the Supreme Court upheld several of these new death penalty statutes that instituted a variety of "guidelines" for the sentencer to follow when deciding whether to impose death. These statutes allowed for the introduction and consideration of mitigating and aggravating circumstances and required that the judge or jury find and identify at least one statutory aggravating factor before imposing a death sentence. *Gregg* also imposed several lasting procedural requirements, including the bifurcation of the guilt and sentencing phases of a capital proceeding.

Although Congress did not act as swiftly to amend the federal death penalty statute, in 1988 it authorized the option to seek the death penalty in a number of crimes associated with the drug trade.[6] Congress expanded the list of death-eligible offenses to sixty in 1994 with the enactment of the Federal Death Penalty Act (FDPA).[7]

Federal Death Penalty Cases: *Moonda, Galan,* and *Lewis*

Despite the lengthy history of capital litigation across the federal criminal system, its history in the Northern District of Ohio is very recent. In fact, prior to 2007, the district had never actually held a death penalty trial. But in that year, it tackled two: the trial of Donna Moonda in Akron for ordering the shooting death of her husband on the Ohio Turnpike and the trial of Thomas Galan in Toledo for a decade-old, drug-related double murder. Although Galan was the first of the two to be indicted, Moonda's trial and sentencing concluded almost five months prior to Galan's, which transformed Moonda's case into the first federal death penalty trial in the Northern District since its creation in 1855.

The Case against Donna Moonda— "The Turnpike Homicide"

The case against Donna Moonda began in 2005 when her lover, Damian Bradford, shot her wealthy husband, Dr. Gulam Moonda. Donna Moonda had told Bradford of her desire to kill her husband in order to dissolve the marriage yet avoid the limitations of a prenuptial agreement. With a promise that she would share her inheritance, she orchestrated a murder plan with Bradford. One day, as she, her husband, and her mother traveled from their home in Pennsylvania to Toledo, Ohio, Moonda pulled onto the shoulder of the highway under the guise of being too tired to drive. Bradford pulled up behind them, approached the car, demanded Gulam's wallet at gunpoint in order to make the crime look like an armed robbery, and then shot him dead. Moonda's attempt at "cooperating" with investigators quickly led them to Bradford, and within weeks, police began to suspect that Moonda and Bradford had conspired to kill Gulam.[8]

Bradford was indicted in the Northern District of Ohio, and the case was assigned in accordance with the district's random assignment procedure to Judge David D. Dowd Jr. By that time, Moonda had stopped cooperating with police, and anticipating that she would be subpoenaed as a key eyewitness in Bradford's impending trial, she preemptively notified the court that she would invoke her constitutional right not to testify. With that decision, Moonda reneged on an agreement that she had made with Bradford to speak on his behalf. Now aware that his lover was refusing to hold up her end of the bargain and that he likely would face a life sentence for the crime without her testimony that he was not the shooter, Bradford cut a deal with the U.S. Attorney's Office mere days before Judge Dowd was set to impanel a jury. In exchange for a recommendation of a seventeen-and-a-half-year sentence, Bradford agreed to testify against Moonda.[9]

Within the month, a grand jury indicted Moonda for several crimes, including murder for hire and the use of a firearm in a crime of violence resulting in death. Most surprisingly, however, the indictment included the "special findings" required to seek the death penalty, and shortly thereafter, the U.S. attorney for the Northern District of Ohio filed official notice of the government's intent to seek a death sentence. Court observers, defense counsel, and even the presiding judge were all surprised. Without a doubt, the case against Moonda in terms of guilt was strong, particularly given Bradford's anticipated testimony. But the U.S. government's decision to make this a test case for federal death penalty litigation in the Northern District was curious for many reasons. The crime, although reprehensible, was not particularly egregious when compared to many of those committed by individuals who occupied federal death row. To be sure, it was premeditated, and Moonda sought to gain a significant amount of money from the murder.[10] Yet the crime stands out more for the things it was not: it was not a multiple homicide, it was not particularly gruesome, and it was not actually committed by the capital defendant.

Additionally, the same prosecutors who sought to execute Moonda had just given the admitted triggerman a deal that, if accepted by Judge Dowd, would likely result in Bradford's release from prison before his fortieth birthday. Finally, the decision to seek the death penalty was unexpected for another reason—Moonda's gender. At the time of the indictment, there was only one woman on federal death row, and no woman had been put to death in a federal case since 1953.[11] Some believed that the government had decided to seek capital punish-

ment in the case of a female just so that it could claim that it did not discriminate on gender lines, despite the general belief that, given Bradford's deal, it was
a poor case in which to develop that theory. As Judge Dowd explained, "A case
in which the target for capital punishment is a woman and demonstrably not the
actual killer" was "a rare event."[12]

Amid the shock at a potential death sentence, the case progressed, and
Moonda requested court-appointed counsel based on her indigency. Judge Dowd
selected Roger M. Synenberg, a local Akron attorney. Moonda asked for two
additional "death-qualified" attorneys shortly thereafter to assist in Synenberg's
preparations, a motion that the government opposed on the grounds that the
defendant was entitled to only one additional attorney and the case was not
particularly complex. Mindful of the frequency of challenges to the adequacy
of counsel in death penalty litigation and even more mindful of the fact that he
was proceeding in uncharted waters in the Northern District, Judge Dowd granted
Moonda's motion and appointed Lawrence J. Whitney of Akron and David L.
Grant of Cleveland. Jury selection began. Again faced with a task never before
undertaken in the Northern District—selecting a death-qualified jury—Judge
Dowd, counsel for Moonda, and Assistant U.S. Attorneys Linda H. Barr and
Nancy L. Kelley spent considerable time drafting a lengthy jury questionnaire.[13]
In an effort to uncover every possible juror bias, the court required jurors to
provide written answers to over fifty questions, which included a detailed narrative identifying salient and potentially inflammatory facts about the ages, races,
religions, and relationships of the victim, Moonda, and Bradford. Moreover,
the questionnaire described in detail the court's trial procedures, required the
jurors to describe their feelings regarding the death penalty, and contained eight
additional questions concerning capital punishment. As Judge Dowd recalled
the jury selection procedures:

> I don't believe in sending the jury questionnaire out [to the prospective jurors]
> ahead of time. I find that if [the jurors] come in and see me they'll get inter-
> ested in the case, [and] have a different attitude. So, I brought in . . . around
> three-hundred jurors in four separate groups. I took them through the ques-
> tionnaire, . . . had them fill it out [at the courthouse,] and gave copies to the
> lawyers. . . . [The jurors] responded thoroughly to the questionnaire. Frankly,
> I was surprised that so many of them answered in a way that you did not have
> to recuse them. . . . [In fact,] of the jurors who filled out the questionnaire, the
> attorneys only disagreed as to two of them. . . . [A]fter we had pared the list
> down, . . . we brought [each juror] in and I went through an additional voir

dire with each juror. . . . Because each side had twenty peremptory challenges you need a lot of people. I got enough jurors qualified . . . so that if [the attorneys] used every challenge, we still had enough jurors . . . I think that we qualified fifty-six jurors.[14]

Ultimately, the court impaneled a jury composed of seven women and five men, and the merits, or guilt, phase of the trial began on June 18, 2007.[15] Moonda maintained her innocence throughout, arguing that Bradford killed Gulam on his own and implicated her only to lessen his sentence. Unconvinced, the jury convicted Moonda on all counts, bringing the guilt phase of the litigation to a close.[16] As the penalty phase loomed, the government's sweetheart deal with Bradford (and one of the facts that made the government's decision to charge Moonda with a capital offense so unanticipated) came to the forefront, where it remained. Judge Dowd was the presiding judge for both the proceedings involving Bradford's plea agreement and Moonda's trial. And with Moonda potentially facing execution, Judge Dowd—notwithstanding his initial skepticism over the propriety of the relatively lenient sentence that the government had proposed in Bradford's plea agreement—made Bradford's sentencing a priority. He intended to ensure that the Moonda jury would be fully aware of the sentence her alleged coconspirator had received: "I was not going to have the jury not know what was going to happen to Bradford."[17] Judge Dowd thus accepted Bradford's plea and the government's recommended sentence of seventeen and a half years.

The penalty phase of the litigation began on July 16, 2007. In an effort to show that their client's actions did not warrant death, defense counsel introduced a variety of evidence in mitigation concerning Moonda's dependent personality disorder, testimony from friends and family, and testimony from a former prison administrator concerning the conditions of confinement that she would face.[18] But Moonda's strongest argument in mitigation was the fact that Bradford had received such a short prison term despite being the individual who admittedly pulled the trigger. It was an "unsettling disparity" for some, and it was a fact with which even Judge Dowd was uncomfortable.[19]

Although federal prosecutors asserted at the time of Moonda's trial that they had "negotiated the plea bargain with Mr. Bradford to strengthen their case" against her,[20] that decision was clearly their undoing as far as a death verdict was concerned. On July 19, 2007, after approximately three hours of deliberation, the jury submitted a question to Judge Dowd, raising a concern that he would remember well. The jury wanted to know whether any sentence other than death or life without release was available. Judge Dowd informed them that the statute circumscribed his discretion: there was no other option. A little more than one hour later, the jury decided to spare Moonda's life and unanimously sentenced her to life without the possibility of release. All twelve jurors agreed that Bradford was equally culpable, and they were greatly disturbed by his comparatively short sentence, even mentioning it in writing. Two jurors even found that Moonda was not the primary offender.[21] Judge Dowd accepted the jury's recommendation and sentenced Moonda.

Even after the proceedings ended, Moonda's sentence still followed Judge Dowd. In fact, some time later he received a letter from a juror who remained very upset with the decision that the jury had to make. As Judge Dowd explained:

> The jury was angry that they didn't have any other choice apart from capital punishment and life imprisonment. . . . And I can't say that I blame them, but there weren't any other choices under the law. And that was hard for them to accept. But think if I hadn't of sentenced the kid. I thought that later maybe I had made a mistake. Maybe I should have left [Bradford's sentence] out of there. . . . [W]hat they really felt angry about was that I didn't give them the chance to [sentence] her as low as [Bradford]. Maybe it would have made it easier for them [if I had not sentenced him]. I hadn't thought of that. I was thinking, . . . it's not fair to her . . . [for the jury] not to know that this kid got a real break. In fact, as I said all along, after he's [released], I think that she's got a really good case for commutation.[22]

Given the facts of the case, the jury's decision to spare Moonda's life was not unexpected, and in many ways, it was in accordance with decisions to reject death sentences in murder-for-hire-type scenarios across the nation. As Kevin McNally, the director of the Death Penalty Resource Counsel Project, explained, a jury's refusal to impose a death sentence in cases such as Moonda's reflected "a recognition on the part of society that there has to be equal treatment for people who are equally culpable."[23]

The Case against Thomas Galan—Double Drug Homicide

Thomas Galan was indicted in early 2006 for the decade-old murder of the Flores brothers—two alleged drug dealers to whom Galan owed a substantial amount of money. In the years immediately following the crime, authorities had little luck connecting Galan to the deaths; in fact, a state grand jury in the county where the murders occurred had declined to indict him, and the case remained unresolved. Interest in Galan was peaked again, however, as federal investigators delved into a large-scale drug-trafficking operation outside Toledo.[24] Based on the information obtained during that investigation, federal prosecutors were able to secure an indictment against Galan for the deaths, and they filed an official notice to seek the death penalty.[25] Judge James G. Carr, then chief judge of the Northern District, was selected to preside over the case.

The court appointed two attorneys from the private criminal defense bar to defend Galan, David L. Doughton of Cleveland and Jeffrey J. Helmick of Toledo. They were tasked with litigating against Assistant U.S. Attorneys Joseph R. Wilson and Ava R. Dustin, both of Toledo. Defense counsel wasted little time in commencing not only their vigorous defense of Galan, who maintained his innocence, but also their crusade to ensure that even if their client were found guilty, a death sentence would be off the table. Counsel quickly moved to strike the possibility of the death penalty based on their claims that the FDPA was unconstitutional, that it violated the Eighth Amendment's proscription against cruel and unusual punishment, and that Galan's capital indictment was faulty. Finding each of these motions to lack merit, Judge Carr denied them all.[26]

As with Moonda, the jury selection was a focal point of Galan's case. His counsel filed several motions related to jury selection as many as eight months prior to the actual start of voir dire; in at least two cases, the motions amounted to memoranda of law reminding the court of the standards for jury selection in death penalty cases as established in Supreme Court jurisprudence. More than two hundred prospective jurors reported to complete the questionnaire over three days in mid-September 2007. And after five days of voir dire, a jury was selected. Interestingly, it was not only the prospective jury that was being asked whether its biases would stand in the way of completing its job, but Judge Carr—having never presided over a capital trial—was reflecting on the issue as well:

> I certainly do not favor the death penalty[,] . . . so I [would] probably . . . best describe myself as being uncommitted one way or the other. . . . And as I approached the prospect of the possibility of having to adopt or reject a jury recommendation of death in the Galan case, I felt that I had to make a conscious decision . . . that I would make th[e] decision [after the jury's verdict] without consideration of or concern about whatever my views about the death penalty are. . . . And I concluded I could. I didn't know what the verdict would be, and I didn't know what the evidence would be, but I was able to say to myself, if [I have] to face that choice . . . I [will] be as confident as humanly

possible that I will look at [the case] . . . in terms of the facts and the law . . . [a]nd make a decision on that basis rather than letting my very substantial lack of enthusiasm for the death penalty and my very substantial doubt about its usefulness, utility, or moral acceptability play a role. And, in thinking, . . . it occurred to me that [such reflection] is simply no more or less than [what] we ask jurors to do. That's why we do voir dire. So, in a sense, I conducted my own internal voir dire.[27]

The trial lasted six days, during which the government presented a wealth of evidence indicating that Galan and one of his friends, Damere Lockett, took a ride as passengers in the Flores brothers' van. Once they were in a rural area, Galan shot both George and Felipe. Although Galan maintained throughout trial that it was Lockett who committed the murders, the jury found Galan guilty. Attention then turned to the highly charged issue of sentencing, but unlike in Donna Moonda's case, attention was focused not only on sentencing outcomes but also on sentencing *procedure*. Galan's counsel had moved for a bifurcation of the penalty phase, proposing that the hearing be further divided into an eligibility phase and a selection phase. The attorneys argued that the jury should be required to deem Galan eligible for a death sentence before hearing "the emotional mitigation and possible non-statutory aggravation evidence" that it would ultimately have to weigh in order to determine whether to spare the man's life.[28] In other words, counsel feared that the jury would be unduly prejudiced if allowed to hear victim-impact testimony and other potentially inflammatory information or evidence when deciding the threshold issue of whether death should even be an option. The government, without much argument, agreed to the division, and Judge Carr granted the motion.[29]

As a result of the bifurcated penalty phase, the jury first heard evidence related to whether Galan was eligible for the death penalty. Ultimately, the jurors found that the government had proven beyond a reasonable doubt that he was at least eighteen at the time of the offense, that he had intentionally killed both victims, and that there existed at least one statutory aggravating factor. In fact, the jury found three: the murders were committed after substantial planning and premeditation, the murders were committed with the expectation of receiving something of pecuniary value, and Galan had killed more than one person in a single criminal episode.[30] After finding the defendant eligible for death, in the selection phase of the penalty hearing the jury heard mitigation evidence regarding his parents' emotional abandonment; his childhood in an environment rife with drug abuse and use; and his lack of criminal convictions, among other evidence from victims about the impact of Galan's crime. The jury then retired to weigh all the aggravating factors against the mitigating ones and determine whether the aggravating factors sufficiently outweighed any of the mitigating factors such that death was justified. On December 15, 2007, the jury elected to spare a death-eligible federal defendant's life. At sentencing, Judge Carr spoke candidly about his opinion of the jury's verdict, admitting that he "was pleased" that the jurors declined to impose a death sentence.[31] Reflecting on the experience of presiding over a capital case, Judge Carr characterized it as emotional and difficult, noting a "level of intensity and attentiveness and commitment" that was unlike other cases. As he bluntly stated, "I think that we all kind of put ourselves in higher gear."[32]

The Case against Antun Lewis—Cleveland's Deadliest Fire

The third federal death penalty case in the Northern District of Ohio stemmed from a May 2005 arson in Cleveland that trapped and killed nine people in a house fire. Eight of those killed were children, some of whom had been invited to the home for a slumber party. Immediately following the tragedy, rumors swirled concerning who could have committed such a terrible crime. Pressure in the community for police to find the perpetrator was high—so high, in fact, that one rumored suspect, Antun Lewis, turned himself in to police on unrelated warrants for "fear that the community would take its anger out on him."[33] For three years, the investigation lagged as disagreements arose over who would investigate the crime and prosecute the eventual suspect and how matters would proceed.

Police and prosecutors ultimately harbored the same suspicions as the community, and on October 1, 2008, a federal grand jury indicted Lewis. In early 2009, Attorney General Eric Holder Jr. approved the prosecutors' plans to seek the death penalty,[34] and Lewis became the third federal capital case to be initiated in the Northern District. Following Lewis's indictment, the first question to arise concerned the basis for the federal government's jurisdiction over an arson. Interestingly, jurisdiction was premised on the fact that the federal government subsidized the lease agreement on the home, which prosecutors argued effectively involved the house in interstate commerce.[35] Given the attenuated federal interest, there was concern regarding why the government decided to bring charges in federal court. The speculation ranged from the belief that a federal trial brought more resources to the belief that a federal jury pool—consisting of individuals from outside the largely black urban area where the crime took place—would be more inclined to impose death. Yet as Kevin McNally, director of the Federal Death Penalty Resource Counsel Project, explained, even though it was extremely rare for a death penalty case to be prosecuted under interstate commerce law, it was unlikely that questions of federal jurisdiction would consume the jurors. "They're looking at the kids that died . . . not whether there's a technical element of a federal offense."[36]

Judge Solomon Oliver was selected to preside over Lewis's capital proceedings. As in the case of Galan, Lewis's three court-appointed attorneys immediately filed several motions in an effort to stymie the prosecution's attempt to seek a death sentence. Counsel filed one particular motion that the Northern District had seen before—a motion to bifurcate jury deliberations. Virtually identical in intent to the motion in Galan's case, the motion from Lewis's counsel requested that Judge Oliver create two phases within the penalty portion of the trial: a death penalty eligibility phase, in the event of a guilty verdict, and a sentencing determination phase. Unlike in the Galan case, however, Lewis's counsel met with great resistance from the U.S. Attorney's Office, which filed a memorandum opposing Lewis's proposed division on the grounds that a bifurcated sentencing would waste judicial resources, confuse jurors, and unnecessarily delay the proceedings. The U.S. Attorney's Office ultimately asserted that any division was simply neither sanctioned nor envisioned by the FDPA.

Given the federal prosecutors' acquiescence to a bifurcated sentencing proceeding in Thomas Galan' case, such vigorous opposition only a few years later came as a surprise to some, but perhaps the about-face was not so unexpected. Although whether to bifurcate the penalty phase of Galan's trial was not a hotly contested matter, this had not always been the case in other districts. For example, in *United States v. Johnson*,[37] one of the principal cases upon which Lewis's attorneys relied, the defendant's request for the same bifurcation that both Galan and Lewis sought became the "most contentious" pretrial issue before the district court. In *Johnson*, the government opposed the motion on the grounds that further division of the penalty phase was contrary to the federal statute. But the district court relied on its gatekeeping power and the belief that there was a great potential for undue prejudice to the defendant in granting the motion. Despite the increasing use of a bifurcated capital penalty phase in federal cases, some courts and legal academics have agreed with the position of the government in *Lewis* and concluded that not only is the further division of federal capital-sentencing proceedings not constitutionally required, it is also impermissible under the plain language of the FDPA, which refers to a singular penalty hearing.[38] Ultimately, Judge Oliver determined that a bifurcated sentencing proceeding was not constitutionally mandated, as Lewis claimed, but he did agree that employing such a procedure was within his discretionary power. And in "balancing" the considerations set forth by both Lewis and the government, the judge concluded that "the concern regarding waste and efficiency" was "substantially outweighed by the risk of unfair prejudice to the Defendant." He granted Lewis's motion.[39]

As Lewis's trial loomed, defense counsel filed an additional, ultimately dispositive motion in an effort to change the status of the case from a capital one: the defense moved for a pretrial determination by the court as to whether Lewis's "mental retardation" precluded the government from even seeking death.[40] During a six-day hearing in October 2010, both parties presented testimony from over a dozen witnesses detailing everything from Lewis's poor academic record and his mother's prenatal habits to his IQ score of 70 and the results of a brain scan.[41] Naturally, the parties disagreed on the significance of the information that the testimony revealed, but in an incredibly thorough, forty-nine-page order, Judge Oliver concluded that Lewis had shown "by a preponderance of the evidence, that he [was] intellectually disabled or mentally retarded"; accordingly, a sentence of death could not be constitutionally imposed.[42] In early 2011, a jury convicted Lewis of arson, but the government's third attempt to seek death in the Northern District had failed.[43]

These Different Cases' Common Ground

Looking at the three cases in which the attorney general has authorized federal prosecutors to pursue the death penalty in the Northern District of Ohio, it is hard to find much in common other than their timing—the indictments were all issued since 2006. But perhaps the key to why they became capital cases actually depends on their relative recency. A U.S. Department of Justice report issued in September 2000 showed a pronounced geographic disparity in the number of death penalty cases that U.S. attorneys submitted to the attorney general for review and the number of cases in which permission to seek a capital sentence was authorized. Essentially, the study revealed that a small number of mostly southern districts were responsible for handling the majority of the federal death penalty litigation. From 1995 to 2000, forty-two percent of U.S. attorney recommendations to seek capital punishment came from just five of the ninety-four federal districts. Twenty-one districts had never submitted a case to be reviewed by the attorney general, and forty of the ninety-four districts that had submitted a case for review always recommended against seeking the death penalty. The Northern District of Ohio fit this latter category. During the relevant time period, the U.S. Attorney's Office from the Northern District of Ohio had submitted four cases to the attorney general for review but ultimately recommended not seeking death in any of them.[44] As Ohio State University law professor Douglas Berman observed in response to questions about the Galan and Moonda cases from a reporter for the *Toledo Blade*: "The rising number of federal cases being prosecuted as capital offenses comes down to a question of 'fairness.' While federal prosecutors in many southern states have sought the death penalty systematically and periodically, northern prosecutors have tended not to use the statute as often. . . . It was a realization that came to light at the start of the Bush Administration. . . . And it was one that led to an increased number of capital cases emerging in northern states."[45]

It is certainly debatable whether "fairness" requires the districts that have seldom sought capital sentences to ratchet up death penalty prosecutions, as opposed to having those districts that frequently seek such sentences refrain from doing so. But regardless of why these cases became the first capital cases in the Northern District, it is clear that the district has been affected by them. The cases have provided judges in the Northern District of Ohio with a greater wealth of knowledge regarding the mechanics of death penalty litigation and the capital sentences that they review with great frequency by way of petitions for writs of habeas corpus. Beyond that, *Moonda* and *Galan* also led to the institution of a new unit within the Federal Public Defender's Office—the Capital Habeas Unit. The unit not only is tasked with litigating the federal death penalty cases filed in Ohio but is now the Northern District of Ohio's "first option when appointing lawyers for state-convicted death row inmates whose appeals have reached the federal level."[46] By employing attorneys "intimately familiar with the federal system," the unit hopes to maintain a high level of advocacy in death penalty cases. Another impetus behind the development of the specialized unit was simple economics. The litigation of Moonda's trial with court-appointed attorneys from the private bar cost taxpayers at least $482,911 in attorneys fees and expert costs, and Galan's case cost over $300,000.[47] As the federal public defender for the Northern District, Dennis G. Terez, explained, unlike attorneys from the private bar, public defenders are not paid on a per case basis, "so the federal government at least gets a bigger bang for their buck."[48]

Habeas Corpus Litigation

An overview of death penalty litigation in the Northern District of Ohio would not be complete without mention of death-sentenced state prisoners' petitions for writs of habeas corpus. Habeas corpus is a civil proceeding where a *state* prisoner who has exhausted his or her remedies in state court brings a claim in *federal* court alleging that he or she is being held in violation of the U.S. Constitution. If the federal court determines that a state prisoner's rights have been violated, then it can issue a writ of habeas corpus requiring that the state court either retry or resentence the alleged offender, depending on the type and magnitude of the constitutional error. It is through this mechanism that prisoners who have been sentenced to death under Ohio's death penalty statute can— and frequently do—challenge in federal court the constitutionality of their convictions and death sentences in the Northern District of Ohio.

Ohio's History of Capital Punishment

The death penalty is imposed much more frequently in the Ohio state courts than in their federal counterparts. Ohio's use of the death penalty began with its statehood in 1803 and continued apace until the U.S. Supreme Court's decision in *Furman*, which the Ohio Supreme Court, in *Vargas v. Metzger*,[49] interpreted as invalidating its then operative capital punishment scheme. Following *Gregg*, Ohio attempted to amend its statute by setting forth a limited number of statutory mitigating factors that a jury could consider in deciding whether to impose death. In *Lockett v. Ohio*,[50] however, the Supreme Court held this limitation on mitigation was unconstitutional, again thwarting Ohio's use of capital punishment. In 1981, after a debate spanning several legislative sessions, the Ohio legislature passed a new statute reinstating the death penalty in the state. Since then, the general statutory scheme has remained largely unchanged.[51]

Capital Habeas Litigation

Prior to 1991, challenges to state-based death sentences in the Northern District of Ohio were virtually nonexistent. Although the writ of habeas corpus was extended to allow state prisoners to challenge their convictions in federal court in 1867, there were substantial limitations on what precisely was cognizable on review. It was not until the middle of the twentieth century that the Supreme

Court extended the scope of the writ to encompass the types of constitutional challenges that are frequent today.[52] In addition to the availability of the writ, the ever-changing Supreme Court jurisprudence on the constitutionality of capital punishment throughout the 1970s also helps explain the lack of filings during that period. When *Furman* was decided, those individuals who were on death row—poised to file federal challenges—saw their death sentences morph into terms of life imprisonment. And for those individuals who had been sentenced to death under the statute that the Supreme Court invalidated in *Lockett*, the same commutations occurred.[53] Thus, any habeas petition that would have started out as a challenge to a death sentence prior to 1972 turned into a challenge to a sentence of life.[54] But when those inmates sentenced within the first years of Ohio's 1981 capital punishment statute started exhausting their state court appeals, the number of capital habeas petitions increased dramatically. In fact, as of March 2012, 103 state prisoners sentenced to death under the 1981 statute have filed petitions for writs of habeas corpus in the Northern District, and there are at least fifteen additional cases ripe for federal review.[55]

Two of the earliest petitions to reach the Northern District—and to be resolved on the merits—were those of David Mapes and John Glenn, both filed in 1991. Both petitioners' federal appeals ultimately led to their removal from death row. Glenn was convicted in Ohio state court for the murder of a deputy sheriff, who was shot as Glenn helped his brother's escape from a patrol car. The crime occurred just three days after the effective date of Ohio's 1981 capital-sentencing statute, and the jury wasted no time in imposing a death sentence. Following the exhaustion of his state appeals, Glenn filed his petition for habeas corpus, arguing that he failed to receive effective assistance of counsel at the penalty phase of his trial because the jury was given virtually no mitigating information about his background, his character, and, most disturbingly, his organic brain damage. Somewhat prophetically, Glenn's claim was one that has resurfaced in the majority of the habeas petitions filed in the Northern District. In a strange twist of fate, Glenn's case was assigned to Judge Dowd. Ultimately, the judge, who adjudicated the petition with no case law yet in place concerning the bifurcated statutory scheme from the governing circuit, denied the writ of habeas corpus, but the Sixth Circuit reversed. Glenn was removed from death row on December 21, 1995.[56]

Like Glenn, Mapes also succeeded in having his death sentence vacated as a result of his federal proceedings, although Mapes's challenge would not be as swift as Glenn's. Mapes had been convicted in Ohio state court of the 1983 aggravated murder of the owner of a bar in Cleveland during an armed robbery. Because Mapes had been convicted previously of a 1972 murder in New Jersey, the Ohio conviction made him eligible for the death penalty. Counsel attempted to introduce some mitigation evidence regarding the New Jersey murder, but the state trial court prohibited the jury from considering this evidence when deciding on a sentence. Finding no relief in state court, Mapes filed a petition for habeas corpus raising fifteen potential bases for relief, including a challenge to his appellate counsel's failure to raise the trial court's evidentiary limitation on appeal.[57] Judge Frank J. Battisti granted a stay of execution pending the resolution of the federal appeal. After almost five years of litigation, in September 1996 Judge Solomon Oliver Jr. adopted the recommendation of Magistrate Judge Jack B. Streepy, who had been handling the case, and conditionally granted Mapes the writ based on ineffective assistance of appellate counsel. Ultimately, the Sixth Circuit affirmed,[58] and Mapes was removed from death row.

Predictably, however, most death-sentenced inmates who have filed petitions for habeas corpus in the Northern District have not fared as well as Glenn and Mapes. In fact, a March 2012 analysis of the petitions filed in the Northern District of Ohio since 1991 indicates that the judges on the court have granted the writ in only seventeen of the more than one hundred cases. The grounds for granting the writ have encompassed a variety of constitutional errors, including ineffective assistance of counsel, faulty jury instructions, withholding of exculpatory or impeachment evidence, violations of the petitioner's right to confront the witnesses against him, and insufficient evidence. Of those seventeen cases where the writ was granted, the Sixth Circuit affirmed in nine instances: eight of these resulted in the petitioner's removal from death row, and in the other, the Sixth Circuit affirmed the grant of the writ only to be reversed by the Supreme Court. In five of the seventeen cases, however, the Sixth Circuit reversed the district court's grant of the writ, and one case is currently on appeal. In the final two of the seventeen cases, the petitions were dismissed after the district court's favorable grants—one by mutual agreement of the parties, resulting in the petitioner being resentenced to life without the possibility of parole, and the second because the petitioner died of natural causes while in custody.

Of the eighty-six other petitioners that have come before the Northern District, as of March 2012, seventeen have proceedings pending before various judges, whether they be awaiting discovery, evidentiary hearings, or the conclusion of miscellaneous proceedings in state courts. In the cases of the remaining death-sentenced inmates, however, the various district judges have denied the petitioners relief. In fourteen of those cases, the Sixth Circuit disagreed with the district court's denials of the writ and reversed. Of those fourteen reversals, nine petitioners have been removed from death row. But in three cases, the Supreme Court in turn reversed the Sixth Circuit, affirming the district court's denial of the writ. In the final two cases, one petitioner awaits a new penalty phase in state court while the other awaits the state's appeal.

As apparent from the Sixth Circuit appellate history of the petitions upon which the judges of the Northern District have opined, reasonable minds can differ as to an appropriate resolution. Not surprisingly, then, several of these cases have made their way to the Supreme Court. One of the first was the case of Robert Buell.[59] Buell was convicted of murdering a young girl and sentenced to death in 1984. Just five days before his scheduled execution, he filed a petition for a writ of habeas corpus, which was assigned to Judge Paul R. Matia. Matia "reluctantly" granted a stay of execution, notwithstanding the fact that Buell's counsel had "deliberately waited until literally hours before the execution to begin the federal court procedures." He then dismissed Buell's petition without prejudice so that the defendant could bring an ineffective assistance of counsel claim in state court. The state court denied the claim, and the Supreme Court denied review. Buell again waited for the state of Ohio to set his execution date before initiating a second set of federal court proceedings. This time, Judge Matia refused to stay Buell's execution, finding it "inexcusable" that he had done "nothing for more than one year" before returning to federal court and giving notice of his intent to file a habeas petition less than two months prior to his execution date. The Sixth Circuit disagreed, however, and entered a stay.

The state immediately appealed to the Supreme Court, seeking to vacate the stay. Although a majority of the Court declined to do so, the Sixth Circuit's decision garnered a sharp rebuke from Justice Antonin Scalia on the grounds that it had "acted effectively without explanation and without any reference to the inequitable conduct described by the District Court."[60] Ultimately, Buell's petition for a writ of habeas corpus was denied by both Judge Matia and the Sixth Circuit, and he was executed on September 24, 2002, a little over ten years to the day after Judge Matia reluctantly granted his first stay. For those legislators concerned about the continual delay in state executions at the hands of the federal government, cases such as Buell's became rallying cries for an overhaul of habeas corpus review. In response, in 1996 Congress passed the Antiterrorism and Effective Death Penalty Act (AEDPA) to combat the "acute problems of unnecessary delay and abuse in capital cases." AEDPA imposed time limits and other procedural restrictions on filing petitions, and it mandated greater federal court deference to claims previously adjudicated in the state forum.[61]

Federal habeas corpus proceedings for petitioners in the Northern District of Ohio have not been the only way for an inmate to escape a death sentence, however, as the case of John Spirko illustrates. Spirko was convicted of aggravated murder and sentenced to death in 1984. Judge James G. Carr denied his petition for habeas corpus on July 11, 2000, concluding that none of Spirko's fifteen claims of alleged constitutional error had merit. On appeal, a divided panel of the Sixth Circuit affirmed, with Judge Ronald Lee Gilman dissenting. In his dissent, Judge Gilman highlighted the wealth of evidence that the prosecution had withheld from the defense during Spirko's trial and concluded that the proper course of action would have been for the court to remand the case to the district court for an evidentiary hearing on this claim. "We are dealing," Judge Gilman stated, "with a capital case where the defendant's conviction and death sentence rest on relatively weak evidence."[62] In 2008, Governor Ted Strickland echoed these sentiments, and in light of "the lack of physical evidence" tying Spirko to the murder "as well as the slim residual doubt about his responsibility," he commuted Spirko's sentence to life without parole.[63] Apparently, reservations about the man's guilt extended beyond the Sixth Circuit and Governor Strickland, as Judge Carr revealed when asked about his involvement in the case: "To speak very candidly, I cannot say that I am without doubt or reservation about Spirko's guilt for that murder, so it seemed to me that Governor Strickland did the right thing, which is the Governor's job to do. It is not my job as a district judge to monkey with the process."[64]

Notwithstanding the fact that there have been relatively few *federal* death penalty cases tried in the Northern District of Ohio, given its location in one of the most prolific capital-sentencing states in the nation the district certainly has seen its share of capital cases on review by way of writs of habeas corpus. Although the stakes for these state-based cases as compared to the federal ones are the same—ultimately, a potential death sentence—they pose distinct dilemmas for the judges and the community in the district. Unlike capital cases originating in the federal system, where the often-posed, albeit nonlegal, question has been *why* this case? and *why* this defendant? when reviewing a state court sentence, the initial *why* is replaced with *was it proper?* As more appeals from Ohio state convictions continue to percolate through the system—convictions stemming from as far back as 1998—the federal review of state death sentences will continue, and the judges in the district will be tasked with determining whether a constitutional error of such magnitude has occurred that vacation of a death sentence is required. But regardless of what type of capital case the Northern District of Ohio faces, the responsibility of ensuring a legally justifiable outcome is an awesome one, requiring judges to wrangle not only with difficult and sometimes novel legal concepts but also with personal views about what is right. Ultimately, however, as Judge Carr stated, the goal is to apply the law to the case at hand and avoid the temptation to substitute personal views about what is right. There should be no monkeying with the process.

Notes

1. The Fifth Amendment demands, "No person shall be held to answer for a *capital* . . . crime, unless on presentment or indictment of a Grand Jury" and further protects against the deprivation "of *life* . . . without due process of law." U.S. Const. amend. V (emphases added).

2. An Act for the Punishment of Certain Crimes against the United States, 1 Stat. 112, 112–17, ch. 9, §§ 1, 3, 8, 14, 23 (1790).

3. An Act to Reduce the Cases in Which the Penalty of Death May Be Inflicted, 29 Stat. 487, ch. 29 (1897); see also Winston v. United States, 172 U.S. 303, 313 (1899) (upholding the constitutionality of the act's dedication of discretion to the jury). For a fuller history of the federal death penalty, see Rory K. Little, "The Federal Death Penalty: History and Some Thoughts about the Department of Justice's Role," *Fordham Urban Law Journal* 26 (March 1999): 360–69, and Christopher Q. Cutler, "Death Resurrected: The Reimplementation of the Federal Death Penalty," *Seattle University Law Review* 23 (Spring 2000): 1192–95.

4. Furman v. Georgia, 408 U.S. 238 (1972).

5. Gregg v. Georgia, 428 U.S. 153 (1976).

6. Continuing Criminal Enterprise, Pub. L. No. 100–690, § 7001(a), 102 Stat. 4181, 4387 (codified at 21 U.S.C. § 848 [1988]); see also Cutler, "Death Resurrected," 1200–8, for a detailed description of the act.

7. Federal Death Penalty Act of 1994, Pub. L. No. 103–322, § 60001–26, 108 Stat. 1796 (codified at 18 U.S.C. 3591 [1994]); see also Little, "Federal Death Penalty," 388–406; Cutler, "Death Resurrected," 1209–16. For current information on individuals sentenced to death under these federal statutes, see Death Penalty Information Center, Federal Death Penalty, available at http://www.deathpenaltyinfo.org/federal-death-penalty.

8. United States v. Moonda, 347 F. App'x 192, 194–97 (6th Cir. 2009).

9. Cary Snyder, "Damian Bradford Admits in Federal Court He Killed Dr. Moonda," *Herald* (Sharon, Pa.), July 24, 2006; Milan Simonich, "Jury Learns of Moonda's Refusal to Testify; Killer Says Cohort's Silence Caused Him to Plead Guilty, Turn against Her," *Pittsburgh Post-Gazette*, June 27, 2007; press release, U.S. Attorney's Office for the Northern District of Ohio, July 24, 2007; Jim Carney, "Plea Deal Paves Way for Wife's Arrest in Killing," *Akron Beacon Journal*, July 25, 2007; Damian G. Guevara, "Plea Deal, New Charge in Doctor's Death," *Cleveland Plain Dealer*, July 25, 2006.

10. United States v. Moonda, No. 1:06 CR 0395, Government's Notice of Intent to Seek Death Penalty, at 3 (on file with author) (setting forth the government's justifications for seeking the death penalty); Joe Milicia, "Wife Who Hired Hit Man Spared Death Penalty,"

Cincinnati Post, July 19, 2007 ("Assistant U.S. Attorney Linda Barr said Moonda deserved a death sentence because she had her husband killed for the worst possible reason: money.").

11. Milan Simonich, "Pursuit of Death Penalty in Moonda Case Surprises Attorney," *Pittsburgh Post-Gazette,* September 24, 2006. For a discussion concerning the imposition of capital sentences on females, particularly in Ohio, see Victor L. Streib, *The Fairer Death: Executing Women in Ohio* (Athens: Ohio University Press, 2006), and Gabrielle Banks, "Could Donna Moonda Join a Rare Breed on Death Row?" *Pittsburgh Post-Gazette,* July 16, 2007.

12. United States v. Moonda, No. 1:06 CR 395, 2006 WL 2990517, at *2 (N.D. Ohio October 18, 2006) (unpublished memorandum opinion).

13. The district court "death qualifies" a jury by excluding persons whose opposition to the death penalty would prevent them from sentencing anyone to death. See Lockhart v. McCree, 476 U.S. 162, 165 (1986).

14. The Honorable David D. Dowd Jr., district court judge for the Northern District of Ohio, interview by the author, June 16, 2010.

15. Both federal death penalty statutes mandate that capital proceedings be bifurcated into a guilt/merits phase and a penalty/mitigation phase. During the guilt phase, the jury determines whether the government has proven beyond a reasonable doubt all of the elements of a charged crime. During the penalty phase, the jury decides whether an individual is eligible for the death penalty and whether he or she should be put to death. To deem an individual eligible for a death sentence, a jury must find certain facts unanimously and beyond a reasonable doubt, including a statutory aggravating circumstance—or a fact that intensifies or makes worse the underlying crime. See 18 U.S.C. § 3591(a) (age); ibid., § 3591(a)(2)(A)–(D) (intent-based factors); ibid., § 3592(c) (statutory aggravating factors); and Ring v. Arizona, 536 U.S. 584, 585–87 (2002). If the jury finds that a defendant is death eligible, then the jury must weigh the aggravating factors (both statutory and nonstatutory) against the mitigating factors. See 18 U.S.C. § 3593(e). Although nonstatutory aggravating factors must be unanimously found by the jury beyond a reasonable doubt, the defendant has the burden of proving mitigating factors by a preponderance of the evidence. Ibid., § 3593(c). If the jury finds at least one mitigating factor, then it decides whether all the aggravating factors "sufficiently outweigh" the mitigating factor(s). Ibid., § 3593(e). After balancing, the jury, by a unanimous vote, must recommend death, life imprisonment without possibility of release, or some other lesser sentence.

16. Moonda, 347 F. App'x 192; Milan Simonich, "Prosecutors Chip Away at Donna Moonda's Truthfulness," *Pittsburgh Post-Gazette,* June 20, 2007; Michael Hasch, "Donna Moonda's Ex-lover Details Murder Plot," *Tribune-Review* (Akron, Ohio), June 26, 2007; Karl Turner, "Jurors Find Donna Moonda Guilty," *Cleveland Plain Dealer,* July 6, 2007.

17. Dowd interview.

18. United States v. Moonda, No. 1:06 CR 395, 2007 WL 2071924, at *1 (N.D. Ohio July 13, 2007) (unpublished). See also Milan Simonich, "Donna Moonda: Too Happy a Childhood?" *Pittsburgh Post-Gazette,* July 18, 2007.

19. Editorial, "Fitting Punishment," *Pittsburgh Post-Gazette,* July 21, 2007; Dowd, interview.

20. Milan Simonich, "Moonda Triggerman Sentenced to 17½ Years behind Bars," *Pittsburgh Post-Gazette,* July 12, 2007.

21. United States v. Moonda, No. 1:06 CR 0395, Jury Verdict Form (on file with author). See also Milan Simonich, "Moonda Gets Life in Husband's Murder," *Pittsburgh Post-Gazette,* July 19, 2007, describing interviews with jurors where several expressed the inability to support a death sentence for Moonda when Bradford received a relatively light sentence.

22. Dowd, interview.

23. Paula Reed Ward, "Death Sentences Rare in Federal Cases," *Pittsburgh Post-Gazette*, October 28, 2007.

24. Erica Blake, "Federal Court in Toledo to Try Its First Capital Case: Fostoria Man Charged in 1996 Drug-Related Killing," *Toledo Blade*, September 30, 2007; Blake, "Prosecutor Says Brothers Shot over Drug Debt," *Toledo Blade*, October 24, 2007.

25. United States v. Galan, No. 3:06 CR 730, Second Superseding Indictment (on file with author); United States v. Galan, No. 3:06 CR 730, Government's Notice of Intent to Seek Death Penalty, November 14, 2006 (on file with author).

26. United States v. Galan, No. 3:06 CR 730, 2007 WL 2902908, at *1 (N.D. Ohio October 2, 2007) (unpublished order); see also United States v. Galan, No. 3:06 CR 730, Defendant's Motion to Strike the Possibility of the Death Penalty Due to the Unconstitutionality of the Federal Death Penalty Act of 1994, January 31, 2007 (on file with author); United States v. Galan, No. 3:06 CR 730, Government's Consolidated Reply to Defendant Galan's Motion Re: Death Penalty Statute, April 20, 2007 (on file with author); United States v. Galan, No. 3:06 CR 730, Motion to Preclude the Government from Seeking Death Penalty (*Apprendi* Violation), May 30, 2007 (on file with author).

27. The Honorable James G. Carr, U.S. district judge for the Northern District of Ohio, interview by the author, June 28, 2010.

28. United States v. Galan, No. 3:06 CR 730, Defendant Galan's Motion for Bifurcation of the Penalty Phase of Trial, November 9, 2007, at 2 (on file with author).

29. The Honorable Alegnon L. Marbley, a federal district court judge in the U.S. District Court for the Southern District of Ohio, employed the first bifurcated sentencing proceeding for a federal capital case tried in Ohio in *United States v. Mayhew*, 380 F. Supp. 2d 936 (S.D. Ohio 2005). See also United States v. Henderson, 485 F. Supp. 2d. 831, 871–72 (S.D. Ohio 2007).

30. United States v. Galan, No. 3:06 CR 730, Jury Verdict Form, December 12, 2007 (on file with author).

31. United States v. Galan, No. 3:06 CR 730, Transcript of Sentencing Proceeding, January 29, 2009 (on file with author).

32. Carr, interview.

33. Gabriel Baird, "Cleveland's Deadliest House Fire Still Unsolved," *Cleveland Plain Dealer*, September 1, 2005; Baird, "Mourning Becomes Anger on News of Arson Report," *Cleveland Plain Dealer*, June 2, 2005.

34. In an effort to reduce geographic disparity and achieve national consistency in the use of the death penalty, the U.S. Department of Justice created a formal "capital case review" process in 1995. This process seeks to centralize federal death penalty prosecutions by requiring U.S. Attorney's Offices across the states to obtain the attorney general's approval to seek a death sentence. The system is described in the U.S. Department of Justice's report, *The Federal Death Penalty System: Supplementary Data, Analysis and Revised Protocols for Capital Case Review* (June 6, 2001), 7, and the U.S. Attorneys' Manual, chap. 9, Capital Crimes, §§ 9–10.010 to 9–10.190, available at http://www.justice.gov/usao/eousa/foia_reading_room/usam/title9/10mcrm.htm. For a discussion of the benefits and shortcomings of the review process, see Little, "Federal Death Penalty," 406. For an up-to-date list of federal capital trials and executions, see Death Penalty Resource Counsel, Federal Death Penalty, available at http://www.capdefnet.org/fdprc/pubmenu.aspx?menu_id=94&id=2094.

35. John Caniglia, "East 87th Arson Witness Is Felon with History of Lying," *Cleveland Plain Dealer*, November 17, 2008; Caniglia, "In Letter, Man Denies That He Set Fatal Fire," *Cleveland Plain Dealer*, October 15, 2008.

36. Thomas J. Sheeran, "Rare Federal Death Penalty Sought in Ohio Fire," *Associated Press*, August 12, 2010.

37. United States v. Johnson, 362 F. Supp. 2d 1043 (N.D. Iowa 2005).

38. See Michael D. Pepson and John N. Sharifi, "Two Wrongs Don't Make a Right: Federal Death Eligibility Determinations and Judicial Trifurcations," *Akron Law Review* 43 (2010): 1–49, and Margo A. Rocklin, "Place the Death Penalty on a Tripod, or Make It Stand on Its Own Two Feet," *Rutgers Journal of Law and Public Policy* 4 (Fall 2007): 788–810, for a discussion of the debate surrounding capital proceeding bifurcation and recent cases.

39. United States v. Lewis, No. 1:08 CR 404, Order, May 10, 2010 (on file with author).

40. Upon a court's finding of "mental retardation," the Eighth Amendment to the U.S. Constitution and 18 U.S.C. § 3596(c) prohibit the imposition of death. See also Atkins v. Virginia, 536 U.S. 304 (2002).

41. Leila Atassi, "Death Penalty Ruled Out for Trial in Arson That Killed 9; Defendant in Case Is Retarded, Judge Says," *Cleveland Plain Dealer*, December 28, 2010.

42. United States v. Lewis, No. 1:08 CR 404, Order, December 23, 2010 (on file with author).

43. In February 2012, Judge Oliver granted Lewis's motion for a new trial on the grounds that the verdict was against the manifest weight of the evidence.

44. U.S. Department of Justice, *The Federal Death Penalty System: A Statistical Survey (1988–2000)* (September 12, 2000).

45. Blake, "Federal Court in Toledo."

46. Reginald Fields, "U.S. Units to Tackle Capital Cases; Public Defenders' Offices to Grow," *Cleveland Plain Dealer*, February 6, 2008.

47. Michael Hasch, "Moonda Defense Cost Taxpayers Nearly $500K, Court Report Shows," *Pittsburgh Tribune Review*, December 28, 2007; Milan Simonich, "Moonda Defense Costs Taxpayers $438,000; Court Appointed Lawyers She Couldn't Afford," *Pittsburgh Post-Gazette*, December 28, 2007; Bill Wekselman, editorial, "Costly Death Defense," *Pittsburgh Post-Gazette*, January 9, 2008 ("This is another illustration of how expensive the death penalty is. If Mrs. Moonda had simply faced a life sentence, the defense would have been less complicated and less costly.").

48. Fields, "U.S. Units to Tackle Capital Cases."

49. Vargas v. Metzger, 298 N.E.2d 600 (Ohio 1973).

50. Lockett v. Ohio, 438 U.S. 586 (1978).

51. There have been several notable alterations. In 1995, for example, one level of direct appeal was eliminated, and cases involving crimes committed after that date now move directly to the Supreme Court of Ohio. Additionally, in November 2001, Ohio eliminated the electric chair as an execution option, and lethal injection was deemed the sole method of execution. For a more complete discussion of Ohio's use of capital punishment and its various death penalty statutes, see, e.g., Andrew Welsh-Huggins, *No Winners Here Tonight: Race, Politics, and Geography in One of the Country's Busiest Death Penalty States* (Athens: Ohio University Press, 2009); David L. Hoeffel, "Ohio's Death Penalty: History and Current Developments," *Capital University Law Review* 31 (2003): 659–90; American Bar Association, *Evaluating Fairness and Accuracy in State Death Penalty Systems: The Ohio Death Penalty Assessment Report* (September 2007), 9–52, available at http://www.americanbar.org/content/dam/aba/migrated/moratorium/assessmentproject/ohio/finalreport.authcheckdam.pdf.

52. Ex parte Hawk, 321 U.S. 114, 118 (1994); Brown v. Allen, 344 U.S. 443, 485–87 (1953); Fay v. Noia, 372 U.S. 391 (1963). For a complete history of the writ of habeas corpus, see Cary Federman, *The Body and the State: Habeas Corpus and American Jurisprudence* (Albany: State University of New York Press, 2006); Eric M. Freedman, *Habeas Corpus: Rethinking the Great Writ of Liberty* (New York: New York University Press, 2001); Paul D. Halliday, *Habeas Corpus: From England to Empire*, (Cambridge, Mass.: Belknap Press of

Harvard University Press, 2010). For statistics on the increase in habeas petitions across the district courts, see, e.g., Nancy J. King, Fred L. Cheesman II, and Brian Ostrom, *Final Technical Report: Habeas Litigation in U.S. District Courts* (August 21, 2007), available at https://www.ncjrs.gov/pdffiles1/nij/grants/219559.pdf. Fred L. Cheesman II, Roger A. Hanson, and Brian J. Ostrom, "A Tale of Two Laws: The U.S. Congress Confronts Habeas Corpus Petitions and Section 1983 Lawsuits," *Law & Policy* 22 (April 2000): 89, 93.

53. When *Furman* was decided, 65 inmates' sentences were reduced to life in prison. At the time the Supreme Court decided *Lockett*, 120 individuals had their sentences commuted. Ohio Department of Rehabilitation and Correction, Capital Punishment in Ohio, available at http://www.drc.state.oh.us/public/capital.htm.

54. One good example is the case of Patricia Wernert. Wernert was found guilty by an Ohio jury of two counts of aggravated murder, and the jury recommended death. Although her conviction was upheld on appeal, the Ohio courts vacated her sentence in light of *Lockett*, and her petition for habeas corpus was thus a challenge to a term of life in prison. Wernert v. Arn, 819 F.3d 613 (6th Cir. 1987). For a detailed history of Wernert's case, see Streib, *Fairer Death*.

55. The calculation of the number of inmates who have filed in the Northern District does not include individuals whose cases were subsequently transferred to another jurisdiction before adjudication, pursuant to the general policy that habeas corpus petitions be handled in the district of the petitioner's conviction.

56. Glenn v. Tate, 71 F.3d 1204 (6th Cir. 1995).

57. Mapes argued that his death sentence was invalid under the Supreme Court's decision in *Eddings v. Oklahoma,* 455 U.S. 104, 100 (1982), which held that the Constitution forbids a sentencer from being "precluded from considering, as a mitigating factor, any aspect of a defendant's character or record and any of the circumstances of the offense that the defendant proffers as a basis for a sentence less than death."

58. Mapes v. Coyle, 171 F.3d 408 (1999); Mapes v. Tate, 388 F.3d 187 (2004).

59. In addition to *Buell,* as of March 2012, five other capital habeas cases from the Northern District have made their way to the Supreme Court—the cases of Gregory Esparza, Kenneth Richey, Frank Spisak, Harry Mitts Jr., and Archie Dixon—and all of them have involved several rounds of opinions, appeals, and remands. The district court granted Esparza's habeas petition on four grounds, and the Sixth Circuit affirmed as to one but did not opine on the remainder. The Supreme Court unanimously reversed the Sixth Circuit, but like the Sixth Circuit, the Court declined to address the additional grounds upon which relief was granted. Thus, almost ten years after first granting the writ, the case is back in the Northern District to determine whether Esparza is still entitled to relief on any other ground. Esparza v. Mitchell, 310 F.3d 414 (6th Cir. 2002); Mitchell v. Esparza, 540 U.S. 12 (2003). *Richey* made its way from the district court to the Supreme Court and back again, ultimately resulting in the vacation of Richey's death sentence based on ineffective assistance of counsel. See Richey v. Mitchell, 395 F.3d 660 (6th Cir. 2005); Bradshaw v. Richey, 546 U.S. 74 (2005); Richey v. Bradshaw, 498 F.3d 344 (6th Cir. 2007). In *Spisak, Mitts,* and *Dixon,* the district courts denied the petitions but were reversed by the Sixth Circuit, which was itself reversed by the Supreme Court. Spisak v. Mitchell, 465 F.3d 684 (6th Cir. 2006); Spisak v. Hudson, 512 F.3d 852 (6th Cir. 2008); Smith v. Spisak, 130 S. Ct. 676 (2010); *Bobby v. Dixon,* 565 U.S.____ (2011); *Bobby v. Mitts ,* 563 U.S.____ (2011).

60. Anderson v. Buell, 516 U.S. 1100 (1996) (Scalia, J., dissenting) (internal quotation marks omitted).

61. H.R. Conf. Rep. No. 104–518, at 111 (1996), *reprinted in* 1996 U.S.C.C.A.N. 944; S. Rep. No.104–23 (1995); Antiterrorism and Effective Death Penalty Act of 1996, Pub. L. No.

104–132, 110 Stat. 1214; see also Alex Kozinski and Sean Gallagher, "Death: The Ultimate Run-On Sentence," *Case Western Reserve Law Review* 46 (Fall 1995): 1, 6–11; King, Cheesman, and Ostrom, *Final Technical Report*.

62. Spirko v. Mitchell, 368 F.3d 603 (6th Cir. 2004); Spirko v. Anderson, No. 3:95CV7209, 2000 WL 1278383 (N.D. Ohio July 11, 2000) (unpublished).

63. Ted Strickland, Governor of Ohio, Warrant of Commutation, January 9, 2008, available at http://www.sconet.state.oh.us/tempx/613189.pdf. Regina Brett, "In Spirko Case, Only Doubt Is Left," *Cleveland Plain Dealer*, January 11, 2008; Bob Paynter, "Spirko Spared the Death Penalty, Sentence Reduced to Life in Prison," *Cleveland Plain Dealer*, January 10, 2008; David Patch, "Spirko Death Penalty Commuted, Governor Says No DNA Proof in Ohio Postmaster's Slaying," *Toledo Blade*, January 10, 2008.

64. Carr, interview.

Carl B. Stokes United States Court House, Eastern Division, Cleveland, Ohio (opened in 2002). Designed by architect Michael McKinnell of Boston, this twenty-four-story structure "resembles a single column," thus symbolically "evoking the law's role as one of society's most significant pillars" ("Justice under One Roof," *Cleveland Plain Dealer*, July 14, 2002, A10). With a stone façade matching the rock quarried for the Howard M. Metzenbaum United States Court House, completed in 1910, this new building is additionally tied to the earlier courthouse by world-renowned sculptor Jim Dine's towering *Cleveland Venus* statue located above the main entrance. The placement of this contemporary rendition of a classical work of art on a modern building draws one back to the ancient roots of modern law and then immediately pulls one forward into the present—a visual acknowledgment of Western law's beginnings, with deference to its continued meaning and application today. *Photo courtesy of Robert Benson Photography.*

Howard M. Metzenbaum United States Court House, Cleveland, Ohio. The stately granite U.S. Court House—the work of renowned architect Arnold W. Brunner—was dedicated in 1911. At the time of its dedication, the building, designated as the Federal Building, comprised the U.S. Post Office, Custom House, and Court House, but the judicial function of the structure eventually entirely encompassed the building as over the years the other federal offices were relocated throughout nearby downtown buildings. This Federal Building—currently known as the Howard M. Metzenbaum United States Court House—was one of the primary components of a civic scheme drawn in accordance with the tenets of the City Beautiful movement of the early twentieth century, which called for and was defined by the carefully considered placement and distribution of principal public buildings within a downtown area.

Howard M. Metzenbaum United States Court House, Third Floor Courtroom East. At the end of the marble-lined corridor on the eastern side of the building is the first of two magnificent courtrooms. Upon entering room 342, one is immediately impressed by the ornate decorative detail: the gold leaf on the ceiling; the huge chandeliers; the rich wood of the judge's bench, jury box, rails, and public seating; the marble pilasters along the walls; and the grand mural behind the judge's bench, called "The Law." Painted by highly regarded muralist Edwin Blashfield, the wide expanse of this piece provides a panoramic montage illustrating the artist's conceptualization of the initial formulation of law, what the law represents, and the derivation of its codification.

Howard M. Metzenbaum United States Court House, Third Floor Courtroom West. Moving down the main third-floor corridor from east to west and into the second grandly ornate courtroom on this level, one also symbolically moves from classical and continental influences east of England and the United States to a representation of the westernization of the law through the development of a social contract. Entering courtroom 301, one is stunned by the gloriously ornamented ceiling; the marble pilasters; the rich wood and woodwork of the judge's bench, jury box, and rails; and the mural behind the judge's bench. This painting by the European-trained American artist H. Siddons Mowbray from Washington, Connecticut, is entitled "The Common Law."

John F. Seiberling Federal Building and United States Court House, Eastern Division, Akron, Ohio

Thomas D. Lambros Federal Building and United States Court House, Eastern Division, Youngstown, Ohio

James M. Ashley and Thomas W. L. Ashley United States Court House, Western Division, Toledo, Ohio

District Judges of the United States District Court
for the Northern District of Ohio

Hiram V. Willson
Charles Taylor Sherman

Martin Welker
Augustus J. Ricks

Francis Joseph Wing
Robert Walker Tayler

John Milton Killits
William Louis Day

John Hessin Clarke
David C. Westenhaver
[CPC]

Paul J. Jones [CPC]
George Philip Hahn

Samuel H. West
Frank LeBlond Kloeb

Robert Nugen Wilkin
Emerich Burt Freed

Charles Joseph McNamee
[CPC]
James C. Connell [CPC]

Paul Charles Weick
Girard Edward Kalbfleisch

Frank Joseph Battisti [CPC]
Ben Charles Green [CPC]

Don John Young

William Kernahan Thomas
[CPC]

Thomas Demetrios
Lambros [CPC]

Robert B. Krupansky

Nicholas Joseph
Walinski, Jr.

Leroy John Contie, Jr.

John Michael Manos

George Washington White
[CPC]

Ann Aldrich
Alvin Irving Krenzler [CPC]

John William Potter
David D. Dowd, Jr.

Sam H. Bell
Alice Moore Batchelder

Richard B. McQuade, Jr.
Paul Ramon Matia

Lesley Wells
James G. Carr

Chief Judge Solomon
Oliver, Jr.
David A. Katz

Kathleen McDonald
O'Malley
Peter C. Economus

Donald C. Nugent
Patricia A. Gaughan

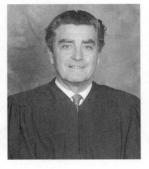 

James S. Gwin
Dan Aaron Polster

John R. Adams
(not pictured)
Christopher A. Boyko
Jack Zouhary

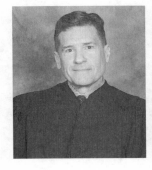 

Sara E. Lioi
Benita Y. Pearson

Jeffrey J. Helmick

United States Magistrate Judges of the Northern District of Ohio. *Back row, from left to right:* Hon. James R. Knepp, II, Hon. Greg A. White, Hon. George J. Limbert, Hon. William H. Baughman, Jr., Hon. Kenneth S. McHargh. *Front row, from left to right:* Hon. Vernelis K. Armstrong, Hon. Nancy A. Vecchiarelli, Hon. Kathleen B. Burke.

Historical Listing of Northern District Court of Ohio District Judges

(see following pages)

District Judge	Hometown	Years in Office	Chief Judge	Date of Death	Nominating President
Hiram V. Willson	Madison County, NY	1855–66		11/11/1866	Franklin Pierce (D)
Charles T. Sherman	Norwalk, CT	1867–72		01/01/1879	Andrew Johnson (D)
Martin Welker	Knox County, OH	1873–89		3/15/1902	Ulysses S. Grant (R)
Augustus J. Ricks	Brookfield, OH	1889–1906		12/22/1906	Benjamin Harrison (R)
Francis J. Wing	North Bloomfield, OH	1901–5		2/1/1918	William McKinley (R)
Robert W. Tayler	Youngstown, OH	1905–10		11/26/1910	Theodore Roosevelt(R)
John M. Killits	Lithopolis, OH	1910–28		9/13/1938	William Howard Taft (R)
William L. Day	Canton, OH	1911–14		7/15/1936	William Howard Taft (R)
John H. Clarke	New Lisbon, OH	1914–16		3/22/1945	Woodrow Wilson (D)
David C. Westenhaver	Berkeley County, WV	1917–28		7/29/1928	Woodrow Wilson (D)
Paul Jones	Youngstown, OH	1923–65	1948–59	8/3/1965	Warren G. Harding (R)
George P. Hahn	Napoleon, OH	1928–37		2/12/1937	Calvin Coolidge (R)
Samuel H. West	Waubeck, IA	1928–38		10/5/1938	Calvin Coolidge (R)
Frank Le Blond Kloeb	Celina, OH	1937–64	1959–60	3/11/1976	Franklin D. Roosevelt (D)
Robert N. Wilkin	New Philadelphia, OH	1939–49		2/23/1973	Franklin D. Roosevelt (D)
Emerich B. Freed	Hungary	1944–55		12/4/1955	Franklin D. Roosevelt (D)
Charles J. McNamee	Cleveland, OH	1951–64		5/2/1964	Harry S. Truman (D)
James C. Connell	Cleveland, OH	1954–73	1960–67	10/30/1973	Dwight D. Eisenhower (R)
Paul C. Weick	Youngstown, OH	1956–59		5/22/1997	Dwight D. Eisenhower (R)
Girard E. Kalbfleisch	Piqua, OH	1959–90	1967–69	4/1/1990	Dwight D. Eisenhower (R)
Frank J. Battisti	Youngstown, OH	1961–94	1969–90	10/19/1994	John F. Kennedy (D)
Ben C. Green	Cleveland, OH	1961–83		1/12/1983	John F. Kennedy (D)
Don J. Young	Norwalk, OH	1965–96		5/10/1996	Lyndon B. Johnson (D)
William K. Thomas	Columbus, OH	1966–98		3/20/2001	Lyndon B. Johnson (D)
Thomas D. Lambros	Ashtabula, OH	1967–95	1990–95		Lyndon B. Johnson (D)
Robert B. Krupansky	Cleveland, OH	1970–82		11/8/2004	Richard M. Nixon (R)
Nicholas J. Walinski Jr.	Toledo, OH	1970–92		12/24/1992	Richard M. Nixon (R)

District Judge	Hometown	Years in Office	Chief Judge	Date of Death	Nominating President
Leroy J. Contie Jr.	Canton, OH	1971–82		5/11/2001	Richard M. Nixon (R)
John M. Manos	Cleveland, OH	1976–2006		7/6/2006	Gerald Ford (R)
George W. White	Duquesne, PA	1980–99	1995–99	11/12/2011	James Earl Carter (D)
Ann Aldrich	Providence, RI	1980–2010		5/2/2010	James Earl Carter (D)
Alvin I. Krenzler	Chicago, IL	1981–92			Ronald W. Reagan (R)
John W. Potter	Toledo, OH	1982–2004			Ronald W. Reagan (R)
David D. Dowd Jr.	Cleveland, OH	1982–Present			Ronald W. Reagan (R)
Sam H. Bell	Rochester, NY	1983–2010		12/23/2010	Ronald W. Reagan (R)
Alice M. Batchelder	Wilmington, DE	1985–92			Ronald W. Reagan (R)
Richard B. McQuade Jr.	Toledo, OH	1986–89			Ronald W. Reagan (R)
Paul R. Matia	Cleveland, OH	1991–2005	1999–2004		George H.W. Bush (R)
Lesley Wells	Muskegon, MI	1994–Present			William J. Clinton (D)
James G. Carr	Boston, MA	1994–Present	2004–10		William J. Clinton (D)
Solomon Oliver Jr.	Bessemer, AL	1994–Present	2010–Present		William J. Clinton (D)
David A. Katz	Toledo, OH	1994–Present			William J. Clinton (D)
Kathleen M. O'Malley	Drexel Hill, PA	1994–2010			William J. Clinton (D)
Peter C. Economus	Youngstown, OH	1995–2010			William J. Clinton (D)
Donald C. Nugent	Minneapolis, MN	1995–Present			William J. Clinton (D)
Patricia A. Gaughan	Lakewood, OH	1996–Present			William J. Clinton (D)
James S. Gwin	Canton, OH	1997–Present			William J. Clinton (D)
Dan Aaron Polster	Cleveland, OH	1998–Present			William J. Clinton (D)
John R. Adams	Orrville, OH	2003–Present			George W. Bush (R)
Christopher A. Boyko	Cleveland, OH	2005–Present			George W. Bush (R)
Jack Zouhary	Toledo, OH	2006–Present			George W. Bush (R)
Sara E. Lioi	Canton, OH	2007–Present			George W. Bush (R)
Benita Y. Pearson	Cleveland, OH	2010–Present			Barack Obama (D)
Jeffrey J. Helmick	Toledo, OH	2012–Present			Barack Obama (D)

Historical Listing of Northern District Court of Ohio Magistrate Judges

Full-Time Magistrate Judges

Magistrate Judge	Hometown	Dates Served
Herbert T. Maher	Lakewood, OH	1971–79
Jack B. Streepy	Rockford, IL	1973–2004
Charles R. Laurie	Cleveland, OH	1977–93
David S. Perelman	Cleveland, OH	1979–2010
James G. Carr	Boston, MA	1979–94
Joseph W. Bartunek	Cleveland, OH	1986–98
James S. Gallas	Wheeling, WV	1991–2010
Patricia A. Hemann	Chicago, IL	1993–2008
Vernelis K. Armstrong	Wyatt, MO	1994–Present
James D. Thomas	Detroit, MI	1995–99
Nancy A. Vecchiarelli	St. Mary's, PA	1998–Present
George J. Limbert	Youngstown, OH	1999–Present
William H. Baughman Jr.	Greensburg, PA	2000–Present
Kenneth S. McHargh	Barberton, OH	2004–Present
Greg White	Willard, OH	2008–Present
Benita Y. Pearson	Cleveland, OH	2008–10
James R. Knepp II	Akron, OH	2010–Present
Kathleen B. Burke	Brooklyn, NY	2011–Present

Part-Time Magistrate Judges

Magistrate Judge	Hometown	Dates Served
John Pietrykowski	Toledo, OH	1971–79
Nicholas Manos	Youngstown, OH	1971–77
Ralph W. Hartz	Akron, OH	1971–77
John W. Ergazos	Canton, OH	1972–76
J. Michael Bernstein	Mansfield, OH	1974–86

Notes on Contributors

ROBERTA SUE ALEXANDER is Distinguished Service Professor of History and professor emerita at the University of Dayton. She earned a B.A. from the University of California at Los Angeles, an M.A. and Ph.D. from the University of Chicago, and a J.D. from the University of Dayton School of Law. Her publications include *Place of Recourse: A History of the U.S. District Court for the Southern District of Ohio* and *North Carolina Faces the Freedmen: Race Relations During Presidential Reconstruction, 1865–67.*

MARTIN H. BELSKY is Dean and Randolph Baxter Professor at the University of Akron School of Law. He received his B.A. from Temple University and his J.D. from Columbia University School of Law. He also has graduate diplomas from The Hague Academy of International Law and Cambridge University. In his career, he served as chief prosecutor in Philadelphia, counsel to the Judiciary Committee of the House of Representatives, and as an administrator of a federal agency. He has served as vice president of the American Judicature Society and now serves as chair of AJS's National Advisory Council. He has written numerous articles and books on the administration of justice, civil rights, constitutional law, privacy, criminal law, international law, environmental law, oceans and coastal law, and professional responsibility.

MELVYN DUBOFSKY is Distinguished Professor of History and Sociology Emeritus, Binghamton University, SUNY. He holds a B.A. from Brooklyn College and a Ph.D. from the University of Rochester. In addition to teaching at several American universities, he served as Distinguished Fulbright Professor at the University of Salzburg, Austria, and the John Adams Professor of American Civilization at the University of Amsterdam. A specialist in the history of labor in the United States, his numerous publications include *We Shall Be All: A History of the IWW; John L. Lewis: A Biography* (coauthor); *The State and Labor in Modern America*; and *Hard Work: The Making of a Labor Historian.*

PAUL FINKELMAN is a visiting professor at Duke Law School, where he holds the John Hope Franklin chair in Legal History. He is the President William McKinley Distinguished Professor of Law and Public Policy and Senior Fellow in the Government Law Center at the Albany Law School. He received his B.A. in American Studies from Syracuse University, his M.A. and Ph.D. in U.S. history from the University of Chicago, and was a fellow in law and humanities at

Harvard Law School. He is the author, coauthor, or editor of more than twenty-five books and more than two hundred scholarly articles. His books, many of which have won prestigious awards, include *Millard Fillmore, Slavery and the Founders: Race and Liberty in the Age of Jefferson, The Political Lincoln,* and *A March of Liberty: A Constitutional History of the United States.* He has held numerous fellowships and has lectured not only throughout the United States, but also in Canada, Europe, Asia, and Latin America.

ALISON K. GUERNSEY is an assistant federal public defender with the Federal Defenders of Eastern Washington & Idaho in Yakima, Washington. She received her B.A. from the University of Michigan Honors College, and her J.D. from the University of Iowa College of Law. Prior to her work as a trial attorney, she clerked for the Honorable Michael J. Melloy, U.S. Court of Appeals for the Eighth Circuit, and the Honorable Karen Nelson Moore, U.S. Court of Appeals for the Sixth Circuit. Her practice is focused solely on federal criminal law.

THOMAS R. HENSLEY received his B.A. from Simpson College, his M.A. from the University of Iowa, and his Ph.D. from the University of Iowa in 1970. His primary research interests are civil rights and liberties, Supreme Court decision making, and the implementation and impact of judicial decisions. He coauthored *The Changing Supreme Court: Constitutional Rights and Liberties* with Chris Smith and Joyce Baugh. His *The Rehnquist Court: Justices, Rulings, Legacies* is forthcoming.

KEITH H. HIROKAWA is an associate professor at Albany Law School. His scholarship explores convergences in ecology, ethics, economics, and law, with particular attention given to local environmental law, ecosystem services policy, watershed management, and environmental impact analysis. He has authored dozens of professional and scholarly articles in these areas and coedited (with Patricia Salkin) *Greening Local Government* (forthcoming). Professor Hirokawa earned his in M.A. and J.D. at the University of Connecticut and his LLM in environmental and natural resources law at Lewis & Clark Law School.

NANCY E. MARION is a professor of political science at the University of Akron. She holds a Ph.D. from the State University of New York at Binghamton, where her focus was public policy. She has published many books and articles on the interplay of politics and criminal justice that demonstrate how the two fields come together and how they affect one another.

DAN AARON POLSTER is a U.S district court judge for the Northern District of Ohio, Eastern Division at Cleveland. Prior to his appointment to the bench by President Clinton in 1998, he served as a federal prosecutor in Cleveland, first as a trial attorney with the Department of Justice, Antitrust Division, and then as an assistant U.S. attorney, handling a wide variety of fraud and corruption cases. Judge Polster received his A.B. from Harvard College and his J.D. from Harvard Law School. Judge Polster is an adjunct faculty member at Cleveland-Marshall College of Law. His publications include "The Trial Judge as Mediator: A Rejoinder to Judge Cratsley."

RENEE C. REDMAN is a sole-practitioner in New Haven, Connecticut, where she focuses on immigration and business litigation. She also teaches immigration law as an adjunct professor at the University of Connecticut and Quinnipiac Schools of Law. Her prior positions include executive director of the Iran Human Rights Documentation Center, New Haven Legal Assistance Association, and legal director of the ACLU of Connecticut. Until 2004, she practiced commercial litigation with Hughes Hubbard & Reed, LLP, in New York City. She clerked for the Immigration Courts in New York City and Newark, New Jersey, and the Honorable Warren W. Eginton of the United States District Court in Bridgeport, Connecticut.

ELIZABETH REILLY, vice provost for academic planning and C. Blake McDowell, Jr. Professor of Law at The University of Akron, received her A.B. from Princeton University and her J.D. from The University of Akron. She is the editor of and a contributor to *Infinite Hope and Finite Disappointment: The Story of the First Interpreters of the Fourteenth Amendment*. She has also published numerous articles and book chapters in the fields of U.S. constitutional law, legal history, and feminist jurisprudence.

RICHARD B. SAPHIRE, B.A., The Ohio State University; J.D., Salmon P. Chase College of Law (Northern Kentucky State University); and LL.M, Harvard University, is professor of law at the University of Dayton School of Law, where he teaches courses in constitutional law, professional responsibility, civil rights, federal jurisdiction, and religion and the law. He has written extensively in the areas of constitutional law and theory, civil rights, federal jurisdiction and administration, and law and religion.

TRACY A. THOMAS is professor of law at the University of Akron School of Law. She earned her J.D. from Loyola Law School, Los Angeles, an M.P.A. from California State, Long Beach, and her B.A. from Miami University, Ohio. She is the editor of *Feminist Legal History* (with Tracey Jean Boisseau) and the author of *Elizabeth Cady Stanton and the Feminist Foundations of Family Law* (forthcoming). Thomas's research focuses on women's legal history and equitable relief.

MELVIN I. UROFSKY is professor of history emeritus and professor of law and public policy at Virginia Commonwealth University. He holds an A.B. and a Ph.D. from Columbia University, and a J.D. from the University of Virginia. He has written widely on constitutional history. His most recent books are *Supreme Decisions* and the prize-winning *Louis D. Brandeis: A Life*.

Index of Cases

General Index

Page references in italics denote illustrations.

abolitionists, 5, 16, 40, 44–45. *See also* Oberlin-
Wellington fugitive slave rescue case
abortion rights, 166, 174–80; Akron ordinance,
175–77, 179–80; Northern District of Ohio
on, 177–79; parental notification case,
180–83; Sixth Circuit on, 178–79, 182; U.S.
Supreme Court on, 179
ACLU. *See* American Civil Liberties Union
Adams, John R., 345, 349
ad coelum, 214–17
Adler, Jonathan, 220
admiralty law, 23–27, 76–77
ADR. *See* alternative dispute resolution (ADR)
AEDPA. *See* Antiterrorism and Effective
Death Penalty Act (1996)
Agin, Carol, 168–69
airspace ownership, 214–17
Akron Beacon Journal (newspaper), 278
Aldrich, Ann, 124, 141, 180–82, 266, 271–72,
275–76, 278, 280–83, 343, 349
Alexander, Roberta Sue, 3, 149
aliens, 3, 19–20, 112
"all deliberate speed" standard, 128
Allen, Florence, 181
alternative dispute resolution (ADR), 124
Ambler Realty, 212
American Center for Law and Justice, 192
American Civil Liberties Union (ACLU), 165,
171, 177, 178, 191–94, 196, 261
American Federation of Labor, 91–92
American Iron and Tube Company, 79
American Law Institute, 174
American Protective League, 103
Angelilli, Adolph F., 296
Antiterrorism and Effective Death Penalty Act
(1996), 327–28
Arbeznik, Gary, 269–70, 272, 275–76, 277,
279–81
Armstrong, Vernelis K., 346, 351
arson case, 320–22
Avery, Charles, 20

Backus, Franklin T., 49, 55, 58
Bacon, John, 37, 41, 48, 50–51, 53, 59, 64, 68
Baich, Dale, 271
Baker, Newton D., 89, 104
Barr, Linda H., 315
Bartholomew, Seth, 53
Bartunek, Joseph W., 351
Batchelder, Alice Moore, 195–96, 197, 343, 349
Battisti, Frank J., 341, 348; on capital punish-
ment, 326; on court, 149–51; death of, 138,
148; on denaturalization trial, 293–301; on
desegregation of schools, 129–42; on hous-
ing discrimination, 143–48; on Kent State
shootings, 257–58, 264; memorial for, 152
Battle of Fort Fizzle. *See* Holmes County draft
riot
Baughman, William H., Jr., 346, 351
Becker, Byron, 270, 277
Belden, George W.: on Oberlin-Wellington
case, 23, 44, 46, 47, 48–51, 53–58, 60–62,
64–65, 67; on obstruction of U.S. mail, 21
Bell, Samuel H., 192, 343, 349
Bell Syndicate, 114
Berman, Douglas, 323
Bernstein, J. Michael, 351
BIA. *See* Board of Immigration Appeals
Bill, Earl, 30
Bingham, John A., 45
Biondillo, Ernie, 235–36
Black, Jeremiah, 49, 62
Black Laws, 10–11n27
Blackmun, Harry, 172–73, 177–78, 179, 180, 182
Blackstone, William, 113, 214
Blanchard, Laurant, 29
Bliss, George, 49, 62
Blosser, Don, 277–78
Board of Immigration Appeals (BIA), 296, 303
Boehme, Charles, 102
Bolitho, Bonnie, 177
Bowers, Claude, 99
Boyer, Elizabeth, 168

Smucker, Greg, 270, 277
Social Democratic Party, 97
Socialist Party, 99, 108–9, 114
Social Security Administration (SSA), 123
Sogg, Linda, 182
Souter, David, 196
Spalding, Rufus P., 48, 53, 54–55, 57–58, 63, 65
Spargo, John, 100
Spicer, Willard F., 175–76
Spiegel, S. Arthur, 282
Spirko, John, 328
SSA. *See* Social Security Administration
Standard Oil Company, 9
Standard Zoning Enabling Act (SZEA), 211
Stedman, Seymour, 104, 106
Steiner, Virgil, 105
Sterling, Edward, 105
Stewart, Potter, 172
St. Louis Proclamation, 99–100, 106
Stokes, Rose Pastor, 111
Stoner, Cyrus H., 111
Stow, Ohio, religious symbols case, 191–94
Streepy, Jack B., 272, 326, 351
Strickland, Ted, 328
strikes, 75, 82–88, 92, 93. *See also* collective action
Strollo, Lenine "Lenny," 235–36
student protests. *See* Kent State University, 1970 shootings
Students for a Democratic Society (SDS), 270
subversion, 22, 27, 28, 46, 98–99
Sutherland, George, 213–14
Swayne, Noah H., 68–69
Synenberg, Roger M., 315
SZEA. *See* Standard Zoning Enabling Act

Taft, William Howard, 81
takings clause, 210
Taney, Roger B., 40, 66
Tayler, Robert Walker, 87, 339, 348
telephone company injunction, 87–89
Ten Commandments case, 194–98
Terez, Dennis G., 323
Thayer, L. C., 60, 61
Thirteenth Amendment, 144
Thomas, Charles, 256
Thomas, James D., 351
Thomas, William Kernahan, 254, 258, 262–63, 264, 282, 342, 348

Tigar, Michael E., 298, 301
Tilden, Daniel R., 23, 65
Toledo Blade (newspaper), 17, 323
Traficant, James A., Jr., 236–41, 243
treason law, 27–28
Turner, Joseph, 106

Underground Railroad, 46
unions. *See* collective action; strikes
unitary status, 138–40, 142, 150
United Freedom Movement, 130
Urban League, 130
U.S. Civil War, 27–29
U.S. Court of Appeals for the Sixth Circuit: on abortion, 178–79, 182; on airspace ownership, 216–17; on capital punishment, 325–28; on denaturalization/deportation, 295, 296–98, 300–301, 303–4; on desegregation of schools, 130, 132, 134, 135, 136–37, 138–41, 145, 150, 152; on draft nonregistration, 282–83; on establishment clause, 193, 195, 199–200, 201–2; on gender equality, 170; on Kent State shooting, 258, 260–61, 263; on labor cases, 75, 82; on RICO cases, 234, 240
U.S. Department of Justice (DOJ), 92, 121–22, 140, 146, 222, 244, 253, 256–57, 266, 269–70, 291–92, 322
U.S. District Court, Northern District of Ohio: on abortion rights, 177–79; on airspace ownership, 208–9, 214–17; on capital punishment, 314–23, 328–29; changes in, 123–24; civil cases, 20, 124; on common-law principles, 75, 77–83, 88; courthouses, 335–38; on Debs trial, 103–12; on denaturalization, 293–301; on desegregation of schools, 129–42; on draft nonregistration, 271–84; on establishment clause, 196–97, 199, 200–203; establishment of, 2, 8, 15–16; on housing discrimination, 142–48; on industrial dispute, 76, 81–93; judges, 339–46, 348–50; and judicial bypass exceptions, 180–83; on Kent State shootings, 254–58, 264; on nuisance law, 209–11; on Oberlin-Wellington case, 22–23, 38, 44–70; on pollution control laws, 217–22; on RICO, 233–44; types of cases, 19–22; on worker injury claims, 74, 76–81; on zoning ordinance in Euclid, 212–14, 221. *See also* specific judges